PHILANTHROPY AND SOCIAL CHANGE IN LATIN AMERICA

Editors: Cynthia Sanborn and Felipe Portocarrero

Published by Harvard University
David Rockefeller Center for Latin American Studies

Distributed by Harvard University Press
Cambridge, Massachusetts
London, England
2005

4236

Library of Congress Cataloging-in-Publication Data

Philanthropy and Social Change in Latin America / editors, Cynthia
   Sanborn and Felipe Portocarrero
         p. cm.
   ISBN-13: 978-0-674-01965-2 (pbk. : alk. paper)
   ISBN-10: 0-674-01965-2 (pbk. : alk. paper)
   1. Charities–Latin America. 2. Social Service–Latin America.
   3. Social change–Latin America.   I. Sanborn, Cynthia.
   II. Portocarrero S., Felipe. ˈ
   HV110.5P47 2005
   361.7ʹ4ʹ098dc22

                                          2005021697

Contents

Leveraging Time and Money: Philanthropy and the Social Deficit in Latin America

John H. Coatsworth

It is impossible to say when Latin America emerged as the world's most unequal region. The European "encounter" brought the subjugation and destruction of Native-American peoples and the subsequent kidnapping of millions of Africans to repopulate the New World. Colonial regimes defined dark-skinned majorities as legally inferior. Long after the abolition of caste systems and slavery, the failure to invest adequately in these human resources still echoes through the modern societies that emerged in the 20th century. Modernization itself intensified pre-existing inequalities by facilitating the concentration of wealth, disproportionately rewarding knowledge and skills because they remained so scarce, and enabling authoritarian regimes of still recent memory to suppress demands for social inclusion for decades at a time.

This volume seeks to determine whether and how philanthropy and volunteerism—as referred to somewhat routinely by North Americans—might contribute to reducing social distances, foster progressive social change, and help to reduce the immense social deficit that Latin America has carried into the 21st century. This is a relatively new question for social scientists who study Latin America, so there is no ready-made or conventional answer to it—apart from understandable skepticism: If governments with their massive resources of money and manpower have not succeeded, what can private individuals, groups, and organizations possibly accomplish?

Latin America's Social Deficit

Latin America consists mainly of middle-income countries with highly skewed distributions of income and assets. The GDP per capita in the region is roughly equal to that of Eastern Europe, but is much more unequally distributed. In Latin America, the top 20% of income earners receive roughly 15 times that of the bottom 20%. In the most unequal Latin American countries like Brazil and Guatemala, ethnic and regional divisions exacerbate inequality even more; there the ratio is about 30:1. In the United States, which is the most unequal of the developed countries, the ratio is 9:1. The countries with the most equal ratios (between 4 and 5:1) are Cuba, Taiwan and Sweden.

The direct consequence of Latin America's extreme inequality can be seen in lagging social indicators, especially in education, welfare, and preventable disease. World Bank figures show that close to 40% of Latin America's population live on less than $2 per day, and 20% earn under $1. These figures imply widespread malnutrition, which may be 30% or higher in such countries as Bolivia and Mexico and even worse in Brazil and Guatemala.

Latin American social progress has lagged behind growth in GDP per capita. Wage levels have remained behind the growth of the Latin American economies for extended periods of time. Governments have failed to invest in human resources, even when they could afford to do so. Thus, Latin America has historically suffered from greater poverty, more preventable disease, higher rates of infant mortality, more illiteracy and other social problems than other regions at comparable levels of GDP per capita.

Roots of Inequality

Simon Kuznets, 1971 Nobel Laureate in Economics, was the first to hypothesize that an initial rise in inequality is to be expected at the onset of economic growth. He and later economists suggest that with prolonged economic growth, a gradual improvement in distribution should occur. They argue that this is what happened in today's advanced countries and that it should occur elsewhere as well. Indeed, something like this pattern can be seen in other world regions, but in Latin America the sharp rise in inequality that occurred with the onset of economic growth in the late 19th century was never reversed.

The obstacles to social progress in Latin America thus appear to be more deeply embedded in Latin America's history than is true for other societies. Historians have offered various explanations for this pattern. First, the region experienced the usual early development problems, such as abundant unskilled labor, scarce skills and scarce capital—the Kuznets effect. But this does not distinguish Latin America from other world regions where the onset of modernization also intensified inequality. The problem in Latin America was that the inequality shock experienced with the onset of economic growth in the late 19th century never got reversed, as it did in other regions. Second, Latin America inherited from the colonial era weak states designed to serve and protect small minorities. This legacy was compounded by post-independence civil strife and international warfare. It took longer for Latin America's governments to acquire the will and the capacity to invest in public goods and provide services to most citizens than in most European societies. Indeed, most Latin American governments did not do so until the massive and politically volatile rural to urban migrations of the 1950s and later. In the larger countries (Argentina, Brazil, Mexico), federalism worked against social progress by compounding regional and ethnic divisions. Finally, political constraints on majorities kept most people from voting until well into the 20th century while periods of military rule suppressed demands for social change and inhibited the development of civil society.

It is true, nonetheless, that substantial social progress has occurred in Latin America during the past 100 years. Life expectancy rose from around 30 years (comparable to the Roman Empire) in 1900 to more than 70 years today. Infant mortality declined from approximately 300 to less than 50 per 1000. The illiteracy rate fell from an average of near 80% to under 10%. Despite these gains, substantial lags persisted throughout the century in most every way. To give a stark example, by 1910, Mexico had reached a level of GDP per capita comparable to the United States in 1800. However, it was not until the 1960s that Mexico attained a literacy rate of over 60%, which the United States had reached in 1800. A similar lag of a half-century to a century or more can be found with respect to many other indicators of social progress in Mexico as well as the rest of Latin America.

Social Change

A broad consensus has emerged in Latin America on the need for significant changes in social and cultural organization. The persistence of high levels of inequality threatens both growth and democracy. Indeed, future economic growth may depend critically on how much and how well Latin America invests in its human resources. The future of democratic political institutions may depend on how well elected governments respond to popular demands for social progress. Fortunately, a window of opportunity for exceptionally rapid progress has already opened and will remain open for the next two decades when population growth rates will continue to fall, dependency ratios (the proportion of populations too young or too old for productive labor) will be unusually low, and the resources potentially available for social investments will rise well above past levels. Governments will be spending less of their scarce tax revenues just to keep up with population growth and thus can devote more to improving the reach and quality of public services.

To make maximum use of this opportunity, however, both public agencies and private service providers will need to change and adapt to new challenges. Three examples will suggest the range of adaptations that may be needed. First, extending social services to marginalized populations in urban slums or remote rural locations, we now know, cannot be accomplished by mechanically applying the models that work elsewhere. Second, improving the quality of social investments may require the creation of effective ways of including the citizenry in the process of designing and implementing public programs, ranging from infrastructure and community development to health care and pension systems. Third, making effective use of new resources will inevitably require a reorientation of efforts from the diminishing problems of yesterday (averting hunger, ending illiteracy, inoculating children) to the critical issues ahead (poor diets and chronic malnutrition, ineffective schools, diseases associated with aging).

Can Philanthropy Make a Difference?

In a purely *quantitative* sense, private philanthropy and volunteering will never be able to provide sufficient material and human resources to change Latin American societies. It is true that the magnitude of giving and volunteering is often underestimated in Latin America, because conventional measures usually omit various kinds of mutual aid and self help as well as traditions of community solidarity, kin-based and family aid, and the more traditional participatory forms of "volunteering." Yet even if every donated peso or cruzeiro were immediately transferred to the poor, the results would be negligible in terms of income distribution, poverty alleviation or social progress. Private philanthropy alone cannot solve Latin America's social problems, because private philanthropy will always be too small.

Nonetheless, philanthropy can play a significant *qualitative* role in fostering social change as a catalyst, energizer and model builder. The essays in this volume suggest at least five key philanthropic activities that could significantly accelerate social progress in Latin America:

First, philanthropy can play a key role in communicating, networking and benchmarking, especially by locating and disseminating information about successes and failures in social programs and policies across nations and regions.

Second, with information on successful cases of mobilizing resources or delivering services, philanthropic organizations can engage in experimentation and model building, testing the applicability of best practices to local conditions.

Third, private philanthropies can publicize and promote the proliferation of successful models to private as well as public agencies.

Fourth, philanthropic organizations can leverage their own resources and experience, both to increase the engagement of others and to enhance the effectiveness and productivity of existing social programs.

Finally, private philanthropy can work to promote the development of vibrant civil societies and the formation of social capital by working to eliminate fiscal and regulatory obstacles to giving and volunteerism, and lobbying for new incentives for such activities.

The essays in this volume are pioneering in the sense that they explore largely unknown terrain. Taken together, their purpose is both to inform and to provoke. If they succeed in luring more travelers to engage in ever more penetrating forays into this developing field of research and analysis, the editors and authors will have succeeded in their efforts.

Editors' Introduction

Cynthia Sanborn and Felipe Portocarrero

Latin America is a profoundly philanthropic region. From the U.S.-Mexican border to the Andean highlands to Porto Alegre in Brazil, there are deeply rooted traditions of voluntary association for the public good and solidarity with the less fortunate. Such traditions have been carried forth by descendents of the diverse indigenous cultures that inhabited vast geographic areas prior to the Spanish and Portuguese colonization. They are also present in the dominant Catholic faith, in other religious communities, and among the associations of immigrants who came to these lands fleeing persecution or seeking new opportunities. Charity and solidarity were fundamental elements in the mutual aid societies, trade unions and professional associations of the 19th and 20th centuries, and in the diverse social movements that emerged during the second half of the last century, involving millions of men and women in efforts to achieve human rights and social justice.

What is exceptional in Latin America is to call all of this activity "philanthropy," as people in this field tend to do in some countries such as the United States and much of Europe. Historically, the term *filantropía* in this region has been used in a more narrow sense, referring to the charitable activities of the Catholic Church and the dominant socioeconomic elite. Such activities have long been oriented towards alleviating the suffering of select groups of the poor and downtrodden, but without aiming to address the causes of their poverty, or to transform an unequal and unjust status quo.

Since the early 1990s, however, there has been a notable increase in the variety of philanthropic institutions and initiatives in this region, and in *expectations* about what organized philanthropy can achieve in society, on its own or in alliances with other forces. We have seen a boom in corporate philanthropy, organized volunteerism and the creation of grant making and operating foundations, as well as national donor networks and associations. Academic centers have been set up throughout Latin America to study and promote philanthropy in its broader sense. Although their objectives vary, there is a tendency among religious and secular philanthropists in Latin America today to stress their distance from traditional charity, and their desire to contribute to the solution of persistent social problems in the region.

How can we explain this change in the philanthropic landscape? Clearly, the privatization of public enterprises and the opening of markets to new foreign investment have generated increased private *wealth* in the last two decades. At the same time, processes of political democratization and the expansion of organized civil society in various countries have unleashed new pressures upon the "haves" to give back more to society. New social movements and NGOs have demanded a greater voice, not just in public policymaking but also in the regulation of private business. Whether out of fear, political astuteness or ethical conviction, numerous corporate leaders and scions of privileged families have expressed a willingness to assume greater responsibility for addressing the region's social problems, through voluntary action and investment.

The catalysts for such efforts are not only domestic. The idea of philanthropy as an instrument for social change coincides with the global movement towards Corporate Social Responsibility (CSR) touted by multinational corporations, multilateral banks and such figures as George Soros, the multi-millionaire Hungarian-born investor who founded the Open Society Institute and a network of associated foundations dedicated to rights, freedom and development around the globe; and Stephan Schmidheiny, the Swiss entrepreneur who founded the World Business Council for Sustainable Development and the Avina foundation, the latter a major promoter of social entrepreneurship in Latin America. While CSR is a broader concept that involves changing corporate behavior on various levels – labor practices, social and environmental impact, legal and tax issues— "strategic philanthropy" tends to be a major part of the package. Indeed, part of the new philanthropy emerging in Latin America can be attributed to the greater presence of multinational companies that have considerable stakes in the region and are highly sensitive to public opinion. Likewise, the vision of philanthropy as a progressive force is promoted by various large international foundations and relief organizations that operate in the region today.[1]

To what extent are these expectations about philanthropy realistic? What are the main characteristics of contemporary Latin American philanthropy, and how much do they actually differ from the charity of the past? Is it practical to think that those who have benefited from the unequal distribution of wealth are going to promote, or even permit, a change in this situation? To date, there have been few efforts to try to answer these questions, either through systematic research or public debate among practitioners. Each chapter in this volume represents a step forward in one or both of these directions.

This volume is the culmination of more than three years of research and public debate on issues related to philanthropy in the Americas, conducted under the auspices of the Program on Philanthropy, Civil Society and Social Change in the Americas (PASCA) at Harvard University. The PASCA Program, jointly sponsored by the David Rockefeller Center for Latin American Studies (DRCLAS) and the Hauser Center for Nonprofit Organizations, was a remarkable effort to tap the convening power and resources of Harvard University in order to achieve the following objectives:

- Promote greater understanding of Latin America's philanthropic and voluntary traditions, and of the factors that shape or hinder philanthropy in the region today.
- Support leadership and teaching on issues related to philanthropy, civil society and social change in Latin America.
- Develop a strong learning network of scholars and practitioners involved in these issues, in the United States, Latin America, and beyond.

Through the PASCA program, visiting scholars and fellows from Latin America examined subjects as diverse as tax codes and community soup kitchens. Conference participants from Latin America, the United States and Europe debated the role of corporate foundations in Colombia, discussed civil society and political change in Peru, and examined community participation and volunteerism in Brazil, while in the corridors of DRCLAS and the Hauser Center connections were made that are still influencing philanthropic practice in the region today. Between 2001 and 2003 PASCA sponsored ten visiting fellows and more than thirty public events, including five international workshops held in Cambridge or Santiago de Chile, as well as numerous lectures and seminars. PASCA staff, fellows and associated colleagues produced at least 30 original articles, working papers and case studies on issues related to philanthropy, and contributed to three editions of *ReVista, the Harvard Review of Latin America*, including a special edition in Spring 2002 dedicated to giving and volunteering in the Americas.

The contributors to this volume are scholars and practitioners from across the Americas and across the disciplines. This collection explores the historical traditions of philanthropy in Latin America, as well as the main current trends in organized giving and volunteering. It examines changing trends in corporate giving and social responsibility, and the challenges to establishing and developing private foundations. The book includes both individual country cases and regional overviews, and takes an in-depth look at some of the public policy issues that affect philanthropy and civil society in this region. Chapters by several Harvard University faculty members also contribute important comparative and U.S. perspectives to this collection.

Scope of Analysis

The term "philanthropy" has multiple connotations and diverse uses in both the Anglo-Saxon and Latin American traditions. Although the authors in this volume vary in their use of the concept, the majority focus on some aspect of *organized* giving or volunteering. More specifically, they examine the activities of three types of institutions—foundations, corporations and religious entities—that publicly undertake social programs and/or make donations to third parties (in cash, in kind, in volunteer time, or through a combination of the three), and hence are subject to some form of public regulation and scrutiny. Additionally, several authors examine the efforts of government agencies and public policymakers to promote or control such activity.

One of the more controversial practices examined in this volume is corporate philanthropy, understanding that to mean voluntary donations made by for-profit organizations to non–profit organizations or activities, through various institutional forms. Although individual giving and volunteering is widespread in Latin America, the largest amount of new organized philanthropy in the region since the 1990s has been corporate in origin. Of course, the motivations for such giving are often not altruistic in nature, but rather related to improving corporate image or community relations, and hence the bottom line. Given the scale of corporate giving and its actual or potential impact on urban and rural communities in Latin America today, however, we believe there is ample justification for independent study of this phenomenon.

As several authors point out, the concept of corporate social responsibility (CSR) is theoretically distinct from philanthropy, implying diverse levels of responsibility on the part of company owners, managers and shareholders, and it is manifested in a variety of ways ranging from responsible tax and labor practices to environmental and political conduct. Because the basic essence of philanthropy lies in its voluntary nature, many believe it should not be considered a "responsibility", much less an obligation, along the lines of due payment of taxes or compliance with labor laws. Nevertheless, one of the observations made in this volume is that in both Latin American and international corporate *practice*, the terms "philanthropy" and "social responsibility" are frequently inter-changeable, and much of what is presented as CSR involves voluntary donations to others.

The editors and participants in this book were all too aware that we could not be entirely comprehensive in the issues covered. For example, we do not examine a large share of the donations and mutual assistance undertaken by and among family members and neighbors in Latin America, informally and privately, including many indigenous and community-based practices that have longstanding, even pre-Hispanic roots. This outcome was not meant to underestimate the value of these practices, especially when diverse studies—including several conducted by authors in this book—demonstrate that these more informal forms of giving and volunteering are extensive, and fulfill a fundamental role in providing social protection and inclusion. To give adequate credit to this line of research, however, would far exceed the capacity of one volume.

The contributions to this collection are grouped into four main cate-gories. While there is certainly a greater diversity of related themes to be explored in the region, the following represent what the editors consider to be the most "critical mass" of research and reflection to date on organ-ized philanthropy in this region.

Latin American Philanthropy: Past and Present

In order to understand the present state of philanthropy in Latin America, it is fundamental to examine its historical roots. Hence the first section begins with a general overview of Latin America's main philanthropic tra-ditions, and of what we know about current trends, drawing on research produced by the editors and various authors in this volume and other sources. Who is giving what, to whom and for what objectives? What has changed, and what has remained the same, in the region's philanthropic landscape? How much has philanthropy *really* shifted from charity to solidar-ity and from there to longer term social change? The following three chap-ters ask similar questions, focusing on the role of individuals – volunteers, organizers, activists—who give their time, energy and resources to diverse social causes, as well as examining the changing institutional and political contexts within which they do so. Silvia Arrom provides a fresh perspec-tive on the role of Catholic charity and volunteerism in Mexico, re-exam-ining the past to help provide insights on the present. Felipe Portocarrero examines volunteering and civic engagement, and the relation between them, in the case of Peru, while Leilah Landim explores change and continuity in the most recent promotion of volunteerism by the Brazilian state.

The Corporate Contribution: Social Responsibility in Changing Times

Felipe Agüero begins this section with an overview piece on the Corporate Social Responsibility "movement" in Latin America, which helps us locate the latest wave of corporate philanthropy within a broader political and economic context. In addition to direct donations or social investment, for-profit companies in Latin America are entering into new forms of alliance with nonprofit organizations, and local and national governments, to tackle broader social problems. Rosa Maria Fischer and Cristina Rojas examine such efforts from independent and critical perspectives in Brazil and Colombia, respectively. Francisco Durand and Mario Roitter look more closely at the evolution of corporate discourse and practice in Peru and Argentina, stressing the evolution of the former as well as some persistent gaps between the two.

Foundations and Frameworks: Creating an Enabling Environment

While direct forms of giving by individuals and companies have long-standing roots in Latin America, the last decade has seen a trend towards the creation of private foundations. In this section, David Winder and Shari Turitz share the results of an important study conducted by the Synergos Institute on grant making foundations in Brazil, Mexico and Ecuador, the majority of which were created in the 1990s. The total number of foundations in Latin America remains small in comparison to the region's vast private wealth and population, however, and this chapter also explores some of the factors that have inhibited further expansion of this type of organized philanthropy.

Of course, the factors that motivate people to donate time and resources vary widely and are often deeply personal. However, as the authors in this section comment, the recent proliferation of organized giving may also be the result of more favorable political, legal and fiscal environments for such activity. The transition from dictatorship to democracy has brought greater freedom of association and action for private donors and voluntary associations, and a greater disposition on the part of some elected governments to promote strong civil societies and philanthropy. Furthermore, governments across the region have entered into collaborative arrangements with private donors and with NGOs, to design, co-fund and implement a variety of public policy initiatives. As Gonzalo de la Maza suggests in the Chilean case, however, such initiatives may have mixed results for all involved. Eduardo Szasi explores the important but unstable alliances that emerged among NGOs, social movements, and donors to influence public policy in the Brazilian case. Such efforts often include demands for greater tax incentives and benefits for donors and their recipients, a controversial topic that is analyzed by Ignacio Irarrázaval, Julio Guzmán and Juan Carlos Jaramillo.

Each of these chapters examines some aspect of the formal regulatory frameworks for philanthropy and nonprofit organizations in the region. In contrast, Rodrigo Villar stresses the need for greater self-regulation within the nonprofit sector itself, through the establishment of common standards, codes of conduct and levels of transparency that can be adhered to voluntarily by private organizations that increasingly operate in the public domain.

Reflections from International Practice

Co-sponsorship of the PASCA program by DRCLAS and the Hauser Center allowed the participants and collaborators to engage in an ongoing dialogue about the nature and limitations of philanthropy in the United States, Latin America, and other regions of the world. Organized philanthropy has a long history in the United States, one that is unique to that country (one historian calls it "The American Creed")[2] and yet serves as an inspiration to many others. In her provocative chapter, Christine Letts examines the differences between organized philanthropy in the United States and Latin America, drawing lessons from both and stressing some of the advantages of the new forms of giving emerging in Latin America today. L. David Brown focuses on the broader issues of the legitimacy and accountability of such private actors who propose to operate for the public good, drawing lessons from his vast experience in Africa, Asia and the Americas. In the final chapter, Merilee Grindle draws on her considerable knowledge about the politics of policy reform in Latin America to suggest ways in which the kind of research and good ideas produced in this volume can be turned into more effective public policies, policies that can strengthen philanthropy and improve its capacity for broader impact.

The Road Ahead

This collection aims to contribute to knowledge about philanthropy, its role in society and its relationship with the State, across the Americas and beyond. We consider it an important step in the creation of an international community of scholars and practitioners, who both analyze and practice philanthropy with an independent spirit. This volume is only one step, however. Much more needs to be done before we can truly understand this phenomena, which in turn may enable us to better promote philanthropy that moves beyond charity to bring about lasting and positive social change.

In most countries, there is still an extremely limited amount of reliable data on giving and volunteering that could permit us to more effectively trace changes over time, and even less that is comparable across national borders. With few exceptions, a huge effort must still be made to convince national census and statistical agencies in Latin America to take into account such activity, as well as to convince tax and regulatory authorities to release what data they have on these phenomenon to independent scrutiny. For their part, both private donors and recipients of philanthropy are often less than forthcoming in opening their records to researchers, though such efforts form part of broader agendas for Corporate Social Responsibility and for self-regulation of the nonprofit sector. Scholars and practitioners alike can work to advance these goals.

The motivations of donors in general are little understood in Latin America, or elsewhere for that matter. In the last decade, several path-breaking giving and volunteering surveys have been conducted in the region (in this volume, Landim and Portocarrero analyze some of the data for Brazil and Peru, respectively), and surveys have also examined attitudes and motives for corporate giving in Peru and Brazil, and individual giving on the part of the wealthy in Argentina.[3] However, more needs to be done to understand what drives people of all socioeconomic backgrounds to give beyond their immediate family and social circles, including both quantitative and qualitative research.

Although this volume touches on the role of the state and political institutions in various ways—as promoters, regulators or obstacles to private giving and volunteering—this is another avenue that needs further exploration. Political Science departments and schools of public policy in developed countries have long given attention to the roles played by civil society, the "third sector" and private corporations, as independent actors and as partners to government. In Latin America far less is known—or even asked, in research terms—about how the private, corporate and non-profit sectors relate. Thanks to efforts by numerous institutions, including The Center for the Study of Philanthropy at the City University of New York, the Johns Hopkins University Comparative Nonprofit Sector Project, the International Society for Third Sector Research and CIVICUS:

World Alliance for Citizen Participation; Latin Americans and other developing country scholars and practitioners have become engaged in global discussions about these issues. In this region's universities and research centers, however, more needs to be done to incorporate these themes into the curricula, produce new knowledge about such links, and train a new generation of leaders across the spectrum who are motivated to use both public and private resources effectively to achieve positive social change.

Acknowledgements

Many individuals and institutions contributed to the research that is contained in this volume as well as to the publication itself. The editors wish to thank Harvard University, and the DRCLAS and Hauser Centers, for their institutional commitment to the study of philanthropy in Latin America, and for providing a truly "enabling environment" for many of the authors between 1999 and 2003. In particular, we thank DRCLAS Director John H. Coatsworth and former Executive Director Steve Reifenberg (now Regional Office Program Director of the DRCLAS Chile office), for launching and promoting the PASCA program, along with former Hauser Center Director Mark Moore and former Hauser Executive Director Shawn Bohen. Harvard faculty Christine Letts, L. David Brown, Merilee Grindle, James Austin and Diana Barrett provided generous and valuable input for this effort. Various authors in this volume have also participated in the Social Enterprise Knowledge Network (SEKN) coordinated by Jim Austin and colleagues at Harvard Business School, which has certainly helped to hone their thinking on these issues.

Our colleague and collaborator Rodrigo Villar played an especially important role in the development of this project, through his efforts as PASCA Director of Programs and subsequently as a promoter of social responsibility and sustainable development in Latin America through the RedeAmerica network of foundations.

We also wish to thank the Universidad del Pacífico, our home institution in Peru, for granting both editors leaves of absence to participate in PASCA; Sanborn for two years to assume the William Henry Bloomberg Chair in Philanthropy, and Portocarrero for a full semester as Visiting Scholar, as well as for maintaining an institutional commitment to the study and promotion of both philanthropy and social change.

Very special thanks goes to the Tinker and Lampadia Foundations for their generous funding and support of the PASCA program and of a share the research presented here. Renate Rennie of Tinker was a colleague and engaged participant as well as a funder, and Joseph Oppenheimer and the late Robert Glynn of Lampadia were welcome sources of advice and constructive criticism. The W.K. Kellogg Foundation and the Ford Foundation also provided support for some of the research presented, and for translation and editing of various chapters. In particular, we thank Andrés Thompson of Kellogg, and Anthony Tillett and Augusto Varas of the Ford Foundation regional office in Santiago de Chile.

Felipe Viveros, Rebecca Raposo, Anna Maria Medeiros Peliano, Valdemar de Oliveira Neto, Anna Cynthia Oliviera, Gabriel Berger and Nelson Colon are among the scholars and practitioners who participated in PASCA, and whose work has been fundamental to the advancement of philanthropy in Latin America. Their ideas and resources have informed this volume through their generous collaboration.

Finally, the authors wish to extend our most heartfelt gratitude to DRCLAS Publications Director June Carolyn Erlick, a dear friend and colleague, whose inherent solidarity and generous donation of her own time and talents were indispensable to the completion of this volume. Each author has reason to thank June personally for improving on his/her original drafts (at times vastly), and the editors have additional reason to thank her for keeping this project on the DRCLAS agenda. Without June, this book simply would not have happened.

Notes

1 The W.K. Kellogg, Ford, Rockefeller, Inter-American and Avina foundations stand out for their efforts to promote philanthropy and corporate social responsibility in Latin America over the past decade. Humanitarian organizations that have shifted from charity and emergency relief to addressing root causes of poverty include the Oxfam affiliates and Catholic Relief Services.

2 In *American Creed: Philanthropy and the Rise of Civil Society 1700–1865* (Chicago: The University of Chicago Press, 2003), Kathleen McCarthy traces the critical role of philanthropy and religious faith in the development of civil society and democracy in the U.S.

3 See Gabriel Berger, Nicolás Ducoté and Lorena Reiss, *Filantropía individual en la Argentina: estudio de opinions, actitudes y comportamiento de personas de alto patrimonio* (Buenos Aires: CIPPEC, 2004)

About the Contributors

Felipe Agüero is Associate Professor in the Department of International Studies at the University of Miami. A Chilean political scientist and sociologist, he has previously taught at Duke and Ohio State University and has been a visiting fellow at the Institute for Advanced Study (Princeton), The Helen Kellogg Institute (Notre Dame) and FLACSO-Chile, and is a fellow at the Wilson Center in Washington, D.C. in 2005–06. He is the author of *Soldiers, Civilians and Democracy: Post-Franco Spain in Comparative Perspective*, and co-editor of *Fault Lines of Democracy in Post-Transition Latin America* and *Memorias Militares sobre la Represión en el Cono Sur: Visiones en Disputa en Dictadura y Democracia.*

Silvia Marina Arrom is Director of the Latin American Studies Program and Jane's Professor of Latin American Studies at Brandeis University. Her research interests are Latin American social history, modern Mexico, women and the family, and social welfare. Her books include *The Women of Mexico City, 1790–1857* and *Containing the Poor. The Mexico City Poor House, 1774–1871.*

L. David Brown is Director of International Programs at the Hauser Center for Nonprofit Organizations and Lecturer in Public Policy at the Kennedy School of Government at Harvard University. He has been President of the Institute for Development Research and Professor of Organizational Behavior at Boston University School of Management. His research and consulting interests include organizational change and inter-organizational relations that foster social transformation and sustainable development. His publications include *Transnational Civil Society: An Introduction* (with Srilatha Batliwala), *Practice-Research Engagement for Civil Society in a Globalizing World*, *The Struggle for Accountability: NGOs, Social Movements and the World Bank* (with Jonathan Fox), and *Managing Conflict at Organizational Interfaces*

John H. Coatsworth is Monroe Gutman Professor of Latin American Affairs at Harvard University, where he also serves as Director of the David Rockefeller Center for Latin American Studies. His recent books include *The United States and Central America: The Clients and the Colossus* and *Latin America and the World Economy Since 1800* (edited with Alan M. Taylor).

Gonzalo de la Maza is Director of the Corporación Innovación en Ciudadanía in Chile. He is a sociologist whose teaching, research and consulting interests include poverty and social development, the evaluation of social programs and the strengthening of NGOs. He was founder and president of ACCION—the Chilean Association of NGOs, and a Ford Foundation DRCLAS/PASCA Visiting Fellow at Harvard University.

Francisco Durand is Professor of Political Science at the University of Texas at San Antonio and Associate Professor of Sociology at the Pontifical Catholic University of Peru. He has published seven books and numerous articles on business and government in Peru and Latin America. He has been a visiting fellow at Notre Dame, Oxford, Harvard and the University of Chicago, and was Director of the Peruvian Institute of Tax Administration (1992–1994) His recent books include *Riqueza Economica y Pobreza Politica, Business and Democracy in Peru*, and *Organized Business, Economic Change and Democracy in Latin America* (edited with Eduardo Silva).

Rosa Maria Fischer is Titular Professor at the School of Economics, Business Administration and Accounting at the University of São Paulo in Brazil. Director of the Center of Social Entrepreneurship and Management of the Third Sector (CEATS), she is a sociologist who specializes in third sector development, corporate social responsibility and cross-sector alliances. She has been on the Board of Directors of the International Society for Third Sector Research and is founding member of SEKN—Social Enterprise Knowledge Network, among other organizations. Her most recent publications include *Social Partnering in Latin America* (as part of SEKN).

Julio Gúzman has worked as an analyst with the Chilean Ministry of Finance and has taught Economics at the Catholic University of Chile. He holds a BA and MA in Economics from the Catholic University of Chile and is completing a PhD in Economics at the University of Chicago.

Ignacio Irarrázaval is a partner in FOCUS, a private consulting firm in Santiago de Chile, and Director of the Diploma in Public Policy at the Catholic University of Chile. He is also associate researcher at the Centro de Estudios Publicos in Chile. He is now conducting the Johns Hopkins Comparative Nonprofit Sector Project case study for Chile. His recent publications include *The Role of Community Organizations in Fighting Poverty*, and *Diagnsitico de incentivos tributarios como fuente de financiamento para la sociedad civil.*

Juan Carlos Jaramillo is a lawyer and specialist in tax regimes for non-profits. He is currently Manager of the Tax Unit of the business group led by the Fundación Social in Colombia, and is also a faculty member at the Universidad de la Sabana and the Universidad Jorge Tadeo Lozano. He has been a consultant to the Colombian Confederation of Non Governmental Organizations and the Fundacion del Banco de la Republica, and is currently consultant to the NEST Foundation for the preparation of proposed new legal and commercial framework for nonprofits in Colombia.

Leilah Landim is a Professor of Anthropology at the Federal University of Rio de Janeiro, Brazil, and a senior scholar at the Institute for the Study of Religion (ISER). She has been a Visiting Scholar at DRCLAS, Harvard University, and Visiting Research Professor at the Center for the Studies of Voluntary Organizations and Service, at the Institute for Policy Studies, Georgetown University. She was involved in the Johns Hopkins Comparative Nonprofit Sector Project as Associate Researcher for Brazil and she has a Post-Doctorate at the *Centre d'Études des Mouvements Sociaux*, EHESS, Paris. Her publications include *Associativismo e Organizações Voluntárias – Estatísticas do Século XX* .

Christine Letts is the Rita E. Hauser Lecturer in the Practice of Philanthropy and Nonprofit Leadership at the Kennedy School of Government, Harvard University, where she also serves as Associate Dean of Executive Programs. Her research interests include high engagement philanthropy and the value exchange between nonprofits and funders. She has been Vice President for Corporate Responsibility of Cummins Engine Company and President of the Cummins Engine Foundation, and has served as Commissioner of the Indiana Department of Transportation and Secretary of the Indiana Family and Social Services Administration. She is co-author of *Virtuous Capital: What Foundations Can Learn from Venture Capitalists*, and *High Performance Nonprofit Organizations: Managing Upstream for Greater Impact.*

Gustavo Morales is professor of International Affairs and Director of the Observatory of International Affairs at the Pontificia Universidad Javeriana in Cali, Colombia. His research interests focus on corporate philanthropy, democracy and the integration process in the Andean Region. His most recent publication is *Comunidad Internacional: Ayuda u Obstáculo a la Superación del Conflicto en Colombia.*

Felipe Portocarrero is Professor of Sociology and Contemporary Social Thought at the Universidad del Pacífico in Lima Perú, and former Director of the University's Research Center (1999–2004). His research interests include history of economic elites and philanthropy in Latin America, giving and volunteering, the third sector and corporate social responsibility. He participated in the Johns Hopkins Comparative Nonprofit Sector Study and the W.K. Kellogg Foundation Leadership in Philanthropy Program, and currently forms part of the Social Enterprise Knowledge Network. His publications include *El Imperio Prado: 1890–1970, Voluntarios, Donantes y Ciudadanos en el Peru* (with Armando Millán and James Loveday), *De la caridad a la solidaridad: filantropía y voluntariado en el Perú* (co-edited with Cynthia Sanborn), *Mas alla del individualismo: el tercer sector en el Peru* (with Cynthia Sanborn, Hanny Cueva and Armando Millan), and *El Pacto Infame: estudios sobre la corrupción en el Perú* (editor).

Mario Roitter is Program Director of the Civil Society and Social Development Department at the Center for the Study of State and Society (CEDES) in Argentina. He participated in the Johns Hopkins Comparative Nonprofit Sector Project, was a DRCLAS fellow at Harvard University, and is now part of the Social Enterprise Knowledge Network. His research interests are on nonprofit organizations and corporate social responsibilty in Argentina, and his publications include *Estudios sobre el Sector Sin Fines de Lucro en Argentina*, *Realidades y promesas del voluntariado*, and *La razon social de las empresas*.

Cristina Rojas is Associate Professor at the Norman Paterson School of International Affairs, Carleton University, Canada. She previously taught at the Universidad Javeriana and the National University of Colombia, and has been a Visiting Fellow at DRCLAS, Harvard University. Her research interests focus on corporate philanthropy, citizenship, comparative social policy, and Latin American political economy. Her publications include *Elusive Peace. International, National and Local Dimensions of Conflict in Colombia* (co-edited with Judy Meltzer) and *Civilization and Violence: Regimes of Representation in Nineteenth Century Colombia*.

Cynthia A. Sanborn is Professor of Political Science and Chair of the Department of Political and Social Sciences at the Universidad del Pacífico in Lima, Peru. Between 2001 and 2003 she was the William Henry Bloomberg Professor of Philanthropy at Harvard University and Director of the Program on Philanthropy and Social Change in the Americas (PASCA). She has been a Program Officer for the Ford Foundation in New

York and Santiago de Chile (1989–1995), and consultant to various foundations and nonprofit organizations. Her research interests include democracy and human rights, civil society and corporate social responsibility. She has a PhD in Government from Harvard University, and her recent publications include *The Pitfalls of Policymaking in Peru: Actors, Institutions and Rules of the Game* (with Eduardo Moron*)*, *Social Justice and Philanthropy in the Andes: Regulating the Extractive Industries* (with Felipe Portocarrero, Luis Camacho and Oswaldo Molina), *From Charity to Solidarity? Latin American Philanthropy in Changing Times, De la caridad a la solidaridad: filantropía y voluntariado en el Perú* (co-edited with Felipe Portocarrero), and *Mas alla del individualismo: el tercer sector en el Peru* (with Felipe Portocarrero, Hanny Cueva and Armando Millan).

Eduardo Szazi is a leading nonprofit lawyer in Brazil and consultant to diverse foundations and non profits, including the major donor's association GIFE. He is also Professor of Third Sector Law at the Getulio Vargas Foundation, the Universidad Mackenzie and the Fundacion Instituto de Administration at the University of Sao Paulo. He was a member of the Working Group on Reform of the Legal Framework for the Third Sector, convened by Comunidade Solidaria, and as such helped produce the new legislation currently in force in Brazil. His publications include *Tercer Setor: Regulación en Brazil.*

Shari Turitz is the Director of Strengthening Bridging Organizations at the Synergos Institute, which she joined in 1996 to run its Latin America programs. At Synergos she has worked with local partners to develop community foundations in Mexico, launch the first foundation network in Ecuador and build Brazil's first community foundation in Rio de Janeiro. She is presently managing the Border Philanthropy Partnership (BPP), a bi-national collaboration of eleven funders and 21 border community foundations working to build community philanthropy and improve quality of life along the US/Mexico border. Previously, she has been Deputy Director of the Guatemala Human Rights Commission/USA in Washington DC, and a Consultant to the Covenant House Latin America programs, Casa Alianza, and worked for the UNICEF NGO Committee on Exploited Children. She holds a BA in Political Science and Latin American Studies from Tufts University and an MA from the Columbia University School of International and Public Affairs.

Rodrigo Villar is a Consultant to the Inter-American Foundation for RedeAmerica. Previously, he was Director of Programs for Philanthropy, Civil Society and Social Change in the Americas (PASCA) at Harvard University. He participated in the Johns Hopkins Comparative Nonprofit Sector Project and worked with the Colombian Confederation of NGOs. As a consultant he has worked with the Inter-American Development Bank, the World Bank, the Synergos Institute, World Education and the Harvard Institute for International Development. His research interests focus on social policy, community development and corporate social responsibility. His publications include *Construír Juntos: Una propuesta para hacer desarrollo de base; Organizaciones de la sociedad civil e incidencia en políticas públicas; El tercer sector en Colombia: Evolución, dimensión y tendencias; Colombia: A Diverse Nonprofit Sector; La Sociedad Civil y la redefinición de lo público,* and *Mujer Campesina y Organización Rural en Colombia.*

David Winder is Interim Director of the Multi-Stakeholder Partnership Program at the Synergos Institute. At Synergos he has developed a foundation building program that provides technical assistance services to foundations and associations of foundations in Latin America, Southern Africa and Southeast Asia and conducts research on the foundation sector. He was previously a mid-career Fellow at St. Antony's College, Oxford University where he conducted research on NGOs in Mexico. He also worked for the Ford Foundation for more than a decade, serving as Representative for Mexico and Central America and for Southeast Asia. Prior to that, he lectured for eleven years in social policy and planning at the University of Manchester, UK, where he acted as Director of the Public Administration Studies Program. His publications include *Foundation Building Sourcebook* and *El Desarrollo: Una Tarea en Comun* edited with Enrique Valencia.

Section

I

LATIN AMERICAN PHILANTHROPY, PAST AND PRESENT

1

Philanthropy in Latin America: Historical Traditions and Current Trends

Cynthia A. Sanborn

> *"Since the Portuguese colonized Brazil as a Catholic community in the 1500s, charities have been present. (. . .) So, what's new in Brazilian philanthropy? Democratization. That is what has changed the face of domestic philanthropy."*
> —Rebecca Raposo, GIFE[1]

> *"The Fundación Carvajal was established in 1961 as an instrument for social justice and Christian charity."*
> —Revista *Credencial Histórica,* Colombia 1999

Persistent poverty amidst great wealth, denial of basic rights amidst formal democracy, profound and morally intolerable inequality: these conditions characterize much of Latin America today. For this reason, numerous leaders in global philanthropy have argued that closing the gap between rich and poor, and empowering the latter, are the most important challenges for this sector in the 21st century (Chen 2002, Harris 2003). But does this not pose a fundamental contradiction? Is it realistic to expect that those who have benefited from the unequal distribution of wealth and rights are going to promote, or even permit, a change in this situation?

In fact, giving and volunteering to help the needy and advance the common good is nothing new in Latin America. The cultural diversity of the region's more than 500 million people is reflected in their many traditions of reciprocity and community self-help, religious and immigrant solidarity, as well as in trade unionism and grassroots movements to challenge the status quo. Furthermore, since the early 1990s, there have been increased efforts in the region to promote new forms of organized philanthropy aimed at achieving lasting social change. Such efforts are being led by international donors and aid agencies, religious organizations and educational institutions, as well as local government and corporate figures.

How much has been achieved by such efforts? How much organized philanthropy is there in Latin America today, and what are its main characteristics and objectives? What historical traditions have had the most influence on contemporary giving, and what changes are most notable? What share of current philanthropy is directed toward addressing the region's most serious social problems, and what impact might this type of philanthropy have? After nearly two decades of research and advocacy around philanthropy in Latin America, it is an opportune moment to pose such questions. This chapter represents an initial effort to answer them. Drawing on the valuable work produced by a growing network of researchers, it paints in very broad strokes a picture of the main trends in Latin American philanthropy, past and present. The many other chapters in this volume provide color, volume, depth and detail to this picture.

Existing research does indeed show that new private giving has been aimed at addressing some priority social problems in Latin America, including education and community development. The persistence of religious charity and *asistencialismo* (or basic service provision), understandable in a region where states alone are incapable of meeting basic needs, has been joined by growing interest among some members of the economic elite in finding longer-lasting solutions to hunger, poverty and violence.

At the same time, much of the new philanthropy in Latin America is still scattered and limited in its impact and capacity to achieve its proposed objectives. Additionally, an important share of private giving remains directed toward activities that primarily benefit—and reproduce—social elites themselves, including support for private schools and universities, wealthy parishes, fine arts institutions, and scientific and cultural events. Such patterns of giving are similar to those in developed countries, and undeniably support worthy initiatives. Nevertheless, in societies with profound social gaps and serious limitations in public resources and capacity, these patterns provoke the suspicions of government authorities regarding the civic virtues of philanthropy, and explain their reluctance in many cases to promote it through public policy, tax or legal or tax initiatives.

The first section in this chapter briefly summarizes the most prominent historical traditions in Latin American philanthropy. The second contrasts these with the basic organizational forms found in contemporary philanthropy—religious, direct corporate, and private foundations—and the third examines the main objectives and intended beneficiaries of Latin American philanthropy today. The fourth section then looks at some of the links between philanthropy, the state and public policy in the region, and the chapter ends with brief reflections on how to increase the impact of philanthropy on social change in this region.

I. Charity and Solidarity: Philanthropic Traditions in Latin America

The inhabitants of this region have longstanding and diverse traditions of charity and solidarity, making it difficult to speak of "Latin American philanthropy" as though it were a homogeneous block. Nonetheless, it is possible to identify some tendencies and experiences common to a large part—if not all—of this region.[2]

The Catholic Church and Christian Charity

It is not surprising that the Catholic Church has played a central role in the history of philanthropy, given that between 80 and 95 percent of Latin Americans consider themselves of the Catholic faith. During the Colonial period, the Church was the principal provider of education, health and social welfare services, and it controlled virtually all of the existing charitable entities. Financed by the colonial government and wealthy elites, Church-provided social assistance was for centuries provided to groups of the poor, in a paternalistic manner and in explicit support of the colonial power structure.

The predominance of the Church in the charitable sphere lasted through the 19th century and the greater part of the 20th.[3] Nevertheless, it would be incorrect to consider the Church's varied activities as a continuum of the colonial model. During the 20th century in particular, the stance of the Catholic Church in Latin America on social issues evolved from a conservative and elitist position toward a preferential identification with the poor and a defense of equitable development and social justice (Fleet and Smith 1997). This turnaround in focus was also reflected in the methods of the different educational and social welfare entities associated with the Church. Furthermore, during the 20th century, important social movements were inspired by the ideals of the new Liberation Theology, and a considerable number of Catholic activists were founders and members of grassroots organizations, NGOs and human rights groups. Although there have always been divisions within the Church concerning the scope and objectives of religiously inspired social work, at the end of the 20th century almost all doctrinal positions within the Church were reflected in hands-on initiatives with preferential concern for the poor.

The State and Central Governments

While predominance of the Catholic Church is a historical characteristic of Latin American philanthropy, another is the controlling role played by the State and central governments. During the 19th century, an important component in the creation of new national states was the effort of governments to centralize power and take control over social services. In Argentina, Brazil, Uruguay and Mexico, a formal separation between state and church took place, and in most countries the state progressively assumed various social functions that had previously been assigned to religious authorities.

Nonetheless, with the exception of Uruguay, the Church maintained considerable power and a notable presence in the social arena as an ally of the state and the local (*criolla*) elite. Yet this was not the case with other forms of private organization. Despite the existence of associative experiences with longstanding traditions, many analysts contend that the creation of organized and consolidated civil societies was subsequent to the creation of independent states in this region, and was strongly conditioned by the same. Moreover, there are those who argue that "modern" civil society in Latin America has developed principally in reaction to the actions and policies of the state.[4]

In regard to the 20th century, the formulation and implementation of diverse social policies on the part of national states must be understood in the context of the general development models that were introduced. While considerable variation existed between countries, for the most part, between the 1930s and 1960s Latin American governments promoted forms of industrialization through protectionist trade policies and the substitution of imports by locally produced goods (known as ISI). These actions privileged and protected the growth of a national industrial sector and internal markets, and motivated the creation of urban interest groups made up of working- and middle-class members interested in promoting diverse forms of social services (Huber 1996: 144). In this respect, expanded public health and education systems allowed for greater coverage and entailed centralized control and administration. Even today, in the wake of neo-liberalism, the education and health services provided by private entities in most countries cover only a reduced segment of the total population. Of the latter, however, the Catholic Church continues to be the privileged partner of the state in the administration of services for the poor.

The Economic and Social Elite

If the state and the church dominated the realm of social welfare, what has been the role of the region's social and economic elites? The involvement of the wealthy in charitable activities during colonial rule and for much of the Independence period was characterized by a paternalistic style inspired by religious motivations and self-interest. The Societies of Public Benefit (*Sociedades de Beneficiencia Publica*) were a leading form of private involvement in social welfare, in which conspicuous members of the upper classes managed the provision of various welfare services (Portocarrero, Sanborn, Llusera y Quea 2000: 233–235). Subsequently, during the ISI period, modernizing sectors of the bourgeoisie became the force behind the creation of new private universities, technical institutions and foundations aimed at promoting national development.[5] Encouraged by the U.S.-sponsored Alliance for Progress in some cases, these private sector initiatives also included diverse campaigns in benefit of the poorer and more excluded sectors of the population. Nevertheless, in societies marked by longstanding discrimination and social exclusion, the generosity of the elite did not always extend to the acceptance of universal suffrage and full citizenship rights for the broader population.

Migrants and Immigrants

In the late 19th and early 20th century, two trends had a significant impact on both civil society and philanthropy in this region: new waves of immigrants from Europe and Asia, and the accelerated flow of migrants from rural areas to the cities. Fleeing from economic poverty and from political or ethnic persecution, waves of Italian, Spanish, Chinese and Japanese immigrants arrived in Latin America, as well as important numbers of European Jews. Each immigrant group established diverse types of mutual aid societies, schools, hospitals and charitable organizations, aimed at providing collective assistance and preserving their cultural traditions. European immigrants also encouraged the creation of trade unions and mass-based political parties in the region.

Weak Liberal Political Traditions

Another factor that bears on the nature of philanthropy is the weakness of liberal political tradition in this region. Although Latin American countries vary in their political histories, and limited forms of democracy flourished early in some societies, authoritarian and populist regimes have been the predominant conduits for exercising state power. These types of regimes have tended to combine the creation or co-option of officially sanctioned social organizations, with the direct repression or indirect control of more autonomous forms of civic association. In some cases, these regimes have achieved important advances in income distribution and social welfare benefits, especially toward better-organized urban labor and professional groups (Peronism in Argentina and the PRI in Mexico are cases in point). Nevertheless, these schemes also involved strict state regulation of society, still partial degrees of political citizenship and social inclusion, and few incentives for—or outright suspicion of—philanthropic initiatives from outside a narrow religious ambit.

The Role of International Cooperation

Between the 60s and the 80s, a wave of new military dictatorships arose in South America, characterized not only by their radical suppression of popular uprisings and armed opposition groups, but also by their modernizing projects for development and state reform. In this context, new organizations for the defense of human rights and social justice also emerged, with strong support in some countries by Catholic Church authorities, including Brazil and Chile, in open confrontation with the authoritarian regimes. The existence of international humanitarian aid and development assistance was also essential for sustaining these activities, because in many cases the local philanthropic elite supported these regimes and looked the other way during the worst periods of state violence. It is important to highlight the role played by international religious agencies of different faiths, such as Catholic Relief Services, Misereor, World Relief and World Vision (the latter two being Protestant) and the World Council of Churches (Fleet and Smith 1997, Smith 1982). The Ford Foundation, the Inter-American Foundation and diverse European donors provided significant international aid to refugees and victims of military dictatorships during the 1970s and 1980s.

With the return of civilian rule in most of the region by the late 1980s, international donors continued to be a fundamental source of support for those civil society organizations that defended the consolidation and expansion of democracy, social justice for the poor, and the extension of equal rights and opportunities to women, ethnic minorities and other excluded groups. With few exceptions, for the most part these were objectives that the economic elite were not ready to support and from which most national donors maintained a prudent distance. According to Fleet and Smith (1997), international aid also remained a key source of support for the social programs sponsored by the Catholic Church in Latin America from the 1980s onward, replacing or complementing available public sudsidies.

As the decade of the 1990s began, therefore, the philanthropic panorama of Latin America included a variety of actors and institutional forms that ranged from the traditional religious charity to new forms of solidarity and support for social justice. Also evident was the persistence of the central state as the predominant provider of basic services, the role of the Catholic Church as the privileged ally of the state in various social tasks, and a still incipient presence of private elites in the philanthropic sphere.

II. Contemporary Philanthropy: Basic Characteristics

What is different about philanthropy in Latin America today? How much organized philanthropy exists, and what are its origins, objectives and institutional forms?

In trying to answer these questions, we can draw on several baseline national surveys of giving and volunteering by individuals in Argentina, Chile, Peru and Brazil (the Portocarrero and Landim chapters in this book are based on the latter two studies). Also, under the auspices of the Comparative Nonprofit Sector Project of The John Hopkins University, research teams in Argentina, Brazil, Colombia, Peru and Mexico produced a series of basic studies of the nonprofit sector. Using 1995 as a base year, these studies examined the history, legal framework, concentration, income, expenditures and impact of the principal forms of nonprofit organizations in each country (Salamon et al., 1999). Furthermore, as demonstrated by other chapters in this book, there are now mappings and case studies of foundations and corporate philanthropy in Argentina, Brazil, Chile, Colombia, Ecuador, Peru and Mexico, using diverse samples and research methodologies.

Although a growing amount of information has been produced about these phenomena, it is still rare to find data that is regularly updated, or that is truly comparable across countries. Similarly, few reliable estimates exist of the actual amount of private donations made in a given country and year, or of the magnitude of resources invested in philanthropic programs, nor do we have baseline data that allows us to confirm whether donations of various sorts have increased or decreased over time. There is very scarce information available with which to assess the direction or impact of philanthropy in specific fields, or to examine the dynamics of existing relationships between donors and beneficiaries.

In spite of these limitations, some basic tendencies and characteristics can be identified in the existing research, and they include the following:

- The Catholic Church continues to play an important role in virtually all forms of philanthropy, even though its historical influence appears to have diminished in comparison with past eras.

- At the same time, there has been a significant increase in organized, secular philanthropy in the last decade, and especially in the number of new foundations and direct corporate giving initiatives.

- Corporate philanthropy appears to be the most extensive and fastest growing form in the region in recent years. Organized community philanthropy has also expanded in several countries, although its scope region-wide remains limited.

- In terms of foundations, there is great heterogeneity behind this legal figure across the region, but to date we have identified very few that are private, autonomous in their management, and possess some form of endowment or permanent source of income. For example, based on reliable data available from seven countries, we have identified 346 foundations that meet these criteria.

- Of the latter group of foundations, the majority (76%) make donations to third parties as part of their activities. However, the majority tend to identify themselves as actors rather than donors, and their direct operation of programs or projects tends to exceed grant making in terms of the amounts of money and staff time invested.

- Charity and the affirmation of religious faith remain the motivations behind the majority of individual philanthropy registered in the region, and also a considerable share of institutional giving. While not explicitly aimed at addressing the root causes of poverty and injustice, the capacity of such activity to lead to broader social transformation should not be underestimated.

- Education and training appear to be the priorities of most private foundations and corporate giving programs in the region, although their philanthropy is also directed toward social services, community development, the promotion of arts and culture, and protection of the environment.

- Children and youth are the declared beneficiaries of most organized philanthropy, followed by the poor and vulnerable in general, and by the residents of specific geographical areas.

- In practice, however, much of the new philanthropy in this region does not have a progressive distributional impact. An important share remains concentrated in large cities, in the best organized sectors of society, and/or within middle and upper class communities, reinforcing rather than reducing the large social gaps in this region.

- A few foundations and corporate donors have developed programs aimed at strengthening other civil society organizations, and have joined forces to promote a more favorable climate for the nonprofit sector as a whole. Yet very few of them support human rights and civil liberties, or promote democracy as a political system.

Religious Charity and Social Change

Amidst the dramatic crises and social transformations experienced by most of Latin America, the social function of the Catholic Church remains one of the most visible characteristics of the region's philanthropic landscape. Local parishes, parochial schools and charitable organizations continue to be the principal beneficiaries of individual donations and voluntary labor, as well as of diverse forms of public subsidy and organized donations.[6]

Among these entities, Catholic-inspired social assistance organizations remain among the largest philanthropic initiatives in the region, in terms of both their resource base and geographic and social scope. One example is the *Nacional Monte de Piedad* (NMP) in Mexico, an organization founded 228 years ago that contributes approximately 40 percent of the total value of all donations made by private foundations in the country, and serves more than eight million people a year through its branches nationwide.[7] Another example is the *Irmandades da Misericordia* in Brazil, a colonial legacy that, according to Thompson and Landim, remains a preeminent symbol of philanthropy in that country (Thompson and Landim 1998).[8]

Of more contemporary origin is the *Hogar de Cristo* in Chile, founded in 1944 by Padre Alberto Hurtado, and its Peruvian counterpart, founded in 1995.[9] In 2001 the *Hogar de Cristo* in Chile offered 848 social programs serving more than 28,000 needy individuals, mobilizing 112,000 volunteers and 568,327 donating members. In the same year, membership fees and self-generated income provided 76 percent of the total income of this institution (Erlick 2002). In addition to its broad coverage, the *Hogar* professes a vision of development that extends beyond traditional charity, emphasizing education and job training as tools for community empowerment.

Some prominent analysts of civil society contend that religiously inspired organizations do not promote civic values or active citizen participation in the public sphere (Putnam 1993: 107–109; Verba et al., 1995: 304, 320–324). However, the situation in Latin America at least partially challenges such assertions. Although the Church is certainly characterized by an emphasis on hierarchy and obedience to ecclesiastic authority, diverse tendencies of Catholicism in Latin America today have institutional expressions that form a part of broader civil society, and have strong political and civic dimensions (Marzal 2002). The *Fe y Alegria* organization, for example, is a region-wide network of schools in low-income communities that is affiliated with the Jesuit order, and promotes the active participation of neighbors, parents and children in the administration of their local schools (Portocarrero, Sanborn, Cueva and Milan 2002: 312–328). Many of the leading human rights organizations in the region also maintain active links with the Catholic Church.

At the same time, it is important to highlight the diversity of religious faiths and organizations operating in the region today, including various strands of Judaism, multiple new and traditional Protestant and evangelical groups, and even small Muslim communities. The philanthropic initiatives of these groups have expanded considerably, and enjoy greater tolerance from both the Catholic Church and the state in comparison with years past. The willingness of people of different faiths to join forces with each other, and with secular civil society organizations, is reflected in many initiatives, including the human rights movement in Peru, the campaign against hunger in Brazil, and the mobilization of humanitarian responses to the recent Argentine crisis. Meanwhile, in the realm of international cooperation, traditional relief organizations such as Catholic Relief Services have extended their work to include a new focus on sustainable development, human rights and social justice, including the empowerment of the low-income communities they have long served.

Nevertheless, there is still little hard data available in Latin America on the majority of churches and religiously inspired social programs currently in operation. While larger, foreign funded organizations are subject to a certain level of regulation and public scrutiny, this is not the case for most parishes, parochial schools and other spheres of religious life. Two recent studies suggest that although the Church continues to be the privileged recipient of the resources and trust of most citizens, the giving of alms and other donations from the faithful to the Church is not sufficient to maintain the operating costs of most parishes and cover other social expenses (Fleet and Smith 1997). In Peru, recent estimates suggest that the role of the Church as a social service provider has also declined, reaching less than one percent of homes through its education, health and food assistance programs (Portocarrero, Cueva and Portugal 2005).

The Corporate Sphere: Philanthropy and Social Responsibility

Over the last decade, the largest amount of resources for organized philanthropy in Latin America came from the business world. Surveys conducted in Argentina, Brazil, Chile, Peru and Colombia show that between 80 and 95 percent of the largest corporations practice some type of direct philanthropy, including financial or in-kind donations, employee volunteer programs and direct operation of social programs (Sanborn 2000). Studies carried out in Brazil, Chile, Colombia, Ecuador, Mexico and Peru also reveal that private companies and their founders or CEOs are the principal promoters of new foundations in the region. Organizations such as *Forum Empresa* (linked to the U.S. organization Business for Social Responsibility) and *RedeAmérica* (associated with the Inter-American Foundation) promote coordination between national-level CSR efforts and greater business leadership in the oversight of social programs and projects (Villar 2003, Aguero in this volume).

The corporate sector in Brazil is particular interesting. According to a survey conducted in 2000 by the *Instituto de Pesquisa Econômica Aplicada* (IPEA), corporate expenditures for social projects in Brazil were estimated at US \$2.3 billion, representing 4 percent of GNP for that year (Avelar 2002). In absolute terms this represents 25 percent of the amount spent by U.S. corporations on similar projects, and in relative terms this figure is four times higher than similar expenditures by U.S. companies (Smith 2003). Furthermore, two out of three companies in the wealthy southeast region report making social investments, and more than a third also promote employee volunteer programs (De Avelar 2002, Raposo 2002).

How can we explain this activity? Various authors in this book address this question, and most analysts tend to cite factors that lie beyond corporate walls. In particular, the transition to democracy in Brazil sparked an increase in both social demands and pressures on the elite, while encouraging new social movements. As seen in Porto Alegre and elsewhere, social movements and NGOs have played a leading role in demanding solutions to hunger, poverty and corruption, on the part of both government and business.

Such solutions are urgently needed. While the Brazilian economy grew in the 1990s, the results did not trickle down very far. Around 60 million people—nearly a third of the population—live in poverty today, a figure double that of Mexico, and 23 million live in extreme poverty, understood as the inability of an individual to feed him or herself properly. Brazil also remains one of the most unequal countries in the world, where the richest 10 percent of the population absorbs more than half of the national income, and the poorest 10 percent lives with less than 3.6 percent (Peliano and de Oliviera Neto, 2003). For many Brazilians, including a new generation of business leaders, this is an unsustainable situation that has motivated them to assign a greater percentage of corporate income to social investment. They have also been encouraged to do so by the Cardoso and Lula governments, and by private intermediaries such as the Ethos Institute—a corporate membership organization—and GIFE, a donors' association.

Business men (and most of them *are* still men) have also assumed greater social and philanthropic leadership in Argentina, Colombia, Mexico, Venezuela and some Central American countries in the last decade, creating new foundations and assuming responsibilities for social policy. These trends reflect broader changes in the relationship between the state, the market and civil society. While these changes vary between countries, the new visibility of corporate philanthropy cannot be understood outside of the economic and political context in which it has emerged.

Private Foundations in Latin America

Direct philanthropy conducted by large companies is a phenomenon with old roots in Latin America, while the creation of independent foundations is a more recent trend in most countries. However, it is important to highlight that there is no one definition regarding what constitutes a "foundation" in Latin America, which makes it difficult to gather comparative data on this sector as a whole. In many countries there is no practical differentiation between foundations and other non profit organizations, or between those that are financially independent and those that are dependent on other entities for financial support and management (including parent companies, churches, political parties and the state itself).

For the purposes of this chapter, we have attempted to identify, in a preliminary way, foundations that share three basic characteristics: 1) they are clearly private and non profit; 2) they are legally autonomous; and, 3) they are dedicated to charitable or social objectives, through the direct operation of programs, donations to third parties, or a combination of both.

Based on available data from seven countries (Argentina, Brazil, Chile, Colombia, Ecuador, Peru and Mexico), we found 346 foundations that meet the above criteria, a small number given the combined population of these countries (see Table 1). The evidence indicates that the majority of these foundations were created during the 1990s, with funds or properties provided by private corporations or individual business leaders, and the majority is secular in orientation in terms of being legally separate from any church.

Table 1. Latin America Foundations—Preliminary Data[1]

Country	Total	Priv / Aut	Grant Making	Priority Areas
Argentina[2]	85	66	66	Education and training, health, arts and culture
Brasil	6000[3]	67[4]	49[5]	Education, arts and culture, citizenship, human rights
Chile[6]	971	42	38	Education and training, health, arts and culture
Colombia	122[7]	111	16[8]	Education, environment, development, arts and culture, health
Ecuador	nd	nd	21[9]	Education, community development, health
México	703[10]	nd	74[11]	Education and training, community development, health
Perú[12]	127	60	nd	Social services, education, research, culture, health
TOTALS	**8008**	**346**	**264**	

1. This table is a tentative effort to estimate the number of private, legally autonomous foundations in Latin America. The sources are diverse and not fully comparable.
2. These results are based on information provided by Verónica Aftalión, from Grupo de Fundaciones, and by Grupo Tercer Sector. Data corresponds to 2003.
3. Based on the number of foundations currently registered by the Centro Brasilero de Fundaciones, provided by Rebecca Raposo.
4. 55 foundations (and institutes) associated with the Grupo de Institutos, Fundaciones y Empresas (GIFE) in 2003 plus 12 cited by Turitz and Winder (2003) not affiliated with GIFE. Turtiz and Winder's survey was carried out during 2000 and 2001.
5. 31 foundations identified by Turitz and Winder (2003) plus 18 associated with GIFE that make grants and were not included in the former.
6. Teixidó y Chávarrí (2001). 971 is the total number of foundations identified. A sample of 94 foundations was surveyed in detail between 2000 and 2001. Based on this survey 42 and 38 foundations were identified as private/autonomous and grant making, respectively.
7. 94 foundations cited by Rojas (2002) plus 28 identified through the Internet.
8. Only those foundations that publicly declare making grants, according to their annual reports or web sites, have been included.
9. Turitz y Winder (2003: 5). The survey was carried out during 2000 and 2001.
10. Data corresponds to the Directorio de Instituciones Filantrópicas, available at www.cemefi.org.
11. Turitz y Winder (2003). The survey was carried out during 2000 and 2001. According to Natal (2002: 21) there could be more than a thousand grant making foundations.
12. Portocarrero et al. (2002). Data corresponds to 1998.

The foundation profile varies from country to country, a result related in part to the relative availability of data and in part to other trends. In Brazil, for example, there are very few private grant-making foundations (we identified just 49) for a country of more than 170 million people; most of these were created in the past decade, and most possess no endowment or assets that generate significant income. Their estimated annual donations are under $70 million total, which is far lower than the estimated US $2.3 billion in social investments carried out directly by private companies in that country. In contrast, Turitz and Winder point out in this volume that in Mexico there are more grant making foundations, and a greater diversity of forms, including corporate, community and family organizations. However, Mexico is similar in terms of having very few foundations that possess endowments or other permanent assets. Furthermore, according to recent studies, an estimated 40 percent of the total amount of donations made by private foundations in Mexico is still made by one organization, the above-mentioned Nacional Monte de Piedad (Natal 2002: 45, 50).

Clearly, international assistance has played a role in the evolution of organized philanthropy in Latin America, particularly in the promotion of foundations and donor networks over the last decade. Some of the large North American foundations in particular have tried to create local counterparts patterned in their own image. Yet as Letts emphasizes in this volume, the foundations in this region tend to have characteristics that differentiate them from their North American counterparts, or at least from the larger foundations that they aspire to emulate.

First of all, although the majority—76 percent—of foundations identified do make donations to third parties, the majority also operate their own programs and projects, and appear to dedicate a larger share of their resources to the latter. Furthermore, the majority appear to identify themselves as actors in a given field or cause, rather than donors per se. This is distinct from the U.S. experience, where few foundations execute their own programs and most prefer to play an indirect role in promoting social change through the efforts of their grantees. However, Letts points out that this is closer to the European experience, where operating foundations are also prominent.

For many of Latin America's civil society leaders, the scarcity of local grant making foundations represents a serious problem, given the chronic need for resources on the part of existing NGOs and community organizations (Turitz and Winder, this volume). Some also see this as an indicator of persistent mistrust of the rest of civil society on the part of social and economic elites. Yet as Letts also points out, both grant making and program operation can be mechanisms for promoting social change. When a foundation has stable resources and dynamic leadership, it can commit itself to the operation of more innovative initiatives, provide sustainability over time and assume risks while protecting the organization from the wear and tear of constant fund raising. Corporate and foundation leaders who are directly involved in a determined cause may also experience a transformation in their own understanding of the problems they aim to resolve. Such transformation in elite consciousness is also necessary for longer term change in this region. Furthermore, operating foundations in this region do not always act alone, and a growing number of them execute initiatives in conjunction with community organizations and local governments.

Of course, the capacity of foundations to have an impact in society is also related to their economic stability and administrative autonomy, and both conditions are weak in Latin America. Most foundations in the region lack endowments or other sources of permanent income. In Latin America, few individuals today dedicate their personal fortunes to philanthropy, and even fewer create foundations. As examined further in chapters by Turitz and Winder, and Irarrázaval et al., the absence of endowments may be associated, at least in part, with a lack of fiscal incentives. Few countries have inheritance taxes and many have strong disincentives to extending inheritances beyond direct heirs. Furthermore, there is a general perception that philanthropic resources should be used to address today's urgent social needs rather than saving for the future.

Nevertheless, it is important to add that the line between what belongs to a corporation and what belongs to the family that founded it, is especially ambiguous in this region. Individuals and families who establish foundations are often majority owners of the sponsoring company, and hence the decision to donate part of the corporate income becomes a highly personal matter. Nonetheless, dependence on a company's annual profits, or on the ups and downs of a given economic sector, creates various restrictions that can affect foundation performance. Meanwhile, those foundations that have neither self-generated income nor regular transfers from a corporate sponsor must dedicate considerable energy to fundraising efforts. This can create a situation where foundations come into competition with the very NGOs and community organizations that they are seeking to support.

III. Philanthropy, Civil Society and Social Change

Christopher Harris of the Ford Foundation asserts that "organized philanthropy plays a crucial role in the promotion of healthy, sustainable and democratic civil society—not only in supporting individual civil society organizations but also in building constituencies for pluralism, civic participation, equity and social justice" (Harris 2003: 47). Many promoters of the new philanthropy in Latin America share this vision. However, if one looks at actual practice in the region, it is important to ask how many donors are actually working toward these objectives. More specifically, where *does* their time and money go?

Charity and Social Services
Direct assistance to vulnerable individuals continues to be the destination of the majority of individual philanthropy and a considerable share of organized philanthropy in Latin America. Feeding hungry children, attending to the indigent sick, protecting adolescent mothers or aiding victims of violence or natural disaster are fundamental acts of human solidarity. As mentioned, parishes and charities associated with the Catholic Church continue to be important beneficiaries of both donations and volunteer work.

Although the majority of this assistance does not propose to attack the underlying causes of poverty and injustice, we should not underestimate its importance in the development of the philanthropic sector and civil society in general. Arrom reminds us of this in her chapter on social Catholicism in 19th-century Mexico. Today, according to Letts, charitable contributions tend to be the first step for a donor, who through these experiences becomes increasingly involved with a given social sector or problem, and may consequently extend the reach and impact of his or her involvement. Additionally, these donors give visibility to the importance of solidarity practices, and may participate in wider alliances to consolidate a third sector in their societies. Something similar can be said in relation to donors with religious motivations whose expressions of faith, in a number of cases, involve a strong commitment to sustainable development and to empowerment of the beneficiaries themselves.

There are various examples of the transformational capacity of so-called *asistencialismo* or basic charitable assistance in Latin America, such as the massive mobilization of support and solidarity efforts in response to the 1985 earthquake in Mexico. Faced with the state's limitations in responding to the disaster and the urgent needs of a devastated population, this cause provided both energy and visibility to a variety of civil society organizations, including new foundations that later contributed to a more extensive democratization effort (Natal 2002). Brazil provides another example. Statistics alone show that the majority of corporate donations in Brazil (54 percent) involve direct charitable assistance, with food aid being the most significant area. Food distribution to the poor constitutes the most traditional form of charity, and for the most part this practice fails to empower the individual beneficiary to overcome his or her condition. However, the Campaign Against Hunger, initiated in 1993 by Herbert de Souza (Betinho) with the support of various NGOs, mobilized numerous business leaders and traditional donors who subsequently participated in other initiatives in favor of democracy and broader social change.

Education and Training

Among recently created foundations, education clearly stands out as the main program priority. Turitz and Winder point out that the majority of grant making entities in Brazil, Mexico and Ecuador support education, and other country studies across the region share this observation. The preference for education represents a step forward in developing philanthropy that can be oriented toward development and social change. Donors, governments and international agencies generally consider education as the key to both economic development and improving social welfare, and business leaders also tend to favor the creation of a more educated and skilled work force. As Turitz and Winder observe, education also represents a relatively low-risk political investment for the donors in highly politicized contexts, and as Irarrázaval et al. show, several governments in the region offer special tax incentives for private donations made in the education sector.

Nevertheless, educational reform experts in Latin America have expressed serious concerns about the impact of private efforts to improve public education and reduce social injustice (Reimers 2001). The challenge for education reform in Latin America today is inequality. How can we close the gap between the quality education received by a privileged and globalized minority, and the deficient education received by the majority of the population, and especially the very poor? How can more resources be more efficiently channeled to the neediest schools, and how can teachers in those schools be better trained and motivated? The majority of private philanthropy in education fails to ask these questions, and a sizeable share of it involves supporting private schools and universities for the elite, thus expanding the social divide.

Although another portion of educational philanthropy is destined to improving educational opportunities for poor children, or toward job training for needy youth, these activities tend to be concentrated in a few large cities and carried out by small and dispersed institutions. Such efforts are rarely coordinated with public sector authorities, and rarely oriented toward making an impact on the large public school systems that serve more than 80 percent of the population in most countries. Additionally, with the exception of Colombia, little national philanthropy goes to supporting policy research or advocacy designed to influence public education.

Arts and Culture

Latin American philanthropists also give an important part of their resources to culture and the fine arts, including museums and galleries, the opera and symphony orchestras, contemporary theater and national cinema. They also participate actively in the preservation of diverse forms of historical and archaeological patrimony. In a region where governments have more urgent priorities, private philanthropy has been critical to sustaining such activities, and is encouraged to do so in some countries through specific tax incentives.

Of course, the majority of wealthy arts patrons do not have equity goals, and the impact of their donations in that sense is not progressive. Cultural philanthropy in Latin America is largely destined toward traditional institutions located in capital cities, and toward the initiatives preferred by an elite public. Few foundations or companies promote art and culture among low-income communities, or in geographic areas far from the capital, and on the whole they show little interest in promoting the less commercial forms of cultural expression.

Community and Sustainable Development

A growing number of foundations in Latin America today are focused on the development and well-being of a specific community or geographical area. Their programs vary according to the needs of that community, and the negotiation and planning processes carried out among diverse stakeholders, ranging from basic charity and public works, to the promotion of employment and accessible credit, to the strengthening and empowerment of community organization *per se*. Although the region's relatively few community foundations by nature operate in this terrain, an important segment of the new corporate philanthropy is also oriented to these objectives.

Community development and the longer-term protection of the environment are the leading priorities of the foundations created by large companies in the extractive industries in the last decade, especially mining and petroleum firms in the Andean region. The creation of such foundations, and the large investments companies are making in such efforts, are primarily the result of new organizing strategies and alliances among communities adjacent to and affected by these industries (Sanborn et al, 2005). Historically, such communities have borne the brunt of environmental degradation, losing access to land and water and seeing little of the huge profits generated by mineral and oil booms. In recent years, however, organizations such as Oxfam, Catholic Relief Services, Environmental Defense, The Mountain Institute and many others have helped local communities to organize and advocate for more effective regulation of these activities and greater participation in the benefits produced. In Peru, Bolivia, Colombia and Chile, the largest mining companies have created foundations to undertake local and regional development programs and promote dialogue with local communities, as part of broader efforts to achieve social acceptance and improve their corporate image.

Philanthropy and Civil Society

In principle, organized philanthropy is an essential part of the growing but fragmented associative panorama of Latin America. At a local level, the community foundations represent an important effort to overcome social and cultural differences in the interests of a specific locale or population. At the national and regional levels, associations of foundations and companies also identify themselves as part of civil society, participate in increasingly wider networks (such as the *Foro del Sector Social* in Argentina), promote legal and tax reforms for the benefit of the entire nonprofit sector, and at times take on leadership positions for the promotion of ethics and transparency within the sector itself.

One of the more interesting areas of new foundation activity today involves efforts to help strengthen other civil society organizations, through technical support and personnel training programs. The basic premise is that the business world and the large foundations have relevant skills that are transferable, and thus they are in the position to aid in improving both the management and efficiency of other organizations. One case in point is the Fundacion Compromiso in Argentina, created by business leaders to support social sector leaders and entities. The Fundacion Corona in Colombia also has a program of building institutional capacities for other organizations, and in Brazil a variety of foundations and companies work along similar lines.

These processes are fairly new, however, and still represent a minority practice within Latin American philanthropy. Many donors continue to lack a sense of identification or significant involvement with their beneficiaries, and do not subscribe to a broader civil society agenda. Some are specifically oriented toward furthering their own business interests and basically consider philanthropy as part of that effort. The relationships established between donors and beneficiaries also do not necessarily promote either the autonomy or empowerment of the latter, and often reproduce more traditional patterns of inequality and dependence between rich and poor. Likewise, many philanthropists are in a position to establish privileged relationships with governments, placing them above other civil society actors in terms of access to power and public resources. Their efforts, in turn, often remain outside the realm of public scrutiny.

Beyond technical assistance and solidarity, how much do foundations and companies contribute, in financial terms, to the rest of civil society? Answering this question is difficult. In the first place, relatively few philanthropic entities donate to third parties *per se*, or fund programs in a given area of activity over time. Furthermore, national philanthropy provides only a small fraction of the overall income of civil society organizations. According to the findings of The Johns Hopkins Comparative Nonprofit Sector Project, an average of roughly 10 percent of the total income of non profit organizations in the region comes from private donations, including private, nonprofit schools and universities, while another 15 percent comes from the public sector, and the rest—nearly 75 percent—is self generated, through membership quotas, fees and sale of services. If international donations and loans are excluded, the total amount of non profit income coming from national philanthropy falls to just single digits in most countries (Salamon et al. 1999). In other words, the majority of civil society organizations in Latin America depend on their own resources, and neither the state nor private elites make significant financial contributions to their development.

Democracy and Human Rights

Finally, there are few national donors who explicitly promote democracy and basic human rights, whether through direct program operation or through support for organizations and leaders which assume these tasks. There are also very few national entities that promote equal rights and opportunities for women, or advocate the social and economic rights of indigenous and native communities, people of African descent or other disadvantaged groups. With the exception of one Colombian foundation and a few entities in Brazil, few foundations (and apparently no corporate donors) have these topics on their agendas. This is explained in part by the continued weakness of a liberal political tradition among the economic elite. Although initiatives for philanthropy promotion in Latin America have made efforts in this terrain, there is a notable reticence amongst the economically powerful to go beyond addressing basic needs, and recognize and support the rights of their fellow citizens.

Of course, most donors in wealthy nations do not support human rights or democracy either, but there is an important (and apparently growing) minority of foundations that do so. In Latin America, organizations that advocate for rights and democracy continue to depend on these foreign donors. This situation allows them an important degree of independence with respect to state interference, but also perpetuates their vulnerability to external changes in donor priorities and internal criticisms regarding their legitimacy and accountability.

IV. Philanthropy, the State and Public Policy

If philanthropists in Latin America have done little for democracy, what has democracy done for them? Do the new democratic governments in this region promote or inhibit philanthropic activity? Does private philanthropy encourage, or reduce, public sector responsibility?

Clearly, the economic liberalization and political democratization of the 90s encouraged the expansion of philanthropy in much of the region. Pressure from international donors and lenders also encouraged many governments in Latin America to include local donors and private, nonprofit organizations in a wide variety of public sector programs. As chapters by Rojas and de la Maza in this volume portray, private foundations and corporate leaders have become privileged participants in the design, planning and implementation of social policy.

Yet philanthropists and NGO leaders alike tend to argue that governments can do more to encourage donations and promote a more propitious environment for the institutional development of the nonprofit sector. In a few countries, there are still onerous restrictions on the freedom of association and the autonomy of voluntary organizations, while in others public sector authorities heavily regulate the sector to the point of suffocating new private initiatives.

Justified concern for reducing tax evasion can also lead authorities to reject any type of tax incentives for private donors. Traditional clientelistic practices often persist, in which key political leaders and parties control the use of public resources and provide access in exchange for partisan support. These practices are hardly propitious to the development of democracy and a plural civil society, and can inhibit the mobilization of those private resources that are in fact complementary to important public policy priorities.

Meanwhile, from the perspective of elected officials in the region, there are legitimate concerns about how to respond when private philanthropy crosses into fields previously dominated by the state or an official church. It is also understandable why some governments, in their efforts to establish priorities in the fight against poverty and inequality, place control over social assistance programs under the auspices of specialized public agencies, even when philanthropy could effectively contribute to these efforts. The general trends in private giving mentioned previously suggest that much of it is not in fact oriented toward achieving significant improvements in the equitable distribution of resources or in the provision of services to the most needy. Furthermore, as other authors in this volume point out, the results of experiments with tax incentives to promote private giving in priority areas—such as education—have not been very encouraging.

Likewise, although corruption and arbitrary exercise of power remain widespread practices in many of the region's new democratic regimes, it is important to ask if various social and developmental programs would be more transparent and effective if they were delegated to private operators. Although there is growing concern among NGOs about issues of legitimacy and accountability, as Villar and Brown explain in this volume, private donors on the whole do not stand out for their willingness to subject themselves to public scrutiny. And as Rojas warns in the Colombian case, when powerful private actors administer public funds and programs the state itself may lose legitimacy, if beneficiaries view such programs as donations rather than part of their rights as citizens.

Certainly, there are numerous cases in Latin America in which the increase in corporate and individual philanthropy is associated with conservative political projects whose objectives do not work in favor of expanding democracy or obtaining social justice. Even where this is not explicitly the case, the results may still be contradictory in terms of democratization. In some cases, the very fact of strengthening the leadership and social authority of certain individuals and companies that are already very powerful, and extending them a privileged relationship with the state, does not constitute an expansion of either citizen participation or the empowerment of the excluded populations, but instead works to the contrary.

Final Reflections

Latin American philanthropy has increased in scope, scale and ambition in recent years, attempting to address a wide variety of public and private concerns. As discussed, much of this activity remains scattered and relatively ineffective at bringing about significant social change—and much of it does not even attempt to do so. Yet encouraging examples continue to emerge. Today there are private foundations supporting peace in war-torn Colombia, and waging war on child exploitation in Brazil. There are business leaders who advocate for education policy reform, as well as supporting poor schools and giving scholarships to promising youths. There are large companies that invest in the long-term development—and political empowerment—of the communities in which they operate. We also find wealthy individuals who look beyond their immediate families and endow organizations that aim to change society on a broader scale, and middle-class professionals who pool their savings to support the causes they believe in. These are all exceptions. Yet through study and dissemination of such efforts, we can identify best practices and draw lessons for others to follow.

How can such efforts be more effective? Research and practice in Latin America suggest that in order to strengthen those philanthropic initiatives that aim to close the social gap, it is necessary to build alliances in which the public sector can participate as an active and legitimate partner. Likewise, it is indispensable that wealthy donors be willing to reflect on the causes of the social problems plaguing Latin America, and to seek greater coherence and effectiveness in their efforts to resolve such problems. It is also fundamental to strengthen other groups in civil society, especially among the poor and marginal, and convert their members into citizens who are carriers of rights and responsibilities, not just recipients of charity. It is only through these means that the beneficiaries of philanthropy will become active partners, capable of making their voices heard on public agendas and participating in alliances for lasting change.

The author wishes to thank Luis Camacho for his excellent assistance with the preparation of this chapter.

Notes

1 Raposo, Rebecca, "Strengthening Civil Society in Brazil," in *ReVista: Harvard Review of Latin America,* Spring 2002, p. 70.

2 The work of Andres Thompson was the primary source for this section. See especially Thompson and Landim 1998.

3 For a better understanding of the associative experiences of the 19th and 20th centuries see Arrom (2002 and this volume), Di Stephano and others (2002) and Forment (2003).

4 These arguments are made by Thompson and Landim (1996, 1997) but questioned by Forment (2003).

5 For example, in 1961 the Fundación Carvajal was created in Columbia (Rojas 2003). The Universidad del Pacifico in Peru was also founded in this period (1962), along with various other educational institutes, supported by the business community for the purpose of forming national leaders with technical capacities and social responsibility.

6 In Peru, for example, the majority of volunteer work is done through religious institutions, followed by organizations providing community development, housing and social services (Portocarrero 2003).

7 The *Nacional Monte de Piedad* operates pawn shops providing loans at low interest rates, and makes donations to over 1,000 other charitable organizations that attend to the needs of children and adults who are impoverished, sick or abandoned. The total income reported by NMP in 2001 was 8 billion pesos, and over the last seven years it has reported donations of 16 billion pesos, a figure without precedent in Mexican philanthropy. See *http://dns .montepiedad.com.mx* and Natal 2002.

8 See *www.santacasa.tche.br/* and Russell-Wood, A.J.R., *Fidalgos e Philanthropics: a Santa Casa da Misericordia da Bahia, 1550–1755,* Brasilia: Editora da Universidade de Brasilia, 1981; cited by Medeiros Peliano, Beghin and de Oliveira Neto (2003). These brotherhoods are supported by member and third party donations and fees from services.

9 For more information on the Peruvian Hogar see Acha, Elizabeth (2003: 125–189).

References

Acha, Elizabeth (2003), "Los guardianes de la caridad: el caso del Hogar de Cristo en el Perú," en Portocarrero, Felipe, y Cynthia Sanborn (eds.). *De la caridad a la solidaridad: filantropía y voluntariado en el Perú.* Lima: Centro de Investigación del Universidad del Pacífico, pp. 125–189.

Berger, Gabriel, Nicolás Duchote and Lorena Reiss (2005), *Filantropía Individual en la Argentina: Estudio de Opiniones, Actitudes y Comportamiento Filantrópico de Personas de Alto Patrimonio,* Buenos Aires: CIPPEC.

Chen, Lincoln (2002), "Philanthropy for Global Equity: The Next Wave?" in *Revista, Harvard Review of Latin America,* Spring 2002. Boston: Harvard University, pp 74–75.

De Avelar, Sonia (2002), "On Corporate Giving and Philanthropy in Brazil: An Overview," in *Revista, Harvard Review of Latin America, Spring 2002.* Boston: Harvard University, pp. 66–69.

Di Stefano, Roberto y otros (2002), *De las cofradías a las organizaciones de la sociedad civil. Historia de la iniciativa asociativa en Argentina. 1776–1990.* Buenos Aires: Gadis.

Erlick, June (2002), "Chile's Hogar de Cristo: Tradition and Modernity," in *ReVista, Harvard Review of Latin America,* Spring 2002, pp. 23–24.

Fleet, Michael, and Brian Smith (1997), *The Catholic Church and Democracy in Chile and Perú,* Notre Dame: University of Notre Dame Press.

Forment, Carlos (2003*), Democracy in Latin America 1760–1900, Volume I: Civic Selfhood and Public Life in Mexico and Peru,* Chicago: University of Chicago Press.

Harris, Christopher (2003), "Making Grants: The Social Justice Gap," *Ford Foundation Report,* Summer 2003, pp. 46–47.

Huber, Evelyne (1996), "Options for Social Policy in Latin America: Neoliberal versus Social Democratic Models," in Esping-Andersen, Gosta (ed.). *Welfare States in Transition.* Londres: SAGE Publications Ltd.

Ilchman, Warren F., Stanley N. Katz and Edward L. Queen II, editors (1998). *Philanthropy in the World's Traditions,* Bloomington and Indianapolis: Indiana University Press.

Marzal, Manuel M. (2002), *Tierra Encantada. Tratado de antropología religiosa en América Latina.* Madrid: Editorial Trotta.

McCarthy, Kathleen D. (2003), *American Creed: Philanthropy and the Rise of Civil Society, 1700–1865.* Chicago and London: The University of Chicago Press.

Medeiros Peliano, Anna Maria T., Nathalie Beghin and Valdemar de Oliveira Neto (2003), *Philanthropy for Equity: The Brazilian Case,* unpublished paper, Harvard University 2003.

Natal, Alejandro (2002), *Recursos privados para fines públicos: las instituciones donantes mexicanas,* México City: CEMEFI, The Synergos Institute and El Colegio Mexiquense.

Paoli, María Célia (2002), "Empresas e responsabilidade social: os enredamentos da cidadania no Brasil," en Boaventura de Sousa Santos, Org., *Democratizar a democracia: os caminhos da democracia participativa,* Rio de Janiero; Civilizacao Brasilieira, 2002, pp. 373–418.

Portocarrero S., Felipe, Cynthia Sanborn, Sergio Llusera y Viviana Quea (2000), *Empresas, fundaciones y medios: la responsabilidad social en el Perú.* Lima: Centro de Investigación de la Universidad del Pacífico.

Portocarrero S., Felipe, Cynthia Sanborn, Hanny Cueva y Armando Millán (2002), *Mas allá del individualismo: el tercer sector en el Perú,* Lima: CIUP.

Portocarrero S., Felipe, Hanny Cueva y Andrea Portugal (2005), *La Iglesia Católica como Proveedora de Servicios Sociales: Mitos y Realidades,* Lima, CIUP.

Putnam, Robert D. (1993), *Making Democracy Work. Civic Traditions in Modern Italy.* Princeton: Princeton University Press.

Raposo, Rebecca (2002), "Strengthening Civil Society in Brazil," *ReVista, Harvard Review of Latin America*, Spring 2002. Boston: Harvard University, pp. 70–71

Reimers, Fernando ed. (2001), *Unequal Schools, Unequal Chances. The Challenges to Equal Opportunity in the Americas*, Cambridge: Harvard University David Rockefeller Series on Latin American Studies.

Salamon, Lester; Helmut Anheir; et al. (1999), *Global Civil Society, Dimensions of the Nonprofit Sector*. Baltimore: Johns Hopkins University.

Sanborn, Cynthia (2002), "From Charity to Solidarity? Latin American Philanthropy in Changing Times," en *ReVista: Harvard Review of Latin America*, Spring 2002, pp. 3–7.

Sanborn, Cynthia, Felipe Portocarrero S., Luis Camacho, Oswaldo Molina and James Loveday (2005), *Social Justice and Philanthropy in the Andes: Regulating the Extractive Industries*, Lima: CIUP, unpublished research report, April 18, 2005. (Presented at international conference on "Funding Change: International Perspectives in Social Justice Philanthropy," Ford Foundation and The City University of New York, May 16 to 20, 2005.)

Sanborn, Cynthia, and Felipe Portocarrero S. (2004), "La filantropía realmente existente en América Latina," in Fundacion PROhumana, editoras, *Los desafíos de las Fundaciones donantes en la construcción de capital humano y justicia social*, Santiago de Chile.

Smith, Brian H. (1982), *Churches as Development Institutions: The Case of Chile 1973–1980*, PONPO Working Paper 50, Institute for Social and Policy Studies, Yale University.

Smith, Tony (2003), "A Philanthropy Rush in Corporate Brazil," en *The New York Times, March 30, 2003*.

Thompson, Andrés (2002), "A Challenge for the Monster: New Directions in Latin America Philanthropy," en *ReVista, Harvard Review of Latin America*, Spring 2002, pp. 8–10.

Thompson, Andrés, and Leilah Landim (1998), "Civil Society and Philanthropy in Latin America: From Religious Charity to the Search for Citizenship," in Ilchman, Katz and Queen, *op cit.*, pp. 355–369.

Teixidó, Soledad y Reinalina Chavarri (ed.), *Mapeando las Fundaciones en Chile: Características y desafíos para el siglo XXI*. Santiago de Chile: PROhumana Ediciones.

Toro, Olga Lucía (2001), *El estado de la investigación sobre el tercer sector y la sociedad civil en América Latina y el Caribe*. International Society for Third-Sector Research.

Toro, Olga Lucía y Elena Vila Moret (2000), *Philanthropy and Volunteerism Programming in Latin America and The Caribbean. Retrospective Evaluation 1994–2000. Summary Report to the Board of Trustees, September 2000*. W.K. Kellogg Foundation.

Verba, Sidney, Kay Lehman Schlozman y Henry E. Brady (1995), *Voice and Equality. Civic Voluntarism in American Politics.* Cambridge: Harvard University Press.

Villar, Rodrigo (2003), *Marco sobre el desarrollo de base y el papel de los miembros de RedeAmérica en su apoyo y promoción*, document for discussion, 15 de junio de 2003.

Villar, Rodrigo (2001), *Análisis comparativo de donaciones y voluntariado en América Latina*, documento interno, Boston: David Rockefeller Center for Latin American Studies, Harvard University, 2001.

W.K. Kellogg Foundation (2001), *Programming Update. Latin America and the Caribbean, Philanthropy and Volunteerism Programming.* W.K. Kellogg Foundation, internal document.

2

Catholic Philanthropy and Civil Society: The Lay Volunteers of St. Vincent de Paul in 19th-Century Mexico

Silvia Marina Arrom

One of the persistent stereotypes about Latin America is that it has a weak "civic culture" (in Gabriel Almond and Sidney Verba's famous phrase[1]) and, as a result, that the "haves" do very little to help the "have nots." This idea, presented in many different forms over the past half century,[2] has been accepted by contemporary social reformers who assert that civil society and philanthropy are new to Latin America. Certainly, it is true that both are now rebounding after the twentieth-century consolidation of central states that weakened non-governmental organizations and discouraged private philanthropic initiatives. Yet it is equally true that Latin Americans have a long and rich tradition of joining civic associations, giving money and resources to aid the less fortunate, and volunteering their time to serve others beyond their family and social group. These efforts were often channeled through Catholic lay organizations that provide continuity from colonial times to the present, but which have barely begun to receive the attention they deserve.

The complete history of Latin American philanthropy has yet to be written. Besides the almsgiving which was central to traditional Catholic charity, historians of the colonial period have long recognized several forms of private poor relief. The Church ran hospitals, asylums, and soup kitchens. Members of lay organizations such as religious *cofradías* and secular guilds took care of their own, including the widows and orphaned children of their members. A few individual philanthropists, usually wealthy members of noble families, stood out for their generosity. It has been widely assumed, however, that these colonial traditions disappeared after independence when republican governments took over the responsibility of providing for public welfare.[3]

The contributions of Catholic philanthropists have particularly been downplayed in Mexico, where Church and State fought bitterly in both the nineteenth-century War of the Reforma (1857–1867) and the revolutionary-period Cristero Rebellion (1926–1929). National histories demonized the "evil" Church and their Conservative (or, in the twentieth century, "counterrevolutionary") allies. They portrayed the nineteenth century as a period when liberalism and secularization prevailed over the dark forces of the past. Hospitals, orphanages, and asylums were transferred from Church to State jurisdiction. Monastic orders were expelled, including those that previously staffed establishments for the ailing poor. Artisan guilds and religious confraternities were abolished. Private giving was presumably deterred by the government's confiscation of the assets of welfare institutions, many of which had originally been donated by pious individuals.[4]

The prevailing wisdom held that these developments were salutary. A typical, if unusually colorful, assessment came from the President of Mexico City's municipal welfare office in 1935. Referring to the 1861 Reform Laws that nationalized welfare establishments and created a government agency to administer them, Rómulo Velasco Ceballos praised that "memorable February" day when "the vigorous hand of the Indian president, señor Juárez, swept away the decrepit, miserable and misguided old beneficence . . . in the hands of the clergy . . . and converted it into public assistance." This shift "forever changed the fortunes of the needy who, instead of having to endure miserable charity accompanied by feigned piety and Latin stutterings, would receive aid as a matter of decorum and justice."[5]

Yet this narrative of progressive secularization accompanied by the marginalization of the Church and of individual philanthropists tells only part of the story. Despite the triumph of the liberal Reforma, the second half of the nineteenth century witnessed a Catholic revival embodied in new lay organizations that proliferated throughout Mexico.[6] My case study of two of these groups shows how devout Catholics joined together to work for their vision of the common good. The male Society of St. Vincent de Paul and the female Association of the Ladies of Charity of St. Vincent de Paul (not to be confused with the well-known order of nuns, the Sisters of Charity of St. Vincent de Paul) were branches of French organizations devoted to assisting the poor. The Mexican chapters have lasted continuously from their foundations in 1845 and 1863 until the present. They provided extensive educational and welfare services. Although some of their activities embodied centuries-old approaches to poor relief, others moved beyond traditional charity to address the root causes of social problems. In organizing to deliver aid to the indigent, the Vincentian volunteers created a national network of local cells, called "conferences," that formed the building blocks of a vibrant civil society. By the late nineteenth century the two groups together mobilized tens of thousands of volunteers and donors in dozens of cities throughout Mexico to serve hundreds of thousands of paupers. The depth and breadth of these organizations reveals a strong tradition of giving and volunteering among the middle as well as upper classes. It also shows how misleading it is to focus primarily on secular initiatives in writing the history of modern Latin American philanthropy.

The Male Sociedad de San Vicente de Paul

In May 1833 a group of university students came together in Paris to create the Conference de la Charité, dedicated to visiting needy families in their houses. In the wake of the secularism and anti-clericalism unleashed by the French Revolution, these devout young men sought to use Christian charity to strengthen the Catholic faith while helping the urban poor. After meeting weekly to pray and deliberate, conference members set off for the homes of ailing paupers to whom they took material as well as spiritual aid. As the small local cells proliferated throughout France, they became the Society of St. Vincent de Paul, named after the French priest who lived from 1581 to 1660 and was canonized in 1737 for his patronage of charitable works. Although the Society was an independent lay organization, it was affiliated with the missionary order founded by St. Vincent de Paul in 1625, the Congregation de la Mission (known as Lazaristes, Paúles, or, in Mexico, the Misioneros de San Vicente de Paul). This missionary order also oversaw St. Vincent's two female organizations: the Confrérie des Dames de la Charité, the charity organization for lay women he founded in 1617, and the Filles de la Charité, the order of uncloistered nuns he founded in 1634 (known in Mexico as the Señoras de la Caridad and the Hermanas de la Caridad, respectively).[7]

The Society soon spread to other European countries and eventually established branches throughout the world. Its global expansion can be seen as an example of French religious imperialism, for it was one of many Catholic organizations exported from France to the rest of the world in the second half of the nineteenth century.[8] It would be a mistake, however, to view the foundation of the Mexican Society as an external imposition. Mexico was home to the first branch of the St. Vincent de Paul Society in Latin America, established only twelve years after the organization was founded in Paris. Unlike many foreign chapters founded by priests, the Mexican branch came as a result of lay initiative. While studying medicine in Paris from May 1833 to June 1836, the Mexican Manuel Andrade

(1809–1848) witnessed the birth of the Society. Upon returning home, he worked to bring several Vincentian organizations to Mexico. As the director of the Hospital de Jesús, Dr. Andrade was particularly concerned with the delivery of health care. Impressed by the nursing services the Sisters of Charity provided in French hospitals, he helped found that religious order in Mexico. After the first nuns arrived in November 1844, he turned his attention to establishing the two male organizations. On December 15, 1844, fourteen pious men gathered to form the first Mexican conference of the St. Vincent de Paul Society. The group immediately petitioned the government to authorize the Congregación de la Misión. Mexican president José Joaquín Herrera approved the *bases* of the Sociedad de San Vicente de Paul on February 8, 1845. The French Society accepted the affiliation of the Mexican chapter on September 15, 1845, and extended to it the indulgences conceded to members of the Society by Pope Gregory XIV. The first missionary fathers also arrived that year.[9]

Table 1 shows that the Mexican lay organization grew quickly. For the first three years it remained in Mexico City, where ten additional conferences were founded by 1849. In that year it began expanding to the provinces, with the original Mexico City conference becoming a Council to govern the emerging national structure. By 1851 there were sixteen conferences in six cities: Mexico City, San Miguel de Allende, Puebla, Oaxaca, Toluca and Guanajuato.[10] The Society had 192 active members. In addition, it counted 6 "honorary" members: benefactors who regularly contributed money, food, clothes, or medicines to the Society's works but did not participate in conference activities. And it had 12 "aspiring" members: youths aged twelve and over who were training to join the Society when they turned sixteen.[11] By 1855 its membership had nearly tripled to reach 567 active members with a solid core of 33 regular donors.

Table 1. Membership of the Mexican Sociedad de San Vicente de Paul, 1851–1896

Members	1851	1855	1858	1865	1868	1869	1870	1871	1875	1885	1894	1896
Active	192	567	558	791	1,094	1,412	1,922	1,665	2,824	1,647	1,536	1,672
Honorary	6	33	90	347	341	507	666	763	640	236	432	633
Aspiring	12	–	164	–	26	309	233	244	–	–	–	–
Total	210	–	812	–	1,461	2,228	2,821	2,672	–	–	–	–

Sources: "Etat du Personnel et des oeuvres…" (1851, 1857), SVP, CC113, Mexique; *Boletín* (1859); *Noticia* (1869, 1870, 1871, 1872); for 1855, 1865, 1875, 1885, and 1894, *Reseña* (1895), p. 47; and for 1896, De Dios (1993), 2: 629.

During the Reforma the Society suffered because of its close ties to the Church and to prominent Conservatives. By laying low and emphasizing that it was apolitical and independent from the Church, the organization avoided the kind of persecution endured by the St. Vincent de Paul Societies in France and Spain (which where outlawed in 1861 and 1868, respectively).[12] Still, at one point in 1861 its President Teófilo Marín and Vice President Manuel Diez de Bonilla were imprisoned by the Liberals for their role in the Conservative opposition. Unsure of their legal status in the wake of the 1859 law that abolished *cofradias* and *hermandades*, many conferences stopped meeting or did so clandestinely.[13] The dramatic expansion of the first decade came to a halt. The few available statistics for the war years suggest that the Society's membership leveled off (see Table 1) and no new conferences were founded in 1855, 1856, and 1863.[14]

Yet the Society began to recover even before the end of Reforma. On May 5, 1861, Francisco Zarco, Liberal President Benito Juárez's Minister of Relaciones y Gobernación, clarified that the Vincentian "charitable Association" was exempt from the Reform laws. Offering it his protection, he encouraged the Society to "persevere in its good works."[15] Then, with the breathing space provided by the conservative restoration from 1863 to 1867, it resumed its growth. Within a month of ousting the Liberals, the new regime commissioned Society member Joaquín García Icazbalceta to report on the state of the capital's welfare institutions, a sign of the close collaboration that would develop between the conferences and the government during the Second Empire.[16] By 1865 the Society had 791 active members and more regular contributors than ever before, with honorary members now 30% of the total. New conferences proliferated. Although the Society was again placed on the defensive when the Liberals returned in 1867, it quickly bounced back from the crisis years. Table 1 shows that, despite occasional harassment,[17] it grew steadily after 1868. With 666 aspiring members by 1871, the Society was successfully recruiting a new generation. By 1875 active membership reached an all-time high of 2,824. Thus, despite the triumph of the liberal Reforma, the Society was stronger afterwards than it had been before.

Expanding its regional coverage, the Society branched out from its core in central Mexico into twenty-one Mexican states and from major cities into a few rural areas.[18] Not all of the new conferences perdured. Some of the provincial chapters folded soon after their foundation, especially in the countryside. In keeping with the geography of piety familiar to students of later Catholic movements such as the Cristero Rebellion, the

Society flourished in the states of Mexico, Jalisco, Guanajuato, Michoacán and Puebla. Beginning in the 1860s it also took root in Veracruz and Yucatán. With scattered conferences in other regions, it attained an impressive national presence, although mostly in urban areas. Indeed, it was one of the first private organizations to operate on a national scale in Mexico.

As the Society grew, the social background of its members became more heterogeneous.[19] At first the lay men listed professions such as *comerciante, abogado, médico, militar,* and *propietario*—as well as one *relojero* in the founding conference. Leading families such as the Mier y Terán and Montes de Oca were represented. Well-known figures like the statesman Luis Gonzaga Cuevas and the writer Joaquín García Icazbalceta served as presidents of the Central Council (in 1849 and 1886–1894, respectively). Although the Society's members remained predominantly well-to-do, especially in the national and provincial Councils, by 1857 several conferences listed men who were *empleados, dependientes, preceptores,* and, occasionally, *artesanos.* In 1865 twenty master artisans created a Mexico City conference to instruct their apprentices and provide work for impoverished journeymen. In 1870 a group of *panaderos* formed a conference in Puebla. By 1874 the applications for aggregation of new conferences included *agricultores, jornaleros,* and *labradores.* In addition, the Society's reports list as honorary members doctors who provided their services free and pharmacists, bakers, and shopkeepers who contributed their goods. Despite excluding most of the rural population as well as the urban poor who were its clients, the Society's members and benefactors reached beyond a small elite to draw from the middle and lower-middle classes. It is therefore wrong to assume that nineteenth-century philanthropy was restricted to the wealthy few.

Nor is it accurate to dismiss the Mexican Society as a pale imitation of the French organization. Although Dr. Andrade was inspired by what he saw in Paris, his plans for his home country responded to local needs and drew heavily on deeply rooted charitable traditions. As explained in an 1846 letter thanking the French Society for approving the Mexican affiliation, "we have been forced to replace some of your customs with others that are more in harmony with our political institutions, our habits, the nature of our country and the education, needs, virtues, and vices of our poor."[20] One of the main differences was that the early Mexican conferences gave a much lower priority to visiting the poor—the central mission of the French organization. Instead, they undertook activities that attempted to fill the gap left by the expulsion of the Hospitaler orders in 1821 and the decline and, finally, abolition of the *cofradías* in 1859.

Shunning publicity, the early French conferences quietly provided parish-level services, mostly hidden inside the houses of their clients. In contrast, the Mexican Society took on highly visible projects, often at the behest of Mexican government or church officials who called upon it to provide public services. In 1845, during its first year of existence, the Archbishop of Mexico entrusted the Society with the Iglesia del Espiritu Santo and the municipal government placed it in charge of the Hospital del Divino Salvador for Demented Women. Both institutions had foundered since the expulsion of the priests who previously managed them. The Society raised money to support the ailing establishments. One of its members, Joaquín Velázquez de la Cadena, volunteered his services as director of the Hospital. Others formed a commission to supervise the institution and appointed a committee of ladies to work directly with the female inmates until the Sisters of Charity took over the nursing tasks a decade later.[21]

A number of special citywide works established during the Society's first five years provide further evidence of the Mexican Society's cooperation with the state in the 1840s, as well as of its discrepancies from the French parent organization. For example, the Mexicans in 1847 printed 12,000 copies of Father Ripalda's catechism for free distribution as a reading primer in the city's elementary schools. During the Mexican American War (1846–48) the Society's members assisted wounded soldiers from both armies and boasted of arranging for many U.S. soldiers to receive the last rites on their deathbeds. Vincentian volunteers cared for victims of the epidemic that came in the wake of the war and in June 1848 claimed the life of the Society's founder, Manuel Andrade. During the cholera epidemic of 1850, at the request of municipal authorities, sixteen Society members joined the Juntas coordinating relief efforts, with two of them serving in each of Mexico City's eight wards.[22] The devout gentlemen of the Mexican conferences were evidently respected for their welfare expertise.

Besides protecting welfare institutions, the early Mexican Society sent its members into public hospitals and prisons to care for the inmates. This institutional visiting continued services provided during the colonial period by the hospitaler orders and by a few confraternities that had taken meals to prisoners and patients.[23] At first the prison ministries were secondary, with only 58 prisoners visited in 1851. In contrast, the Society reported tending to 9,204 sick and dying paupers that year by taking them food and clean bed linens, offering them solace, praying with them, and arranging for proper Catholic burials. In later years the balance shifted. By 1860, for example, the Vincentian volunteers assisted 2,460 prisoners but only 647 hospital inmates.[24]

The hospital and prison ministries did not follow French precedents. Indeed, when the French Society became more bureaucratized in the 1850s and began furnishing preprinted report forms to its branches, it did not include the categories of *sick and dying assisted, cadavers buried,* or *prisoners visited.* The Mexicans had to add these categories by hand to the printed forms.[25] As Albert Foucault explained in his centennial history of the international St. Vincent de Paul Society, "the visiting of prisons, so flourishing abroad, was only introduced to Paris in 1927."[26] Thus it cannot be said that the Mexican Society was a mere carbon copy of the parent organization.

The most striking departure from the French model was that the Mexicans did not at first visit the poor. A letter to Paris dated March 2, 1846, confirms that no home visits were conducted during the Society's first year, a failing its President promised to rectify by organizing young men into new conferences where they could "begin practicing visits to poor families and thereby ignite their love of our impoverished brethren."[27]

Home visiting apparently began soon thereafter. By 1851 conference members visited 213 families, and the numbers increased steadily to 520 families in 1860, 712 families in 1870, 851 in 1885, and 1,110 in 1894.[28] The Society's annual reports indicate that the gentlemen visited their adopted families regularly, usually going once a week in pairs to avoid any scandalous appearances that might arise from the contact of an unaccompanied man with the women in these families.[29] The visitors provided for the material needs of their clients by giving them food, clothes, bed linens, cigarettes (at the time considered a necessity), and rent money. They arranged for doctors, medicines, and legal aid when needed. They helped place the children in school or the men in jobs, and occasionally bought tools so a breadwinner could work to support his family. By the end of the century they also placed women as servants. Moreover, the visitors tended to spiritual needs by making sure the family members knew Christian doctrine and the children were baptized and took first Communion. They offered advice and consolation, encouraged their clients to attend Mass and other religious functions, and when necessary attempted to dissuade them from their "vices."

Yet home visiting did not come easily to the Mexican chapters. In 1856, when the Society was already a decade old, the volunteers visited many more inmates of welfare institutions (9,202) than families (213). Although the number of families had more than doubled by 1860 (to 520), they were few compared with the 3,107 inmates assisted. The problem persisted even as the number of client families increased at the end of the nineteenth century. In 1887 the Society's president, Joaquín García

Icazbalceta, complained that "conferences in the *campos* and *pueblos*, generally composed of poor people with little education . . . who do not understand the bylaws, fail to give home visits the capital importance they hold among us."[30] This failure was more widespread than he admitted, however. When the Mexican Society printed aggregation forms for new conferences it considered it necessary to explain (in a footnote to the section where each conference was to list its activities) that "The *obra* of visiting poor families in their domiciles, is the first one that should be listed because it is the fundamental and characteristic *obra* of the Society of San Vicente de Paul and the only truly essential one. The others, such as the rehabilitation of illicit unions, . . . the patronage of children and apprentices, the instruction of workers, soldiers, and prisoners, the visitation of hospitals, etc., are secondary."[31] Despite such admonitions, home visiting fell proportionally after 1851: whereas 192 active members visited 213 families in 1851 (1.1 families per member), each active member only visited .5 families in 1855 and 1865. As the membership soared in 1875, the rate dropped even further, to .25. Only in 1894, after years of tutelage under García Icazbalceta, did visiting rise to .72 families for each of the 1,536 active members.

If by the end of the nineteenth century the activities of the Mexican Society were thus closer to those of the French organization, they were still not identical. After the Reforma the Society severed most of its ties with municipal institutions. In July 1867, after ousting the imperial regime, returning Liberals took control of the Hospital for Demented Women, which the Society had managed for twenty-two years.[32] Society members were no longer openly called upon to help public institutions. Indeed, municipal authorities occasionally prohibited the Vincentian volunteers from visiting hospitals and prisons.[33] Yet they continued their prison ministry. In 1871, the last post-Reforma year for which such figures are available, they visited 1,467 prisoners. By then the hospital visiting had been largely abandoned, though it may have resumed later in the century.[34] In fact, when the Mexican Society began printing its own report forms after 1868 it did not include the category *sick visited* (or the French category of *soldiers instructed*). Reflecting local practices, however, the Mexican forms included *dying assisted* and *cadavers buried* (a minor activity, with only 143 and 119 aided in 1871), as well as the all-important *prisoners instructed*.[35]

The post-Reforma Mexican Society increasingly devoted itself to creating its own network of welfare institutions, as well as to visiting the poor. It had already begun establishing schools, soup kitchens, and lending libraries by 1858. The 1859 *Boletín* reported that, instead of just paying the school tuition and food costs for individuals in their adopted families, a few conferences founded their own establishments to serve a wider public. In Mexico City, for example, with the help of a generous member who spent 913 pesos from his own pocket, the conference of Nuestra Señora de los Dolores on November 1, 1858, opened a *cocina económica* serving hot meals to 200 paupers a day. In 1859 two other conferences planned to open similar cafeterias. In 1858 the Society also opened a library in the capital to lend religious as well as morally uplifting works to its members and client families. The Morelia, Michoacán conferences had by 1859 established two *talleres* (workshops) to give young artisans religious instruction as well as train them to become carpenters and shoemakers. As time passed the Society created primary schools, night schools for adults, homeless shelters, clinics, and—by the 1880s—*cajas de ahorro* (credit unions) to help their clients save money. The most numerous of these foundations were the elementary schools. The Society's statistics show that the numbers of *niños patrocinados/jovenes instruidos* grew from some 300 in 1856–58 to over a thousand in 1868–1871. Society-run schools apparently increased in subsequent decades. In the city of Mérida, Yucatán, for example, local conferences operated eight primary schools and four catechisms that educated 627 students by 1894.[36]

Although the conference members occasionally volunteered in these institutions, they turned most of the work over to hired employees. The gentlemen personally served meals at the opening of the first *cocina económica*, and sometimes taught a catechism class or awarded prizes to the best students in their schools. But they quickly arranged to hire nurses for their hospitals, teachers for their schools, cooks for their soup kitchens, and laundresses to provide clean bed linens for the sick.[37] The eight primary schools in Mérida employed 23 teachers by 1894, for example. The Society rarely used nuns to staff its institutions, in part because of the suppression of conventual orders in 1861 (though the Sisters of Charity received a reprieve until 1874), and in part because, even before that, there were relatively few nuns in Mexico compared with Europe. The Vincentian institutions therefore provided steady work for lay people, usually women struggling to make ends meet.

In the process, the conferences made important contributions to the development of the Mexican welfare system. Although their system of home relief and institutional visiting remained the province of amateur volunteers, they were beginning to professionalize the delivery of many of their services. The visitors used the Vincentian system of vouchers which, much like modern food stamps, their clients used to obtain food, clothes, and shoes directly from local shops.[38] Since the volunteers did not have to deliver all the goods themselves, they maximized their impact with the assistance of participating shopkeepers. In addition, the visitors who went into poor people's homes foreshadowed the role of social workers because they investigated each family before "adopting" it, and then determined what the family required to survive a crisis and get on its feet again, arranged for medical and legal services, and provided job placement, education, and training.

As the Society expanded its services, it did not apparently encounter opposition from the State. Although the regime of Porfirio Díaz (1876–1910) left the anti-clerical Reform Laws on the books, it mended fences with the Mexican Church.[39] And it welcomed the contributions of private philanthropists. Indeed, the Society was only one of several private groups founding hospitals, asylums, and schools during the Porfiriato.[40] Although the official version of Mexican history claims that the government took over the provision of public education and social assistance after the Reforma, it in fact allowed non-governmental—including Catholic—organizations to supplement its meager resources. As a result, private philanthropy was thriving in the late nineteenth century.

Yet the Society itself stagnated. By 1895 membership had declined 45% since 1875, from 2,824 to 1,536 active members. The Society was nonetheless larger and more active than in the middle of the century. It counted 120 chapters throughout Mexico. With 432 honorary members, it enjoyed the support of many more benefactors than in the early years—evidence that it had developed a network of businessmen donating goods, doctors donating services, and individuals donating money to help the Vincentian projects. The growth of its expenditures, from 20,084 pesos in 1855 to 39,116 in 1885 and 54,170 in 1894 (not including in-kind donations), suggests that its welfare programs were healthy.[41] And membership recovered slightly in the next two years, returning to the level of the 1880s (Table 1). Between the "outdoor relief" offered to paupers in their houses and the "indoor relief" delivered in both its own and public institutions, the Society was helping at least 10,000 people a year.

If membership in the Society declined, it was not because giving and volunteering had failed to take root in Mexico. Instead, participation in Vincentian organizations had become highly gendered, with women more likely to provide personal service and men more likely to serve as honorary members donating money and goods. A sexual division of labor had also developed in the visiting of public institutions, with the men specializing in the rougher prison ministry and relinquishing most of the hospital ministry to the ladies (both the Sisters of Charity and the lay volunteers). Consequently, the leveling off of the male Society at the end of the nineteenth century is not a good indicator of the state of private Catholic philanthropy. The Society's increased spending suggests that the men were delegating much of the work to the employees in their welfare institutions, as well as leaving it to their loosely affiliated sister organization whose members were often their wives and daughters.

The Female Asociación de las Señoras de la Caridad

Far less information is available on the Ladies of Charity than on the male Society of St. Vincent de Paul. The picture that emerges from scattered documentation is nevertheless remarkable. Although the Asociación de las Señoras de la Caridad was founded in Mexico nearly two decades later than the men's Society, it quickly outstripped them with more members, more supporters, more chapters, and far more paupers assisted each year.

Table 2. Membership of the Mexican Señoras de la Caridad de San Vicente de Paul, 1864–1910

Members	1864	1865	1866	1868	1872	1878	1888	1892	1895	1896	1901	1909	1910
Active	566	997	2,251	–	–	3,003	7,344	13,371	9,875	11,264	14,933	18,034	20,188
Honorary	839	1,863	5,226	–	–	5,709	10,601	25,120	12,777	18,550	21,047	24,338	23,018
Total	1,405	2,860	7,477	12,274	20,212	8,712	17,944	38,491	22,652	29,814	35,980	42,372	43,206

Note: Statistics cover the fiscal year which ran from July 1 of the previous year to June 30.
Sources: De Dios (1993) 1: 544, 550 for 1864 & 1868 and 2:641, 645–46 for 1872, 1888, 1901 & 1909; *Memoria* (1865, 1867, 1879); *Rapport* (1893, 1896, 1897); González Navarro (1985), p. 62 for 1910.

The two organizations were not identical. One of St. Vincent de Paul's original foundations, the Association de Dames de la Charité was already centuries old in Europe when the men's Society was created. Yet the ladies' organization blossomed during the nineteenth century, began to expand internationally at about the same time as the male conferences, and had such similar purposes and structure that the Dames even applied for membership in the men's Society, which rejected the petition on the grounds that its bylaws only authorized it to admit men.[42] Although the Dames continued to function under their old rule, which emphasized home visitation of the sick, in practice they performed a broad array of charitable activities similar to those of the men's conferences and drew their support from the same social classes. The major difference between the two groups (aside from the sex of their members) was that the Ladies were directly controlled by the Vincentian order of the Congregation de la

Mission and maintained a very close relation with the Church.[43]

The Asociación de las Señoras de la Caridad was established in Mexico City on August 2, 1863, by Father Muñoz de la Cruz, a Vincentian missionary priest.[44] Under the relative safety of the Second Empire, the Association took off like wild fire. In July 1864, after only one year of operation, the Señoras held a national assembly and published a *Memoria* of their activities. They reported 566 active members and 839 benefactors in 21 conferences, 12 of them in Mexico City and 9 in the states of Mexico, Puebla, Guanajuato and Guadalajara. They had already established a Superior Council to govern the local chapters. They had also created a shelter for young women, the Asilo de la Caridad de Nuestra Señora de la Luz, soon to be followed by several primary schools and orphanages.[45] Thus, the Señoras quickly caught up with the older men's Society.

Thereafter the Ladies' Association grew so dramatically that it dwarfed its brother organization (see Table 3).

Table 3. Comparison of Male and Female Societies, 1865–1895

	Active Members		Families Visited		Expenditures (pesos)	
	Male	Female	Male	Female	Male	Female
1865	791	997	374	–	17,743	16,767
1875/78*	2,824	3,003	714	1,151	23,793	49,243
1894/95*	1,536	9,875	1,110	70,537	54,170	96,206

*First dates are for the male conferences, second dates are for the female.
Sources: Information on male Society in *Reseña* (1895), p. 47; information on female Association in *Memoria* (1865, 1879), and *Rapport* (1896).

By 1866 there were 87 female conferences, including 6 composed of *niñas* training to become full-fledged members when they turned 18.[46] By 1868 the Señoras counted 12,274 active and honorary members, compared with only 1,461 for the male Society. In just five years, the Ladies were thus mobilizing eight times more volunteers and donors than their male counterparts. These discrepancies persisted for the rest of the century. By 1894 there were only 1,536 men active in 121 conferences, compared with 9,875 women active in some 400 conferences by 1895. With branches in nineteen states, the ladies were broadly distributed across Mexico, although they were strongest in Jalisco, home to nearly half their members.[47] They were backed by an impressive 12,777 benefactors, compared with only 432 supporting the men's conferences. The 96,206 pesos they spent on good works (not including the value of in-kind donations) was almost twice what the gentlemen disbursed. The ladies reported aiding 21,428 sick people and visiting 70,537 families, compared with only 1,100 families visited by the men. Each lady thus visited an average of 7.1 families regularly, compared with the .7 families visited by each man.

The Señoras' growth continued without interruption until the outbreak of the Mexican Revolution. A report of the international association listed 19,000 *niñas* in 1895, an indication that the ladies were training a sizeable new generation of members.[48] In 1901 there were 14,933 volunteers and another 21,047 regular contributors. In 1910, on the eve of the tumult, active membership had risen to a historic high of 20,188. The volunteers visited 135,344 families and 32,000 hospital patients. They distributed 1,779,849 meals, 132,481 prescriptions, and 27,000 articles of clothing, which they often sewed themselves.[49] In addition, they managed a large national network of elementary schools, asylums, cafeterias, clinics, and pharmacies to provide low-cost medicines to the poor. In 1909 these included 32 hospitals, 20 schools, and 17 orphanages throughout Mexico, with a large number concentrated in the Guadalajara region. The schools alone reached 25,000 children that year.[50] By comparison, the male Society languished.[51]

It is tempting to argue that the success of the female organization reflects the feminization of piety in the nineteenth century.[52] But there is a more complicated explanation for the disparity between the male and female conferences. Many of the benefactors who supported the female volunteers were men. Male piety flourished in other organizations. Catholic laymen in the late nineteenth century published Catholic periodicals and founded numerous devotional and mutual aid associations. In the early twentieth century they joined Catholic trade unions and attended Catholic conferences.[53] These men were not afraid to display their religious fervor openly, yet few of them joined the Vincentian organization.

The phenomenal growth of the Asociación de Señoras de la Caridad is partially due to the organizing efforts of Vincentian priests. Unlike the foundation of the male conferences, the ladies' groups apparently owed little to lay initiative. Indeed, the 1865 *Memoria* attributed the success of the Ladies of Charity during the first two years entirely to the "zeal" of the missionaries, and did not name a single woman as a founder.[54] The Church began encouraging the formation of lay organizations after the *cofradías* were outlawed in 1859, and increased its pace after 1874, when the expulsion of the Sisters of Charity left a glaring gap in ecclesiastical welfare services. A Pastoral Instruction of 1875 explicitly called on "Catholic ladies" to join the conferences of St. Vincent de Paul to continue the work of the Sisters of Charity in providing for "the instruction of destitute children, the needs of ailing paupers in hospitals, and the relief of all sorts of misery."[55] According to the 1894 *Rapport* of the international Dames de la Charité, the Mexican chapter was the largest in "the world" (although perhaps this only meant outside of France) because the Mexican poor were "deprived . . . of the succor provided by the hospitaler communities."[56] Thus the unusually difficult Mexican Church-State relations provided the impetus for priests to promote the Ladies of Charity.

Still, if priests promoted the organization, it was lay women who enthusiastically joined. As women's education improved in the nineteenth century and the ideal of feminine seclusion declined, many ladies sought outlets where they could apply their talents. Since upper- and middle-class women rarely worked outside the home, the conferences gave them a socially acceptable way to serve the larger society beyond their families. The growth of the conferences reflects the larger trend of the feminization of charity in nineteenth-century Mexico, also visible in women's membership on the boards of public welfare institutions, as well as in their increased role in managing them.[57] But these provided opportunities for very few women. The suppression of conventual orders in 1874 left Mexican women with few service organizations they could join. In 1869 laywomen flocked to the new Sociedad Católica de Señoras y Señoritas, but its demise in 1878 left them without that avenue for philanthropic activities.[58] Filling a void, the Ladies of Charity gave tens of thousands of Mexican women a structure for contributing to the common good.

The Vincentian conferences also provided a community, source of prestige, and arena where women could become leaders, acquire new skills, and interact with people they might not otherwise meet. In addition to their charitable activities, the Señoras met in their local conferences weekly, made speeches, and prepared reports. Whereas Mexican women were barred from voting and holding public office until the mid-twentieth century, they could do both as Señoras de Caridad. Each conference elected a president, secretary, and treasurer as did the central and provincial councils that governed the local chapters. They voted to approve the entrance of new members. After a six-month trial the *aspirantes* who proved their capacity to perform the demanding work of serving the poor were inducted, in annual assemblies whose ceremonies included the granting of a diploma to each new *socia* (as the active members were called). In providing welfare services, the ladies also managed large sums of money and developed organizational skills.

Although the conferences held their weekly sessions in the protected precinct of the parish church, the volunteers went out from there into public spaces. Working in pairs, the ladies were not alone while visiting the dingy rooms of their "adopted" families or the filthy wards of public hospitals and prisons, but they were not sheltered, either. In carrying out their good works they might be subjected to shocking sights and rude insults. For example, the triumphal story of one lady, who endured a dying patient's vulgar screams and after several tries convinced him to accept the last rites, was narrated in the 1865 *Memoria* as an inspiration to others.[59] Even when serving as teachers or supervisors in their own supposedly spotless schools, orphanages, shelters, and clinics, the ladies were operating in the public arena. And it was not an exclusively female sphere they entered. The volunteers offered services to men as well as women. They maintained close contact, not only with the priests who helped each conference, but also with the doctors and pharmacists who assisted them. Indeed, the statistical reports for each conference recorded the number of associated priests, doctors, and pharmacists—usually numbering about one dozen—immediately after listing the number of active members and benefactors. The ladies' fundraising efforts entailed not only attending charity balls and raffling off donated items among their friends, but also collecting alms in public plazas and approaching the leading men in the community, including the director of a circus, Señor Chiarini, who in 1865 donated the 910 peso earnings of one performance to the Association.[60] Thus, without overtly challenging social norms, the Ladies of Charity expanded women's roles and ventured into new spheres.

Men had less need for these outlets, for they had alternate sources of prestige and sociability, as well as alternate avenues for serving others, defending their faith, and reforming the modern world. They could do so through work, government service, or—for the most devout—the priesthood, options closed to women of the upper and middle classes. They could also join the mutual aid societies, clubs, masonic lodges, and political parties that were closed to their mothers, sisters, and daughters. Moreover, many gentlemen were deterred from joining the conferences because of the kind of commitment they required.

In the highly gendered world of nineteenth-century Mexico, the Vincentian demands for regular face-to-face contact with the poor and for hands-on caregiving were considered more suited to women than to men. The Pastoral Instruction of 1875 that called on women to join the conferences noted the special feminine disposition for serving the poor and sick. So did the 1863 Mexican edition of the *Reglamento* of the Señoras de la Caridad, which noted that, in addition to having "greater compassion for the sufferings of others," women were already "accustomed to carrying out certain chores in their houses." The *Reglamento* added that the "the principal ladies of each town" were ideal members of the Association because "they are always at home and less distracted than the men, who are ordinarily occupied with their business and frequently out of the house and even the city."[61] Many men were thus simply too busy to engage in Vincentian philanthropy, except as donors and behind-the-scenes supporters.

The *Reglamento* recognized that this female advantage was restricted to the higher social classes where women "had no need to work for their subsistence like the women of an inferior class." Yet it bears emphasizing that the members of the female conferences were not all wealthy. For example, in 1865 the conference of San Antonio de las Huertas in Mexico City consisted entirely of seamstresses, and few well-known last names appeared in the membership lists of the other conferences that year.[62] Still, it is likely that few of the middle-class *socias* held jobs and that most had servants to care for their homes and children, thereby freeing the ladies to devote themselves to charitable activities while their male relatives were at work.

Moreover, after anti-clerical Liberals won the War of the Reforma, men may have realized that their career advancement would be hindered by membership in a Catholic organization that had close ties to the defeated Conservatives—especially if they had ambitions to serve in public life. Indeed, although several members of the early Mexican Society held political office, this was no longer the case in later years. The importance of the political variable is confirmed by two recent studies of the St. Vincent de Paul Society in other Latin American countries: in Chile and Colombia, which had far less conflictive relations between Church and State, the male conferences continued growing at the end of the nineteenth century, and there appears to have been less of a disparity between male and female Catholic lay organizations.[63] These structural factors, and not necessarily women's stronger devotion, help explain why the conferences of St. Vincent de Paul attracted more Mexican women than men.

Contributing to Social Change

With their multiplicity of functions, the Vincentian lay associations combined both traditional and modern approaches to alleviating poverty.[64] The rhetoric in the bylaws and reports recalled the centuries-old discourse of St. Vincent de Paul with its emphasis on imitating Christ, loving the poor, and showing humility and abnegation. The conference members practiced charity not only out of a desire to help others but also to gain their own salvation, aided by the indulgences granted to those who joined the organizations. The Ladies of Charity even engaged in such customary

Catholic practices as inviting twelve paupers to dine on Maundy Thursday and having the conference members wash and kiss their feet.[65] Both societies maintained paternalistic relations with "their" adopted families. Moreover, a large part of the members' efforts went to providing the Seven Acts of Mercy: feeding the hungry, housing the wayfarer, dressing the naked, giving drink to the thirsty, visiting the sick, caring for orphans, and burying the dead. These older types of assistance characterized the work with hospital patients and prisoners that was so important to both the male and female conferences. Much of the thrust of home visiting also offered only temporary remedies to destitution.

Yet the works of the Vincentian lay societies should not be dismissed as mere throwbacks to traditional Catholic charity. Instead of accepting poverty as a normal condition and merely relieving its symptoms, they often tried to treat its causes. The emphasis on providing elementary schooling, adult education, vocational training for youths—and in one case music lessons so that a blind man could support his family as a musician[66]—aimed to prevent their clients' future destitution. The curriculum in their schools included not only Christian doctrine but also history, science, music, calculus, and line drawing that prepared their graduates for employment.[67] The credit unions that encouraged savings were designed to help their clients achieve financial independence. The job placements and provision of tools likewise went beyond palliative measures.

Unlike traditional almsgivers, Vincentian volunteers did not hand out aid indiscriminately. The societies shared the liberal critique of almsgiving as encouraging idleness. Thus Mexico's numerous beggars were rarely among their clients except, according to the Society's 50th anniversary review, "when there is some hope that we can convert them into useful members of society."[68] Instead, these Catholic activists used philanthropy as part of a broader strategy to achieve social change.

The volunteers coupled their assistance with religious and moral instruction because they wanted to transform their clients, not just to save their souls, but also to serve their project of Catholic renewal. The Vincentians taught doctrine to the children in their schools, the orphans and homeless in their asylums, and the prisoners, patients, and apprentices they aided. The *Boletínes, Memorias,* and *Noticias* boasted of cases where the volunteers brought a recalcitrant prisoner or hospital patient back to the Church after many decades of having strayed, converted a Protestant, or convinced an unmarried couple to enter the sacrament of marriage. They proudly reported the number of children taken to baptism or prepared for the first Communion, the dying given the viaticum, and the paupers brought to confession. Unafraid of being intrusive, the visitors also tried to "moralize" their clients by pressuring them to end illicit relationships, conciliating divided families, persuading the debauched to give up drunkenness, and even providing separate beds for the boys and girls. Putting a high priority on instilling the work ethic, they made sure the youths they patronized were gainfully employed so they would not turn to prostitution or crime. Far from exalting the poor, then, the societies tried to change popular values and customs.

The Vincentian ladies and gentlemen were convinced that their philanthropy helped combat the major ills of the nineteenth century.[69] They blamed the French Revolution, that "horrible" movement that separated the Church from public life, for unleashing the secularizing forces that caused the loss of faith and led to the immorality, materialism, individualism, alienation, and class conflict of modern times. They were also increasingly on the defensive against the incursions of Protestantism. Their solution was to propagate the Catholic religion and Catholic values, and to do it in such a way as to restore social harmony. It was therefore essential for Vincentian volunteers to establish a personal relationship with the people they aided. These intimate—though clientelist—bonds helped further the desired reconciliation between the rich and poor. Indeed, the President of the Society's Central Council in 1894 proclaimed his organization's type of philanthropy as far superior to public welfare, which "is haughty. . . and leaves the poor in the isolation, indifference, and oblivion that offend him more than his material deprivations."[70] Clothed in religious rhetoric, then, were fundamental civic concerns.

Although the Vincentian project was profoundly anti-Liberal, it responded to contemporary problems and represented some modern approaches to social problems. To be sure, the conferences resembled the colonial *cofradias* in many ways. Conference members worshipped together just as the *cofrades* had, and practiced special devotions such as attending spiritual retreats and celebrating the feast day of St. Vincent de Paul on July 19. Their annual assemblies included a sermon and closed with a prayer. Like the confraternities, the societies' basic cell was a small group that in theory should not exceed 33 members (the age of Christ when he died).[71] Although it was not part of the French bylaws, the male conferences also functioned like confraternities by praying for sick and deceased *socios* and even, when Dr. Andrade died in 1848, carrying his body on their shoulders from the center of Mexico City to the distant cemetery of Santa Paula.[72] The Vincentian associations thus provided continuity from the colonial period.

Yet they represented a departure as well. Unlike most *cofradías,* the conferences did not exist primarily to protect a particular church or religious image, or to care for their own members in times of need. Instead, their principal activity was to assist total strangers.[73] If Catholicism was customary in Mexico, this brand of Catholic activism was not. In particular, the practice of home visiting had to be learned and disseminated.[74] It was far easier (especially for elite men) to give money to the poor rather than donating time and personal service. For most ladies, active participation in the public sphere and administration of welfare organizations were not customary practices either.

Moreover, the Vincentian conferences helped build a democratic culture and shape republican citizenry. Adhesion to the conferences was voluntary, with membership based on ideological affinities. The *socios* were not even required to pay mandatory dues. Both organizations governed themselves democratically with a written constitution, elected officers, and members voting as equals. Indeed, the bylaws of the Ladies of Charity dictated that elections be held by secret ballot.[75] These organizations consistently defended freedom of speech and assembly. In calling for Mexicans to join the Catholic conferences, for example, the 1875 Pastoral emphasized that "the Constitution of the Republic formally and expressly recognizes the right of all Mexicans to associate for any honest and licit end."[76] Ironically, it was the Liberals who tried to restrict the conferences' rights of association in 1861 and 1868, and who as late as 1889 limited their right to publish by insisting that the societies' publications could only be distributed to their own members.[77] It is therefore misleading to label the societies as simply "conservative," for they shared in many modernizing tendencies.[78]

In some respects these lay associations presaged the progressive Catholic social movements that emerged in the wake of the papal encyclical *Rerum Novarum* in 1891. Like later groups, they represented an organized effort to challenge secularization through "an orthodox adherence to Catholic dogma and a progressive critique of liberal[ism]."[79] From today's perspective, we might denigrate the societies' aid as paternalistic and controlling, since self-righteous visitors tried to impose their values on those they assisted and aimed to "help" rather than empower their clients to demand equality. Yet the conference members did not merely reinforce the status quo. Instead, they viewed themselves as social reformers combatting poverty, hunger, sickness, illiteracy, homelessness, class conflict, moral degeneration, and alienation. Besides proselytizing and practicing individual acts of charity, they created institutions like elementary schools, night schools for adults, and credit unions to achieve a greater measure of social justice. They tried to give needy families the resources to become independent. Although they did not organize Catholic trade unions—the hallmark of twentieth-century Social Catholicism—they established "patronages" for workers and apprentices that offered vocational training and mutual aid along with religious instruction. And they worked tirelessly to shape public opinion both by catechizing their clients and by distributing Catholic almanacs, missals, and edifying works designed "to combat the pernicious influence of the novel and the newspaper."[80]

It is difficult to know what the recipients thought of this mix of material assistance and moral regulation. In his brief, critical discussion of the Vincentian associations, Moisés González Navarro ridiculed them for "exacting communions in exchange for a loaf of bread."[81] Yet there was no shortage of paupers willing to tolerate the presence of intrusive visitors, even agreeing to pray with them and accompany them to church in return for assistance. The families that petitioned the conferences for help evidently incorporated the societies' services into their survival strategies. Those who cooperated not only received aid and protection during their lifetimes but also avoided the dishonor of a pauper's funeral. The stories of grateful clients in the *Boletínes* and *Memorias* may not have been pure fiction. In a country where rich and poor shared a Catholic culture, some of the societies' clients may even have appreciated the opportunity to strengthen their faith. In any case, given the paucity of public relief in Mexico, the destitute had few other places to turn to in times of need, especially if rather than entering into demeaning public institutions they preferred to continue living in their homes with dignity.

In the process of constructing an extensive network of local organizations to assist the poor, Catholic activists from the upper and middle classes also created the building blocks of a vigorous civil society. The conference members met together in their local chapters week after week, year after year—for some forty years in the case of García Icazbalceta and longtime Society secretary Jesús Urquiaga—forming social networks that have been overlooked by social historians. Forging personal bonds with less fortunate members of society, the volunteers constructed a community that united members of different social classes. The neighborhood-level cells were tied into a complex national and international structure that was independent from the Mexican State. By only tracing the formation of civil society in secular organizations, the recent literature has missed an important locus of associational life. The size and longevity of these associations challenges the view so widespread in the older social science literature that, unlike the Americans observed by Alexis de Tocqueville, Latin Americans were not "joiners." Historians have simply ignored some of the kinds of groups they joined.

Although in Mexico these Catholic groups were weakened in the early twentieth century by the twin attacks of the Revolution and the defeat of the Church during the Cristero Rebellion, their strength in the second half of the nineteenth century shows that participation in civil society, democratic practices, and volunteering to help others are not emerging today for the first time, as is so often affirmed. Neither is highly organized philanthropy. The Vincentian societies had written bylaws, officers, central and regional governing bodies, annual meetings, published reports, and correspondence with the parent offices in Paris. They also had formal programs to recruit, train, and deploy volunteers in an extensive network of relief organizations. Moreover, their services—as well as their critique of secular liberalism and vision of Catholic renewal—reached a large clientele. We should beware of exaggerating the Vincentian accomplishments. Their assistance only reached a minority of the Mexican poor. Largely confined to cities and towns, it barely touched the deeply ingrained rural and indigenous poverty. Yet this record should not be scoffed at, since it compares favorably with what the Mexican government offered at the time.

Conclusion

Mexico was not unusual in having a dynamic tradition of Catholic philanthropy. Indeed, Catholic activism may have been stronger in other Latin American countries that did not experience such fierce anti-clericalism— and where, unlike Mexico, the conferences received state funding for some of their initiatives.[82] If in 1844 Mexican laymen pioneered the new Vincentian approach to social reform, by the end of the nineteenth century the St. Vincent de Paul Society was established in eighteen Latin American countries.

A recent study of Colombia shows that the male conferences thrived there until the 1920s, when they were increasingly supplanted by Acción Católica and the Círculos de Obreros Católicos whose political activism and syndicalism appealed to a new generation.[83] The Mexican Association of the Ladies of Charity may have been the largest outside of Europe in 1894, but by 1892 the French central office listed branches in Brazil, Costa Rica, Ecuador, Guatemala, Martinique, and Peru.[84] Vincentian ladies conferences were also active in late nineteenth-century Argentina, although they voted against affiliating with the international body in order to avoid paying dues.[85] And the Ladies of Charity continued spreading to other countries, such as Colombia, in the early twentieth century.[86]

Table 4. Foundation Dates of American Branches of the St. Vincent de Paul Society (19th century)

1845	Mexico*	1866	Ecuador
	United States*	1872	Brazil
1847	Canada*	1878	Haiti
1854	Chile	1881	El Salvador
1857	Colombia	1883	Peru
	Trinidad and Tobago		Panama
1858	Uruguay*	1885	Costa Rica
	Guyana		Guatemala*
	Cuba	1894	Paraguay
1859	Argentina	1897	Nicaragua

*There are some discrepancies in various sources about these dates. For Mexico and the U.S. I have used the foundation dates of 1845 accepted by both national organizations. For the other countries I follow Foucault (1933), pp. 87–88; and Société (1933), pp. 281–303. On the U.S. foundation, see Glazier and Shelley (1997), p. 1249.

These were not the only groups dedicated to helping the poor. As historians become disillusioned with the achievements of public welfare, they are increasingly turning their attention to the private sector. Numerous benevolent societies, both secular and religious, are coming to light in nineteenth- and early-twentieth-century Latin American cities.[87] My interviews with elderly Cubans suggest that not so long ago visiting the poor under the auspices of other Catholic groups, such as the Damas Isabelinas, was an important activity for many middle and upper-class women. Businesses and individuals regularly donated goods and money to assist the less fortunate. Medical doctors sometimes set aside one day a week or a month to treat the destitute without charge. These practices merit further study. Although private initiative was eclipsed in the second half of the twentieth century when government agencies took over the provision of health, education, housing, and welfare services, it did not disappear. Understanding Latin America's charitable traditions in the time when citizens did not rely on the State is fundamental to strengthening philanthropy and civil society in the region today.

Acknowledgments

An earlier version of this chapter appeared in *ReVista: Harvard Review of Latin America* (Spring 2002), pp. 57–59. It benefited from the valuable comments of Ann Blum and participants at the LASA meetings in September 2001, the Seminario de Historia Social of the Colegio de México in June 2002, and the Harvard Latin American History Workshop in October 2002.

Notes

1 Almond and Verba (1963).

2 For a recent review of this literature see Forment (2003), chap. 1. Forment likewise challenges the stereotype that 19th-century Latin America lacked a democratic tradition and civil society.

3 A cogent expression of this view appears in Centro para la Filantropía (1996), pp. 185–87. For a review of the historical literature on Mexican welfare, see Arrom (2000), pp. 8–9 and 303–4, fn. 28–38.

4 Even Moisés González Navarro, one of the few historians to recognize the persistence of private charitable groups after the Reforma, portrayed their efforts as inferior to public welfare (1985). A revisionist work that recognizes the importance of private philanthropy in the late 19th century is Blum (2001).

5 Velasco Ceballos (1935), pp. 103–4.

6 See, for example, Adame Goddard (1981); Ceballos Ramírez (1991) and (1999); Hanson (1994), esp. chaps. 1 and 2; and Matute, Trejo and Connaughton (1995).

7 See Société (1933); and Foucault (1933).

8 See Serrano (2000), pp. 18–27.

9 De Dios (1993), 1: 65–77, 521–22; and *Acta* (1945), pp. 8–9. The Presidential decree is cited in AHDF, Hospitales, vol. 2312, leg. 1, exp. 3, f. 3v.

10 The 50th-anniversary *Reseña* lists the foundation dates and locations of all conferences as well as national and provincial councils (1895), pp. 25, 50–57.

11 For a definition of these terms see Société (1933), p. 102.

12 The French General Council was prohibited from meeting between 1861–70. Foucault (1833), pp. 183–4, 204.

13 See *Reseña* (1895), p. 39; letters to Paris of 23 Sept. 1860, 28 Oct. 1861, and 27 April 1861 (SVP, CC113, Mexique); *Boletín* (1860), p. 6; and "Las Conferencias de San Vicente de Paul, Dictamen del Sr. Castañeda," *La Unión Católica* (15 June 1861), pp. 1–2.

14 The only other years when no conferences were founded were 1847 (during the Mexican American War) and 1877. See *Reseña* (1895), pp. 50–57.

15 "Dirección General de los Fondos de Beneficencia Pública," *La Unión Católica* (13 June 1861), p. 1. Partially quoted in *Reseña* (1895), pp. 27–28.

16 Although García Icazbalceta presented his report to Emperor Maximilian in July 1864, it was only published posthumously (1907). Tomás Gardida, another Society member, served as alderman in charge of welfare institutions during those years. De Dios (1993), 1: 527; and Arrom (2000), p. 229–33.

17 De Dios (1993), 1: 525, 537–38, 553; and *Reseña* (1895), pp. 27, 30, 39.

18 See list of conferences in *Reseña* (1895), pp. 50–57.

19 See the "Etats du personnel et des oeuvres," in SVP, CC113 and CC114, Mexique; *Boletín* (1859), p. 204; *Noticia* (1871), p. 15; and 7 March 1868 "Boletín de Agregación de la Conferencia del Santíssimo Sacramento," SVP, CC114, Mexique. I am indebted to María Gayón for informing me that Juan Santelices, a founding member of the Society, is listed as a clockmaker in the 1848 census.

20 Letter of 2 March 1846 to the Central Council in Paris, SVP, C113, Mexique.

21 See *Reseña* (1895), pp. 23–24; García Icazbalceta (1907), p. 63; and AHDF, Hospitales, vol. 2312, leg. 1, exp. 3.

22 *Reseña* (1895), pp. 17, 31; and De Dios (1993), 1: 522–24.

23 Belanger (1997), p. 277.

24 "Tableau Statistique . . ." (1851), SVP, CC113, Mexique; *Boletín* (1860).

25 See Tableaux Statistiques, SVP, CC113, Mexique.

26 Foucault (1933), p. 395.

27 Letter of 2 March 1846 to the Central Council in Paris, SVP, C113, Mexique.

28 "Tableau statistique…" (1851), SVP, CC113, Mexique; *Boletín* (1860); *Noticia* (1871); *Reseña* (1895), p. 47 for 1885 and 1894 figures.

29 Explained in footnote 5 to the *Reglamento* (1851), p. 8.

30 Letter of 17 November 1887 to the Central Council in Paris, SVP, C113, Mexique.

31 See Boletines de Agregación, 1865–74, SVP, CC114, Mexique.

32 *Reseña* (1895), p. 31.

33 The *Reseña* does not give dates for these bans (1895), p. 42.

34 Visiting the sick was adopted as a special *obra* by the provincial council of Orizaba, founded in 1884. *Reseña* (1895), p. 34.

35 See statistics in *Noticia* (1869, 1871) and *Memoria* (1872).

36 See *Boletín* (1859), pp. 194–95, 204–5; De Dios (1993), 1: 518, 526–7, 539; and *Reseña* (1895), pp. 31–46.

37 See, for example, letter to Paris of 4 Jan. 1853, SVP, CC113, Mexique.

38 *Reglamento de la Sociedad* (1851), p. 8; *Reglamento* (1863), p. 22.

39 See Cuevas (1928), vol. 5, chap. 6; and Hanson (1994), pp. 52–67.

40 See Blum (2001); González Navarro (1957), pp. 495–509.

41 *Reseña* (1895), p. 47.

42 *Reglamento* (1851), fn. 2, p. 6; Foucault (1933), p. 218; and *Memoria* (1867).

43 See *Reglamento* (1863) and (1911), esp. 47. Because of the suppression of conventual orders, the Mexican Señoras at times reported directly to the Archbishop.

44 Earlier attempts to establish the ladies' conferences in Mexico, beginning in Puebla in 1848, did not succeed, De Dios (1993), 1: 544–49. The organization later recognized 1863 as its foundation date, *Memoria* (1922), p. 5.

45 De Dios (1993), 1: 544–49; *Memoria* (1865).

46 *Memoria* (1867).

47 Statistics for male conferences in *Reseña* (1895); for female conferences in *Rapport* (1896), tableau no. 7. In 1895 the Ladies of Charity had branches in the following states, in decreasing order of membership: Jalisco, Michoacán, Yucatán, San Luis Potosí, Mexico, Guanajuato, Sinaloa, Veracruz, Nuevo León, Zacatecas, Coahuila, Querétaro, Puebla, Chihuahua, Guerrero, Tabasco, Aguascalientes, Oaxaca, and Durango.

48 The *Rapport* explains that the Mexican girls' groups, the Enfants de Marie, were "puissantes auxiliaires des Dames, et . . . les premieres dignitaires de l'Oeuvre" (1896), p. 83. De Dios suggests that the Hijas de María were an autonomous organization which concentrated more on strengthening the faith of its members than on training to become Ladies of Charity, however (1993), 1: 563–66.

49 González Navarro (1985), p. 62; and (1957), pp. 505–9. The *Memoria* (1879) also lists high numbers of *raciones ordinarias* (385,110), *raciones extraordinarias* (60,273), *recetas* (50,662), and *piezas de ropa* (8,664) distributed the previous year.

50 De Dios (1993), 2: 644–46.

51 De Dios quotes an editorial from the 1910 *Boletín* as lamenting the low membership of the Society, but does not provide figures (1993), 2: 630.

52 See Chowning (2001). Serrano notes that the Chilean Church hierarchy consciously harnessed women to play new roles in the late 19th century (2000), pp. 13–38, 71–75, 94. So did the Argentine government, Little (1978).

53 Adame Goddard (1981); Ceballos Ramírez (1991) and (1995); De Dios (1993), 2: 627–28; Hanson (1994), pp. 83–130; and Pani (2001).

54 *Memoria* (1865), p. 8.

55 Quoted in Olimón Nolasco (1995), p. 289.

56 *Rapport* (1894), p. 45.

57 For a fuller discussions of these trends, see Arrom (1985), esp. chap. 1; and Arrom (2000), pp. 180, 228, 244–47, 260–61, and 267–68.

58 Cuevas claims that in 1873 the female branch of the Sociedad Católica de México had 20,000 members (1928), 5: 383–84. See also Adame Goddard (1981), pp. 19–27. A few religious orders were reintroduced to Mexico at the end of the nineteenth century, but they did not apparently flourish as they had in the past.

59 *Memoria* (1865), p. 7.

60 *Memoria* (1865), p. 6.

61 *Reglamento* (1863), p. 4.

62 *Memoria* (1865).

63 Ponce de León Atria (2001); Serrano (2001); and Castro (2001). In contrast, male conferences did not apparently catch on in Argentina. See Mead (2001), p. 100, fn. 23.

64 For a discussion of shifting notions of poor relief in Mexico, see Arrom (2000), esp. pp. 7–8, 32–33, 38–39, 59–62, and 72–74.

65 *Memoria* (1867), p. 10.

66 *Boletín* (1859), p. 200.

67 *Reseña* (1895), p. 11.

68 *Reseña* (1895), p. 12.

69 This philosophy, expressed in the Society's by-laws and reports, is elaborated on in the book by conference member and 1849 Central Council president Luis Gonzaga Cuevas (1851).

70 Agustín Rodríguez, quoted in *Reseña* (1895), p. 71.

71 De Dios (1993), 1: 513.

72 See *Reglamento* (1851), p. 8, fns. 4 and 6; and De Dios 1: 73, fn. 2.

73 See De Dios (1993), 1: 513–17; and Belanger (1997).

74 Home visiting did not come easily to the Chilean or Colombian conferences either, which likewise failed to practice it in the early years. Castro (2001), p. 198; Ponce de León Atria (2001), p. 1.

75 *Reglamento* (1863), p. 7.

76 Quoted in Olimón Nolasco (1995), p. 289.

77 *Boletín* (1889).

78 On this point for Chile, see Serrano (2001), pp. 3–4; and Valenzuela and Valenzuela (2000), p. 210.

79 Entry on "Catholic Social Movements" in *New Catholic Encyclopedia* (1967), 13: 321. See also articles on "Social Action," 13: 310–12; and "Rerum Novarum," 12: 387.

80 *Reseña* (1895), p. 13.

81 González Navarro (1957), p. 496.

82 In Argentina, for example, the conferences received cash and land donations from the federal and municipal governments, and in Colombia they not only received government funding but also were charged with administering state-run welfare institutions. See Mead (2001), pp. 102, 104, 107–8; and Castro (2001), pp. 192, 202–3.

83 Castro (2001), esp. chap. 4. See also Foucault (1933), pp. 270–331; and Société (1933), pp. 281–303.

84 *Rapport* (1893). The Mexican Ladies of Charity was also one of the earliest, if not the first, in Latin America. The *Memoria* (1865) listed only one other Latin American branch by the end of 1864, in Peru (final chart).

85 Mead (2001), esp. p. 100.

86 Castro gives a foundation date of 1925 for the national organization, although some local conferences had already been founded by then (2001), pp. 209, 227–28.

87 See, for example, Castro (2001), esp. chaps. 3–4; Farnsworth-Alvear (2000), pp. 53–54, 77–90, 100–1; Forment (2003); Londoño (2000), pp. 155–56, 163–64; Matos Rodríguez (1999), chap. 5; Serrano (2000), pp. 34–38 and (2001); and Valenzuela and Valenzuela (2000), pp. 210–14.

References

Archives Consulted

AHDF   Archivo Histórico del Distrito Federal, Mexico City
AL   Archives Lazaristes, Paris
BNM   Biblioteca Nacional de México, Mexico City
INAH   Instituto Nacional de Antropología e Historia, Mexico City
SVP   St. Vincent de Paul Archives, Paris

Published Primary Sources—Sociedad de San Vicente de Paul:

Acta de la Asamblea General Extraordinaria celebrada el día quince de septiembre de 1945, en ocasión del Centenario de la agregación de esta sociedad a la de Paris. [SVP, Mexique: Rapports nationaux, 1868–1952]

Boletín de la Sociedad de San Vicente de Paul. Nos. 7 (1859) and 11 (1860). [SVP, Méxique, Rapports nationaux]

Memoria de las Obras de las Conferencias de la Sociedad de San Vicente de Paul . . . durante el año de 1871. Mexico City: Imp. de la V. e Hijos de Murguia, 1872. [SVP, Méxique, Rapports nationaux]

Noticia sobre las Conferencias de la Sociedad de San Vicente de Paul . . . 1868/1869/1870/1871. México: Imp. de la V. e Hijos de Murguía, 1869/70/71/72. [SVP, Méxique, Rapports nationaux]

Reglamento de la Sociedad de San Vicente de Paul, 1835. Mexico City, 1851. [SVP, CC113, Méxique]

Reseña del Quincuagenario de la Sociedad. Mexico City: Imp. y Lit. de Francisco Díaz de León, 1895.

Published Primary Sources—*Señoras de la Caridad:*

Memoria que el Consejo Superior de las Asociaciones de Señoras de la Caridad del Imperio Mexicano dirige al General de Paris, de las obras que ha practicado y cantidades colectadas e invertidas en el socorro de los pobres enfermos, desde 1 de julio de 1864 a 30 de junio de 1865. Mexico City: Comercio, 1865. [Harvard-Houghton]

Memoria que el consejo superior de las asociaciones de señoras de la caridad de México, dirije al general de Paris, de las obras que ha practicado y cantidades colectadas e invertidas en el socorro de los pobres enfermos, desde el 1o de Julio de 1865 a 30 de Junio de 1866. Mexico City: Mariano Villanueva, 1867. [BNM, Lafragua]

Memoria que el Consejo superior de las Señoras de la Caridad de Méjico leyó en la Asamblea general verificada en la Iglesia de la Encarnación de esta capital el dia 23 de julio de 1878. Mexico City: Tip. Religiosa de Miguel Torner y Cía, 1879. [NY Public Library]

Memoria sobre la obra de las Señoras de la Caridad de San Vicente de Paul en México, Año de 1921. Mexico City: Imp. 'La Moderna,' 1922. [INAH Fondo Reservado]

Rapport sur les oeuvres des Dames de la Charité pendant l'Année [1892/ 1893/1895/ 1896] Lu a l'Assemblée Générale . . . Paris: 95, Rue de Sevres, 1893/ 1894/ 1896/ 1897. [AL]

Reglamento de la Asociación de las Señoras de la Caridad instituida por San Vicente de Paul en beneficio de los pobres enfermos, y establecida en varios lugares por los Padres de la Congregación de la Misión con licencia de los ordinarios. Mexico City: Imp. De Andrade y Escalante, 1863. [INAH Fondo Reservado]

Reglamento de la Asociación de las Señoras de la Caridad . . . formado según el original de Paris y mandado observar por el Director General de la República. Mexico City: Iglesia de la Inmaculada Concepción, 1911. [INAH Fondo Reservado]

Secondary Sources:

Adame Goddard, Jorge. *El pensamiento político y social de los católicos mexicanos, 1867–1914.* Mexico City: UNAM, 1981.

Almond, Gabriel, and Sidney Verba. *The Civic Culture: Political Attitudes and Democracy in Five Nations.* Princeton: Princeton University Press, 1963.

Arrom, Silvia Marina. *The Women of Mexico City, 1790–1857.* Stanford CA: Stanford University Press, 1985.

————. *Containing the Poor: The Mexico City Poor House, 1774–1871.* Durham NC: Duke University Press, 2000.

Belanger, Brian C. "Cofradías." vol. 1: 276–79 in *Encyclopedia of Mexico: History, Society & Culture.* Ed. Michael S. Werner. Chicago: Fitzroy Dearborn Publishers, 1997.

Blum, Ann S. "Conspicuous Benevolence: Liberalism, Public Welfare, and Private Charity in Porfirian Mexico City, 1877–1910." *The Americas,* 58, 4 (July 2001): 7–38.

Castro, Beatriz. "Charity and Poor Relief in a Context of Poverty: Colombia, 1870–1930." Ph.D. Dissertation, Oxford University, 2001.

Ceballos Ramírez, Manuel. *El catolicismo social: un tercero en discordia, Rerum Novarum, la 'cuestión social' y la movilización de los católicos mexicanos (1891–1911).* Mexico City: El Colegio de México, 1991.

————. "Las organizaciones laborales católicas a finales del siglo XIX." Pages 367–398 in *Estado, Iglesia y sociedad en México: siglo XIX.* Ed. Alvaro Matute, Evelia Trejo, and Brian Connaughton. Mexico City: UNAM-Porrúa, 1995.

Centro Mexicano para la Filantropía. "Understanding Mexican Philanthropy." Pages 183–191 in *Changing Structure of Mexico: Political, Social, and Economic Prospects,* ed. Laura Randall. London: M.E. Sharpe, 1996.

Chowning, Margaret. "From Colonial Cofradías to Porfirian Pious Associations: A Case Study in the Feminization of Public Piety in Mexico," Unpublished paper presented at the LASA meetings, Washington, D.C., Sept. 2001.

Cuevas, Mariano. *Historia de la Iglesia en México.* vol. 5. El Paso TX: Ed. "Revista Católica," 1928.

De Dios, Vicente. *Historia de la familia vicentina en México (1844–1994).* 2 vols. Salamanca: Editorial Ceme, 1993.

Farnsworth-Alvear, Ann. *Dulcinea in the Factory: Myths, Morals, Men, and Women in Colombia's Industrial Experiment, 1905–1960.* Durham, NC: Duke University Press, 2000.

Forment, Carlos A. *Democracy in Latin America: Civic Selfhood and Public Life in Mexico and Peru.* Chicago: University of Chicago Press, 2003.

Foucault, Albert. *La Société de Saint-Vincent de Paul: Histoire de Cents Ans.* Paris: Editions SPES, 1933.

García Icazbalceta, Joaquín. *Informe sobre los establecimientos de beneficencia y corrección de esta capital . . .* Mexico City: Moderna Librería Religiosa, 1907.

Glazier, Michael, and Thomas Shelley, eds. *The Encyclopedia of American Catholic History.* Collegeville, MN: The Liturgical Press, 1997.

Gonzaga Cuevas, Luis. *Porvenir de México, o juicio sobre su estado político en 1821 y 1851.* Mexico City: Imp. de Ignacio Cumplido, 1851.

González Navarro, Moisés. *El Porfiriato: Vida Social.* vol. 4 of *Historia Moderna de México.* Ed. Daniel Cosío Villegas. Mexico City: Editorial Hermes, 1957.

———. *La Pobreza en México.* Mexico City: El Colegio de México, 1985.

Hanson, Randall S. "The Day of Ideals: Catholic Social Action in the Age of the Mexican Revolution, 1867–1929." Ph.D. Dissertation, Indiana University, 1994.

Little, Cynthia J. "Education, Philanthropy, and Feminism: Components of Argentine Womanhood, 1860–1926." Pages 235–54 in *Latin American Women: Historical Perspectives.* Ed. Asunción Lavrín. Westport CT: Greenwood Press, 1978.

Londoño, Patricia. "The Politics of Religion in a Modernising Society: Antioquia (Colombia), 1850–1910." Pages 143–65 in *The Politics of Religion in an Age of Revival: Studies in Nineteenth-Century Europe and Latin America.* Ed. Austen Ivereigh. London: Institute of Latin American Studies, 2000.

Matos Rodríguez, Felix V. *Women and Urban Change in San Juan, Puerto Rico, 1820–1868.* Gainesville FL: University Press of Florida, 1999.

Mead, Karen. "Gender, Welfare and the Catholic Church in Argentina: Conferencias de Señoras de San Vicente de Paul, 1890–1916." *The Americas*, 58, 1 (July 2001): 91–119.

New Catholic Encyclopedia. 15 volumes. New York, McGraw-Hill, 1967.

Olimón Nolasco, Manuel. "Proyecto de reforma de la Iglesia en México (1867 y 1875)." Pages 267–92 in *Estado, Iglesia y sociedad en México: siglo XIX.* Ed. Alvaro Matute, Evelia Trejo, and Brian Connaughton. Mexico City: UNAM-Porrúa, 1995.

Pani, Erika. "Democracia y representación política: la visión de dos periódicos católicos de fin de siglo, 1880–1910." Pages 143–60 in *Modernidad, tradición y alteridad: la ciudad de México en el cambio de siglo (XIX-XX).* Ed. Claudia Agostoni and Elisa Speckman. Mexico City: UNAM, 2001.

Ponce de León Atria, Macarena. "La Sociedad de San Vicente de Paul en Chile: nuevos vínculos con la jerarquía eclesiástica y los pobres urbanos, 1854–1870." Unpublished paper presented at the LASA meetings, Washington, D.C., Sept. 2001.

Serrano, Sol. "Asociaciones católicas en el siglo XIX chileno: política, caridad y rito." Unpublished paper presented at the LASA meetings, Washington, D.C., Sept. 2001.

———, ed. *Vírgenes viajeras: diarios de religiosas francesas en su ruta a Chile, 1837–1874.* Santiago: Ediciones Universidad Católica de Chile, 2000.

Société de St. Vincent de Paul. *Livre du Centenaire: L'oeuvre d'Ozanam a Travers le Monde, 1833–1933.* Paris: Gabriel Beauchesne et ses fils, 1933.

Valenzuela, Samuel J., and Erika Maza Valenzuela. "The Politics of Religion in a Catholic Country: Republican Democracy, Cristianismo Social and the Conservative Party in Chile, 1850–1925." Pages 188–223 in *The Politics of Religion in an Age of Revival: Studies in Nineteenth-Century Europe and Latin America.* Ed. Austen Ivereigh. London: Institute of Latin American Studies, 2000.

Velasco Ceballos, Rómulo. *El niño mexicano ante la caridad y el estado.* . . . Mexico City: Editorial Cultura, 1935.

3

Volunteers and Donors: Patterns of Civic Engagement in Contemporary Peru

Felipe Portocarrero

Reflection on volunteering and giving in Latin America is uncharted territory. Academically speaking, in Peru, as in the rest of the continent, the study of cooperation has been insufficiently explored. Newspapers have reported case histories, and television programs highlight out-of-context good deeds. However, the common denominator of these journalistic endeavors has been to emphasize the altruistic behavior of individuals and institutions, without regard to historic processes. Peruvian civil society is now at a complex stage in which ancient practices of reciprocity and exchange—with roots stretching back to the pre-Hispanic past—have been combined and redefined with new humanist-inspired collective behaviors. In this redefinition, sociability and freedom find in "others" the source, purpose, and framework for their action (Todorov 1998, 52–57).[1] However, the broader social context is not free from tensions and ambiguities with frequent ups and downs. Contradictory discourses co-exist: from those who base their practices on the above-mentioned values of solidarity and participation to others whose thinking and action are guided by an individualistic and self-sufficient stance, rather than a concern for promoting stronger citizen rights in a community where the existence of "others" is subordinate to personal realization (Portocarrero G. 2001: 3).

Although the study of volunteering and giving in Latin America remains *terra incognita*, it is a controversial and intensely debated academic field. For some, the study of volunteering is part of an Anglo-Saxon tradition in which concepts such as the volunteer and the good citizen replace those of the militant and the activist. The former are those who do their civic duty and abstain from proposing major social changes, while the latter are players from parties, unions, or social movements more generally associated with critical questioning of the *status quo*. Given official neglect of basic needs, these groups have sought to compensate for their shortcomings by resorting to old practices of reciprocity and several forms of community self-help. Some consider that terming such social manifestations "volunteering" is a mistaken analytical perspective: in the end, governments have sought to obtain free labor by instrumental and clientelist utilization of such traditions of solidarity among the poor in exchange for access to housing, education, and food programs.

Although these critical observations should be taken into consideration, we believe that sufficient research has not been done to give them adequate empirical support. The debate cannot progress in a meaningful way unless we have a more precise view of the social reality on which these criticisms are based. Only then will we be in a position to answer such questions as: How extensive are volunteering practices in Peru? What are the principal volunteering activities and which organizations carry them out? Are there significant differences if these practices are examined from the perspective of religion, sex, age, and socioeconomic bracket of the volunteers? What motivates citizens to donate part of their time and money? Is it possible to build a typology based on the various forms of volunteering current in Peru? What is the relationship between practices of this type of solidarity and building citizen values?

Using the previous observations as background, the present study is intended to focus our attention on behaviors of solidarity, that is, on the nature and extent of volunteering and giving in contemporary Peru. To accomplish this, in 2001, the *Universidad del Pacífico* research center conducted the First Peruvian Survey on Volunteering and Giving (EDV 2001).[2] In addition, a number of in-depth interviews were conducted during the First Peruvian Volunteer Fair in Lima in late 2001 to provide a more complete overview of what motivates people to undertake this sort of civic involvement. In the pages that follow, we will summarize our most significant findings.[3]

The presentation is divided into two sections. The first examines the major features of volunteering and giving in Peru, as well as public perceptions and attitudes toward these practices. The second section concludes with some thoughts seeking to explore the relationship between practices of solidarity and citizenship-building in Peru.

Volunteers and Donors: A Quantitative Approach

Profile of Peruvian Volunteering

The notion of volunteer work is complex and at the same time controversial. Neither its meaning nor its scope has been clearly defined, especially in Latin America (Roitter 2002: 3, Landen 2003: 2). Far from becoming identified with a particular social group, volunteering traverses the entire social structure. It finds expression in different ways under diverse circumstances: major natural disasters (earthquakes, floods, famine) or manmade disasters (international or civil wars causing death and displacement of huge contingents of the population) also arouse in human beings solidarity, compassion, altruism, social and political responsibility (Thompson and Toro 2001: 1). Under less extreme conditions, however, numerous forms of expressing solidarity emerge from individuals and civil society organizations that donate time and money to meet unfulfilled basic needs and defend the rights of society's most vulnerable sectors.

To complicate matters further, old stereotypes still persist alongside more positive images of volunteering and giving. The old cliché about volunteer work is that it involves small groups of members of a social *elite* seeking to pacify their consciences with work of this nature (Ibid:3).[4] Ignorance and prejudices held by the population in a common sense sort of way have given the concept a meaning associated with older charitable and welfare activities of Christian inspiration. Indeed, from a long-term historical perspective, this was the sort of volunteer work that prevailed during the Colonial period, when philanthropic practices were introduced by the Spanish and Portuguese authorities in close coordination with the Roman Catholic Church (Portocarrero F. 2002: 53–54). Owing to a singular transfer of meanings, this kind of practice has remained most forcefully rooted in the contemporary collective imagination and only lately, in the last few decades, has this traditional association between volunteering and charity begun to be questioned.

In any event, the very breadth and indetermination of concepts, in which ambiguous and diverse social concepts—ancient and modern— mingle, are its greatest attraction and, at the same time, its most visible weakness. In fact, the tendency to generalize the positive features and virtues of volunteering has perhaps led to excessive expectations about its ability to bring about social change, strengthen civil society, and achieve economic development. Given such disorder and confusion, it becomes particularly important to establish some basic facts about the scope and nature of volunteering. Only an empirical approach to this social phenomenon will help to dispel errors, determine its scope of action, and assess its actual impact.

Bearing in mind the exploratory nature of the present study, for operational purposes we have defined volunteering as organized unpaid work channeled through some social organization and carried out for the benefit of others or the society as a whole. This definition excludes the type of volunteering done as personal services or favors to individuals, relatives, or friends. In practice, this definition applies to diverse sectors with varying degrees of commitment, motivations, goals, and expectations. Thus, the study results include not only traditional activities conducted in favor of third parties (such as helping the sick or the elderly) and actions associated with policies aiming at social change, but also numerous activities undertaken by popular associations focusing on self-help and family survival.

How many volunteers are there? According to EDV 2001 data, one out of every three persons interviewed (34%) had volunteered during the previous year. In addition, while most of these volunteers (74%) were linked to a single organization, about one-third (27%) did volunteer work with one or more organizations. Comparatively speaking, the presence of volunteer work in Peru, while significantly lower than in a country with such a long-standing civic tradition as the United States (56%),[5] is comparable to some European countries, for example, the Netherlands (36%), Germany (34%), or Romania (33%).[6] Moreover, volunteering in Peru is more than 10 percentage points higher than the figures from similar surveys conducted in other Latin American countries: 26% in Argentina,[7] 14% in Uruguay,[8] 16% in Brazil.[9]

Studies on volunteering in Latin America are few and the methods used differ—which is why only general comparisons are possible. However, where there is available information, certain trends are clear (Villar et al. 2001). That is, volunteering in Latin America mostly addresses those areas in which government action—in spite of the immense expansion of coverage and improvement in the quality of services in the past two decades—has not managed to completely satisfy certain demands of the population. In all the countries studied, primary social services such as education and health and activities aiming at community and neighborhood development figure as common denominators.

To what sphere are the volunteer host organizations connected? Organizations connected with the neighborhood, the locality, or the volunteer community—representing the local sphere—accounted for 52 percent of the organizations (see Figure 1). Volunteering takes place in limited spaces, usually linked to specific immediate needs arising from daily life and directly affecting living conditions. These characteristics indicate that volunteering was motivated by concern for questions of mere survival rather than by ideological questions or abstract political principles.

Figure 1. Links of volunteering[1]

1. Percentages do not add up to 100, due to multiple-choice responses.

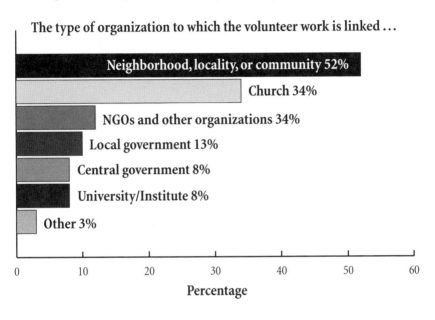

The type of organization to which the volunteer work is linked ...

Neighborhood, locality, or community 52%

Church 34%

NGOs and other organizations 34%

Local government 13%

Central government 8%

University/Institute 8%

Other 3%

Percentage

Base: Total volunteers (487 persons)
Source: *Encuesta Nacional de Donaciones y Trabajo Voluntario* 2001
Developed by the author.

The Church, linked to 34% of volunteer work, was second to the local sphere in importance. Because of the way the question was posed, this option may represent a sort of "umbrella" covering many local activities, that is, activities connected with parishes or churches particularly close to the daily life of the volunteers. More significantly, however, this figure confirms the significance of religion's role in producing a sense of belonging to a community through a powerful set of symbols that it spreads to the population. Indeed, by generating the possibilities for social interaction through collective practices and rituals and shared beliefs, religion encourages the formation of networks while promoting creation of social capital and community integration (Turner 1991: xi; Foley et al. 2002: 215–216).

Figure 2. Areas of Volunteering and Types of Organizations

Areas	Organizations
Culture and Art	1. Musical, artistic and cultural groups
	2. Other culture and art (museums, cultural associations, media, etc.)
Sports and Leisure	
	3. Departmental/provincial/district clubs
	4. Sports clubs
	5. Service clubs (Lions, Rotary, etc.)
	6. Other sports, games, and leisure
Education and Research	
	7. Day care and nursery school educational programs
	8. Primary and secondary education
	9. Higher education, technical institutes
	10. Associations for technical training and capacity-building
	11. Youth formation (Boy Scouts, etc.)
	12. Other education and research
Health Administration	
	13. Health care centers, emergency clinics (Local Health Administration/CLAS etc.)
	14. Hospitals and clinics
	15. Rehabilitation (including drug & alcohol addiction)
	16. Health education and prevention (AIDS, reproductive health, etc.)
	17. Other health (mental health institutions, asylums)
Social Services	
	18. Child aid centers, day care, nurseries
	19. Glass-of-milk committees
	20. Soup kitchens
	21. Emergency social services (Red Cross, Civil Defense, etc.)
	22. Other social services (aid centers for youth, senior citizens, women, disabled or displaced persons)
Environment	
	23. Urban sweeping, park area embellishment
	24. Other environment (conservation of national parks and reserves, animal protection and care)
Development and Housing	
	25. Urban patrols
	26. Neighborhood organizations
	27. Women's clubs
	28. Housing associations
	29. Organizations for supporting development
	30. Other development and housing
Civic Organizations	
	31. Human rights and women's rights organizations
	32. Volunteer Firemen of Peru
	33. Other civic organizations (criminal rehabilitation, consumer protection, etc.)
Philanthropy and Charity	
	34. Foundations and charitable organizations (e.g. fund-collecting)
	35. Other philanthropy and charity
Religion	
	36. Parish groups
	37. Religious groups or associations
	38. Churches, synagogues, mosques and other places of religious worship
	39. Other religion
Other	
	40. Trade, business, professional associations and unions
	41. Other areas and organizations

Source: *Encuesta Nacional de Donaciones y Trabajo Voluntario* 2001
Developed by the author

Following local organizations and the Church, we have non-governmental organizations (NGOs), local government, central government,
universities and other institutions that—especially in the case of NGOs—
are more closely associated with democratic values, defense of citizen
rights, and community action.

In what areas do volunteers work? EDV 2001 defined a set of 41 specific
organizations where volunteers work. These organizations, according to
their focus, goals and particular interests, form various operating areas, as
summarized in Figure 2. In practical terms, these areas and organizations
represent the vast and heterogeneous universe of solidarity practices that
Peruvian citizens carry out, which will have to be borne in mind in the following pages.

Analysis of the information in this comprehensive and diverse
panorama reveals that in the case of Peru, only six of the above areas are
particularly significant, i.e.: (i) religion; (ii) development and housing; (iii)
social services; (iv) education and research; (v) sports, games, and leisure;
and, finally, (vi) health. In fact, Figure 3 shows that the largest amount of

Figure 3. Nationwide Volunteering by Area[1]

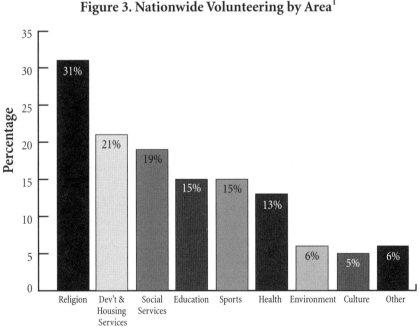

1. Percentages do not add up to 100 due to multiple-choice responses.
Base: Total volunteers (487 persons)
Source: *Encuesta Nacional de Donaciones y Trabajo Voluntario* 2001
Developed by the author.

volunteering is done in the area of religion; a second group comprises volunteering in areas of social interest, namely development and housing, and social services; and, last, the third group is composed of traditional government-related social sectors and sports-oriented organizations. The remaining groups, with lower percentages, form a fourth group, heterogeneous by nature.

Drawing on this first overview of volunteer practices in Peru, we may reach some preliminary conclusions. In the first place, religious volunteering is strongly linked to the Roman Catholic Church; development and housing, to the neighborhood; social services, to the neighborhood and central or local government institutions; universities and NGOs also play a significant role. Second, while volunteer work in the areas of sports and leisure is closely linked to local affairs, volunteering in the health care area—in addition to connection with the neighborhood and the community—is closely linked to central, and to some degree, local, government. Again it may be concluded that, in most areas of volunteer work, the scope of action is limited, geographically circumscribed to the locality and primarily—although not exclusively—concentrated in community organizations. This finding confirms the conclusions of other studies concerning the weakness of civil society organizations as nationwide political or social interlocutors.[10]

To ensure that this first approach to volunteering in Peru is properly reflected, Figure 4 presents the types of organizations in which the population surveyed prefers to practice solidarity.

Figure 4. Main Types of Organizations Where Volunteering Took Place, Nationwide

Type of organization	Percentage
Parish groups	20
Neighborhood organizations	12
Glass-of-milk committees	12
Sports clubs	10
Primary and secondary education centers	7
Health care centers and emergency clinics	6
Religious groups or associations	6
Parishes, synagogues, mosques	6
Urban sweeping, park areas	5
Musical, artistic, and cultural groups	5
Childcare centers	4
Hospitals and clinics	4

Source: *Encuesta Nacional de Donaciones y Trabajo Voluntario* 2001
Developed by the author.

How dedicated are the volunteers? To answer this question requires examining not only the economic contribution that volunteers make, but also the degree of involvement shown by those who choose to practice solidarity in this way. In terms of economic contribution, a volunteer devotes an average of 196 hours per year to volunteer work, that is, a little more than 16 hours per month, or the equivalent of 2 working days per month.[11] To the extent that volunteering, by definition, receives no monetary compensation, correctly assessing its economic value is no easy task. Notwithstanding, following the method suggested by Portocarrero and Millán (2001: 9), we may estimate the minimum economic value of volunteer work. This value amounts to US $281,103,581, equivalent to 0.63% of Peru's GDP for 2000.[12]

In regard to the level of involvement, it is interesting to note that in 42% of all cases of volunteering,[13] the volunteer worker had been involved in that work for more than one year. In addition, if the observation is extended to volunteers with six months' involvement, the proportion increases and becomes quite significant—63% of all cases of volunteering. This is not, therefore, a group of citizens who practice solidarity during a marginal portion of their lives, or whose involvement is sporadic, intermittent, and uncertain. On the contrary, these persons adopt a steady pattern of behavior, are uninterruptedly involved in social causes, and have made commitments that make up a central part of their daily lives. This perception is in fact reinforced by the finding that in 28% of cases of volunteering, the volunteer worker is willing to work in this manner four or more times weekly.

Another indicator of the extent to which volunteering is institutionalized in Peru is the level of citizen membership in the various organizations demanding their services. The survey data reveal that 43% of the persons who did volunteer work were members of the respective organizations. Although this is a significant percentage, the extent of volunteer involvement is considerably more complex than just organizational membership. Theoretically, a high degree of membership indeed tends to be associated with stronger commitment, since formal registration in an organization has required deeper reflection and involved a well-scrutinized decision with the advantages and disadvantages of such a decision being carefully weighed. Nevertheless, a closer look reveals other issues associated with this phenomenon that first need to be examined.

In principle, an examination of all the organizations of which volunteers claimed to be members shows that three kinds of membership may be described, based on the perception of those interviewed. First, *classic membership* is associated with organizations requiring formal member registration, that is, members are duly registered and usually provided with an identity card or other form of personal identification. This form of membership ensures member training, group activities, and (explicitly or implicitly) imposes a shared vision on members' behavior. Membership thus takes on a permanent character and reflects a major volunteer commitment toward the institution that welcomes him or her. Organizations with this form of membership include sports clubs, social clubs and organizations providing emergency services, among others. Second, *open membership* is associated with local organizations operating to ensure survival, that is, oriented toward fulfilling the basic needs of the population. In this case, the organization does not require formal registration and members are considered as part of the organization as long as their participation lasts. Thus, this form of membership is more volatile and entails more turnover in the course of a relatively short period. Organizations with this form of membership include women's clubs, urban patrols, neighborhood organizations and glass-of-milk committees, among others. Finally, *emotional membership* involves volunteer identification with an institution with which an individual shares values, beliefs and moral standards. This form of membership is to be found in all organizations connected to the religious sphere.

Based on this typology, it is clear that classic membership requires a more profound commitment from volunteer workers than the other two types. Although all organizations require a sort of contract—often informal and implicit—between the volunteer worker and the organization, in the case of classic membership, the contract is a formal one, often requiring a written agreement whereby the volunteer undertakes a number of obligations and responsibilities. Undoubtedly, this form of membership potentially ensures more extensive and stable involvement and level of civic commitment. In fact, the evidence clearly shows that membership has a positive relationship with the number of hours devoted and the length of association with volunteer activities. On average, member volunteers did indeed devote more than twice the number of hours than simple collaborators in 2000, the monthly average being 17.7 hours for the former, and 7.6 hours for the latter. In addition, 31.2% reported having engaged in such activities for more than three years. Thus, this relatively stable and socially committed volunteering ensures continuing projection into the future.

Figure 5. Volunteer Organizations and Form of Membership*

Type of organization	Membership
Musical, artistic, and cultural groups Departmental, district, and provincial clubs Sporting clubs Service clubs (Lions, Rotary, etc.) Centers for youth formation (Boy Scouts, etc.) Hospitals and clinics Rehabilitation centers (including drugs and alcohol) Emergency social services (Red Cross, etc.)	Classic
Technical training and capacity-building associations Health care centers and emergency clinics Child aid centers, day care and nurseries Glass-of-milk committees Soup kitchens Urban patrols Neighborhood organizations Women's clubs Housing associations Primary & secondary education centers	Open
Parish groups Religious associations or groups Churches, synagogues, mosques	Emotional

*This table shows information on the types of organizations where volunteers claimed to be members. The *Encuesta* did not register "membership" with organizations not listed above. So though it may appear questionable for a volunteer of any religious faith to declare him or herself a member, this information was collected from his/her own perception and self-classification as such.
Source: *Encuesta Nacional de Donaciones y Trabajo Voluntario* 2001
Developed by the author.

What do volunteers do? Close to 41% of the volunteers claimed that their collaboration involved physical labor rather than the type of work needing special educational or training. This finding is consistent with the observation that more volunteers who have performed such tasks belong to socioeconomic levels D/E (63%) than C (37%) or A/B (21%). The reverse is true for activities associated with teaching, training, and capacity-building, the second-ranking category of volunteer work (18%), which by their very nature require some degree of specialized knowledge. Here, the number of volunteers from levels A/B amounts to 42%, whereas the percentages of volunteers from levels C (23%) and D/E (25%) are practically the same. The remaining activities are fairly homogeneous and of comparable importance. It is worth pointing out that the socioeconomic levels used for the survey were established according to a set of variables including level of education, occupation of the head of household, nature of dwelling, area of residence, and ownership of other real or personal property. In broad terms, level A/B is equivalent to high and medium-high brackets, level C to medium sectors, and level D/E to poor and extremely poor sectors.

Who are volunteers? EDV 2001 confirms that there are no significant differences in the numbers of male (51.1%) and female (48.9%) volunteers. This finding, which came up in the first survey of giving and volunteering conducted in four Peruvian cities in 1998 (Portocarrero and Millán 2001: 20) and was confirmed in the survey of Lima youth in 2000 (Portocarrero et al. 2001: 20), casts doubt on the common belief that volunteering is a mostly female form of activity. The similarity between the sexes also applies to the number of volunteers, hours devoted, type of work done (except in "planning and organization" where 21% are males and only 8% are females), as well as the ratio of collaboration and membership. Slight differences are observed only in frequency of activities, in which women score 6 percentage points higher in the "6–7 times a week" category.

Notwithstanding, major differences between men and women arise in areas and types of organization, with division of labor according to sex adhering more closely to traditional patterns. Whereas women stand out in social services (7% men vs. 33% women), especially in glass-of-milk committees, women's clubs, and other community food-related organizations, men are more numerous in the area of sports and leisure (23% men vs. 7% women), particularly in sports clubs. Men are also slightly more numerous than women in education, development and housing.

In regards to age, generally no major differences are observed between young people and seniors in area of action, radius of influence, working hours devoted to volunteering or motivations. Individuals between 25 and 39 tend to participate more in primary and secondary education than younger people (9% vs. 1%), a finding related to more active participation in parent associations by parents of school-age children. On the other hand, individuals between 40 and 70 tend to participate more actively than younger people in neighborhood organizations, a fact that may stem from their greater tendency to be householders or heads of households. In regard to type of work, younger persons tend to participate more in information campaigns than the 40- to 70-year-olds, while the latter tend to be more active than younger people in administrative support.

In terms of socioeconomic level, the distribution of volunteer workers is fairly similar to the general distribution of the population, with a slight over-representation of individuals from high and medium brackets. In addition, the data show that 80% of the volunteers come from medium (level C) and poor and extremely poor (level D/E) sectors of the population. However, this distribution is only indicative of the high levels of economic deficiencies prevailing in Peru, making it more likely to find poor rather than non-poor volunteer workers—rather than suggesting that the poorest do more volunteer work than others. A survey of volunteering per socioeconomic sector, shown below, rather suggests the reverse, that level A/B is more likely to do volunteer work than level C or level D/E.

Figure 6. Composition of Total Surveyed and Volunteers Per Socioeconomic Level

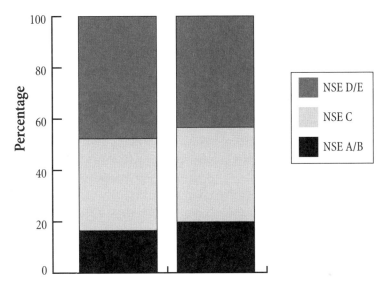

Base: Total (1,414 persons); Volunteer workers (487 persons)
Source: *Encuesta Nacional de Donaciones y Trabajo Voluntario* 2001
Developed by the author.

   In a scenario such as the above, in which most volunteer workers belong to the poorest sectors of the population, it is to be expected that many activities would be associated with survival and unfulfilled basic needs. Examination of the linkages of the organizations where volunteer work was done reaffirms the importance of the local character of participation among these sectors of the population. While 50% of volunteers from levels C and D/E claim that the organization where they performed volunteer work was connected with their "neighborhood, locality, or community," the equivalent figure for level A/B is only 29%. On the other hand, the relatively uniform rate of volunteering associated with the Church is noteworthy at all levels of the population surveyed.

Volunteering and religion. Having identified the religious area as the one with the highest concentration of volunteer work, the nature of this relationship calls for more detailed examination. Is there a causality between volunteering and adherence to some religion? The evidence suggests that, as in the case of Brazil (Landim and Scalon 2000: 60), no statistically significant differences are found between the proportions of religious and non-religious volunteers. If this is true and bearing in mind that most Peruvians (96% of the survey population) profess some religion, the next step is to determine whether affiliation with a specific creed is a crucial factor in the decision to do volunteer work. According to the findings, evangelicals account for a larger percentage of volunteers (43%) than Roman Catholics (33%). It is interesting to note that these findings agree with those of Putnam (2000: 76–77) for the United States.

However, considering that the vast majority of the population surveyed identify themselves as Roman Catholic,[14] it is perhaps more meaningful to relate volunteering to active religious involvement. In this context, a particularly useful indicator is personal participation in ritual celebrations. The evidence suggests that there is a larger proportion of volunteers among active practitioners of their religion. Whereas 39% of those who attended religious services did volunteer work, only 20% of those who did not attend engaged in the same work. Moreover, stressing the above relationship, the proportion of volunteers is higher among persons who attend religious worship more frequently. Thus, 26% of individuals who occasionally attended religious services engaged in volunteer work, in comparison to 46% of those who attended on a weekly basis.

As Putnam points out in connection with the United States, religious institutions directly support a wide range of social initiatives extending beyond strictly pastoral activities and worship (2000: 66). Indeed, parishes play a major role in community development, so it is essential to equate their projection efforts toward the community with volunteering. In this context, findings show that participating in parish activities is also positively linked to volunteering: 28% volunteer workers among persons who do not attend parish activities contrast with 52% volunteer workers among individuals who do attend them.

Giving: Between Charity and Solidarity

Donations are a different form of solidarity and commitment for those who give them. Donation size, composition, destination, and nature, however, have not been properly studied. As observed below, the degree of citizen involvement involved is significantly different from that of volunteering. It is therefore advisable to examine the principal characteristics:

What is the number and destination of donations? First of all, more than half the Peruvian population (51%) made donations. Half of the donations made in 2000 were intended for individuals, although this percentage rises to 59% if we take into account those who also made donations to social organizations. In turn, 41% of donations were directed toward an organization, although again this percentage rises by half when those making donations to individuals are included. In other words, if we look at the joint destination of donations, a relative balance is found among the main beneficiaries, that is, between individuals and organizations. This finding is particularly interesting in that it has major consequences in the process of organizing institutions that promote creation of social capital in the country. Donations to individuals, usually associated with charitable practices of Roman Catholic origin, will hardly promote larger or stronger social networks, formation of shared values, or a sense of belonging to a community. Informality, sporadic occurrence, and lack of institutional organization, restrict the social impact of these donations and make them difficult to sustain over time. On the other hand, donations made to organizations have better prospects of involving recipients by providing them with spaces for socializing, possibilities for exchanging information, and forming broader shared values. In addition, economies of scale and improved identification of recipients ensure greater efficiency that may contribute substantially in reducing the costs of intervention.

Organizations benefiting mainly from donations include those connected to the Church (52%) or linked to some independent institution (32%), such as charitable institutions that take up yearly collections. Furthermore, the low percentage of organizations linked to the neighborhood, locality, or community (13%) is striking and in clear contrast with the ranking held by volunteering which is most often carried out in the context of the community sphere. A closer look, however, reveals that the very fact of making donations in money or in kind need not be circumscribed to a specific space.

What do Peruvians donate? According to available information, 87% make donations in clothing, 46% in money, 39% in provisions, while a second less important group donated books, toys and newspapers. As in the case of volunteering, financial contributions may be examined in terms of the types of organizations that make up each of these areas.[15] In light of these findings, money donations appear to have a clearly charitable logic, since the main areas and types of beneficiary organizations (religion and philanthropy) are closely linked to general donations (church and independent organizations). This finding suggests that donations in general, as well as donations in money, show fairly traditional characteristics and can be categorized as charity, that is, aid for the needy.

How much do Peruvians donate? EDV 2001 shows that in 2000 donors contributed an average of 92.7 *soles* (US $26.30). Now, considering the population represented in this survey, the amount of donations in that year totaled US $37,861,468, equivalent to .07% of GDP.[16]

Who donates? The data gathered confirm that women (64.1%) donate more then men (46.9%), though the difference is not considerable. Some behaviors differ, however, and are worth examining. To begin with, the data show that while women tend to donate clothing more than men (75% of female donors vs. 68% of male donors), men tend to donate more money than women do (51% vs. 41%). Second, women usually donate more to institutions linked to NGOs and other organizations (36%), as well as to organizations linked to neighborhood, locality, or community (17%), than men do (28% and 9%, respectively). Finally, there are no significant differences in the areas and types of organizations to which financial contributions were made, except for parish groups, where 29% of the women claimed to have made a contribution during 2000, compared to 17% of the male donors.

The results obtained lead to an unsurprising causality: greater financial capability can influence the decision to make (or not to make) a donation. This finding, however, tells little about citizen willingness to help each other,[17] since that would require examining the value of donations compared to individual income levels. Thus, we could say that a higher portion of income spent on charity implies greater commitment and sacrifice. Since it is very difficult (if not impossible) to assess total donations because they often involve second-hand goods of undetermined value, such an examination would have to be limited to money donations that interviewees claimed to have made in 2000. In this context and in absolute terms, total donations in the year averaged 114 *soles* (S/) at level A/B, S/.

111.14 at level C, S/. 45.43 at level D/E.[18] In regards to income bracket, EDV 2001 results contradict the assumption that persons in the top brackets donate a larger proportion of their income.[19] While 0.41% of net monthly income was donated at level A, 0.73% was donated at level C, and 0.64% at level D/E. Thus, the highest economic brackets do not show a greater disposition to help one's neighbor by donating money.

Giving and religion. As in the case of volunteering, EDV 2001 shows that religious organizations are closely linked to donations, absorbing 47% of contributions made during 2000. However, to declare oneself a follower of some religion or otherwise makes no difference at all to the making of donations. This assertion is borne out in the case of volunteering, as well as data collected in Brazil (Landim and Scalon 2000: 42). If the issue is to be pursued, the next step is to examine the differences in the percentage of donors according to the religion they profess. On this subject, however, it is worth noting that though differences exist, they are not significant for the two most important religions (Roman Catholic and evangelical), which account for 91% of the survey population. In any event, it is worth mentioning that, unlike in the case of volunteering, the proportion of donors is slightly higher among Roman Catholics that among evangelicals (53% vs. 47%).

Perceptions and Attitudes in Respect of Volunteering and Donations
In the matter of helping the neediest, tensions exist between personal responsibility and government obligation, as noted in survey interviews on charitable activities. And this tension is part of the collective imagination—not only of those who donate goods or money and perform volunteer work, but also of those who observe them.

Volunteer work. As might be expected, society perceptions of volunteering are varied. According to EDV 2001, 75% of individuals disagreed or totally disagreed with the statement *"I do not believe in volunteer work"* and 87% with the statement *"People who do volunteer work are naïve/foolish."* Accordingly, there is a socially positive assessment of these practices of solidarity. Nonetheless, interviews conducted by our team allowed a richer shade of meaning to be captured. Points of view ranged across a broad spectrum of opinions, from acceptance to rejection, including in some cases irony, disbelief, or simple disinterest: "they don't criticize, they can tell me, it's good that you're doing that," "some people do recognize our effort," "sometimes we get laughed at. Me, for example, my friends call me the doctor lady," "in this world, you find all kinds," "this doesn't concern me."

In general, volunteers perceive that their work is hard to understand for people unfamiliar with the experience, who are therefore incapable of appreciating something they do not really know: "it's like a world apart, they don't understand, it's very hard to realize in theory, volunteering is a living experience," "you have to live through it to understand it, otherwise it's no good," "perhaps you can't appreciate what you live through in volunteering until you do it," "many people don't really understand it."[20]

Based on these statements, two central issues can be singled out. First, volunteers themselves describe their work as a world apart that needs to be personally discovered in order to learn to appreciate it: the living experience and direct contact with beneficiaries of this form of aid are essential for realizing its profound sense and meaning. Second, obviously connected to the first issue, ignorance and lack of information are limitations to increasing citizen participation in these types of activities. In fact, not infrequently interviewee responses showed an interest in understanding better what these practices were about, to whom they were addressed, which organizations conducted them. The evidence points to the existence of potential civic energy that might be channeled by means of appropriate information campaigns to increase citizen involvement.

Donations. For the great majority of the survey population, the government has the principal responsibility for helping the needy (80%). Hence it is not surprising that a considerable proportion (60%) of citizens also feel that *"if the government met this responsibility, donations would not be necessary."* Nevertheless, interviewees recognize that ineffectual social programs and policies, the persistence of inequities and Peru's complicated economic position make the need to donate greater. There is also a clear perception of a religious and moral mandate to make donations, a fact with its philosophical and doctrinal base in the concept of Christian charity. Indeed, 70% of the survey population said they agreed, or fully agreed, that *"every citizen has a moral obligation to give,"* while 63% feel that *"charity is part of religious beliefs."*

Simultaneously, however, this moral and religious obligation coexists with the belief that this kind of aid fails to resolve the underlying problems. Curiously enough, no significant differences are found between donors and non-donors in response to the statement *"charity is a symbolic gesture that fails to resolve the underlying problems."* If those who donate believe that their contribution fails to resolve the structural poverty situation, then why do they do it? According to Landim and Scalon (2000), there may be two reasons that need not be mutually exclusive. As previously mentioned, one reason is that donating is closely linked to the notion of Christian charity, in which helping one's neighbor and generally concerning oneself with the less fortunate is part of a scale of values imposed on the good believer as an inescapable mandate. In other words, we are faced with an obligation that individuals feel they must fulfill beyond assessing its results. Second, the donation may be viewed as a palliative in an emergency situation, not necessarily meant to resolve the root of the problem but only its more visible manifestations (Ibid: 65–66).

This finding is in contrast with the case of volunteer workers, who do indeed believe that their efforts are capable of bringing about major changes in society. This comparison opens up an additional explanation of how donations are perceived: that they may be used to dispel feelings of guilt, as a mechanism to unburden one's conscience in view of the difficulties that certain groups in the society undergo.[21]

Final Conclusions: Solidarity Practices and Citizenship

What does the study of solidarity practices among Peruvians tell us about their position as citizens? Are volunteer workers and donors more active citizens in the social and political setting than those who fail to engage in such practices? Does the dynamics of association stemming from volunteer work strengthen the democratic system and creation of social capital? The answer to these questions far exceeds the objectives for which EDV 2001 was designed, its purpose being to map the nature, scope, composition, and destination of volunteering and donations. Nevertheless, some of the questions included in the survey provide a starting point that future studies must approach in more breadth and depth.

In principle, no very significant differences are to be discerned among practitioners and non-practitioners of these actions of solidarity, especially in regard to their perception of personal economic circumstances, in addition to those of the nation as a whole. Moreover, EDV 2001 offered interviewees the option of agreeing or disagreeing with various statements connected with individualism, solidarity, and democratic values. No remarkable discrepancies are apparent on these topics either, except for one single statement. When interviewees were asked whether they agreed with the phrase "*today, in order to rise you must think of yourself first rather than of others,*" 52.8% of volunteer workers said they agreed or fully agreed, while the percentage rose to 56.2% for non-volunteer workers. Even though the difference is minimal, volunteer workers seem to tend less toward a characteristic trait of individualism. The gap between groups is clearer in the case of donations. Here, 50.8% of donors said they agreed or fully agreed with the above statement, in contrast with 59.8% for non-donors. Here the difference is wider but not particularly revealing.

The same contrast arises when we examine the importance of politics for the general citizen at three levels: the interviewee's daily life, the locality or community where he or she lives, and the nation in general. For both donors and volunteer workers, differences are minimal, lower than the survey error margin. To the extent, however, that percentages of volunteer workers and donors are higher than those of non-volunteers and non-donors, a positive view of politics is higher among citizens practicing altruistic behaviors.

If the foregoing is true, is there other evidence to reflect such a positive relationship between practices of solidarity and greater civic involvement? (Cohen 2001: 225). Though clearly insufficient, EDV 2001 provides some indications in this context. We may observe, for instance, what happens when we examine affiliation with political groups or movements and distinguish among citizens according to their altruistic behavior. For example, donors and particularly volunteer workers tend to belong to political organizations more frequently than the average 7% of the general population. In other words, there is a positive association between the behaviors examined and participation in the nation's politics.

Similar results may be found when examining the levels of citizen participation in activities connected with the neighborhood, the parish, or management of local organizations; in all cases, the involvement of volunteer workers is considerably higher than that of non-volunteers. A similar scenario exists in regard to donors and non-donors. Although the gap is still minor in comparison with the case of volunteering, the difference is quite wide on the item "keeping informed," with no significant differences apparent between volunteers and non-volunteers.

In summary, the limited evidence available points to a positive relationship between altruistic behavior and participation in political or social organizations. Concern for becoming involved in social problems affecting the fate of the nation does not seem to be an alien characteristic among citizens who engage in practices of solidarity.

Notes

1 Here we follow the definition of humanism supplied by Todorov, for whom this line of thinking ". . . is at once *anthropology* (describes how human beings are: a species apart whose members are sociable and partly indeterminate — and for that reason led to exercise their freedom), *morals* (describes how human beings ought to be: they ought to love human beings for themselves and accord the same dignity to all), and *politics* (privileges the régimes where subjects can exercise their autonomy and enjoy the same rights)." (Ibid: 54)

2 The survey was conducted on a sample numbering 1,414 persons between 18 and 70 years of age and from all socioeconomic strata of the population, in the eleven most important cities of the country. Survey results, duly adjusted to Peruvian circumstances, were based on the framework used for the Comparative Project on the Third Sector, at Johns Hopkins University.

3 The present paper is based on a more extensive and detailed study by Portocarrero S., Felipe, Armando Millán, and James Loveday (2004).

4 In the study of volunteer work, Thompson and Toro recognize four not necessarily mutually exclusive approaches: (i) volunteering as social resource following the crisis of the Welfare State; (ii) volunteering as a hinge for developing and sustaining democracy; (iii) volunteer associations as strategies for strengthening and capacity-building; and, finally, (iv) the individual volunteer worker: between interest and utilitarianism (Ibid: 5).

5 See information supplied by the U.S. organization Independent Sector on the Internet at www.independentsector.org.

6 Information from the Nonprofit Comparative Research Project at Johns Hopkins University.

7 See Federal Ministry for Family Affairs, Senior Citizens, Women, and Youth 2000: p. 22.

8 See The Civil Society Development Foundation 1996: p. 16.

9 See Landim and Scalon 2000: p. 22.

10 This is in keeping with the conclusions of Tanaka and Zárate (2000: 23): "In Peru, social organizations do exist, but are very weak, they fail to extend beyond local and immediate limits, and cannot become nationwide social or political interlocutors." Macassi (1999: 19–23), however, makes an exception to this view in the case of youth, pointing out that despite an ongoing process of reappropriation or reterritorialization of local public spaces, especially by males, young people often ignore the internal dynamics of their own district and are more concerned for metropolitan and national problems.

11 For this calculation we considered a working day equivalent to 8 hours of work.

12 This method was actually based on that used for the Comparative Project for the Third Sector at Johns Hopkins University. To estimate the same economic value, the number of volunteers was calculated on the basis of the population

between ages 18 and 70 in the largest cities in the country. This information was used to calculate the total number of hours of volunteering (number of volunteer workers per city times the average number of hours per year devoted to volunteering). The resulting figure was converted to daily terms, based on 8 working hours per day, 22 working days per month. Lastly, the opportunity cost was based on the legal minimum wage (S/.400.08 per month, or S/.2.38 per day) and the average exchange rate for 2000, at S/.3.52. According to *Banco Central de Reserva*, GDP in 2000 amounted to US $53,512 million.

13 A distinction needs to be made between "volunteers" and "cases of volunteering," because one individual may do volunteer work for more than one organization. Accordingly, the *Encuesta* registers 487 volunteers in 667 cases of volunteering.

14 Of the total surveyed, 83% declared themselves Roman Catholics, 8% Evangelicals, 5% Jews, Muslims, and others, while 4% claim to be atheists or agnostics.

15 To identify types of organizations and their respective areas, see Table No. 1.

16 To estimate the total amount donated, in the first place, the number of persons who made donations in money in 2000 was calculated (percentage volunteers in money times the population between 18 and 70 in each city), then the result was multiplied by the average amount donated per individual in each city. According to *Banco Central de Reserva*, GDP in 2000 amounted to US $63,512 million.

17 As Putnam (2000: 123) puts it: "to measure our philanthropic generosity, we need to know how our giving compares to our income, not merely how many dollars we are handing out."

18 In monthly terms, the amounts were 9.5, 9.26, and 3.79 new *soles*, respectively.

19 Similar evidence was found for the Brazilian case. See Ladim and Scalon (2000).

20 This feature of relative isolation in volunteering *vis-à-vis* other activities was also perceived in a qualitative study conducted among the youth of Metropolitan Lima. See Portocarrero *et al.* (2001).

21 As mentioned in the section dealing with donations, this is more frequent in the case of donations of goods for which the benefactor finds no further use or donations in money when equivalent to a reduced percentage of the benefactor's income.

References

Acha, Elisabeth, "Los guardianes de la caridad: el caso del Hogar de Cristo en el Perú," in Portocarrero S., Felipe y Cynthia Sanborn, *De la caridad a la solidaridad: filantropía y voluntariado en el Perú*, Lima: Centro de Investigación de la Universidad del Pacífico, 2003.

Becerra, Silvia, "Asociación de Damas de Ayuda al Instituto de Enfermedades Neoplásicas: una experiencia de voluntariado de los sectores altos," en Portocarrero S., Felipe y Cynthia Sanborn, *De la caridad a la solidaridad: filantropía y voluntariado en el Perú*, Lima: Centro de Investigación de la Universidad del Pacífico, 2003.

Calvo, César y Oswaldo Molina, "Programa Nacional de Voluntariado de EsSalud," in Portocarrero S., Felipe y Cynthia Sanborn, *De la caridad a la solidaridad: filantropía y voluntariado en el Perú*, Lima: Centro de Investigación de la Universidad del Pacífico, 2003.

Cohen, Jean, "Trust, voluntary association and workable democracy: the contemporary American discourse of civil society," en Warren, Mark, E., *Democracy & Trust*, Cambridge: Cambridge University Press, 2001.

Federal Ministry for Family Affairs, Senior Citizens, Women and Youth, *Volunteering in Germany. Results of the 1999 Representative Survey on Volunteering and Civic Engagement*, Münich, 2000.

Foley, Michael W., John D. McCarthy y Mark Chaves, "Social Capital, Religious Institutions, and Poor Communities," en Saegert, Susan, J. Phillip Thompson y Mark R. Warren (Editors) *Social Capital and Poor Communities*, New York: Russell Sage Foundation, 2002.

Landim, Leilah, *As campahas pelo 'novo voluntariado' e o contexto brasilero*, Rio de Janeiro: 2003

Landim, Leilah y Maria Celi Scalon, *Doacoes e trabalho voluntário no Brasil: uma pesquisa*, Rio de Janeiro: 7Letras, 2000.

Macassi, Sandro, *Sondeo de Opinión: Jóvenes y políticas de juventud. Una mirada a los jóvenes desde la experiencia local*, Lima: Asociación de Comunicadores Calandria, 1999.

Martin, Mike, *Virtuous Giving. Philanthropy, voluntary service and caring*, Indiana University Press, 1994.

Panfichi, Aldo y Marcel Valcárcel, *El significado de la juventud en las ciencias sociales*, en Panfichi, Aldo y Marcel Valcárcel (eds.), *Juventud: sociedad y cultura*. Lima: Red para el Desarrollo de las Ciencias Sociales en el Perú, 1999.

Portocarrero, Gonzalo, *Hacia una cartografía de los sentidos comunes emergentes: las nuevas poéticas del sujeto en la sociedad peruana*, Lima: Pontificia Universidad Católica del Perú, mimeo, 2001.

Portocarrero S., Felipe, "Peruvian Philanthropy: A historical perspective," en *Revista*, Harvard Review of Latin America, Spring 2002.

Portocarrero S., Felipe y Armando Millán, *Perú: ¿país solidario?*, Lima: Centro de Investigación de la Universidad del Pacífico, 2001.

Portocarrero S., Felipe, James Loveday y Armando Millán, *Donaciones y trabajo voluntario: los jóvenes de Lima Metropolitana*, Lima: Centro de Investigación de la Universidad del Pacífico, 2001.

Portocarrero S., Felipe, Armando Millán y James Loveday, *Voluntarios, donantes y ciudadanos en el Perú*, Lima: Centro de Investigación de la Universidad del Pacífico, 2004.

Putnam, Robert, *Bowling Alone: the collapse and revival of American community*, New York: Simon & Schuster, 2000.

Roitter, Mario, *Realidades y promesas del voluntariado: estado del arte sobre una práctica social y sus representaciones*, Buenos Aires: CEDES, 2002.

Roitter, Mario e Inés González Bombal (comp.), *Estudios sobre el sector sin fines de lucro en Argentina*, Buenos Aires: CEDES, 2000.

Salamon, Lester M., Helmut K. Anheier, Regina List, Stefan Toepler, S. Wojciech Sokolowski y asociados, *Global Civil Society. Dimensions of the Nonprofit Sector*, Baltimore: The Johns Hopkins Center for Civil Society Studies, 1999.

Sen, Amartya, *Rational Fools: A Critique of the Behavioral Foundations of Economic Theory*, en Mansbridge, Jane (ed), *Beyond Self Interested*, Chicago: The University of Chicago Press, 1990.

Tanaka Martín y Patricia Zárate, *Valores democráticos y participación ciudadana en el Perú*, Lima: Instituto de Estudios Peruanos y USAID, 1999.

Tarazona, Bruno, "El Larco Herrera: ¿Hospital o asilo?," en Portocarrero S., Felipe y Cynthia Sanborn, *De la caridad a la solidaridad: filantropía y voluntariado en el Perú*, Lima: Centro de Investigación de la Universidad del Pacífico, 2003.

Tarazona, Bruno, "Los olvidados: el caso del Puericultorio Pérez Araníbar," in Portocarrero S., Felipe y Cynthia Sanborn, *De la caridad a la solidaridad: filantropía y voluntariado en el Perú*, Lima: Centro de Investigación de la Universidad del Pacífico, 2003.

Turner, Bryan S., *Religion and Social Theory*, London: Sage Publication, 1991.

Thompson, Andrés and Olga Lucía Toro, *El voluntariado social en América Latina. Tendencias, influencias, espacios y lecciones aprendidas*, mimeo, Fundación W.K. Kellogg, 2002.

Todorov, Tzvetan, *La vida en común. Ensayo de antropología general*, Madrid: Taurus, 1995.

Todorov, Tzvetan, *El jardín imperfecto. Luces y sombras del pensamiento humanista*, Barcelona: Paidós, 1999.

The Civil Society Development Foundation, *Romanians' Philanthropic and Associative Behavior*, mimeo, 1996.

Thompson, Andrés y Olga Lucía Toro, *El Voluntariado Social en América Latina*, mimeo, 2001.

Villar, Rodrigo, *Análisis comparativo de donaciones y voluntariado en América Latina*, documento interno, Boston: David Rockefeller Center for Latin American Studies, Harvard University, 2001.

4

A "New Volunteering" in the Brazilian Context

Leilah Landim

Why do people give and volunteer? Motivations are manifold, and so are the ways people engage in voluntary actions. The challenge in analyzing voluntary actions becomes all the greater because of rapid changes in the area. On the one hand, these practices are currently the focus of attention and generalized campaigns around the world that have spread reasonably homogeneous discourses and values. On the other hand, giving and volunteering are different realities in accordance with the traditions and cultural heritage of the various national contexts where they develop.

This chapter seeks to present the results of a quantitative survey on practices that can be seen as *donations* and *volunteering* in Brazilian society. In commenting on these findings, we will consider some background characteristics of this society and the recent context in which governmental organizations or civil society are making new appeals to donate time and money, or to create a new volunteering.

The volunteering wave and its background

Such emphatic and visible public dissemination of donations and volunteering as items to be considered on the social agenda is quite a recent phenomenon in Brazil. That is to say, the "volunteering wave" that of late has spread throughout the country via the media with regard to governmental or non-governmental social projects, renewed national and international circuits of meetings, ideas, agents and values, is another of those phenomena that arrive on the field of social action with the alacrity typical of the times in which we are living.

Of course, there have always been actions in Brazilian society that we can recognize and identify as donations and volunteer work, even if the people involved do not always use these terms. I believe that in daily life and in the representations of the vast majority of the population, "helping" actions are generally restricted to the personal and private domain and are rarely seen as a matter of public and civic nature, as they are in North American society. In this sense, the discourses being elaborated over the last ten years, especially by private institutions engaged in social action, by certain governmental or multilateral agencies, or by private sector groups that invest in social action, are a novelty. This can be seen, for example, in the growth of television programs or newspaper material on exemplary initiatives, prizes, campaigns and appeals to the public to donate to social causes, the dozens of pages on the Internet supplying and demanding volunteers, skill-building courses, promoting business sector volunteering and other such initiatives. New images are thus being created of what, in terms of public benefit and citizenship, can be meant by voluntary work and donating to nonprofit organizations.

Although this is not the purpose of the study, it is nevertheless worthwhile to recall that these phenomena occur in the context of known global processes such as redefining the role of the state and retracing the policies of social protection, the predominance of market logic and the aggravation of poverty and exclusion, unemployment and changes in the world of labor that have led to the crisis of old forms of solidarity and sociability. The literature—especially Durkheim-inspired European literature—has underscored the growing process of negative individualization and social disaffiliation involved in these changes, together with a weakening of participation in collective action organizations (Castel, 1995). These are some of the elements that entail reconfiguring social action in contemporary societies, where voluntary work comes to occupy a new place.

This background contains tendencies and generic characteristics that play themselves out in different and specific ways, according to each national context. In the case of donations and volunteering, we find new campaigns that dialogue and contact or lose contact with various organizations, values, conceptions and practices that exist in Brazilian society in respect to solidarity. The impact of these appeals still calls for careful analysis and is not an *a priori* given.

When we think of donations and volunteering in this society, we necessarily recall traditional practices. These are the omnipresent relations permeated by informality, personalization, reciprocity (which does not exclude the frequent presence of hierarchy and political cronyism), corresponding to specific forms of solidarity that characterize society throughout history. This "culture of donation" or "culture of assistance," though generally fragile as regards civic components, is very important in forming a mindset, as well as in the material survival of the poorer segments of the population. The borderline between the religious and the secular may also not be very clear.

On the other hand, a vigorous field of organizations geared to social action appears alongside these forms of sociability. A recent associativism, characterized by collective action and egalitarian values and dedicated to social change and forging rights, remains relatively small in number but politically and socially significant. In this case, the agents of these organizations prefer the term "militancy" or "activism" to define their actions (though *volunteering* is not excluded).

In analyzing the term *volunteering* and its various meanings, the role of governmental organizations and public policies should be borne in mind because of the weight and visibility that official and legal concepts possess within society.

With regard to Brazil, the hypothesis may be raised that the terms "donation"—and especially "volunteering"—given their particular history, have taken on a negative connotation, notably in the circuits related to building citizenship and civicmindedness, or within the sociological line of thinking generally characterized by liberal or republican conceptions. This bad reputation certainly stems from the role of these terms and practices in the usually flawed processes of relations between state and society as a consequence of a long history of patrimonialism and corporativism. In the minds of segments of the population—and opinion makers—this demoralization of philanthropic actions is due in part to their frequent association with political cronyism, exchanges of favors and embezzlement of public funds into private hands. The history of the term *volunteering* in the Brazilian context is bound to include some governmental initiatives and the forms taken by their relations with society. A broad program to stimulate volunteering (prior to the one inaugurated in 1994 by the Fernando Henrique Cardoso administration) lasted from 1979 until the early 90s: PRONAV—the National Volunteering Program of the now-defunct LBA (the "Brazilian Legion of Assistance," a governmental organ then entrusted to undertake social programs in collaboration with nonprofit organizations). This program functioned through Volunteering Nuclei; a 1987 report informs us that 1,040 Volunteering Nuclei with 5,454 volunteer groups were then working in the country, as well as conducting various donation campaigns. "Civil society" and "citizenship" were at that time not part of the official rhetoric, as they are today, as can also be seen reading these reports. The President of Honor was the First Lady, and PRONAV's structure was centralized, with the First Ladies of the states acting as state coordinators and mayors' wives acting as municipal coordinators. This organizational scheme followed the classic model of centralizing and facilitating political cronyism and charity "assistencialism" on the part of women of the elite, which only tended to reproduce inequalities and hierarchies—a situation accentuated by the context of the military regime that held power for part of the program's duration. It might be supposed that such a lengthy and generalized governmental initiative did not go unnoticed, marking the somewhat ambiguous meanings given socially in the country to volunteering and donations.

These meanings contrast with recent campaigns and intense media appeals stimulating the practices of giving time and money. Renewed government initiatives complement these campaigns to encourage donations of time and money, especially in the case of volunteering, which for the first time is the object of legal regulation.[1]

Also relevant was the launching of the Volunteers Program in November 1997 by the Community Solidarity Board, an organization set up during the previous administration, presided over by First Lady Ruth Cardoso, and made up of representatives of civil society and the federal government. Volunteering Reference Centers scattered throughout the country were also set up for the purpose of skill-building, constructing databases and mediating between institutions and candidates for volunteering. These Centers were founded with the prospect of becoming autonomous, relying on civil society organizations in each different site for their implementation.

Through the Volunteers Program, Community Solidarity aimed at "implanting a modern culture of volunteering concerned above all with the efficiency of services and qualification of volunteers and institutions." While recognizing pre-existing practices and provisions: "Recognizing the vigor and scope of the generous efforts of citizens and institutions," the Program's mission was nonetheless to "contribute to promoting, valorizing and qualifying voluntary work in Brazil," adding that "[the] new view of voluntary work has nothing to do with charity and alms, nor with occupying the time of those suffering from tedium." It did have to with "participative citizenship" and with "efficiency and results" (Document of Community Solidarity, no date). The law on volunteers came at an opportune time when, as expressed by Miguel Darcy de Oliveira, then a board member of Community Solidarity, "the very concept of volunteering (was) going through a profound process of transformation in the country" (Agir, 1997).

The Luis Inácio Lula da Silva administration, inaugurated in January 2003, did not renew this program, since it was created and linked to the

Community Solidarity Board, an initiative conceived by the First Lady of the previous administration and part of a political project of assistance criticized by the political forces that now came to occupy the new mandate. The Reference Centers mentioned above, however, remained active, with campaigns and interventions on the level of civil society. Through the Centers, this "modern culture of volunteering" has been discussed, reproduced and amplified. Internationalized channels composed of mostly U.S.-based foundations and business sector entities have also promoted this modern volunteer concept. Civil-society organizations in different places are involved in increasingly more projects to qualify and promote voluntary work as defined above.

So what one witnesses today in the above-mentioned instances and spaces is a revival of terms and practices of volunteering, accompanied by a process endeavoring to re-semanticize and find a new social niche to create professionalized and civic voluntary action.

The Research: What Brazilians Claim to Do

In 1998, a national survey on donations and voluntary work, summarized below, was carried out. Although it was not yet known that the year 2001 would be chosen by the United Nations as the International Year of Volunteers, the theme had already started to circulate more intensely in society as part of the official agenda, as well as that of foundations, NGOs and other groups.[2]

The questionnaire was based on formats of analogous research carried out in other countries (principally by the Independent Sector and Comparative Nonprofit Sector Project at Johns Hopkins University). At the same time, we adapted the questions to the Brazilian context and to our specific inquiries. Using this focus, the questionnaire went beyond the intent of measuring "donations and volunteering," adding a variety of other practices. In this context, we used open-ended questions as much as possible.[3]

How many donate and volunteer?
As previous qualitative research had already pointed out, the frequency with which those interviewed mentioned engaging in this type of practice (in 1998) is not small: in Brazil, 21% of adults donate money to institutions, while 29% donate goods.[4] In other words, 50% of the adults in the country practice some sort of donating to institutions. That means 44,200,000 individuals, the equivalent of the population of South Africa. If we add to that total those who make donations only to people directly

(without including institutions), that makes an additional 30%, so we reach almost 80%, close to 70,000,000 people. Those statistics mean that four out of every five adults at some moment donate something to some organization or person.

The quantity of "volunteers" is more reduced, as also happens in other contexts: 22.6% donate some of their time in volunteering to help some entity or person outside their family and close friends, that is, 19,748,388 persons. Those who engage in volunteering only in the institutional context number 16%, or 13,905,532 persons, with six hours monthly the average time donated.

Donations

If we add up all the money donated in 1998 by individuals to some institution, we arrive at the impressive amount of close to two billion reals: R$ 1,703,000 (at the time, practically the same value in dollars).

These donations are incredibly dispersed; suffice it to say that the average per individual is R$ 158 per year. As expected in the light of the economic situation at the time, this forms an ocean of small contributions: 65% of the donations are made for less than 100 reals a year, with 41% of the people contributing to institutions less than 20 reals per year. In other words, people donate little, but nonetheless do donate.

Is this a lot or is this a little? This question, part of the conventional wisdom in the field of the above-mentioned current projects and campaigns, immediately tends to introduce a comparative numerical criterion: it might be a lot or a little when compared with numbers in other national contexts. In this case, the champion would necessarily have to be the United States, where national surveys enable us to trace a consistent numerical series over the last 15 years and where 69% of individuals (counted per households) donate money to institutions (68.2 million people, about US $111 billion donated, the average value of the donation being about one thousand dollars a year per unit). Taking the example of another developed country, in France, the number drops to 45% of individuals who donate money to institutions.

International quantitative comparisons have constituted an important procedure in studies on the "third sector" and like themes such as volunteering. In this case, one should note that the question about "a lot or a little" can lead to comparisons that remove the data from their contexts, thereby tending to hide or devalue the inquiry into the different meanings that such practices have in each individual case. The amounts donated in this case should be examined in the light of the different political and civic cultures, the associative traditions and the various forms of configuring relations between state and society, among other factors. In addition, of course, the extent of poverty within each society must be taken into consideration. In this case, Brazil certainly ranks among the champions; it might actually come as a surprise to see such willingness to donate money to social action institutions, thus calling for further explanations of the phenomenon. Poorer people—in Brazil, the very poor—make donations in money to institutions with reasonable frequency. This case suggests caution as to the inferences made only on the basis of comparisons between numbers, which tend to construct evolutive schemes to evaluate the "voluntary spirit" in each country, with "less" and "more civilized," "pre-," "growing," and other comparisons. A good example of this type of distortion is an editorial of the most widely read magazine in Brazil on the subject of donations and voluntary work, under the title "This is what Brazil needs," in which we are told that "In the more civilized countries, the presence of philanthropy—also known as 'the third sector'—is more noticeable. In the socially less developed nations, voluntary work is more embryonic. Brazil is an intermediate term" (*Veja Magazine*, 2001).

What goods are donated?

Food donations largely predominate: 40% of those people who donated goods answered "only food" as donations. Adding to this figure the number of people who claimed to have donated other items (generally clothes and/or shoes) as well as food, one sees that food is donated by 68% of those who make their donations in the form of goods.

Materially and symbolically, donations in goods reflect meeting the basic necessities for survival, helping the poorer, and suggest the fundamental action of helping those who lack what is basic. The most elementary gesture of Christian charity is evoked through the emphasis on donating food: "give food to the hungry." It also recalls the daily practices of reciprocity to be found in family or neighborhood groups, where exchanging food is common. The logic of these relations may also permeate the donations to institutions at play here, which would nevertheless tend to depersonalize the relation between donator and receiver. Compared to donations in clothes and shoes (generally used items), this may imply a deeper engagement in action, seeing that food has to be bought, or cooked. On the other hand, when compared with giving cash, food donations may offer the donor more security as regards the proper destination of his donation.

Profile of the Donors

Those over 40 years old are the most willing to make donations. And the higher the educational level, the greater the propensity to make donations: those who donate to institutions have on average 6 years of schooling, while those who do not make donations spend an average of 4.3 years in school (all of them, it should be pointed out, in the educational bracket of most of the Brazilian population).

Income, as may be expected, correlates with the likelihood of donating money: 49% of the adult population with a family income above 20 minimum wages donate to institutions, a proportion that falls as less income is available. Note that the proportion of people who donate goods does not present significant correlation with income. However, another reading of these last data offers us something to think about: among the poorer—in the Brazilian case, substantially poorer—some people contribute part of what they have in cash donations: about 8% of those who earn up to one minimum wage (US $70) do so. Furthermore, among people whose family income stands at between one and two minimum wages, 13% donate money to institutions (here the proportion of those who donate goods— 26%—is the same as those who earn more than 20 minimum wages). That is a lot of people. What percentage of their income do they donate? Nothing less than 3.6% of what they possess—a far higher proportion that that observed for the better-off: for those who earn above 20 minimum wages, the amount donated amounts to only 0.8% of their income.

Poorer Brazilians demonstrate their "generosity" by donating proportionally more than the wealthy to institutions. It is obvious that any small donation represents a higher proportion to a very low income. Yet conventional wisdom also says that it still makes a dent in the budget. Here we are obviously dealing with different "budgets" and their destinations and priorities. What is at stake here may be considered to be the relations of reciprocity and belonging that are specific to the daily life and survival of certain strata of the population, including relations with churches.

Religion is one of the most outstanding variables in this sphere. Although mere religious belonging has not proved statistically relevant to the disposition to make donations, what does count a great deal is effective religious practice: the more frequent attendance of religious services, the greater the propensity to make donations, in both money and goods. So, for example, 54% of those who made donations in money to institutions worship once or twice a week, whereas a scant 5% of them declared they never frequent religious services (of statistical relevance were the Catholics, Evangelicals and Kardec spiritualists).

Indeed, half of these donations are made through churches, parishes or other religious centers—in other words, through spaces in which not only confessional activities are performed but also, as is well known, a great deal of social work, which the research did not allow to disaggregate and which as a matter of fact is in some cases difficult to separate. In addition to this, 46% of the donations go to institutions dedicated to social assistance. Only 2.8% of the amount donated is earmarked for other institutions (health, education, defense of rights, community action). Everything seems to indicate that the profile of the field of donations is quite traditional.

Voluntary work

Those who claim to engage in voluntary work, according to the open-ended definition of our questionnaire, intersect with those who make material donations only in terms of the types of institutions that they choose to help. The religious and social-assistance institutions monopolize almost all the volunteers: 57% and 17% respectively, making a total of 74%. The rest is distributed in small portions among the areas of health, education, defense of rights and community actions.

Nonetheless, the proportion of people who declare they perform non-remunerated activities in these last two areas is relatively significant (defense of rights and community action, practices that often appear in combination): 8%. This is the terrain of the most recent Brazilian organizations, characterized by the emphasis on building actions and values linked to citizenship (such as the so-called NGOs), which are significantly less numerous than the philanthropic entities.

Once again, the question arises of how to evaluate the significance of these figures. As in the case of donations, the United States is also the champion, with 49% of the population engaging in volunteer work for an average of 4.2 hours a week. However, using one of the above-mentioned international comparative numerical scales—relating to the 22 countries surveyed by the Johns Hopkins University Program—the average of volunteers per country would stand at around 28% of the population. So, rich and poor are not so far apart when voluntary work is at stake (in France, for example, the proportion is 23.4% of the public).

Over half (52.7%) of the activities carried out by volunteers in Brazil is connected to the daily maintenance of the organization's infrastructure: office work, maintenance of premises, meals and other general services that do not demand any great level of qualifications on the part of the volunteers.

Lagging far behind are fund-raising activities, which can include anything from campaigns and relations with the media to small church bazaars and fêtes (15.3%). A similar proportion is given to activities connected to religious practices (14.2%). Note that the number of activities rather than the number of people is being considered here, and that the former can overlap for the same volunteers.

The profile of the volunteer is similar to that of the common citizen, the average Brazilian (in numerical terms comprising the poorer segments): people of different ages, income, levels of education and religions offer to donate their time—none of these variables proved to be significant in differentiating those who do and those who do not do volunteer work.

Nevertheless, two variables proved to be of relevance: first, those who engage in volunteer work have a greater propensity to make donations, or vice-versa. Second, frequency of religious attendance matters: among those who attend services more than once a week, 27.8% donate some time to volunteer work, whereas only 1.4% of those who stated they did not attend worked voluntarily.

According to research in other countries, one factor that counts in the tendency of people to donate their time is belonging to associations or certain social networks (which this research did not measure, except with regard to religious spaces).

Attitude and Opinion

Interviewees, basing their answers on a scale of approval, indicated a generally positive view of giving and volunteering. The answers were consistent for both those who engage in these practices and those who do not. And two sets of logic exist, both in the perceptions of and the reasons for donating goods or money.

On the one hand, there was a high degree of agreement as to the affirmations referring to the domain of reciprocity and moral/religious obligation, as well as to forms of sociability. These affirmations included statements like "making donations to people in greater need is a way of expressing gratitude for the opportunities that have arisen in life," and "doing charity through donations is part of my religious belief," or else "dedicating myself to activities without remuneration to help others is part of my religious belief," or even "one advantage of collaborating with institutions is to be able to meet and get to know other people." More than 75% of the population interviewed agreed completely with these assertions.

Yet the same proportion of agreement holds true for affirmations that resort to ideas on citizen participation and consequences for society, such as "all citizens should donate something to improve society" or "volunteer work is part of citizenship and helps to build a better society."

It is significant to observe that in the mind of the interviewees none of this contradicts the idea that it is up to the government "to assume its responsibilities" or "fulfill its duty" in this area of social needs. On the one hand, it is important for people to do voluntary work, for various reasons; on the other hand, the state has the duty to do so.

In interpreting these results, we might mistakenly venture the hypothesis that here is yet another affirmation of the celebrated Brazilian statist culture—or, more likely, a reaction to the even greater precariousness of social policies today. In fact, as far as social action is concerned in Brazil, this conception of "waiting for the state to do it" (there is no evidence here of "demanding a right of the state") has always lived hand in hand with the values associated with personalized or similar charities, seen as belonging to the private domain. These two faces of the coin—either state (usually seen outside the perspective of representativity) or "disinterested" charity—left little space for recognizing a "private, but public" action in this field, according to Anglo-Saxon models or in keeping with the ideas of private social action disseminated at this turn of the century. Some authors claim that in Brazil the historical difficulties in establishing two-way routes between state and society are due to a lack of dynamics in social construction of the political (Carvalho, 2000).

Reflections: Some Challenges

The results of this research, complemented by other localized studies and observations, suggest that people in Brazil made, make and most likely will continue to make donations or contributions, and to offer help to institutions, based on different motivations and values that circulate, blend and change in society. The figures reinforce the arguments in the sense that these practices permeate Brazilian society from top to bottom, with a reasonable degree of vigor and legitimacy granted by a large portion of the population, as actions that are welcome and necessary, and with astonishing intensity shown in the cash donations made by the poor. And all this, as we have seen, is based on different yet not divergent reasons and values, in the opinion of the majority of the interviewees. Our studies also disclose that not always— or perhaps rarely—are these practices called "volunteering."

The data also reinforce the predominantly traditional profile of such practices, in which the imprint of religious values and institutions is strong, combined with those of an "assistencialist" nature, tenuously perceived as civic actions or else as a public benefit. However, it should be mentioned that practices relating to the field of citizenship also made their appearance in the research (as the 8% who stated they acted without remuneration in organizations dedicated to "development and defense of rights").

The terms used aside from "volunteering"—such as "militancy," "help," "assistance," and "contributions"—are all expressions commonly referring to the subtleties that for those involved differentiate intentions, values, relations and networks active in society. This is obviously not a static framework, that is, various imaginaries and relations overlap within a dynamic that will affect the democratic construction of Brazil.

This was the context in the second half of the 90s when projects appeared to "implant a modern culture of volunteering," such as that proposed by Community Solidarity or, as some North American foundations active in Brazil put it, "creating a culture of giving." These proposals hover tenuously between transforming existing cultures and "creating" another culture, supposedly in areas where they are lacking.

There are some possible novelties in these ideas now being disseminated. First of all, the channels of institutions and agents who support this type of initiative are new: multilateral organizations, the government, foundations and companies. This change, accompanied by intense diffusion by the media, has an impact on the new position of volunteering and donations in the social and political sphere.

Secondly, these channels spread renewed conceptions of terms and practices throughout the scenario of Brazilian social action. These new conceptions associate volunteering with ideas such as the quality of the action, competence, efficiency, results, autonomous individual choice and talent. What is proposed is a "modern culture of volunteering" which blends together the idea of civic action and a logic that belongs to the area of the market and involves standards of professionalization and qualification—something unheard of in the national context. This is the first time volunteering has been mentioned as an item to be included as a professional qualification in a curriculum vitae in Brazil.

The question of possible consequences of these processes for society is a recent one and calls for specifically focused studies. Nevertheless, the long waiting lines of applicants for voluntary work in answer to current campaigns on the Internet or other media enables the hypothesis of these values and practices to echo among middle-class segments of large urban centers in Brazil. Similar to what is happening on the international level, in Brazil, one can identify a will to participate and engage socially on the part of strata of the population more subjected to the processes of individualization, secularization and social isolation. New people—such as the young who find it difficult to break into the labor market—are being mobilized in times of exclusion, unemployment and a crisis of ideologies. The relevance has been pointed out of these engagements as supports to create identities and spaces of belonging.

If this is true, some questions deserve our attention as to the possible negative social consequences of these processes.

First of all, in their present form, these recent campaigns sometimes tend to be unaware of—and consequently erase from the social map—the vast world of practices, relations, values and organizations that have always peopled Brazilian society and that make up a terrain rooted in more traditional ties and networks of solidarity. The campaigns run the risk of conveying the idea that in a context such as Brazil there is a "minus" sign in this field and that now, finally, it is time to correct these practices and/or stimulate "correct volunteering." The symbolic effect of these disseminated conceptions can be disastrous if they become characterized as a "civilizing" campaign: this would create in society, especially in its many poorer segments, a negative image of themselves by not recognizing or not legitimizing the forms of solidarity and organizations that already exist and with which they are involved daily, thereby configuring yet another process of "destitution of discourse."

Add to this non-recognition another more obvious and radicalized one, namely that these campaigns run the risk of also making *tabula rasa* of the broad field of civil society organizations that make up the space for the defense of interests and the conquest and effectuation of rights and recent democratic experiences in the country. This is a relevant field in building civic culture and the public sphere in a society that is so lacking in these attributes and spaces. These forms of collective action that also promote social inclusion and solidarity are excluded from the meaning of "doing your part" or else remain obscured in the generally disseminated idea of voluntary individual action. If we analyze the current discourses of the above-mentioned campaigns, as well as the alliances and partnerships privileged by them, we see that conceptions are implicitly propagated that minimize or are unaware of a broad area of collective activism involving many thousands of individuals, created and consolidated over the last 30 years and geared toward social and political changes on behalf of rights and democracy. The state's attributions and society's relations with public government have often been eclipsed as issues in depoliticized versions of the meaning of voluntary individual action.

In short, although these campaigns can be effective in creating new practices and organizations, there would be serious consequences if, in a society as unequal and with such precarious rights as Brazil, the idea is conveyed of solutions produced only through each individual's sense of solidarity and altruistic action (besides causing the cultural destitution mentioned above).

The field of social action is in itself varied and comprised of different organizations and values, ranging from militancy to charity, via help, assistance and contemporary forms of volunteering. All of these are legitimate and involve representations, feelings, organizations and networks of relations that are not necessarily exclusive, that live together and even blend with one another, but are nevertheless quite plural in their meanings, roles, possibilities and scope. The debates in the field of politics and the agents of social action would gain by trying to understand and live with this actual diversity.

This work was made possible thanks to the support of the Ford Foundation of Brazil.

Notes and References

1 The Volunteering Law, enacted on 18 February 1998, contains an official definition of what "*is considered to be voluntary service*": "*non-remunerated activity rendered by an individual to a public entity of any nature or private nonprofit institution with civic, cultural, educational, scientific, recreational or social-assistance objectives, including mutuality*" (Law number 9.608, Diário Oficial da União, 02/18/98).

2 This paper was written under my supervision with the collaboration of Maria Celi Scalon (Professor of Sociology at IUPERJ [University Research Institute of Rio de Janeiro]) in the area of statistics, through a public-survey institute (IBOPE). See Landim, Leilah, and Scalon, Maria Celi—*Doações e Trabalho Voluntário no Brasil—uma pesquisa*, Rio de Janeiro: 7 Letras, 2000.

3 The research consisted of a national survey by means of household interviews held in May 1988. A stratified representative sample was used of Brazilians aged 18 or over living in cities with more than 10,000 inhabitants.

4 The group that "donated money" (21%) may include people who also donated goods. As for donors of goods (29%), these only donated goods, never money. This procedure enables us to draw international comparisons of those who donate money and to compose exclusive universes (donors of goods and donors of money), which can then be added together.

Agir. Informativo do Programa Voluntários. 1997–98. São Paulo: Núcleo de Coordenação do Programa Voluntários.

Castel, Robert. 1995. *Les Métamorphoses de la Question Sociale*. Paris: Gallimard.

Carvalho, José Murilo de. 2000. "A Cidadania na Encruzilhada," in *Pensando a República*. Belo Horizonte: UFMG.

Veja Magazine. August 2001. São Paulo: Ed. Agir.

Section

II

THE CORPORATE CONTRIBUTION: SOCIAL RESPONSIBILITY IN CHANGING TIMES

5

The Promotion of Corporate Social Responsibility in Latin America

Felipe Agüero

Philanthropy is nothing new for business leaders in Latin America. Even in the previous context of a statist sociopolitical matrix,[1] in which all socially oriented expenditure was viewed as an exclusive state responsibility, business leaders promoted donations and foundations, created universities and technical schools and developed social assistance initiatives toward the poorest groups, often alongside church programs.[2] What is new, however, is the discourse of corporate social responsibility, and the flurry of initiatives undertaken under that concept, including the creation of organizations by business leaders with the specific purpose of advancing it.

Corporate social responsibility (CSR) is often presented as distinct from the idea of philanthropy, which is presumed to follow altruistic motivations, with little or no expectation of a direct benefit for the firm, using resources that come from profits and involving only individuals or, at most, the board of directors. Philanthropy is exerted in fields not necessarily associated to the activity of a particular business or firm. In contrast, CSR, in its ideal version, seeks benefits for the firm that may include image and reputation, improvements in productivity, and sustained earnings while simultaneously pursuing community improvement. It relies primarily on the firm's general budget, equipments and human resources, and not necessarily on profits and, still ideally, on the participation of officers and workers at all levels of the firm, and sometimes of shareholders.[3] In this way CSR brings in a more strategic perspective involving planning, targets, impact, and evaluation.

In the language of international meetings and of major foundations involved in the promotion of philanthropy the terms are either used indistinctly or CSR is viewed as one subset of philanthropic activity. In Latin America, the prevalent use of one or another concept to capture both sets of activities varies according to national context and experiences. However, it is the more demanding concept of corporate social responsibility that has pervaded the recent discourse on business' social orientation.

The recent adoption of this concept among significant sectors of the business elite might have appeared unlikely in the context of market reforms, increased international competition, and sluggish growth. Milton Friedman's dictum that there is no social responsibility for corporate officials "other than to make as much money for their shareholders as possible," or its updated formulation in *The Economist*—"The proper business of business is business. No apologies required"—could have sufficed as legitimacy buffers to resist or at least postpone the admission of an active social role for business.[4] Yet, and despite the actual gap between discourse and reality, the dissemination of the idea of corporate social responsibility (CSR) has taken off and expanded vigorously across the region.

Beginning in the late 1990s organizations created by business to promote this concept began to sprout throughout the region. The vigorous Instituto Ethos in Brazil was created in 1998, followed by Acción Empresarial in Chile in 1999 and *Fundemas* in El Salvador in 2000. "Older" organizations, such as the Mexican Center for Philanthropy (Cemefi), created in 1988, or *Peru 2021*, founded in 1994, began engaging in the promotion of CSR at about the time of the founding of their younger partners in the region. Similar organizations emerged in countries such as Argentina, Colombia, and Panama.

What accounts for the emergence of all this activity in a short period of time and in a context that could not be seen as the most propitious? Perhaps the answer must be sought in the heightened visibility of the private sector in a context provided by a relatively weaker state, the social impact of sluggish and uneven growth,[5] and the inegalitarian consequences of economic reform. Viewed in this way, CSR provides a defensive buffer against the threat of social discontent. At the same time, economic internationalization, accompanied by features of globalization such as the development of transnational networks and movements,[6] has demanded ethical behavior and social responsibility on the part of firms, particularly if these firms export to developed markets or are based in advanced countries.[7] These networks facilitate the circulation of ideas and their reflection in international norms, influencing the expansion of CSR promotion to Latin America.

A distinctive feature of the recent wave of social responsibility promotion is its internationalized origin. Most of the organizations mentioned above developed a close relationship with Business for Social Responsibility

(BSR), a leading organization in the United States founded in 1992 and based in San Francisco. Beginning with a preliminary meeting in Miami in 1997 of a group of individuals interested in gauging the state of business social responsibility in Latin America, this relationship strengthened the following year with the participation of Latin American business leaders in BSR's annual conference. The San Francisco based BSR played an important role in providing models for the Latin American organizations and in advising them in their early stages.[8]

Furthermore, these organizations established a tightly knit network and have developed common platforms for the region, as expressed in Forum Empresa, whose Governing Council is formed by the top leaders of BSR, Instituto Ethos, Peru 2021, Acción Empresarial, and Fundemas. Other members include Cemefi, the Prince of Wales International Business Leaders Forum (U.K.), and Empresa Privada para la Responsabilidad Social (Panama). This regional alliance set forth a mission "to strengthen and help establish national and regional business organizations committed to social responsibility."[9] However, the most dynamic activities have sprung from the national organizations and their direct interactions with sister organizations in the region.

The Latin American organizations have established a vast network with local and international NGOs, government agencies (in their countries and the U.S., such as the Inter-American Foundation), multilateral organizations (such as the Inter-American Development Bank), universities (locally and abroad, especially the US), think tanks, research centers, and foundations (such as the Kellogg Foundation, the Synergos Institute, the Ford Foundation, and Avina). They participate, promote and sustain a hectic calendar of national and international conferences and workshops, and have begun documenting social responsibility practices by business in Latin America. CSR activities and organizations have in fact acquired the ability to engage a variegated set of civil society organizations, international organizations, and government agencies, in debates and practices with important implications for the future of business, state, and society relations.[10]

This chapter provides an overview of the activities of CSR organizations in Argentina, Brazil, Chile, and Mexico. This group includes the largest countries in the region and displays differences in those organizations and the manner in which CSR is conceived and promoted. The chapter presents a preliminary explanation for the recent impulse of socially oriented activities by business under the wrappings of business social responsibility. Toward the end several questions are raised for future research.

The Origins of CSR in Latin America: A Preliminary Framework

Three interrelated factors can be posited as the basis for the emergence of CSR in these countries: a) social mobilization or pressures from below; b) changing views among business leaders; and c) developments in management theory and practice. These are presented here in the manner of hypotheses that require further research, especially in terms of the different ways in which they combine in each of the countries of concern.

The factors have operated in the new context of an invigorated business sector after the termination of state-led inward-oriented development strategies that prevailed in Latin America until two or three decades ago and the promotion of market oriented reforms. The contrast with the situation of business a few decades back is stark.[11] Dependent on the dynamics of the public sector and public policy, business was subdued by controls and regulations ranging from price controls to tariffs through exchange rates, quotas, and wages. Today, although with variation across countries, a much weightier private sector often is the one that sets the tone for the public sector.[12] The change in the balance of power, raising the visibility of business and its leaders, presents new issues of legitimacy and accountability.

Within this context the role of social pressure, business leaders' views, and management concepts in the promotion of CSR in Latin America may be addressed.

Social pressure. Interest in programs that portray business as concerned with social problems must be viewed, in the first place, as a response to social pressure. In fact, some scholars have made it part of the definition of CSR. David Vogel, for instance, views CSR as "those business policies that are primarily undertaken in response to changes in political or societal pressures, norms or expectations."[13] In Latin America, social pressure appears in the context of economic reforms that have had dramatic social effects jointly with enhanced opportunities for political expression of previously suppressed social and political actors. Argentina, Brazil, and Chile saw the end of military rule at different points in the 1980s, and social and political actors that had been severely repressed under those regimes found new opportunities for organization and expression.[14] Except in Chile, neoliberal reforms were pursued only after democratic rule had been attained. Also in Mexico liberalization and eventual democratization of the political regime went along with economic reforms, also opening up avenues for civil society organization and opposition. In all of these cases, high levels of unemployment combined with high rates of poverty and levels of inequality, and often with a dramatic expansion of urban crime and violence, laid bare the shortcomings of a weakened public sector as well as the responsibilities of an ascendant private sector. Business organizations for CSR emerged at about the time in which these pressures were being felt.

At the level of individual firms, business executives became more aware of public scrutiny of the behavior of firms and of a better educated and demanding consumer. Firms increased their resort to consulting in communications and public relations and their attention to public opinion surveys that focus on the public's perception of the behavior of firms and its consequence on consumer loyalty.[15] Many businesses also became sensitive to empowered social and civil organizations at the local and national level, and felt urged to propose solutions to social problems in areas adjacent to their particular area of activity and to anticipate crises through the establishment of links to the community. Social pressure from below operates objectively, as an increase in popular mobilization and organization, but most often operates subjectively, as business' anticipated response to a perception of crisis or social pressure, and as awareness of the magnitude and complexity of social problems.[16]

Changing views among business leaders. The initiative of enlightened individuals in the business community and the development of new ideas among significant sectors of this community have helped conceive strategies for business that address its social responsibility in the face of large and complex social problems. In many ways, in some elite sectors, this development may best be captured as a transition from a segmented and particularistically oriented mindset and behavior, to one decidedly more assertive and national-universalistic in orientation. This movement can be presented in Mancur Olson's terms as the passing from a narrower *strategy of redistribution* to a broader *strategy of collective gain*; from the pursuit of particularistic gain in a zero-sum game, to the pursuit of gain by collective improvement.[17] Put differently, a stronger and wealthier business sector is freer to think beyond its corporate boundaries and to consider taking on responsibilities that were previously the exclusive domain of the public sector. Beyond defensive corporate claims, business may now aspire to assume a national leadership role in shaping debates over modes of social organization and coordination, taking on directly the role of disseminating a private, market-based ethos throughout society.

A parallel development has been the strengthening of the role of economists in public policy and political leadership, and, more generally, of a cadre of intellectuals with diverse disciplinary foundations.[18] Business relations with this cadre—its "organic intellectuals"[19]—have helped it advance a view about the connection between an improved social context (stable political relations, an educated work force, expanded consumption opportunities) and business performance. These intellectuals have aided in challenging business to move beyond its corporate frontiers into collective-universalistic pursuits.[20] Along these lines appears the recent development of the notion of social entrepreneurship, supported by business school programs in major U.S. and European universities, a trend which is beginning to develop in Latin America.[21]

Changing views among business leaders are also often the result of religious inspiration. This is the case with Uniapac (International Christian Union of Business Executives), "an ecumenical movement of business executives who take inspiration from the Christian social thinking and ethical principles of Christianity concerning their economic and social responsibilities toward enterprise and society, in order to accomplish their tasks and professional duties."[22] This organization, with members in Latin America, stands for liberalism, globalization, and subsidiarity, and maintains close relations with other organizations similar in its Christian inspiration, including the International Christian Democracy. However, this older Christian organization, dating back to the 1930s, appears to be less influential in the current tide of CSR than are recent strands of more conservative Catholic organizations, such as the Legionarios de Cristo, influential in Mexico and Chile. In most cases, however, CSR promotion is secular in orientation and has often been aided by orientations generated from within early immigrants' associations.

Management theories and practice. A third factor in the emergence of CSR comes from developments in management theory and practice that stress new roles for the corporation and new tasks for effective long-term management that emphasize links with the community. In this view the corporation is a part of society, and responsiveness to the community must be built into the daily practices of the firm and into its management and strategic design. This ultimately makes business sense as is reflected in the ability to attract better quality employees and in its beneficial impact in "human resource management, culture building, and business generation."[23]

In the ideal type presented by these new concepts CSR emerges as business that integrates a concern for ethics, people, the community and the environment both in the daily operations of the firm and in its strategic planning and decision-making process. It ideally engages all or most of its human resources, and includes an internal dimension focused on labor relations, personnel, working standards, and management practices, and an external dimension focused on respect for the environment, a commitment to aiding the community's economic and social development, and the conduct of responsible trade and marketing practices.[24]

This requires establishing partnerships with groups or organizations outside the company.[25] Stakeholdership is the general concept connecting these partnerships, in which stakeholders are "those key groups of people who can influence the business or are directly affected by its activities, and also the natural environment."[26] Core stakeholders may include suppliers, employees, voluntary representatives, retailers, customers, the local community, investors, the environment, shareholders, as well as government, and other societal actors and organizations to which corporations must be responsible and accountable. This means integrating society's and the community's concerns to daily management and strategic planning. Firms then operate according to the expectations of all those concerned that they will behave in a socially responsible way.[27] A generalized practice of CSR would ideally create a chain connecting firms, suppliers, consumers, and the financial sector in ways that multiply the impact of social responsibility by conditioning those relationships to socially responsible practice.

In part this means that CSR includes the adoption of all the internationally defined norms of quality management along with social responsibility norms. The internationalization of Latin America's economic scenario, including its increasing export orientation, makes the adoption of these norms a matter of both legitimacy and competitiveness. There appears to be a growing demand by companies for advice and training in quality management that includes social responsibility.

Zadek, Pruzan and Evans presented a similar set of factors in explaining social and ethical accounting and auditing in the advanced economies. They identified a public interest/accountability factor by which business responds to changing interests and needs; a value shift factor, and a managerialist/stakeholder management factor. They also identified historical landmarks in the development of the practice of ethical and social reporting, all of which have been business responses to what it perceived as crisis, such as the depression of the 1930s, the nationalizations of the 1960s and the social unrest of the same period. Progress in CSR concepts became harder in the 1980s, a time in which business found more of a green light to set its own terms for relationships with society. Progress resumed, in the view of these authors, in the 1990s, with the proliferation of communication technologies and international information networks, by circulating and sharing concepts and experiences around the world.[28]

The short recent history of the emergence of CSR in Latin America also appears related to crisis: the enduring signs of poverty and inequality in the 1980s and 1990s, in the context of a less able state and a vastly more powerful private sector. Business perceives political and societal pressures, and reacts alongside a network of civil society organizations, think tanks, research centers, and multilateral agencies that circulate, multiply, and legitimize ideas about social responsibility. Across the different countries, the factors listed above combine in different and particular ways, confronting their own specific landmarks of crisis. History, politics, and culture are important factors in establishing these differences. A comparative research agenda in this field should aim precisely at determining the role of all these factors.

Promoting CSR in Latin America: Four Cases

Distance from the ideal type of CSR is large in deed among Latin American companies and only a few firms approximate it. However, an increasing number engage in CSR reporting, especially in Brazil. At a comparative level, CSR should be viewed as materializing somewhere along a continuum that goes from CSR as defined above and philanthropy. On one end, CSR activity in Brazil tends to be closer to the CSR end of the continuum whereas in Mexico there is more activity closer to the philanthropy end. Argentina may be viewed in between these cases, while activity in Chile is comparatively smaller on either end.

Organizations that promote CSR insist that, whatever their inspiration, they are not promoting religious or political views and they do not discriminate on those bases. They are not, for instance, to lobby public institutions for specific policies. Here too, however, some kind of gradation is found across countries. In Mexico, CSR activity is occasionally understood as the promotion of particular political or sectoral goals by business organizations. Brazil, again, may be found at the other extreme, with Argentina close to it. In Chile, the leading organizations emphasize this dimension of neutrality, although several factors have tended to counter this emphasis: overlap in membership in religious organizations, and a more active political stance by the business leadership. The country review below starts with Brazil, undoubtedly the most advanced country in Latin America regarding CSR.

Brazil

Brazil displays the most advanced practice and set of institutions in CSR in the region. Instituto Ethos de Empresas e Responsabilidade Social along with GIFE (Grupo de Institutos, Fundações e Empresas) and IBASE (Instituto Brasileiro de Análises Sociais e Econômicas) have been the most influential organizations in the emergence and current discussion and practice of CSR.

At the basis of the movement leading to the institutionalization of business's social concerns has been the role of an activated social and labor movement, and the perception of this activation by an enlightened business leadership. Civil society and the labor movement expanded and became more active toward the twilight of the military regime (1964–1985). A concern and an interest with this mobilization, jointly with the challenges opened by the process of liberalization and democratic transition, led business groups to initiate broad discussions on issues of national interest and national policy beyond narrow corporate boundaries. They, especially the most liberal groups, signaled a willingness of business to contribute to the solution of problems of inequity and injustice, and its urban violence consequences, which the political opening had unveiled. This very opening facilitated the activation of independent social and political activity from outside the state, expressed through political channels—new political parties, mobilization campaigns such as the campaign for direct presidential elections in the mid 1980s—and ultimately articulated in the post-authoritarian constitution of 1988.[29]

During the first years of democracy, corruption at the highest levels and the impeachment process of president Collor added stimulus to business's concern with the promotion of ethics in business and politics. This gave the final impetus for the consolidation of a group of private donor organizations interested in social projects, which created GIFE in 1995 (in actual existence since the turn of the decade) and approved a code of ethics. GIFE strengthened the activity of those groups seeking partnership between the state and organizations in civil society for the solution of social problems and inequality.[30] Amcham, expressing the role of multinational corporations in Brazil, played an important part in this movement.

The campaign against hunger started in 1993 by the sociologist Herbert de Souza (Betinho) from IBASE offered another opportunity for diverse groups including social and business organizations to come together.[31] GIFE and IBASE were actors in, and expressions of, this mobilization, playing their own independent role. GIFE articulated foundations and companies with a social concern and an interest in increasing the effectiveness, professionalism, and visibility of social investment and its requisite alliances. IBASE, bringing together civil society organizations, carried out its campaign for democracy, equity, and *cidadania empresarial* (business citizenship) and pushed for the idea of the *balanço social* (BS—social reporting).[32]

The Christian inspiration of some business leaders organized in a local chapter of Uniapac, and in IDE (Instituto de Desenvolvimento Empresarial), which later became FIDES (Fundação Instituto de Desenvolvimento Econômico e Social), played a role in the mobilization of the 1980s and 1990s. These groups had been expressing a concern with the extremes of poverty since the 1960s, calling for a social conscience among businessmen and specifically proposing a *balanço social* for companies.[33]

However, the major thrust in business mobilization in the late 1980s and 1990s and its socially progressive concerns originated in the action of a group of businessmen organized in the PNBE (Pensamento Nacional das Bases Empresariais), a dissident group within the Business Federation of São Paulo.[34] This group started its activities in the 1980s but became institutionalized in the 1990s, participating in public debates through the media and gathering an important following in the business community. PNBE sought a modernization of industrial relations at a time in which labor issues lay at the center of social and political conflict. Toward the end of the 1980s this group participated in the debate and mobilization around environmental and consumer defense issues, and produced think pieces with which to contest the leadership of the official business federations.

Another important element in this process was the creation of the Abrinq Foundation in 1990 to fight for the rights of children and adolescents, and specifically against child labor.[35] A small group from this initiative, and especially Oded Grajew, a leading toy manufacturer and founder of Abrinq Foundation, took time off to study the way social responsibility was approached in Europe and the U.S. This led to contacts with BSR in San Francisco and soon after to the organization of the 1997 Miami meeting, which was attended by 12 business people from Brazil that became the founding core of Ethos.[36]

Ethos developed spectacularly since its foundation in 1998 and the first international congress it organized in 1999. It is the undisputed center of reference for most CSR activity. It started out with a group of 11 associated firms; in 2002 it claimed a membership of 443 associated firms; by December 2003 the number climbed to 793 firms whose total earnings represented about 20 percent of the country's GDP. By May of 2005 the figure had reached 1006 members representing 30 percent of Brazil's GDP.[37]

A distinctive feature of this organization is that its governing councils are not representative. Its members are co-opted, not elected. Members are companies, not individuals. Free from electoral and representational considerations, it may function as a politico-cultural vanguard of the business sector pushing it in the direction of social responsibility. Its purpose is not principally to manage or implement large projects, but to promote a new culture in business management based on responsiveness to stakeholders. It seeks to identify a network of people in the media and academia that can help promote the agenda of CSR, to be always ahead, to be alert to new trends, and to articulate these trends back to its expanding membership.[38]

Ethos's vision of its role as cultural promoter leads it to emphasize work on what it calls *agentes indutores*, i.e., those that may most quickly and efficiently influence business toward adopting CSR behavior and culture. Primary among them are financial actors such as pension fund administrators and banks, which should use CSR criteria for their loan policies and risk assessments, and could stimulate their clients in the right direction.[39] Consumers are another important *agente indutor* approached through the Akatu Foundation, a spin-off from Ethos. A third important agent is the media addressed via training programs for journalists. About one hundred of them participate in a network with its own website. Journalists are rewarded annually for their work with a special individual award, the Prêmio Ethos do Jornalismo.[40]

Young executives and professionals also are especially targeted, and there is a special award for students—Prêmio Ethos-Vâlor.[41] An agreement with the ministry of education sought the inclusion of CSR in the curriculum in economics, administration, social communication, and engineering. Ethos also sought to include the concept of social responsibility as a criterion in the evaluation of higher education centers and to include it in the *Lei de Diretrizes e Bases Curriculares* (bill on curriculum bases and guidelines). At the same time, Ethos started organizing a network of researchers, claiming to already have one with 180 professors with the goal of advancing an instructional capacity at the graduate and undergraduate levels.[42] Consulting firms are viewed as another important *agente indutor* because of their concern with and expertise in quality management.[43] Finally, the state itself is a target for action, in which Ethos supports legislation or puts pressure at the top executive level for the inclusion of relevant criteria and clauses in trade agreements. Ethos's view is that the state must be strengthened so that it may perform its part in the social responsibility area.[44]

Ethos also works in the production of standards and indicators. One of its four units was, for instance, devoted to "knowledge management" which collects and disseminates relevant information, develops standards, indicators and manuals, and keeps the organization up to date with the latest developments in the literature. Ethos offers the most advanced set of indicators in the region in *Indicadores Ethos de Responsabilidade Social Empresarial*, which include seven major categories: values and transparency (self-regulation of conduct; transparency of relationship with society); internal public (dialogue and participation; respect for the individual; respect for the worker); environment (management of environmental impact; responsibility before future generations); suppliers (selection of and partnership with suppliers); consumers/clients (social dimension of consumption); community (relations with local community; philanthropy/social investment; volunteer work), and government and society (political transparency; social leadership).[45]

Brazil is the only country in the region in which companies engage in serious social responsibility reporting. Seventy-one companies submitted results on *Indicadores Ethos* in 2000, of which 58 percent were Ethos associates. The majority of them (70.3 percent) were large size (more than 500 employees), and also a majority of them were private domestic companies. A study by Ethos considered a benchmark group made up of those 10 with the best scores, of which nine were large firms located in the southeast, mostly private domestic companies. The benchmark group pointed to the small number of firms that carry out social responsibility to very high levels according to Ethos standards.[46]

Many of those companies that do IBASE's social reporting overlap with those doing the Ethos questionnaire. While Ethos emphasizes reforms in companies' strategic planning and management, especially in the relations with stakeholders and community involvement, IBASE emphasizes accountability. Sixty-nine companies turned in the BS in 2000, versus 18 that did it in its first year, 1998. By 2004, 734 businesses had filled out the report.[47]

In comparison to other organizations in Latin America, the Brazilian organizations stood out for their emphasis on human rights. This is very much a part of the mission of IBASE while Ethos calls for observance of the Universal Declaration of Human Rights and its relevance for companies: child labor, forced labor, freedom of association, discrimination, health and security. Also distinctly, Ethos emphasizes ethical attitudes in, as well as actual reporting of, campaign and political party financing on the part of business.

Argentina

There has been no central organization in Argentina claiming officially to carry the CSR torch, although the Consejo de Fundaciones (Council of

Foundations) (GDF), a comparatively modest equivalent of GIFE in Brazil, does in practice approach this role. Created in 1995 and formed by 15 donor foundations, the GDF's mission is to promote and professionalize private social investment initiatives and to develop a culture of business social responsibility. The GDF was preceded by the Consejo Empresario Argentino para el Desarrollo Sostenible (Argentine Business Council for Sustainable Development) (CEADS), created in 1992 and formed by 37 firms as the local chapter of the World Business Council for Sustainable Development. CEADS conceives of corporate social responsibility as a tool for the larger aim of sustainable development. More recently, the smaller Instituto Argentino de Responsabilidad Social Empresaria (Argentine Institute of Business Social Responsibility) (IARSE), formed by 19 firms and business organizations (membership is open to civil society organizations as well), also claims a mission to promote the concept and the practice of CSR in order to support Argentina's sustainable development through information networks and cooperation.[48]

Dispersion is possibly the result of competing claims to leadership that are likely related to the fractious history of Argentine business associations.[49] It is also connected to the complexity and multilayered nature of the country's philanthropic practice and tradition. There has been a tradition of large companies carrying along company-associated foundations. In turn, these foundations and the philanthropic tradition in general have been associated with more diversified migration patterns than is the case in many other countries in the region. The origin and mission of some of the foundations and companies could be traced to ethnic lines. This, in turn, is related to a greater pluralist tradition in the social realm than, especially, neighboring Chile. This is reflected, for instance, in differences between Catholic and Jewish groups, as well as within each one of them.[50] The study of the ways in which migration patterns connect with philanthropic traditions seems especially relevant in this case.

This picture of a variegated philanthropic tradition in the contemporary scenario began to change recently, in the course of the last decade, as a result of privatization and neoliberal reforms started in the early 1990s. They profoundly affected changes in the structure of ownership with a heavy emphasis on denationalization. The tradition of large locally owned companies that acted as self-enclosed welfare systems for its employees simply disappeared. The picture has also been influenced by recurrent economic crises and a very profound crisis of legitimacy of the state. The state, mired in corruption and stalemate, was perceived as unable to place the country along a path of economic growth.[51]

The recent emergence of the notion of business social responsibility, as distinct from philanthropy, has affected traditional philanthropic patterns. This is partly the result of the presence of internationally connected organizations and businesses that have installed the notion of CSR, generating its own dynamics.[52] In turn this should be seen as resulting from other, deeper factors at play: a more complex network of civil society organizations, changes in business sectors and their perceptions, and a more pressing push from foreign companies.

A more complex civil society developed along with democratization started in the 1980s. The pioneering human rights movement that reacted to the massive atrocities conducted by the military regime activated in new ways a culture of rights in Argentina. This was followed by a number of organizations that enlivened a citizens movement and organizations devoted to social policy, solidarity and philanthropy.[53] This process was accompanied by a greater professionalization of civil society organizations, which resulted in better management and exercise of demand capacities.[54] Notable examples are, of course, Poder Ciudadano, and the Centro de Estudios Legales y Sociales and, with more direct relevance to our subject, the Fundación Compromiso, inspired in the notions developed by Peter Drucker.

Also relevant has been the Foro del Sector Social, which emerged in 1996, a continuation of the Alliance against Poverty organized by the World Bank. The Foro helped articulate social sector organizations and operated as a bridge between the state and business for social sector issues. The Foro claimed to represent 220 organizations, for a total of about 3000 associated institutions.[55]

Another important factor has been a change in the disposition of the business sector, willing more systematically to embrace CSR through the traditional conduit of foundations. Whether or not in the Grupo de Fundaciones (many large and effective foundations operate on their own), foundations have moved in the direction of improved professionalized management of their philanthropic activity.[56] These changes in attitude and organization followed a double realization of the growing incapacity of the state to efficiently handle social demands, and the worsening social conditions in the context of stagnant growth and maldistribution of wealth. This realization took place against a background of fear of violent social eruption. Experiences of public anger with respect to business failure in the context of economic crisis, even before the collapse of the De La Rúa administration in December 2001 and the subsequent economic collapse, greatly influenced the willingness of sectors of the business community to consider the inclusion of the CSR discourse.[57]

Accompanying this process of gradual expansion of the idea of CSR was the independent and active publicity it was given. *El Cronista Comercial* devoted a permanent section to this issue and another daily, *La Nación*, gave it a monthly special section. *La Nación* had had its own experience of personnel reduction and devoted this section to responsible ways of handling similar cases by numerous other companies in the context of state and economic reform.[58] *Apertura*, a business monthly published in collaboration with *Business Week*, and greatly legitimized in business circles for its neoliberal orientation, was also an outlet for CSR activity. Its yearly issue exclusively devoted to CSR was more profitable than regular editions. Publicity for CSR also came from the Ciudadanía Empresaria award granted by Amcham, which started in 2000. All this activity, in the context described above, had increased the concern by business for developing some form of CSR, especially the marketing aspect, in an economic situation that had grown increasingly harsh.

Chile

CSR organizations in Chile are newer than in the other cases and still of modest scope, although recently with a greatly increased level of institutionalization. Acción Empresarial (AE), created in May 2000, is officially connected with BSR and Forum Empresa. Now, with its new name, *Acción RSE* hosts the Chilean chapter of the World Business Council for Sustainable Development (WBCSD). With a small staff, Acción RSE's membership keeps growing, from 29 associates in 2002 and 37 in 2004 to more than 50 in 2005. Its origins can be traced back to Generación Empresarial (GE), an organization that brings together individuals to promote a business culture centered in the person, seeking to bring about personal change among business people and executives through the practice of Christian values and social responsibility.[59] Initially, the membership of GE and AE overlapped substantially, with AE's first president also a GE vice-president, but those strong initial links have since been severed. The impetus in the formation of AE from GE was complemented by an interest from the Confederación de la Producción y el Comercio (Confederation for Production and Commerce—CPC), the main organization of business, industry and commerce, concerned with improving the public image of business by publicizing the actual social role it claims to perform. At the time of its founding, AE was officially sponsored by CPC, and most of its meetings were held in CPC facilities.

In the United States, BSR played a major role by initiating contacts with the CPC and a group of Chilean and foreign firms seeking to find a partner from within business for the development of an organization in Chile.

BSR contacted GE and provided a fellowship for one of its members to get to know BSR first hand. BSR and GE subsequently entered into an agreement to create Acción Empresarial.[60] The idea was to create a distinct organization that resulted from an association of companies and not individuals (such as GE), and that was free of representational and lobbying interests (such as the CPC).

This confluence of interests and inspirations must be viewed in the context of economic and political transformations that had taken place in Chile. Advancement of CSR toward the end of the century was partly a delayed response to processes of economic transformation initiated during the Pinochet regime. Early neoliberal reforms and widespread privatization had significantly empowered the private sector while inequality worsened, with poverty affecting 40 percent of Chileans. The first democratic administration inaugurated in 1990 had to tackle this problem through social spending financed by increased taxation on profits. Despite initial opposition, business reluctantly agreed to increased taxes because of awareness of skyrocketing poverty and inequality.[61] Very high rates of growth in the 1990s and targeted policies helped reduce poverty rates without decreasing inequality. Neoliberal reforms and policies highlighted the visibility of the private sector. In conclusion, an empowered business sector, a leaner state and the haunting specter of recalcitrant poverty should be viewed as factors behind the introduction of CSR.[62]

Business also became conscious of a more demanding consumer, regularly carrying out surveys on the public perception of companies. Citing one such survey requested by CPC and AE, the CPC president showed that nearly half the respondents took responsible business practices into account in forming an opinion about a particular company, and that 37 percent has considered punishing irresponsible conduct. In consequence, he argued, "Once business fulfils its essential mission . . . [growth and employment] . . . it must extend its action toward a commitment with public goals and insertion in the community [. . .] because it has been demonstrated that businesses that behave like good corporate citizens [. . .] obtain the recognition of public opinion, which is a competitive variable of great importance."[63]

The introduction of CSR is also a delayed result of the internationalization of the economy. The most internationalized economy in Latin America is vulnerable and sensible to quality and social norms prevailing in international markets and business communities. One consequence is that the most extensive CSR experiences in Chile have been conceived abroad and adapted to the local scenario, for instance, by Shell, BellSouth and

Fundación Telefónica. Of the nine members of the Chilean chapter of the WBCSD, eight are transnational corporations which already participated in the council from their headquarters and elsewhere.[64]

Promotion of CSR encountered some unique difficulties in Chile that came from cultural and political divides inherited from its democratic transition that resulted in opposing pro-Pinochet and pro-democracy camps. The leadership of business organizations (CPC and the Sociedad de Fomento Fabril—Society for Manufacturing Promotion—SOFOFA) were perceived as venturing too often outside their representational corporate concerns into the political realm. This perception was reinforced by their stance during the evolution of the Pinochet detention in London in 1998 and 1999, and reflected in their opposition to government proposals on issues such as labor and tax reform, and in their support for rightist opposition parties. Another source of difficulties, especially for the development of partnerships, was the misgivings from a perception of a conservative Catholic inspiration of many business leaders, connected with the *Legionarios de Cristo*. All these factors resulted in distrust between business organizations and other civil society organizations. A round table on CSR held in 2001 concluded that "the high levels of distrust between different sectors were explained in the light of the absence of a consensus national agenda."[65] This distrust also extends to labor organizations, expressing itself in a failure to include labor relations within businesss' notion of social responsibility.[66]

In recent years, however, the atmosphere for the reception of CSR ideas has improved visibly. This stems in part from changes in business leadership and from greater institutionalization and professionalization of organizations involved in CSR promotion. The leadership of the major business associations started to change toward the end of the 1990s—but in particular beginning in 2001—with the election of a younger generation. This new leadership cooperated with the government in the negotiations of trade agreements with the United States and the European Union, especially in devising strategies to confront recessionary trends, such as the joint promotion with the government of the so-called pro-growth agenda. In January 2002, the SOFOFA president (simultaneously the president of CPC) and government ministers announced the conclusion of a joint project that would clear the way for resumed growth. The joint taskforce involved 28 technical committees with proposals for microeconomic changes and institutional reforms at all levels, some of which would require legislative action. This agreement signaled the end of the confrontational stance of previous leaders and the acceptance of social issues in the agenda.

Reception of CSR ideas also increased as a result of electoral dynamics that have led rightist parties and their presidential hopefuls to adopt centrist positions by emphasizing unresolved problems of poverty and inequality. As the 2005 presidential election campaign began to take off, candidates' rhetoric converged on these issues, which marked a shift in rightist positions.[67]

On the other hand, the acceptance and dissemination of CSR ideas have gained impulse from its official adoption by SOFOFA, which renamed its previous Social Area as Sofofa Responsabilidad Social (SRS). This organization now grants SOFOFA's award on social responsibility, which started in 1998, and has established an alliance with Acción RSE jointly to develop a data bank on cases of social responsibility in several areas (for instance, it had more than 50 cases in the area of community services in 2005). However, at the same time that the alliance for CSR expands and gains in institutionalization, SOFOFA's incorporation, with its much stronger resources, may be viewed as an attempt to control and define CSR in a more restrained way. Its mission statement places CSR as a pillar of sustainable development and states that SOFOFA "will promote the development of an ethical framework that aids in the establishment of a contributive environment that fosters the due fulfillment of juridical norms and the cooperation and understanding among shareholders, partners, workers, customers, and suppliers." SOFOFA "considers relevant to encourage the development of CSR in the internal and external practices of the firm, viewing it as an element of competitiveness, sustainability and positioning vis á vis market and society."[68]

Finally, PROhumana, an independent organization for the promotion of philanthropy and social responsibility, has been a major contributor to the promotion of the idea of CSR. Created in 1998, prior to Acción RSE, to promote a culture of social responsibility among business, individuals, institutions and civil society organizations, PROhumana specifically seeks to bridge business and citizen social responsibility. With support from the Kellogg Foundation, the Ford Foundation, the UNDP and other major organizations, it develops a hectic agenda of international and national seminars, conferences, workshops, colloquia and a social responsibility fair with exhibits from major companies and civil society organizations. PROhumana has developed a broad network that includes business, universities, individuals, civil society organizations, media, and government agencies and a vast array of sponsors for its many activities. It undertakes research on cases of CSR in collaboration with international organizations and with SOFOFA, with which it co-sponsors the Premio Fundación PROhumana

RSEtica (PROhumana's award in ethics and business social responsibility) to a firm selected from an independent committee, jointly with AcciónAG (the top association of NGOs), the General Secretariat of the Presidency of the government, and the CPC. PROhumana has competently positioned itself as an interlocutor and facilitator with local social organizations and international networks. It is active in the circulation of ideas and research and publishes the quarterly Filantropía y Responsabilidad Social en Chile. PROhumana and SOFOFA, each from its distinct perspectives and agendas, have helped expand and institutionalize the debate on CSR from its business origins in AE and the CPC.

Mexico

The development of modern CSR organizations in Mexico should be viewed in the context of political liberalization and democratization gradually advanced in the past two decades, and its complex interaction with business mobilization against nationalization in the 1980s and business's role in the promotion of neoliberal reforms in the 1990s.[69] This processes had as a background the political activation of organized groups as well as new forms of mobilization by an emergent civil society interested in the solution of sectoral issues and problems.[70] CSR is best understood as a response to these developments, which also encouraged greater connection between business and civil society organizations.[71]

Mexico's most important organization in CSR promotion—the Mexican Center of Philanthropy (Cemefi)—is also the oldest (1988) of the new wave of such organizations in Latin America.[72] It brings together companies (59), foundations and associations (93), and individuals (45) for the promotion of a philanthropic culture, civic engagement, and the sustainability of nonprofit organizations. Through its program on government and public policy, it conducts research and lobbying for legislation that facilitates inter-sectoral social investment, and provides advice and consulting to business on these issues. Cemefi has been supported by organizations such as the Kellogg Foundation, Synergos Institute, the Ford Foundation, and the Inter-American Foundation.

Cemefi started a business social responsibility program in 1997, although it really did not take off until later. By 2001 it brought together 32 companies and 14 business foundations, figures which had risen to 70 and 26 respectively in 2005. Cemefi claims this to be the first and only group formed by business solely for the purpose of debating and advancing CSR.[73] Business foundations meet separately, with participants coming from a group of about 20 fee-paying members. Cemefi also promotes sectoral alliance workshops, including business, government, foundations and social organizations around specific topics, mostly in regions.

Cemefi's founder, Manuel Arango, was instrumental in organizing the first CSR conference in the Americas and took the 3rd Congress to Mexico in 2000, which allowed him to bring together a number of relevant organizations in Mexico that had so far remained dispersed: universities, the CCE, Coparmex, Desem, Usem, and Aval (which develops business's codes of conduct).[74] This experience led to the creation of ALIARSE (Business Social Responsibility Alliance) with all those organizations, with a coordination secretariat at Coparmex. However, this alliance has not become well institutionalized, although it, with Cemefi, granted the social responsibility seal, which 85 companies received in 2005.[75] Through work for the award Cemefi was improving on the construction of objective indicators.

Despite those signs of institutionalization much work revolved around the personal activities of influential individuals associated with large companies and their foundations. Such is the case of Lorenzo Servitje, from the *Bimbo* group, Roberto Hernández, from Banamex, and Carlos Slim from *Telmex*. Servitje has been a leading member of Indesoc (Christian Social Doctrine Institute) and an influential member of USEM (Mexico's Uniapac affiliate), while Carlos Slim has led the powerful Telmex foundation, which supports a number of large socially oriented projects, and gives to conservative Catholic organizations. Although these individuals participate in councils and informal settings where some coordination takes place, there is for the most part little systematic interaction and many activities remain highly personalized.

Cemefi maintains intense contact with public entities, and with the inauguration of the Fox administration it was called to participate in numerous programs and became an important bridge in the connection between business and public policy in social areas. Cemefi was called by the Presidency of Mexico to form a monitoring group on the national development plan, jointly with some of the companies that have received the Cemefi recognition. Collaboration with the Fox administration, particularly with Alianza Ciudadana, the office in the presidency for relationships with civil society, SEDESOL (the social development secretariat), and the economy secretary, has been facilitated by the incorporation into government of business people (many from Coparmex) and leaders from social organizations previously associated with Cemefi.[76]

Independently of Cemefi, business organizations that have entered into alliance with it claim to develop their own brand of business social responsibility. For instance, Coparmex, the employers' union founded in 1929, carries out social programs on education, the environment, and other top-ics—courses, workshops, and conferences—through its regional centers. The centers assume leadership and local coordination roles in times of cri-sis. For instance, Coparmex takes credit for starting the initiative in Chi-huahua after the flooding that led to the creation of the successful FECHAC, the Chihuahuense Entrepreneurs' Foundation.[77] However, Coparmex's role in expounding principles of social responsibility often appears to mean a concern with issues of policy, from its mission of defending business's interests and influencing public policy. In fact, Coparmex prides itself for being a seedbed of political leaders at the local and national level, viewing itself as the "conscience of the private sector" and advocating a "market economy with social responsibility" based on the human person and a system of liberties under Christian inspiration.[78]

Also business's peak association, the CCE, formed in the midst of busi-ness's fight against the policies of President Echeverría in the 1970s, claims to provide guidelines for business to engage in social responsibility, and is now, for instance, the host of ALIARSE. The CCE's own view of social responsibility, however, often includes the promotion of a market econ-omy, the rule of law, and business culture.[79]

The implantation of new ideas in management that incorporate social responsibility is making inroads, albeit slowly.[80] Much slower appears to be the expansion of modern CSR views among businesses, despite the philanthropic tradition and the expanded CSR rhetoric. An important area for investigation relates to the greater role that religion plays in pub-lic life as a result of the rise of the National Action Party (PAN) and the Fox administration, and the influence of religion in philanthropy aimed at the support of Catholic conservative organizations.

Final Reflections

This chapter focused on efforts to promote CSR from ad-hoc business organizations and highlighted important differences among the cases reviewed in regard to both the magnitude and the depth of those efforts. There is no question that Brazil stands apart on both counts. Nowhere but in Brazil does the number of companies associated with CSR reach signif-icant numbers.[81] Only in Brazil does these companies' output amount to nearly one third of the national economy. Brazil also displays a density of networks and partnerships at the city and state level that is alien to all other cases. Furthermore, the rigor, expanse and depth of the dimensions considered in CSR and that are the subject of reporting and accountabil-ity are the most advanced, reaching to areas that are inconceivable in other cases. They include, as noted above, issues of transparency in political contributions and issues of human rights, broadly understood, inside and outside the company. The contrast between Brazil and the rest calls for comparative research that should help illuminate the relative role of the different factors mentioned earlier in helping to adopt, disseminate and develop notions and practice of social responsibility. Here only preliminary suggestions may be made.

The main explanatory factor should be found, I suggest, in the combination of social mobilization and business leadership in the period preceding the rise of CSR. What is perhaps distinct of Brazil is the absence of a clear opposition between emergent business leadership and social mobilization. At the risk of oversimplifying, one may say that in most other cases there was, more or less directly, a reactive factor involved, a response to a perceived crisis that called for the adoption of CSR (in the different meanings given by business in the different countries, often quite divergent from the ideal type). In the case of Brazil, an emergent business leadership stood, to different degrees, in opposition to the military regime, especially in its final stages, and this led it to share interests with a social mobilization that included labor and a growingly mobilized and organized civil society. In other cases of democratic transition business had sided with the military regimes, except in Peru, but in this case business's stance did not lead it to coalesce with labor or social mobilization. Neither was the case in Mexico's gradual transition from civilian one-party state.

Recent waves of CSR promotion may be associated with a fear of the consequences of extreme poverty and inequality in Chile, with a response to state policies in Mexico, and with a fear of social explosion in Argentina in the context of drastic neoliberal reforms. In Brazil, in contrast, sectors of an emerging business leadership, particularly in São Paulo, started developing ideas that were congruent or at least not overtly incompatible with other sectors' interests in social reform and democratization. This, I suggest, is what makes it possible in Brazil for business leaders to go farther and deeper, to include goals and a language of human rights, as well as specific policies, that are alien to the other cases. A more systematic comparison would shed light on the specific role that each factor has played in the different countries, and at the same time would provide bases for different kinds of expectation about the future of CSR in the region, in terms of both magnitude and orientation.

Such a study would need to draw from knowledge about the dynamics of change in the culture, politics and the sociology of business. On the other hand, work done on civil society, social movements, and the labor movement must be integrated with studies of business in order to understand the role of pressures from below as well as the opportunities created for solidarity and alliances. Social science studies must also address the impact of trends in management schools and theories, as well as integrate the studies of change in the firm and the corporation. Motivations such as the different kinds of religious inspirations that are found within and across cases and the emergence of conservative views such as Opus Dei and Legionarios de Cristo inspirations in CSR in some countries also demand deeper study. Integrated comparative study of these developments should help gain comprehensive understanding of CSR dynamics in the region.

Another aspect that emerges from the case reviews in this chapter is the gap between ideal type CSR and the actual conceptions that prevail and are advanced in each case, and between those types and conceptions and the actual practice of social responsibility. Measurement of actual activity and results is difficult but must be developed for a critical review of these practices. The recent emergence, circulation and adoption of the notion of business social responsibility, which proliferates in conferences, documents, events, and practices, indicate that, as different groups try to make sense of this concept, they also attempt to dominate its definition according to their interests and preferences. Future research must approach conceptually, as Roitter proposes in his chapter, the influence on social representations about social and public life that results from business social action, an influence that reaches the agenda of critical actors in the state, society and multilateral agencies.

An important part of this involves the normative idea of the *empresa*—the firm or the company—as the leading agent of social change that often appears in the way that CSR is presented by business organizations. Peru 2021, the Peruvian organization that is part of the network expressed in Forum Empresa, has, for instance, stated that "businessmen are the main agents of development, of increasing and expanding welfare and the quality of human life. Businessmen are the main creators of personal, social, and cultural wealth."[82] What is the idea of social order implied in such a view, and what is the ranking of other social and political actors involved in its construction? What is the notion of politics, of public space and agents? What is the role of the state? Besides ideas, the actual mode of promotion of CSR in the context of the neoliberal project and a less resourceful state leads to a centrality of business and corporations in the already atomized handling of social and public issues, around which converge civic organizations individually addressing them in fragmented manner. This lends much credence to the notion of a "perverse confluence" that Evelina Dagnino has suggested exists between the neoliberal project and the participatory project entailed in the activation and strengthening of civil society,[83] and which becomes most salient in Brazil where such a participatory project has been advanced and where CSR is the most developed.

Acknowledgements

Research for this chapter was generously supported by a grant from the Ford Foundation.

Notes

1 Manuel Antonio Garretón et al., *Latin America in the Twenty-First Century: Toward a New Sociopolitical Matrix*. Miami: University of Miami/North-South Center Press, 2002.

2 Cynthia A. Sanborn and Felipe Portocarrero, "La filantropía realmente existente en América Latina," presented at the international seminar "La filantropía en América Latina: los desafíos de las fundaciones donantes en la construcción de capital humano y justicia social," Fundación Ford and Fundación Prehumana, Santiago, Chile, 17–20 November 2003.

3 See Baltazar Caravedo, Pilar Mariscal, Karem Salinas and Juan Carlos Villacorta, "Responsabilidad Social: una nueva forma de gerencia," Lima: Universidad del Pacífico, SASE, Peru 2021, octubre 2000. In some accounts, between philanthropy and CSR stands the notion of social investment.

4 "The Good Company: A Survey of Corporate Social Responsibility," *The Economist*, January 22nd 2005, p. 22. The quote by Milton Friedman may be found in Simon Zadek, Peter Pruzan and Richard Evans, eds., *Building Corporate Accountability: Emerging Practices in Social and Ethical Accounting, Auditing and Reporting*. London: Earthscan Publications, 1997, p. 18.

5 During the 1990s the region grew at more than double the rate of the 1980s, although at 3.3 percent growth was far inferior to the 5.6 percent growth rate of 1945–80. GDP per capita growth rate was only 1.6 percent in 1990–2000. Jorge Katz and Giovanni Stumpo (2001), "Regímenes Sectoriales, Productividad y Competitividad Internacional," *Revista de la CEPAL*, 75, p. 140.

6 Margaret E. Keck and Kathryn Sikkink, *Activists Beyond Borders*. Ithaca: Cornell University Press, 1998; and Sanjeev Khagram, Kames V. Riker, and Kathryn Sikkink, eds. *Restructuring World Politics: Transnational Social Movements, Networks, and Norms*. Minneapolis: University of Minnesota Press, 2002.

7 See George Kell and John Ruggie, "Global markets and social legitimacy: the case of the 'global' compact," in Daniel Dreche, ed. *The Market or the Public Domain: Global Governance and the Asymmetry of Power*. London: Routledge, 2001.

8 BSR seeks to establish worldwide presence for the principles of CSR through local organizations. It helps BSR's own goals by keeping track of developments in the field, creating synergy, and by allowing BSR to play a facilitator role for U.S. and European companies interested in Latin America. Bob Dunn, President BSR, interview, 8/31/01. However, the presence of Canadian and European transnational corporations helps to influence views in Latin America. Aaronson and Reeves, looking at the U.S., Canadian, and European experience argue that CSR contains different emphases according to its national origin. Susan Ariel Aaronson and James T. Reeves, *Corporate Responsibility in the Global Village: The Role of Public Policy* (Washington: National Policy Association, 2002), p. 2.

9 See www.empresa.org.

10 See in this regard James Austin et al., *Social Partnering in Latin America: Lessons Drawn from Collaborations of Business and Civil Society Organizations.* Cambridge: Harvard University David Rockefeller Center for Latin American Studies—Harvard University Press, 2004.

11 "A organização empresarial já se apresenta como o ator social mais poderoso do nosso tempo." Carlos Alberto Rabaça, sociologist and professor, "Empresas socialmente responsáveis," article published in *Jornal do Brasil* and reproduced in Ethos' website (www.ethos.org.br) on February 7th, 2001.

12 Sebastian Edwards, *Crisis and Reform in Latin America: From Despair to Hope.* Oxford University Press, 1995; Shahid Javed Burki and Sebastian Edwards, *Dismantling the Populist State: The Unfinished Revolution in Latin America and the Caribbean.* Washington D.C.: World Bank Publications, 1996.

13 David Vogel, *The Market for Virtue: The Potential and Limits of Corporate Social Responsibility.* Washington, D.C.: Brookings Institution Press, 2005.

14 Manuel Antonio Garretón and Edward Newman, Eds. *Democracy in Latin America (Re)Constructing Political Society.* Tokyo: United Nations University Press, 2001.

15 Interviews with directors at Tironi y Asociados in Santiago and Lima, at Burson-Marsteller in Santiago and São Paulo, and Compite in Mexico. A "combination of enlightened self-interest and looking to the long-term generates both good will and respect among stakeholders." Richard Aylard (European Environment Director, Burson-Marsteller), "Sustainability Expectations of the Corporate Sector," Allied Domecq Lecture, Committee for Interdisciplinary Environmental Studies, Cambridge University, 30th January 2001.

16 Although market reforms, as many argue, have weakened the ability of popular sectors to organize, coordinate and mobilize. See, for instance, Marcus Kurtz, "The Dilemmas of Democracy in the Open Economy: Lessons from Latin America," *World Politics* 56 (2): 262–302, January 2004.

17 Mancur Olson, *The Rise and Decline of Nations.* New Haven: Yale University Press, 1982.

18 Veronica Montecinos, *Economists, Politics and the State: Chile 1958–1994.* (Latin America Studies No. 80), and Verónica Montecinos, "Los Economistas y Las Élites Políticas en América Latina." *Estudios Internacionales* Nos. 119–120, July–December 1997.

19 For this Gramscian concept see Joseph Femia, *Gramsci's Political Thought: Hegemony, Consciousness, and the Revolutionary Process* (Oxford University Press, 1981), p. 130. The Gramscian connection has been established by others in this field as well. See, for instance, Peter Utting, "Regulating Business Via Multistakeholder Initiatives: A Preliminary Assessment," UNRISD, 2001.

20 Through these intellectuals "the development and expansion of the particular group are conceived of, and presented, as being the motor force of a universal expansion, of a development of all the 'national' energies." Antonio Gramsci, *Selections from the Prison Notebooks,* excerpted in David Held, ed. *States and Societies* (New York University Press, 1983), p. 121.

21 Just to name a few, Columbia, Stanford, Duke, Yale, and Oxford have developed programs in social entrepreneurship of one kind or another. Stanford has launched the first academic journal on the subject: *The Stanford Social Innovation Review.* See Emily Eakin, "How to save the world? Treat it like a business," *The New York Times,* A19–A21, December 20, 2003.

22 Uniapac, n.t., n.d., 2.

23 "Don't think that this is a charitable thing where you will get rewarded in heaven. You get rewarded right away because you'll be known as a company that is conscious of its social responsibility, you'll attract better quality employees, your stock will sell at a higher multiple." John Whitehead, former Chairman of Goldman Sachs, cited in James E. Austin, "The Invisible Side of Leadership," *Leader to Leader,* no. 8, Spring 1998.

24 See, for instance, Acción Empresarial, "Acercando la Empresa a la Comunidad: Guía Práctica sobre Inversión Social Empresarial," Santiago, May 2001.

25 For recent studies on Latin America, see James Austin et al., *op cit.*

26 Richard Evans, "Accounting for Ethics: Traidcraft plc, UK," in Simon Zadek, Peter Pruzan and Richard Evans, eds., *Building Corporate Accountability: Emerging Practices in Social and Ethical Accounting, Auditing and Reporting.* London: Earthscan Publications, 1997, 86.

27 R.E. Freeman, *Strategic Management: a Stakeholder Approach* (Boston: Pitman Publishing, 1984).

28 Simon Zadek, Peter Pruzan and Richard Evans, *op cit.,* 19–20.

29 Ana Claudia Chaves Teixeira, Evelina Dagnino and Carla Almeida Silva, "La constitución de la sociedad civil en Brasil," in Evelina Dagnino, ed. *Sociedad Civil, Esfera Pública y Democratización en América Latina: Brasil.* Mexico: Fondo de Cultura Economica and Editora Unicamp, 2002, and Paola Cappellin, Gian Mario Giuliani, Regina Morel, and Elina Pessanha, "As organizações empresariais brasileiras e a responsabilidade social," in Ana Maria

Kirschner, Eduardo R. Gomes, and Paola Cappellin, eds. *Empresa, Empresários e Globalização*. Rio de Janeiro: Relume Dumará, 2002. See also, for an earlier work, Fernando H. Cardoso, "Entrepreneurs and the Transition Process: The Brazilian Case," in Guillermo O'Donnell, Philippe C. Schmitter, and Laurnece Whitehead, Eds. *Transitions From Authoritarian Rule: Comparative Perspectives*. Baltimore: The Johns Hopkins University Press, 1986.

30 See the chapter by Turitz and Winder in this volume.

31 Ciro Torres, "Responsabilidade Social das Empresas (RSE) e Balanço Social no Brasil," in César Augusto Tibúrcio Silva and Fátima de Souza Freire, eds. *Balanço Social: teoria e prática*. São Paulo: Editora Atlas, 2001. Ibase was created in 1981 as a federal nonprofit public interest organization with the mission of aiding in the construction of democracy, fighting against inequality, and promoting citizen participation.

32 BS's first antecedent in Brazil comes paradoxically from the military dictatorship, which in the 1970s made it mandatory for businesses to issue an annual report on social activities. *Ibid.*, 17. This idea developed later and matured under the notion of *empresário cidadão* (citizen businessperson) developed by Betinho. See Herbert de Souza, Betinho, "O Empresário Cidadão," in Sonia Joia, ed. *O Empresário e o Espelho da Sociedade*, Rio de Janeiro: Banco Arbi, 1994, and Herbert de Souza, "Empresa Pública e Cidadã," *Folha de São Paulo*, 26 March 1997, 2–2.

33 For a depiction of different national and international landmark initiatives on social responsibility reporting, see Instituto Ethos, *Guia de Elaboração de Relátorio e Balanço Annual de Responsabilidade Social Empresarial, Versão 2001*. Sao Paulo, Junho 2001, 10–11. See also, Ciro Torres, "Um pouco da história do *Balanço Social*," *www.balancosocial.org.br*.

34 Eduardo R. Gomes and Fabricia Corrêa Guimarães, "Empresários, o Brasil em reformas e o corporativismo em transição: um estudo sobre o PNBE—pensamento nacional das bases empresariais," in Ana Maria Kirschner and Eduardo R. Gomes, eds. *Empresa, empresários e sociedade*. Rio de Janeiro: Sette Letras, 1999.

35 In 1989 the Brazilian Association of Toy Manufacturers (Associação Brasileira dos Fabricantes de Brinquedos—Abrinq) created within its structures a unit for the defense of the rights of children, which joined other organizations pressing at the time for the passing of the Bill of Children and Adolescents. It is noteworthy that it was business groups that led the fight for these rights. A 1994 campaign resulted in the creation of a special "Friends of Children" certificate to be awarded to companies that met set requirements. The group stepped up its concerns to broader issues of business citizenship.

36 Valdemar de Oliveira Neto, Superintendent, Instituto Ethos, interview 8/2/01. According to Oliveira Neto there was a generational factor at play: people which had had a part in the active generation of 1968 had come of age, in their 50s, now in leadership positions but maintaining a special social sensibility.

37 *www.ethos.org.br*

38 In this view of Ethos provided by Oliveira Neto one could hardly get closer to Gramsci's notion of the organic intellectual.

39 For instance, Unibanco—the 4th bank in Brazil and whose president is on the board of Ethos—produces social environmental profiles of Brazilian companies for foreign clients.

40 O Globo is a member of the board, and close work is done with Valor, Gazeta Mercantil, and Exame, and CBN radio station that broadcasts relevant news twice daily. All this work is supported by a staff of 5 in Ethos, a substantial number of its small overall staff.

41 In its first edition in April 2002, 156 students submitted applications, from which 12 were selected as finalists, with the help of 56 volunteer referees.

42 Ethos is also helping produce case studies for use at the University of São Paulo and Harvard and other higher learning centers abroad, and helped the School of Marketing in São Paulo develop a curriculum in stakeholder management for its executive MBA.

43 There is a large "quality management" movement well established in Brazil. However, consulting services admit to the pervasiveness of cosmetic concerns by companies that feel the pressure to produce some form of social report. Ramiro E. Prudencio, President and CEO, Burson-Marsteller Brazil, interview, 8/2/01.

44 Public agencies are receptive to CSR public activity and the partnerships that may result. Ruth Cardoso's Comunidade Solidaria was a good example, as are local level interactions with the state. The Câmara Municipal de São Paulo, for instance, awards the Empresa Cidadã seal to companies that report a high quality balanço social. It is noteworthy that there has been almost no work with trade unions, although Ethos claimed to have offered seminars and training programs to trade union leaders.

45 See Instituto Ethos, "Indicadores Ethos de Responsabilidade Social Empresarial: Versão 2001," São Paulo, Junho 2001, 7.

46 For a study of the magnitude of companies' involvement in CSR see Anna Maria T. Medeiros Peliano (coord.), *A Iniciativa Privada e o Espíritu Público*, Brasilia, IPEA (March 2000 for the Southeast; April 2001 for the Northeast; May 2001 for the South).

47 João Sucupira, Ciro Torres, and Claudia Mansur, IBASE, interview 8/7/01.

48 IARSE and the GDF joined efforts in 2003 in promoting the Ethics and Business Social Responsibility National Award for university students submitting essays on the subject.

49 Ben Ross Schneider, *Business Politics and the State in Twentieth-Century Latin America*. Cambridge: Cambridge University Press, 2004, p. 173–4.

50 Javier Martini, Fundación Antorcha, interview, 7/18/01; Mario Roitter, CEDES, interview, 7/18/01.

51 Hector Schamis, "Argentina: Crisis and Democratic Consolidation." *Journal of Democracy* 13, no. 2 (April 2002): 81–94. See also, Steven Levitsky and Maria V. Murillo, Eds. *Argentine Democracy: The Politics of Institutional Weakness*. University Park: Penn State University Press, 2005.

52 See Mario Roitter and María Andrea Campetella, "La razón social de las empresas: Una investigación sobre los vínculos entre empresas y sociedad en Argentina," Documento CEDES 115, Buenos Aires, 1996. I am grateful to Mario Roitter and Gabriel Berger for helping me understand the Argentine landscape in this area.

53 Enrique Peruzzotti, "Emergencia, Desarrollo, Crisis y Reconstrucción de la Sociedad Civil Argentina," in Aldo Panfichi, ed. *Sociedad Civil, Esfera Pública y Democratización en América Latina: Andes y Cono Sur*. México: Fondo de Cultura Económica and Fondo Editorial de la Pontificia Universidad Católica del Perú, 2002.

54 *Indice de Desarrollo de la Sociedad Civil de Argentina: Formosa/Jujuy/Mendoza/Rio Negro/Santa Fe*. Buenos Aires: PNUD-BID, 2000.

55 María Rosa Martini, President, *Foro del Sector Social*, interview, 7/20/01.

56 Silvio Schlosser, Repsol/YPF Foundation, interview, 7/19/01.

57 One of these experiences was the reaction against "Spanish capital and investments" that was blamed for taking Aerolíneas Argentinas out of business. The airline had been Argentina's flagship national air carrier prior to privatization. Another experience concerned Chilean investors in poorly managed public utilities in Buenos Aires that resulted in protracted blackouts.

58 Javier Comesaña, *Fundación La Nación*, interview, 7/19/01.

59 See *www.generacionempresarial.cl* (2001).

60 Javier Cox, president AE, interview 7/5/01.

61 See Delia Boylan, "The 1990 Chilean Tax Reform," *Latin American Research Review* vol. 31 no. 1 1996, and Eduardo Silva, "Organized Business, Neoliberal Economic Restructuring, and Redemocratization in Chile," in Francisco Durand and Eduardo Silva, Eds. *Organized Business, Economic Change, and Democracy in Latin America*. Miami: North-South Center Press, 1998.

62 In the view of Juan Francisco Lecaros, director of the Corporación Simón de Cirene and a board member at AE, business in the 1990s was tremendoulsy empowered by the privatizations of the previous decade. This change resulted in a stronger, talented and organizationally efficient private sector. However, this did not result in radical diminution of poverty ("The fight against poverty is no longer being won"). According to Lecaros, philanthropy must be actively promoted among business so that it may bring its methods, talents

and time closer to the organizations that are in the fight against poverty. Lecaros' organization conducts training workshops in management for social organizations. Over 100 social organizations participated in such workshops during the year 2000. Interview with J.F. Lecaros, and Corporación Simón de Cirene, *Memoria 2000*.

63 Ricardo Ariztía (CPC president), inaugural speech at the 2nd CSR international seminar organized by AE, June 2001. *www.accionempresarial.cl/ponencia_ariztia*. My translation. More dramatic and demanding figures are found in "Los Chilenos Opinan: Responsabilidad Social de las Empresas. Análisis de la Encuesta MORI," PNUD-PROhumana, Santiago, Chile, abril 2002.

64 Two studies of CSR cases are Soledad Teixidó, Reinalina Chavarri, and Andrea Castro, *Responsabilidad Social: 12 Casos Empresariales en Chile*. Santiago: PROhumana Ediciones, 2002, and "Diagnóstico y Estrategia para Promover la Filantropía Ambiental en Chile," Cipma, Ecología y Desarrollo, UACH, July 2000.

65 "PROhumana y PNUD coordinan mesas redondas sobre RSE," *Filantropía y Responsabilidad Social en Chile*, no. 5, March 2001, 14. See also, "Responsabilidad Social Empresarial en Chile," Informe de Mesas de Trabajo, PNUD & PROhumana, Santiago, March-September 2000.

66 According to Eugenio Tironi, head of one of the leading consulting firms in business strategic communication, business has been unable to overcome the "traumas" inherited from a deeply polarized business-labor relationship of three decades ago, significantly harming business's ability to genuinely move forward in the field of social responsibility. Eugenio Tironi, "RSE en Chile: una mirada desde la sociedad," presentation at Acción Empresarial Seminar, 19 June 2003.

67 Former SOFOFA president and advisor to rightist candidate Lavín maintained that wealth concentration "must be corrected because otherwise it generates anger and that could lead to the destruction of the system. . . . The system is efficient but it generates inequality. . . . Corrections must be made soon because the model is not functioning as it should. For instance, the economy grew 6.2% in 2004, but where did that growth go if salaries remain stagnant?" Statements made in a speech at Universidad San Sebastián in Puerto Montt, Chile on May 12, 2005. *La Tercera*, May 13, 2005. My translation.

68 *www.sofofa.cl*, my translation.

69 Rocío Guadarrama Olivera. *Los empresarios norteños en la sociedad y la política del México moderno: Sonora (1929–1988)*. México: Universidad Autónoma Metropolitana, El Colegio de México, el Colegio de Sonora. 2001.

70 Alberto J. Olvera, "Las Tendencias Generales de Desarrollo de la Sociedad Civil en México," in Alberto J. Olvera ed. *Sociedad Civil, Esfera Pública y Democratización en América Latina: México*. México: Fondo de Cultura Económica y Universidad Veracruzana, 2003.

71 See Gerardo Lozano-Fernández, "Mexico: The Business Sense of Cross-Sector Alliances," in James Austin et al., *op cit.*

72 For earlier philanthropic activities see Patricia Greaves, "Empresas y Empresarios: Algunas Tendencias Actuales de la Filantropía Corporativa en México," Trabajo presentado a la 4a. Conferencia ISTR, Mexico, 5–8 July 2000.

73 Juan Felipe Cajiga Calderón, Coordinator for Business Social Responsibility and Research, Cemefi, interview 8/21/01, and *www.cemefi.org* (2005).

74 Coparmex (Confederación Patronal de la Republica Mexicana) is the Employers' Union of Mexico. The Consejo de Coordinación Empresarial (Business Coordination Council) is the peak organization bringing together the chambers of commerce, industry, banking, agriculture, and insurance. Desem (Desarrollo Empresarial Mexicano), promotes entrepreneurial spirit among youth.

75 ALIARSE's website is not in function and information on it could be found only within the CCE's website. Concamin—the Confederation of Industrial Chambers—also joined the alliance. ALIARSE claimed to have collaborated with the Fox administration to help it design a Binational Recognition on Social Responsibility with the U.S.A. It is revealing, however, that the American Chamber of Commerce has played no role in CSR in Mexico, in contrast to other places in Latin America. Amcham in Mexico was, for instance, unaware of the existence of the San Francisco-based BSR in the U.S. Interview with John Brutton, Executive Vice-president of AmCham-Mexico, 8/20/01.

76 F. Cajiga Calderón, interview 8/21/01.

77 The Fundación del Empresariado Chihuahuense (FECHAC) formed in 1990 to face a severe flooding in the region. On the request of business leaders, government passed a special tax that generated resources then administered by the Foundation. It has been reported in a study by Columbia University supported by the Synergos Institute, which makes it a case study of an innovative private-public initiative. See Patricia Greaves, *op cit.*, also for a descriptive study of six cases of work by foundations, and FECHAC's website at *www.online.com.mx/plaza/fechac/.*

78 Jorge Espina Reyes, president Coparmex, interview 8/16/01.

79 Federico Müggenburg, Director, Center for Social and Political Studies, CCE, interview 8/20/01. See also Ricardo Tirado, "Mexico: From the Political Call for Collective Action to a Proposal for Free Market Economic Reform," in Francisco Durand and Eduardo Silva, Eds. *op cit.*, and Benn Ross Schneider, *op cit.* 81–88.

80 See studies conducted by Cemefi and the Instituto Tecnológico y de Estudios Superiores de Monterrey *(ITESM)* and by Zimmat, cited in Greaves, *op cit.*

81 It should be noted, however, that the number of companies reporting on the Ethos indicators are only a fraction of the large number of companies that are Ethos associates.

82 Cited in Denis Sulmont and Enrique Vásquez, Eds., *Modernización empresarial en el Perú*. Lima: Red para el Desarrollo de las Ciencias Sociales en el Perú, 2000). My translation.

83 Evelina Dagnino, "On confluences and contradictions: the troubled encounters of participatory and neo-liberal projects," Paper prepared for delivery at the XXIII Congress of the Latin American Studies Association, Dallas, Texas, March 27–29, 2003.

6
Intersectoral Alliances and the Reduction of Social Exclusion

Rosa Maria Fischer

Ever since the mid-1990s, corporate social action has grown noticeably in Brazil, with alliances created with civil society organizations. The media and other groups promoting the concept of social responsibility have furthered this trend and provided it with visibility, thus strengthening the participation of organized civil society.

Until 1998, the notions of corporate social action and alliances between businesses and civil society organizations were virtually unheard of in Brazil. Companies with social projects rarely advertised these activities or their relationship with Third Sector organizations. Social initiatives were considered relevant only to the internal life of the organizations and to the personal decisions of the company owners, and systemized data on the subject was therefore negligible. Since 1998, however, surveys, academic studies and institutional advertising materials have proliferated, as well as ample media coverage describing the social actions undertaken by organizations working in partnership.

The watershed in 1998 came about when the Center for Social Entrepreneurship and Administration in the Third Sector—CEATS (Centro de Empreendedorismo Social e Administração em Terceiro Setor) conducted the first Brazilian research on cross-sector collaboration for developing social projects. This study formed part of a more comprehensive project[1] undertaken by the Boston-based Institute for Development Research. The study, an analysis of enterprises involving civil society groups and market organizations, was designed to compare cases in India, South Africa and Brazil.

Cases of cross-sector collaboration were mapped and described, thus permitting the identification of corporate social action trends in Brazil and companies' promotion of social action activity through alliances with civil society organizations, government agencies and, occasionally, other private enterprise groups.[2]

The comparative study of the cases in the three countries, prepared by Darcy Ashman[3] of the IDR team, permitted the identification of the common elements among the alliances under investigation:

- Social action efforts were primarily focused on the areas of education, training and social assistance.

- The alliance produced good results for the partners. Civil society organizations benefited from institutional strengthening, management improvement and increased funding. Companies enjoyed the strengthening of their image and the capacity to deal with innovation.

- Managing these cross-sector alliances is not an easy process and does not ensure the success of the social undertaking. Some of the challenges that were pinpointed were:

  - The need for sharing control in decision-making,

  - The need to make different organizational cultures compatible and

  - Adaptation of management tools to make the flow of communication easier and to guarantee consistency in the evaluations.

Despite these inherent difficulties, the cross-sector organizational collaboration model is growing as a strategy for achieving significant results in social undertakings. As Brown says, "I suspect that we may be at an institutional 'culmination point', in which the patterns of the past and the cross-sector distance between civil society and the market organizations can change rapidly to a new pattern of cross-sector collaboration on many different fronts."[4]

The Brazilian political context of the 1990s was one of the determining factors in creating a favorable environment for this collaboration between organizations from different sectors. Brazil's re-democratization was consolidated, thus expanding the social space for the exercise of citizenship and for organized kinds of participation. The 1988 Constitution began to ensure civil rights for all and to strengthen democratic principles of social relations. The proposal for the state's administrative decentralization, despite delays associated with difficulties in implementing tax reforms, opened the door to the emancipation of local communities.

In this context, the Comunidade Solidária (Community of Solidarity) emerged as a channel—semi-official and semi-officious—for efficient dissemination of the partnership concept. Created as a space for generating programs and projects, directed by a council with representatives from all sectors, and led by the charismatic personality of then-First Lady Ruth L. Cardoso, this innovatively designed organization contained within its own name the integrating concept: solidarity—the joining together of different organizations in order to achieve common results in the field of social action.

In 1999, the Comunidade Solidária Council asked CEATS to conduct research to map out corporate social action in order to identify whether companies were stimulating volunteer work by their employees. Besides seeking to understand a situation for which it had no prior information, the study had the pragmatic objective of generating input for the Volunteer Program, one of the innovative activities of the Comunidade Solidária.

This program sought to expand the "volunteering culture" in terms of stimulating people to create or join volunteer centers in which they would develop structures for training and guidance in this kind of work. One of the areas considered fertile for developing these practices was the internal environment of the companies, since it brought together people and resources that could provide support for services by philanthropic, charitable or community groups.

The corporate volunteering concept was not a familiar one in Brazil, and the study made use of the theoretic and empiric framework developed in the United States and Canada, mainly through the works of Kenn Allen and the Points of Light Foundation.[5] This mapping effort resulted in the "Corporate Strategies in Brazil: Social Performance and Volunteering" (*Estratégias de Empresas no Brasil: Atuação Social e Voluntariado*) study. This found that 57% of a representative sample (consisting of 1200 companies from diverse sectors of the economy) were developing actions and projects aimed at reducing or eliminating social problems that were not within the scope of its business mission or of its strategic business objectives. Out of this group of companies dedicated to social performance, 48% also followed practices to stimulate, or at least facilitate, employee involvement with the voluntary rendering of services to a social cause or entity.

This pioneer survey led to many other subsequent studies on corporate social action, but even more significantly, it study identified a trend that concurred with the proposal for cross-sector collaboration—the growing frequency with which companies were seeking to establish partnerships with civil society organizations to carry out their social performance projects.

Throughout the same period, from the late 90s through the beginning of the new century, the media began to systematically publicize these business initiatives. Specialized columns and sections appeared in the most popular newspapers in the economy and business sections. Radio spots and television programs were created for national broadcasting channels. *Exame* magazine, with widespread circulation in business circles, published an insert in 1999, named the Guide to Good Corporate Citizenship, which in subsequent years became a substantial publication in which companies began to compete for space.

On the one hand, "popularization" of corporate social responsibility propositions and of cross-sector alliances designed to make social projects feasible provides an optimistic perspective on the collaboration between organizations. Yet, on the other hand, one must notice the lack of a deeper understanding of these developments.

This chapter seeks to complement the effort to produce systematized knowledge about these alliances and understand their characteristics in the environment of the companies involved, as well as the impact and tendencies created through the performance of these partnerships. In this context, the preliminary results of a CEATS survey presented here acquaint the reader with corporate social performance and the ways to establish partnerships between organizations in different sectors to implement social projects.

The current phase of this project is comprised of preliminary qualitative analyses. This chapter discusses some key issues:

- How and why are corporate efforts in the area of social performance being intensified? How are these initiatives regarded by civil society organizations?

- What are the characteristics of the alliances and partnerships that have been established between organizations in the three sectors (State, Market and Civil Society Organizations) in order to implement social projects? How are these alliances managed? What are the benefits that they bring to each partner?

- What are the effective results of these initiatives on the poverty and social exclusion indicators? Do they contribute to the strengthening of civil society organizations?

Socio-Economic Context

Cross-sector alliances designed to undertake social action for the purpose of combating exclusion must be understood in the context of Brazilian poverty. Although some socio-economic indicators have been modified throughout the last decade of the 20th century, Brazil still presents a scenario of profound distortions that hinder a sustained social development project.

Brazil currently has 170 million inhabitants, with 86.5% living in urban areas. Brazilian government data show that at about 32% of that population lives in conditions of poverty. Of this percentage, it must be pointed out, an estimated 15 million people live in a situation of misery—that is, below what is considered the poverty line.[6] Even more noteworthy is the inequality created by Brazil's income distribution. The poorest half of the population has access to only 13% of the national income while the richest 10% continue controlling approximately 52% of it.

Although it is classified among the ten largest economies in the world, Brazil is positioned among the four countries with the worst income distribution, in accordance with the data of the United Nations Development Program (UNDP) annual report, which evaluates human development in 173 countries.

The 2002 report shows an improvement in some significant indicators in the past two years:

- Brazil went up from the 75th to the 73rd position in the Human Development Index ranking (HDI);
- The life expectancy of the population increased from 67.5 to 67.7 years;
- In the country's richest regions (as in the cities of São Paulo and Rio de Janeiro and in the Federal District), 98% of school-age children are enrolled in schools;
- The *per capita* income went up from US $7,030.00 to US $7,625.00.

Other positive trends point to a scenario in which there is growth in social development such as, for example, the decrease in the infant mortality rate and of child labor in economic activities.[7]

Nevertheless, these positive changes do not minimize the portrait of the structural iniquities that persist in characterizing the economic and social scene of this country. The matter of education, for example, stands out because it is essential to the equation of the trinomial of poverty × work × income. Although the country has elevated its school attendance rate for children between 7 and 14, only 15% of this population actually reaches high school level. The grade repetition rates are going down, but still apply to almost 24% of the school children. Dropout and failures mean that 27% of the available spots are wasted, with an average loss of 2.3 years of study per student.

These disturbing indicators in the area of basic education not only point to a problematic future, in which the continuation of unequal educational opportunities will keep a significant part of the population excluded from the economic processes that could increment Brazilian competitiveness, but also reinforce the evidence of strong regional imbalance. While the richest regions of the country (like São Paulo, Rio de Janeiro and the Federal District) present elementary school coverage of 98% of the school-age population, in the northeastern states—affected by drought and poverty— more than 40% of the children will not have access to education. If, aside from this quantitative data, we analyze the teaching quality in public schools, these regional differences are even more negative. Even in the city of São Paulo, where most wealth is concentrated, the public school system presents mediocre learning results for schools serving poor neighborhoods on the city outskirts, These reflections on Brazil's poverty, especially the nature of exclusion in meeting the educational needs of the population, reinforce the fact that the state does not possess conditions to assume total responsibility and leadership in the processes directed at overcoming these deficiencies. Decentralizing implementation of social policies and increasing the participation of civil society in their formulation are essential means for redirecting them to ensure the inclusion of all social classes in the sphere of public service.

As Augusto Franco, a member of the Solidarity Community Council, points out, the country's recent history and its current development scenario prove that the presence of the State is needed but that it is insufficient to cover the extension and complexity of the social problems. This perception guided the strategy of this entity, created and directed by Ruth Cardoso, who sought to stimulate and create alliances between organizations in the three sectors.

In her words, "in view of the limitations of state action and the nature of the phenomenon of social exclusion, only by extensive social mobilization will it be possible to bring together sufficient resources to confront the problem. It is therefore necessary to seek partners outside the State, that is, within society or, more specifically, in private companies and the third sector. The growing mobilization of private resources for public ends represents a break with the traditional dichotomy between public and private, in which the public was synonymous with the state and the private, with profit. The participation of citizens and the investment of businesses in social action configures the appearance of an unprecedented nongovernmental public sphere and of a nonprofit and nongovernmental Third Sector whose growth contributes to the resizing of the State as well as of the Market." [8]

Seen from this perspective, it may be said that the growth of the so-called Third Sector emerged in Brazil as a positive factor in the strengthening of civil society. Through philanthropic organizations, foundations, business institutes, rights defense organizations and the most varied organizational forms, civil society manifests itself as a dynamic center for social performance.

For the private companies active in the country, social inequality poses a threat for the future of their business. The domestic market, with potential for becoming one of the largest of the world, tends to shrink because large segments of the population have low purchasing power. The labor force with its precarious levels of schooling and professional skills lowers the levels of competitiveness in the productive sectors. Poverty contributes to the increase in indexes of criminality and violence, while diminishing the quality of life for the entire population. The rule of law and democratic stability, achieved with much effort after a long period of dictatorship, are fragile due to the social imbalance that establishes an unfair distribution of citizenship rights.

Businessmen and executives active in Brazil are gradually becoming conscious of the fact that these unfavorable conditions in the country's socio-economic structure place strong restrictions in terms of their business profitability. These obstacles may even be greater with respect to companies seeking to internationalize themselves with significant positioning in the globalized economy.

This growth in corporate awareness of the risks that arise from this scenario of poverty and inequality may be observed through the increased mobilization around social responsibility. In 1990, the Abrinq Foundation was created by a group of Brazilian businessmen committed to the notion of investing in improving the living conditions of children and youth. So it is not surprising that part of this group of people had founded, in the 1980s, the PNBE (National Thinking of the Business Bases) which was a renewal movement in the associative organs of the business class, such as the FIESP—Federation of Industries of the State of São Paulo.

In 1982, AMCHAM—the American Chamber of Commerce—instituted the Eco Award, the first initiative designed to honor companies that developed actions that denoted responsibility for the socio-environmental consequences of their performance. In 1989, GIFE (Group of Institutes, Foundations and Enterprises) appeared, as a formal organization for associating the "social arms" of the companies. The 25 associates in the foundation grew to 67 in 2002, increasing the scope of their performance in marketing, training and support activities for the social undertakings of companies associated with the group.

More explicitly geared to the dissemination of the concept and practices of corporate social responsibility, Ethos Institute (Companies and Social Responsibility) was created in 1998 in the presence of various people connected to Abrinq Foundation and to GIFE. Ethos grew from 11 associated companies to 682 in 2002, representing more than 28% of the Brazilian Gross Domestic Product (GDP).

It is not a mere coincidence that these organizations for corporate mobilization appeared in the city of São Paulo, where 34% of the transformation industry and 12% of the service companies of the entire country are concentrated. Since the beginning of the 20th century, São Paulo has transformed itself into the dynamic heart of the Brazilian capitalist economy.

The Study of Cross-Sector Alliances

The above-described scenario of a troubling socio-economic context associated with the mobilization of organized civil society caused the phenomenon of cross-sector alliances to come to the attention of researchers. In order to analyze the characteristics and the roles of these alliances, use was made of some data and analyses resulting from the "Strategic Cross-Sector Alliances," research done by CEATS in 2001/2002, with the support of the Ford Foundation.[9]

The research was designed in a series of phases that included theoretical studies to consolidate the conceptual background for the area of cross-sector alliances, which tends to be generic and imprecise. Next, a survey was made that outlined the social performance practices of companies with headquarters in Brazil, highlighting the cases in which such actions were accomplished through partnerships of the company with other organizations, thus characterizing the formation of cross-sector alliances. After this phase, qualitative data was sought and analyzed and case studies were prepared, focusing on the theme of the organizational cooperation relationship for making social projects and enterprises feasible.

During the survey phase, an extensive questionnaire was sent out to an intentional sample of 2085 companies acting in Brazil that had a history of social performance, with a representative sample of 385 returned and valid questionnaires. Of this sample, 85% handled their social projects and programs through cross-sector alliances. A sub-sample of 60 companies participated in the following phase, in which qualitative data was sought and analyzed about the forming and maintaining of alliances. In this sub-sample, 41 organizations allied to these companies were identified, of which 73% were from the Third Sector, 20% were government agencies and 7% were other companies. In the subsequent phase, the characteristics of these alliances, their implementation and their accomplishments became the object of thorough analysis, generating content for the structuring and discussion workshops, in which the main topics were questions such as:

- What are the difficulties that need to be overcome to ensure the longevity of a partnership?
- How can the power of decision and command be balanced between partners from different sectoral backgrounds?
- Are the objectives and expectations that lead to the setting up of an alliance executable?
- How can the results of social action implemented by these alliances be evaluated?
- Do these results have a social impact?
- How can these processes of collaboration between organizations be managed and monitored?

This methodological design is based on research-action, a kind of social research with an empirical basis, conceived and done in strict association with an action, or with the solving of a collective problem. Thus, researchers and representative participants in the situation or problem are involved in a cooperative and participatory manner. This method focuses on solving real problems and improving the practices under study; the investigative activities are simultaneous with the structuring of the tools and procedures and can thus generate didactic-pedagogic content for teaching and dissemination activities.

The Matter of Conceptual Inconsistency

Probably because it acquired such great and rapid notoriety, the matter of corporate social action has been the object of a diverse and controversial combination of ambiguous and inconclusive definitions, both in broadcast media and publications and in the more specialized literature.

The terms Social Marketing, Corporate Citizenship, Social Responsibility and Corporate Responsibility are used indiscriminately. Social action and private social investment are more modern nomenclatures that try to be distinguished from corporate philanthropy, a concept which, in turn, is associated with notions of charity and protective assistance that are considered obsolete and inadequate.

Some initiatives seek to organize the field of the ideas and practices of social enterprise. The IBASE—Brazilian Institute of Social and Economic Analyses—an NGO left over from popular social movements, for example, suggests the use of social balance as an instrument for managing the social activity of organizations. It offers a model constituted by an instruction manual that can be used by the company to commence its social initiatives. The GIFE (Group of Institutes, Foundations and Enterprises) supports its members with multiple advisory services, information, trainee instruction and juridical/legal assistance, with the objective of stimulating companies to develop their social action with the same economic and administrative efficiency rationale with which they run their business.

Some authors have proposed definitions (Fischer, 99; Peliano, 99), generally within the framework of specific studies. The term most used is that of "Social Responsibility," which includes the social functions that traditionally are associated with the company in the modern capitalist system, with emphasis on the most frequent ones—job creation, capital payment, the payment of taxes to the State, labor costs and specific taxes, as well as adherence to the standards and legislation that regulate the country's economy.

Social changes brought about the broadening of the significance of this concept at various moments in recent history. For example, the elevation of the level of schooling of the population and its easier access to information stimulated the awareness of consumer rights, obliging the companies to become responsible for the quality of their products and to improve their relationship with the market. The dissemination of measures to preserve the environment and nonrenewable natural resources incorporated to its sphere of responsibility the need to adopt practices that would avoid environmental damages.

Thus, a progressive growth in the extent of the actions that represent corporate social functions can be observed, even though analysts and leaders that have a contrary opinion are constantly contesting this process. Their arguments point out the division of duties and responsibilities among the state, civil society and the market, demarcating the private economy sector with exclusive attributes of production and distribution of property, wealth and profit.

The economic globalization scenario is fanning this argument. In the light of the ache of social exclusion and the imbalance of income distribution, reinforced by the distance between the countries that have a developed economy and the numerous miserable outskirts, the conclusion is that the responsibility for human development should be distributed among all social actors whether they be in government or business organizations or a civil society participant.

Social Responsibility is taken as a broad concept in which the company, while maintaining its business commitments, creates methods, plans and ethical incentives so that, internally and externally, it can collaborate with society's expectations for balance and justice, going beyond the roles that have been established by law and its own interests that are an integral part of its business.

The Survey

In order to survey the data that describes corporate social performance, the project used an intentional sample of 2085 companies. This sample was extracted from the records of corporate associations that advertise Social Responsibility commitments and from the lists of companies that participated, in the past five years, in various competitions that award social projects.

The companies were initially approached by telephone in order to check the identification data. This preliminary survey was necessary because, despite the spread of news about corporate social action, there are no standards for procedures that permit locating the organizational areas and the professionals in each company that were responsible for running these projects and that were acquainted with the data necessary for the mapping proposed by this survey. This feature was one of the indications that, in most of the cases, social performance is still a new phenomenon that has not been totally incorporated into management practices and, frequently, is little known within the framework of the company itself.

Questionnaires were then sent out, via electronic or regular mail, to the group of companies that had been identified. Four hundred twenty-three of these returned them, which was more than 20% of the initial sample. This was deemed to be in line with the objectives of the survey, especially upon consideration of the difficulty experienced in obtaining the primary data about the topic of corporate social performance.[10] Since the survey was based on the detailing of the social performance practices developed by the respondent companies, the existence of such practices was the main criteria used to validate the questionnaires received, as well as their having been filled in correctly. The result was a final sample of 385 participating companies.

This final sample presented the following characteristics:

- Gross sales—37% of the companies stated that this was less than 50 million reals per year, 31% between 50 and 500 million and 23% over 500 million reals.

- Number of employees—only 22% of the companies had less than 100, while 34% had between 100 and 1000 employees and 35% employed more than 1000 people.

- Of the companies that responded, 69% had mostly national capital, while those that had foreign capital made up 23% and the state ones 5% of the sample group.

- As for the economic sectors, the respondent companies were mostly industries (51%), followed by the companies that provide services (32%) and ones in commerce (10%). The remaining sectors made up 4%. These were agriculture/extractive and construction industries.

- Of these companies, 22% practiced their social activities through a specific entity—a foundation or a corporate institution.

Social Performance Characteristics

Although there is much heterogeneity in the social performance of these companies, it is possible to highlight various results of the survey that allow for some generalization:

- More than a fad propagated by the media, corporate performance is being intensified in activities related to support of social programs and to the development of projects directed at a cause. These practices seem more and more integrated to the set of corporate strategies that govern the business, and thus are no longer activities of secondary importance to the top-level administration.

- Although it is starting to position itself in the sphere of strategic decisions, corporate social performance is still quite disorganized. The company finds it hard to choose the areas in which it will perform and to use its organizational competencies so as to obtain greater efficiency and efficacy in the social actions that it undertakes.

- Reiterating the results of previous research, as observed in Figures 1 and 2 below, the preferred area in which the companies promote these projects and programs is that of education. The target population that receives most attention consists of children and adolescents. In contrast, ethnic minorities, prisoners, the unemployed and the chemically dependent are groups rarely contemplated by corporate action.

Figure 1. Social Performance Areas

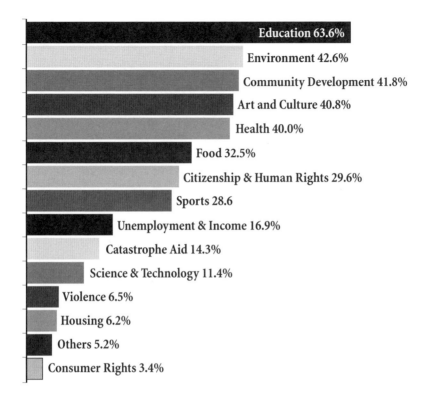

- Corporate action is still preponderant in its philanthropic forms such as donations, sponsorships, and helping with campaigns to support institutions or specific programs. Figure 3 allows the identification of more innovative trends in corporate social action: 49% of the companies promote some kind of volunteering, a practice which has been much stimulated since the UN promotion of the International Year of the Volunteer in 2001. 39% of the companies developed direct projects. More rare are the examples of companies that dedicate themselves to cause-related marketing, probably because this is a scarcely known practice in the country.
- Multinational companies are encouraged through global corporate policies to perform actions within their communities and with the civil society organizations in the regions in which they

Figure 2. Target Groups of Social Performance

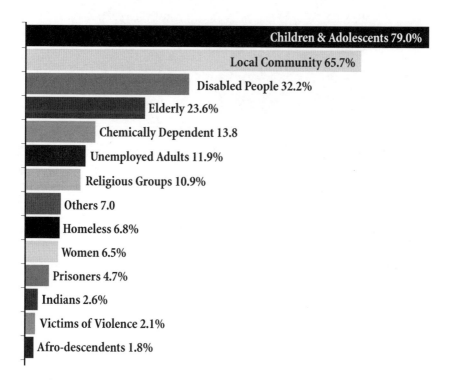

Children & Adolescents 79.0%
Local Community 65.7%
Disabled People 32.2%
Elderly 23.6%
Chemically Dependent 13.8
Unemployed Adults 11.9%
Religious Groups 10.9%
Others 7.0
Homeless 6.8%
Women 6.5%
Prisoners 4.7%
Indians 2.6%
Victims of Violence 2.1%
Afro-descendents 1.8%

Figure 3. Social Performance Practices

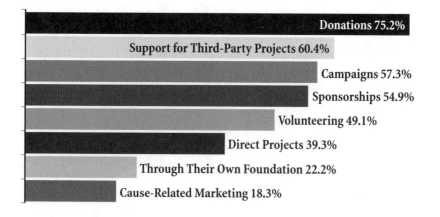

Donations 75.2%
Support for Third-Party Projects 60.4%
Campaigns 57.3%
Sponsorships 54.9%
Volunteering 49.1%
Direct Projects 39.3%
Through Their Own Foundation 22.2%
Cause-Related Marketing 18.3%

are located. A deeper analysis of these initiatives indicates that, generally, they face some problems. For example, a global social action strategy may not meet the specific needs of a local community or it might even create conflicts with the regional cultural standards.

- It is not possible to verify a cause-and-effect relationship between globalization and the greater presence of foreign capital in the Brazilian economy and the volume of funds invested in social initiatives by these companies. What may be inferred is that the growth in corporate social action during the past five years, in Brazil, may be linked to the country's presence in the world economic system and to the new standards of corporate competitiveness stemming from globalization. Many demands have emerged from this marketplace positioning, such as transparency in policies, management practices and procedures and the need to be on a par with "global standard" companies.

Characteristics of Partnerships and Cross-Sector Alliances

Partnerships and alliances are defined, in this study, as all forms of joint collaboration or work that the company maintains with other organizations in civil society and in the State in order to achieve its social performance practices. The term "partnership" acquired great popularity, mainly because of the success of the Solidarity Community proposals that have been disseminating the concept and stimulating the approximation of businessmen and community leaders as they seek solutions for local social problems.

The "strategic alliance" concept, coined by James Austin (Austin, 2001), is still quite innovative for the scenario of relations in organizational cooperation in Brazil. This term is based on the tri-sector theory, which classifies existing organizations as belonging to the first sector when they are public organs connected with governmental administrative structure. The second sector includes all kinds of organizations dedicated to producing goods and services for the market while the third sector, to which civil society organizations belong, may be characterized by public aims using private resources.

The cross-sector alliances are, in this context, the collaborative relationship established between two or more organizations, each of which is inserted in one of the three sectors. These alliances are constituted in order to prepare and implement projects and programs that aim at benefiting a community, eradicate or reduce some social problem, meet the needs of underprivileged groups or promote or defend a cause in the public interest. By proposing the strategic alliance concept, Austin seeks to highlight the partnership relations that acquire characteristics of deeper integration between the allied organizations. In a similar fashion to the business world (where companies created productive chains between themselves and their suppliers, in order to strengthen their productive capacity and their market position), the social development initiatives also sought organizational forms that would increase efficiency and ensure the efficacy of their actions.

This "principle of organizational collaboration" has shown itself to be more complex when applied to the field of social responsibility, because the organizations that should form alliances are very different from one another. They belong to diverse sectors, have different natures stemming from their origins, and are positioned at different distances with respect to the social development objective that motivated the partnership.

In the study conducted, several of the companies with a more consolidated social performance as well as some civil society organizations that were more accustomed to the cross-sector relationship were observed to be developing an interest in the creation of more structured and integrated forms of partnership. Yet, this is such a recent and immature trend that it is hardly noticeable in the survey results, except by some indications from the comprehensive interviews and the case studies that are being conducted by the project.

The survey underscores the plurality of existent collaboration forms because, for many companies, the partnership concept can vary from a single relationship (through one donation to support a certain entity) up through the joint development of projects that are common to the various organizations involved. By analyzing the collected data, an attempt was made to categorize and evaluate the various kinds of cross-sector collaboration:

- 15% of the respondent companies do not have any kind of alliance.
- Another 15% declare that they maintain collaboration in all the social practices developed.
- 37% are in alliances so as to accomplish the majority of their social projects.
- 33% maintain their social performance with very little setting up of partnerships.

Figure 4. Tri-Sectoral Model – Partnership distribution by sector

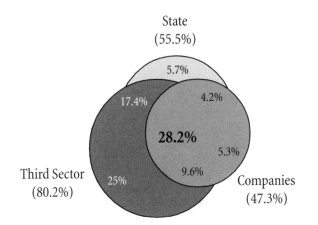

Figure 4 above presents the sectors with which the companies that had responded to the survey (which said that they used alliances as a means to accomplish their social performance practices) established their partnerships. Each circle represents a sector, with the internal numbers representing the percentage of existing partnerships among the respondent companies and the organizations from each sector. The numbers in the intersections are the percentage of partnerships of companies with more than one sector. The first conclusion is that the majority of these companies have alliances with Third Sector organizations, showing up in the sample at a rate of 80.2%, while 55.5% of them declared partnerships with State organs and 47.3% with other market enterprises.

Nevertheless, as the percentages themselves indicate, most of the time these alliances were not made exclusively with organizations in only one sector, since:

- 17.4% of the companies establish alliances with Third Sector and State organizations, simultaneously;
- 4.2% establish alliances with State organizations and other market companies;
- 9.6% establish alliances with Third Sector organizations and with other market companies;
- 28.2% of the companies establish alliances with organizations in the three sectors, taking up the central space of the figure, in which

the relationships of more complex alliances take place, but which are also those with greater potential to achieve their objectives.

These percentages indicate the intensity of the cooperation between the sectors that is being verified in Brazil so as to make it possible for the companies to adopt social performance practices.

It may be observed that 47.3% of the companies surveyed made alliances with organizations within the private sector itself. This result is probably due to the search for competencies in the performance area, which means that, when companies at first decide to initiate their social action, they seek government or nongovernmental organizations that already have know-how in social management.

Furthermore, since companies have been dealing with social performance as a differentiating factor in competitive environments, this is often considered to be an exclusive differential and they do not demonstrate the capacity to accept other companies as their partners. This is a factor that has been frequently cited as a complicating aspect in the making and maintaining of cross-sector alliances. Upon incorporating certain standards typical of business competition, some companies limit the possibilities of growth and consolidation of partnership networks. Many times, this demand for exclusivity causes Third Sector organizations to avoid partnership with the company or, when it does form one, a conflicting relationship results, in which the entity feels that its autonomy has been reduced.

Another side of this scenario, however, has been the trend to increase the synergy of the collaborative alliance between companies that constitute a productive chain. In this case, the familiarity already established through the business connection facilitates the creation of the partnership for social efforts and neutralizes the problems that would come with competition. It has been common for suppliers and service providers to ally themselves with the companies that are their clients in order to establish a joint social project.

It is of interest to observe that the percentage of alliances of the respondent companies with organizations in the three sectors is higher than the percentage of alliances with only one of the sectors. This could mean that the involvement of the company with cross-sector alliances causes it to increase its awareness of social problems and its desire to participate, with other persons and organizations, in the search for solutions.

When asked to identify the roles played by their partners, 75.4% of the respondent companies referred to the donation of non-financial resources, and 63.1% to the donation of financial resources. 63.4% indicated incentives to employee participation, which were generally encouraged to take part in corporate volunteering programs.

Roles that demonstrate a more integrated collaboration, which is what would be closest to the cross-sector strategic alliance model, appear in smaller, although significant, percentages: 54.5% of those that use partnerships declare that they monitor and evaluate the results, while 50.8% are discussing and defining guidelines with their partners.

Other important indicators that result from this analysis are:

- The top echelon of the company accompanies the organization of the partnership, in detail, in 74% of the companies surveyed that work with cross-sector alliances.

- 71% of the partnerships between companies and organizations from other sectors are developed with various joint activities, starting from the planning through the control of the actions undertaken.

- 82% of the companies that use cross-sector alliances state that they maintain relatively frequent relations with the partner organizations.

As may be observed in Figure 5 below, the potential for better quality in social action is the main motive offered by the companies surveyed for forming the alliances: 73.8% believe that this kind of performance results in gains in efficiency. Allied to this factor, the recognition that the partner organizations possess better know-how in the area of the social problem appears as the second reason pointed to by the participating companies, representing 64% of the cases.

Upon analyzing the motives presented by the companies for participating in alliances, and crossing these with the origin of the predominant capital, one perceives that, for foreign capital companies, efficiency and know-how are much emphasized (being listed by more than 70%), while the visibility item was below 19%. This fact might be justified by the work culture of this kind of company that values very clear procedures and focuses within its business, thus transferring this kind of thinking also to its social performance. The little interest that these companies have in developing specific competencies for their social performance confirms this observation, since it indicates that they prefer that these competencies be among the attributes of their partners.

On the other hand, state-owned companies are characterized by a lesser valuing of the know-how of the partner organization, when compared to

Figure 5. Reasons for Performance Through Alliances

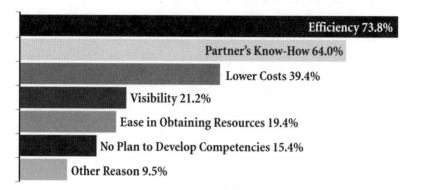

Efficiency 73.8%

Partner's Know-How 64.0%

Lower Costs 39.4%

Visibility 21.2%

Ease in Obtaining Resources 19.4%

No Plan to Develop Competencies 15.4%

Other Reason 9.5%

others, considering the cost distribution as the most important reason for sharing their social performance. This might be explained by the greater familiarity that these organizations have with the social questions, as well as with the lack of resources that state-owned companies face, reducing their financial capability for social performance. Another factor that proves this point of view is the extremely high amount of responses coming from these companies, in comparison to others, for the item "greater ease in obtaining additional resources," which demonstrates that, for the state-owned companies, the alliances are valuable ways for promoting institutional involvement.

Of the total number of 385 companies that responded to the survey, 15% said that they preferred to work without setting up alliances. Figure 7 below presents the main motives declared both by the companies that adopted this option as well as by those that work through alliances.

"Control of resources" was considered to be the main reason for the three groups of companies preferring not to work through alliances, which denotes a certain resistance to sharing resources, the lack of effective management tools for doing this and, most likely, distrust in connection to the partner's control capacity. Nevertheless, these groups present different views as to the other reasons given. While the companies that did not use these alliances believe that their social performance would be more efficient if handled individually, the others, who are accustomed to using alliances, also do some projects individually in order to develop specific competencies for this activity, especially those that mostly act without alliances. This investment in the development of internal competencies may point to two nearly opposite points of view, that will need more data to be explored: this trend may be related to the search for more effective types of integration

Figure 6. Per Predominant Capital – Reasons for Performing Through Alliances

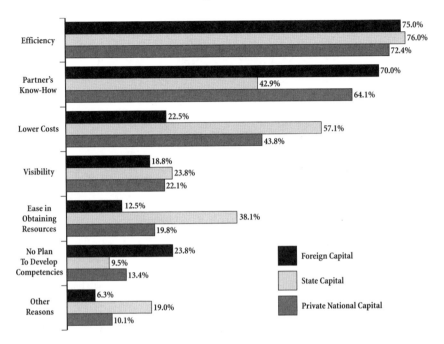

with the social problems, which somehow start to be incorporated in the company's day-by-day activities or it may represent a concern with respect to the administrative capacities of the partner organizations.

When grouped according to the origin of the predominant capital, all companies also consider "better control of resources" as the main reason for not working through alliances, especially the state-owned companies. There were, however, several variations within the other items. The companies with foreign capital and private national capital considered the development of internal competencies to be the second most important reason. On the other hand, the state-owned companies considered "greater efficiency" to be the second most important reason.

It is important to observe that the "greater efficiency" reason is used to explain both the need for establishing alliances as well as for avoiding them. Even though this seems contradictory at a first glance, it may be related to the companies' previous experiences with respect to social performance. Those that enjoyed successful partnerships and experienced synergy with their partners, consider it to be more efficient to work in this manner while those that did not have any experience with alliances, or that

Figure 7. By Kind of Social Performance – Reasons for Not Working Through Alliances

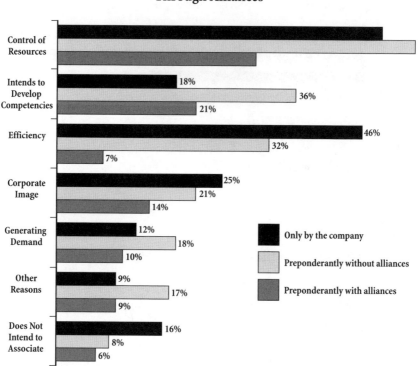

found them to be disappointing, tend to believe that working in an isolated fashion would be more efficient.

These survey results, and the qualitative analyses that are being made, allow for the identification of new social actors—the companies, the company owners, the executives and the employees—that are becoming incorporated into the social development scenario. It seems clear that reducing social exclusion and finding the means to obtain sustainable development are no longer deemed to be the exclusive responsibility of the State. Neither should this be restricted to charitable entities, non-governmental organizations or social movements.

Nevertheless, the data only shows the existence of this trend, and is still very restricted in ensuring that the corporate social performance initiatives are having an effective impact on structural problems such as the inequalities in income distribution or the educational discrepancies cited in this chapter.

Figure 8. Per Predominant Capital – Reasons for Not Performing Through Alliances

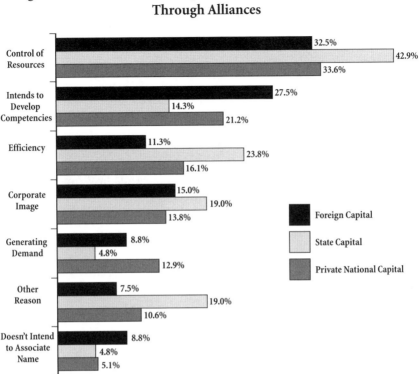

Similarly, the survey allows for the identification of that social mobilization that has made possible the forming of organizational alliances with the objective of promoting social action. These partnerships seem to have a strong potential for becoming long-lasting and more integrated and thus ensuring, on the one hand, the continuity of programs and projects. On the other hand, they contribute to the strengthening of civil society organizations so that these become more well-known, more visible and, often, more capacitated due to the experience of working in collaboration. The results of this survey, however, do not demonstrate whether the cross-sector alliances are the organizational structure that best guarantees efficiency to the projects focused on reducing poverty.

It was, evidently, not within the scope of this work to arrive at highly generalized conclusions but, rather, to point out the trends and the possibilities that they suggest for social undertakings and for the exercise of corporate responsibility.

Considerations

When taken to the workshops, promoted by the study, with the social actors of the alliances surveyed, the data, the analyses and the questioning resulting from the research made possible the advancement of the considerations on this topic.

It may be observed that, even considering the complexity of building and managing cross-sector alliances, they are seen as a fertile and innovative path to social performance, not only for companies but also for individuals and organizations in general.

Among the greatest management difficulties, the following stand out:

- The power imbalance between the allied organizations, either because the companies control financial resources and management competency or because the Third Sector organizations exclusively control the know-how and the access to the populations being assisted.

- Alliances with public administrative agencies are turned down, mainly by private companies, because of bureaucratic impediments, slow decision-making processes and the lack of the administrative continuity that characterizes the First Sector.

- The absence of planning and of mutual awareness of the expectations, in addition to the previous lack of definition of the anticipated results, contributes to the failure of the alliances or transforms them into an ineffective partnership that is maintained because of institutional interests.

- The process of making diverse organizational cultures compatible and the lack of adequate management technologies appropriate to these innovative organizational structures constitute great challenges to their development.

- Among the priority needs for improving the functioning of cross-sector strategic alliances, evaluation and monitoring systems and indicators must be stressed. Their nonexistence makes alliance planning and forming difficult, especially in that which concerns aligning the partners' expectations, assessing the results of the actions undertaken and evaluating the social impact resulting from the alliance performance.

From these debates, the participating social actors obtained guidelines for perfecting their competencies to form and manage cross-sector alliances. They also offered significant contributions so that CEATS could prepare instructional materials and propose management tools to be used by the organizations interested in developing collaborative social alliances.

Out of the experience resulting from this study, some considerations should be stressed with respect to the key questions that directed the research. Social performance management practices have been growing in the country during the past five years, stimulated by public visibility and by the actions of entities that disseminate the ideals of Social Responsibility. Companies that have already developed actions of this nature have increased their performance and gone on to advertise it or demonstrate their importance even more. Companies that did not adopt systematic social performance practices are starting to seek information and technical orientation so as to incorporate them in their management model.

Partnerships do not constitute an exclusive manner, but they are one of the most frequent ways in which companies perform their social actions. There is a noticeable trend to seek this kind of arrangement or to consider that this way of working might be more efficient and reduce the costs of social performance. A significant portion of the companies, however, prefers to stick to the autonomy and exclusivity of their actions. Issues such as lack of trust, shortage of data and frustrating experiences permeate this trend to reject working in collaboration.

The civil society organizations showed themselves to be quite ambivalent about the trend of these companies taking interest in acting toward the solution of social problems. Those that have a positive perception of the partnerships in which they participate emphasize the benefits—perfecting management capacity, expanding the network, image strengthening and increased access to resources. Those that avoid making alliances, or those that have had frustrating experiences, highlight the incompatibility of the logic and the rhythms of the work, the lack of knowledge or sensitivity of the company about the specific nature of the social problems, the arrogant and imposing, or the paternalistic and condescending attitude with which the company relates to the entity, the lack of clarity as to the intentions of the company and the values which guide its actions, and the uncertainty as to the duration of the relationship.

It may be said that, throughout the duration of the partnerships, the civil society organizations tend to oscillate between these two positions, which indicates that they depend on business initiatives and decisions. Therefore, a step forward on the path to perfecting cross-sector alliances would be to stimulate the proactive stance of the civil society organizations and to influence companies in the direction of maintaining a more balanced relationship in that which concerns the decisions that are vital to the destiny of the alliances.

The study also demonstrates that the field is wide open for administrative, technical and management improvements so as to make cross-sector strategic alliances effectively possible. From the way in which they are currently created and run, one may deduce, but not prove, that they accomplish effective results in reducing the poverty indicators and social exclusion.

According to this evaluation, they currently constitute more a proposed model than a consecrated methodology. They can also not be thought of as a single solution but rather as a way of working that should be associated to other measures, if that which is intended is to generate an effective social impact.

From this study, it is possible to infer that the cross-sector alliances work toward institutional strengthening, promote responsible citizenship concepts and make specific social projects and programs possible. If a strategic component should be adopted, they might set out to influence public policies by creating, with their actions, facts and results that would redirect the strategies and guidelines of the State. In this sense, these might become valuable guides in the processes for structural changes in the socio-economic context of the country, effectively contributing to its social transformation.

Notes

1 "Non-Governmental Organizations and the Marketization of Development" was a study program made by the IDR with the support of the Ford Foundation, coordinated by Prof. L. David Brown of the Hauser Center for Non-Profit Organizations.

2 Some of the studies described in this project have been analyzed in the book *The Challenge of Collaboration—Social Responsibility Practices between Companies and the Third Sector* (*O Desafio da Colaboração—Práticas de Responsabilidade Social entre Empresas e Terceiro Setor*) by Rosa Maria Fischer, Editora Gente, São Paulo, 2002.

3 Ashman, Darcy. "Towards a Model of Empowered Civil Society Collaboration with Business," IDR, 2000.

4 Brown, L. D. Preface of the book, *The Challenge of Collaboration—Social Responsibility Practices between Companies and the Third Sector* (*O Desafio da Colaboração—Práticas de Responsabilidade Social entre Empresas e Terceiro Setor*) by Rosa Maria Fischer.

5 Kenn Allen is an international specialist in strategies for stimulating business volunteering. He was the President of the International Association for Volunteer Effort (IAVE) and Vice-President of the Points of Light Foundation, a North American network of volunteer centers.

6 The survey indicates that about 50 million people live on a monthly income of less than 30 American dollars and that, of these, around 15 million live with much less than a dollar per day. This information can be found, for example, in the Map of the End of Hunger in Brazil (*Mapa do Fim da Fome no Brasil*) Survey, (Getulio Vargas Foundation—FGV, 2001), based on the National Household Survey (*PNAD*) and on the Human Development Index (HDI) of the United Nations Development Program (UNDP).

7 Between 1991 and 2000, the infant mortality rate went down from 47.8 to 29.6 per thousand live births. From 1995 to 1999, a decrease of 25% was registered for child labor (data source: Demographic Census of the Brazilian Institute of Geography and Statistics—IBGE).

8 Cardoso, Ruth. "Corporate Citizenship: The Challenge of Responsibility" (*Cidadania Empresarial: O Desafio da Responsabilidade*), Update Brochure Brazil-USA, special supplement, AMCHAM, São Paulo, no. 8, p. 117, August 2000

9 This survey was part of the "Organizational Citizenship and the Third Sector" program that was created by the CEATS/FIA/USP with the support of the Ford Foundation in order to generate studies, publications, teaching and capacitating activities as well as instructional materials focused on social management and enterprise.

10 Although the subject offers positive visibility to the companies, the majority of these do not have systematized data on their social performance or prefer not to provide them in a precise fashion.

References

Anheier, H.K.; Salamon, L.M. *The Nonprofit Sector in the Development World: a Comparative Analysis*, New York: Manchester University Press, 1998.

Ashman, D. *Towards a Model of Empowered Civil Society Collaboration with Business*, [s.l.]: IDR, 2000.

Austin, J. E. *Parcerias—Fundamentos e Benefícios para o Terceiro Setor*, São Paulo: Editora Futura, 2001.

Borger, F. G. *Responsabilidade social: efeitos da atuação social na dinâmica empresarial*, Tese (Doutorado em Administração)—Departamento de Administração da Faculdade de Economia e Administração e Contabilidade. São Paulo: Universidade de São Paulo, 2001.

Brown, L. D. Prefácio. In: Fischer, R.M. *O Desafio da Colaboração—Práticas de Responsabilidade Social entre Empresas e Terceiro Setor*, Editora Gente, São Paulo, 2002.

Cardoso, R. Cidadania Empresarial: O Desafio da Responsabilidade. *Revista Update*. São Paulo: Câmara Americana de Comércio (AMCHAM), suplemento especial no. 8, ago. 2000.

Carroll, A. *A Three-Dimensional Conceptual Model of Corporate Performance*, Academy of Management Review, [S.I], no. 4, 1979.

Carroll, A. Corporate Social Responsibility, Business and Society, [S.I], vol. 28, no. 3, set. 1999

Dwight, F.; Dennis, R. *Corporate Philanthropy at the Crossroads*, Bloomington: Indiana University Press, 1996.

FGV. Fundação Getúlio Vargas, *Mapa do Fim da Fome no Brasil*. Estudo—Rio de Janeiro: Fundação Getúlio Vargas, 2001.

Fischer, R.M. *O Desafio da Colaboração—Práticas de Responsabilidade Social entre Empresas e Terceiro Setor*, São Paulo: Editora Gente, 2002.

Fischer, R.M. *Alianças Estratégicas Intersetoriais, do Programa Cidadania Organizacional e Terceiro Setor*, Relatório de Pesquisa—CEATS/FIA/USP/Fundação Ford, São Paulo: [s.n.], 2002.

Fischer, R.M. A Responsabilidade da Cidadania Organizacional. In: Fleury, M. T. L (Org.) *As Pessoas na Organização*, São Paulo: Editora Gente, 2002.

Fischer, R.M.; Falconer, A. Desafios da Parceria Governo e Terceiro Setor, *Revista de Administração*. São Paulo: FEA/USP, vol. 33, no. 1, p. 12–19, 1998.

Fisher, J. *Non-Governments: NGOs and the Political Development of the Third World*, West Hartford: Kumarian Press, 1998.

Fisher, J. *The Road from Rio: Sustainable Development and the Non-Governmental Movement in the Third World*, London: Prager Publishers, 1993.

Kanter, R.M. From Spare Change to Real Change—The Social Sector as Beta Site for Business Innovation. *Harvard Business Review*, Boston: Harvard Business School Publishing Corp., vol. 77, no. 3, p. 122–133, mai/jun 1999.

Neto, F.P.M.; Froe, C. *Gestão da Responsabilidade Social Corporativa: O Caso Brasileiro*, [s.l.]: Qualitymark, 2001.

Os Novos Desafios da Responsabilidade Social Empresarial. São Paulo: Instituto Ethos, julho 2001 (Série Instituto Ethos Reflexão ano 2, no. 5).

7

Private Contributions to the Public Sphere: Corporate Foundations in Colombia

Cristina Rojas and Gustavo Morales

Private corporations, nonprofit organizations and families play significant roles in the provision of social services. International institutions such as the World Bank and United Nations consider corporate social responsibility as part of their strategies to solve global social problems.[1] Despite the role that corporations play in the provision of social services, most specialized literature on social welfare focuses only on the state. The debate on private involvement in public matters is far from being settled.

This chapter examines the capacity of corporate foundations to make a positive impact on improving social welfare, arguing that this capacity depends on the creation of public spaces of democratic deliberation from which citizens can demand their social rights. The need to create public spaces for democratic deliberation makes the study of private contributions imperative, since civic participation leads to the advancement of social causes. The public sphere is a form of solidarity, and it is from this sphere that public policy is steered (Calhoun 2002, 287). The public sphere—as opposed to the private—must serve as a criterion to assess the potential for social change, as detailed in the first part of this chapter. The chapter then takes a look at the application of this concept to Colombia's corporate foundations, where their involvement in social issues has been widespread for a long time. The high rates of exclusion from social services, rampant inequality and violence in Colombia make the call for public involvement a pressing task. Colombian corporate foundations have not isolated themselves from this process of civic involvement, as reflected in their participation in peace initiatives, social reform programs and monitoring of state and political institutions. Private actors are thus contributing to the formation of a public sphere of civic involvement. However, the risk exists that this involvement could become privatized as illustrated through the analysis of different modes of private intervention in social issues.

The Public Sphere, Democracy and the Social Question

Social concerns cannot be defined by clear public or private boundaries. The "social" hovers strategically between the political and the economic and between the public and the private sectors. This location allows "the social" to intertwine and connect private and public logics in different ways, transforming their boundaries in this process.

The ability of the social to move between the public and private sectors helps us in turn to understand the particularistic character of Latin American democracies. One problem, as Guillermo O'Donnell points out, is the privatization of social concerns manifested in practices like clientelism (1996, 40). A second related problem is the presence of "low-intensity citizenship" referring to both the large percentage of the population without basic social rights and protections and to the absence of basic civic rights, especially lack of legal protection (O'Donnell 2001, p. 601). Without political and civil rights "policies against poverty and inequality will continue being captured, and distorted, by ingrained practices of clientelism and paternalism" (p. 608). International organizations such as ECLAC (CEPAL 2000, 17) have identified strengthening citizenship—the effective participation of social actors—as key to improvement of social conditions. Citizens are not just recipients of social services, but participants in collective life by exerting control over governments and steering proposals for social change.

This chapter uses Hannah Arendt's (1998) double meaning of the concept "public." One refers to transparency: "everything that appears in public can be seen and heard by everybody and has the widest possible publicity" (57–58). The other refers to the public sphere as a scenario for world making (Warner, 59). She sees this process as a construction of a world "common to all of us and distinguished from our privately owned place on it." For Arendt, a common world does not mean a world in which people are one. Instead, she advocates a pluralistic concept of the public sphere relying "on the simultaneous presence of multiple perspectives and aspects in which the common world presents itself and for which no common measurement or denominator can ever be devised" (1998, 57).

The public character of social practices does not derive from the place where it is located, i.e., if they belong to public or private institutions. The public is a mode of intervention characterized by its political role of mediation, not only between citizens and the state but also within society. The public is a space "in-between" that both separates and unites individuals.

According to Arendt "the world, like every in-between, relates and separates men at the same time" (1998, 52). She claims that individuals are mobilized around a shared world while maintaining their plurality. Anything that suppresses the mobilization around a shared interest, in-between, suppresses the public. For example, charity suppresses mediation between people. Thus, charity cannot create a public realm "of its own" because its very nature is of a non-political, non-public character. The suppression of distance also applies to such practices as clientelism or nepotism. These practices involve exchanging favors and are of a private rather than public nature.

This pluralistic vision of the public also brings into question practices such as populism and corporatism. Organic visions of society based on biological and holistic representations suppress politics because they "see a multitude—the factual plurality of a nation or a people or society—in the image of one supernatural body driven by one superhuman, irresistible 'general will'" (1963, 54). The idea of a unified and indivisible will stifles exchange of opinions and eventual agreements among them (71). Contributions to the public sphere must come about through diversity of opinions and debate. This vision also questions communitarian or paternalistic practices where members are represented as a family; in Arendt's view, in the public sphere, innumerable perspectives co-exist without a common denominator (1998, 57).

This concept of the public helps us understand how the social can be articulated with the public or private spheres. The realm of necessities is not political *per se*, without denying the possibility of making them political. As Warner argues, "the conditions of gender and necessities can be treated not simply as the given necessities of the laboring body but as the occasion for forming publics, elaborating common worlds" (2002, 61).

Thus the question of whether corporate foundations can contribute to the formation of the public sphere is evaluated according to the extent that they:

- Subject their action to public scrutiny.
- Contribute to the expansion of possibilities of individual or group formation in a way that these individuals or groups increase their capacity to demand for civil and social rights.
- Open room for opposition and negotiation between competing publics, and with the state.
- Influence state or corporate practices toward the expansion of social rights.

- Create networks of solidarity rather than particularistic relationships inspired in favors or clientelism.

Following these criteria, we will analyze three different philanthropic modes of intervention: assistance to the poor, developmental aid and public governance. Although these modes of intervention were originated at different historical conjunctures, it does not mean that one replaces the other; they co-exist.

Private Contributions to Social Services in Colombia

The extent of private involvement in social issues within the Latin American region has not been studied yet in a comparative manner. The best efforts are the studies of the John Hopkins University on the Third Sector[2] and the Ford Foundation's study on philanthropy.[3] According to the results of the Johns Hopkins study, Latin America does not have a strong tradition of nonprofit organizations as compared with European or North American countries.[4] In Latin America the most important sources of income for nonprofits are self-generated, largely through fees and the sale of services, which constitute 74 percent of total nonprofit income as compared with 49.3 percent for industrialized countries (Villar 2001, 108). In terms of private donations from foundations or individuals, Colombia boasts the highest percentage (14.9 percent of total nonprofit income), compared to Peru with 12.9 percent, Brazil with 10.7 percent and Argentina with 7.5 percent (*Ibid,* 109).

This result is consistent with the strong tradition of philanthropy in Colombia, one of the oldest in the Latin American region. Philanthropy accompanied Colombia's industrialization process at the beginning of the 20th century, when entrepreneurs guided by a sense of paternalism created local forms of welfare capitalism (Farnsworth-Alvear 2000; Arango 1992). As documented by Farnsworth Alvear, companies projected themselves as families in which workers were cast as children and employers as their protectors (149). Women made up the majority of textile workers, for example, and their protection included safeguards against sexual dangers. Indeed, in some factories, virginity was a condition for employment of young women (148). Paternalism included the protection of workers against communism through provision of material benefits, including medical insurance, housing, and factory schools and cost-of-living bonuses (149).

Religious organizations also created their own philanthropic institutions. One of Colombia's largest corporate foundations, the Social Foundation, for instance, was founded in 1911 by the Spanish Jesuit priest José

María Campoamor as the Workers' Circle, "La Obra'" and the Workers' Circle Co-operative. The groups focused on the education of poor children in the principles of Catholic religion, as well as basic education. A group of women, known as *las Marias,* were trained to teach the children in the *Granja,* an institution of the Circle. Dubbed "nuns without vestments" by Padre Campoamor, these women worked in tasks like printing, selling and bank clerking for a symbolic payment, making their labor virtually free.[5]

Health services in the first half of the 20th century also depended mainly on private contributions, making the state the recipient of private and philanthropic activities (Abel 1996, p. 15). Both church and individual philanthropists focused on hospitals for their philanthropic activities (p. 65). A national social security system did not exist until 1946, when the Instituto Colombiano de Seguros Sociales, ICSS (National Institute of Social Insurance) was created. Employers did not react in an uniform way to the creation of the ICSS; for example 36 companies, including the largest textile companies, asked not to be included in the ICSS. The National Association of Industrialists (ANDI) complained that the ICSS demanded more than what the national industry could give (Abel 1987, 281; Safford and Palacios 2002, 321). Three decades after its creation, ICSS coverage was still very low, reaching only 15% of the population (López de Rodríguez 1980, 164).

Although private associations opposed state-sponsored social security, they actively provided social services to their members. In 1954 ANDI created the first private security system for their members' families (*Cajas de Compensación Familiar,* or benefit societies to distribute family subsidies*)* COMFAMA. Three years later the military government made compulsory the creation of *Cajas* (benefit societies) as mechanisms to distribute subsides. In 1991, 67 *Cajas* provided health, education, housing and recreation services to a significant part of the population (Villar 2001, p. 78).

Another example of private involvement in public matters is the Colombian Federation of Coffee Growers (FNC), a very powerful interest group. Created in 1927, the Federation became a "co-government with regard to matters affecting coffee" (Safford and Palacios: 2002, 270). By 1980, the federation marketed 95% of the country's coffee exports, but its importance extended beyond commercial interests. In addition to negotiating international coffee agreements, it also negotiated with the government in such broader fiscal matters as taxes and exchange and monetary policies. The federation is also involved in meeting social needs, sharing with the state the responsibility for construction of schools, health posts

and roads in coffee-growing areas (p. 271). Nevertheless, while large cof-
fee-growers and the state built mutual trust to influence economic policy,
small coffee growers were subject to the patronage systems used for power
and control. Thus, it could be said that the relationship between the large
growers and the state was a horizontal one, while the relationship between
them and small growers was a vertical one (Thorp and Durand: 1997,
222). Furthermore, managers of the FNC did not lobby on social issues
with the same degree of effectiveness that they look for favorable economic policies (235).

Corporate Foundations

Corporate foundations first appeared in the 1960s. They have the legal
character of a foundation and are created and financed by a private corporation. Colombian legislation defines a foundation as a legal entity that
aims to pursue the public good; in securing that common objective,
donors contribute material goods. Rather than being associations of people, foundations are composed of material goods linked to a common
objective. In the case of corporate philanthropy, the foundation originates
in assets donated by a corporation or businessperson or in a portion of
corporate profits dedicated to financing the foundation. Some foundations participate as a company shareholder. Philanthropic foundations are
regulated by a special system of taxation.[6]

Whether measured by the scale of corporate foundations' economic contributions or in terms of the diversity of responses to social issues, Colombia is an outstanding case in the region. In 1997, 94 corporate foundations
with almost a billion dollars in assets represented one percent of Colombian
GDP and five percent of total public expenditures.[7] In Argentina, a country
with a GDP more than three times that of Colombia, there are 200 corporate foundations, most of them created in the past 20 years. (Luna: 2001, 7).
Mexico and Brasil do not have a significant number of corporate foundations (Roitter: 1996, p. 41). In Peru 10 out of 127 foundations are corporate
foundations (Portocarrero, Sanborn, Llusera, Quea 2000, 97).

A high proportion of resources are concentrated in Colombia's largest
foundations, with the 10 largest foundations accounting for 97.7% of total
foundation assets. Most of the foundations are highly institutionalized and
heterogeneous, and 60% of these foundations are 15 years old and older.
Their assets range from US$90,000 to US$360 million. Most concentrate
their activities in the social sector, and their income is equivalent to 2.5%
of Colombia's social expenditures.

Foundations create a varied and complementary network between philanthropic and commercial activities with social and economic benefits for both the foundations and the companies. One cannot simply characterize this type of philanthropy as only favoring private interests or as merely guided by public principles. Corporate philanthropy is a good positioning strategy since consumers prefer companies with a friendly, humanistic image. Identifying particular companies with noble causes or altruistic activities provides significant benefit to a company in terms of image vis-à-vis consumers. *Dinero* (1998) magazine and the firm Invamer Gallup undertook a survey of 301 Colombian businesspersons in the biggest cities. This survey confirms that the firms that garnered the most admiration were those that had foundations. The three highest ranked were Bavaria, Carvajal and Exito, all of which maintain their respective philanthropic company. However, what is most interesting is the inclusion of the variable *commitment to the community* alongside the more traditional management, innovation, product quality, and ability to attract and maintain personnel, to evaluate the performance of businesspersons and their companies. In turn, foundations can use resources derived from these commercial activities and/or donations from the parent company, thus relying on a favorable economic situation to accomplish their social objectives.

Finally, as a social dividend, one cannot discount the possibility that corporate foundations help entrepreneurs to come out of their isolation in the economic sphere, creating a greater feeling of social identification. Faced with high levels of insecurity and uncertainty, philanthropy becomes an instrument of social articulation that permits a company to ensure the continued development of its commerce. Foundations are extensions of the company; in order to create linkages with the community, they usually adopt the family name or the name of the parent company.

This hybrid conception of philanthropy that is neither public nor private helps explain the evolution and rapid growth of corporate foundations in Colombia. On the one hand, foundations share with non-governmental organizations (NGOs) the benefits of being a nonprofit organization that seeks the public good. However, unlike traditional NGOs, foundations can accomplish their objectives through assets guaranteeing the achievement of their mission. In the 1970s, the concept of foundations changed somewhat with a shifted emphasis on the ability to obtain resources, rather than a foundation's initial assets. Assets held by foundations after this change in requirements for the establishment of foundations amount to only 9% of the total foundation's assets, reflecting the change in conception and possibly explaining foundations' sustainability.

The hybrid character of foundations can also account for the size of the corporate foundation sector in Colombia: the early differentiation in the legislation of the notions of nonprofit and surplus benefit. A nonprofit is an organization that does not distribute its profits among its members. Colombian legislation differentiated between profit (*lucro*) and surplus benefit (*beneficio*). Thus, nonprofit organizations could perform commercial activities generating surplus benefits for social development. What has recently been called "new social entrepreneurism" (Draimin: 2001) was happening in Colombia as early as the 1960s. The case of Fundación FES is perhaps the best example. Created in 1964, FES developed as a university institution created by 12 individuals who contributed with less than US$300 each. Growing into the Colombia's largest financial broker institution, FES promoted philanthropy by giving financial support to civil society organizations (CSOs) through a special financial mechanism known as Permanent Endowment Funds. Since its inception, the foundation has garnered donations of US$55 million.

Since corporate foundations are closer to the business world, they have taken a position of leadership in sponsoring programs of economic development like micro-enterprises. They are more prone than NGOs or community organizations to take an entrepreneurial role, as can be seen in the cases of FES and Fundacion Social. This type of foundation is known as a *fundación propietaria* (proprietary foundation) because the foundation owns the company. By 1997, Fundación Social owned 19 companies in the construction, insurance, banking, leasing and communication fields, employing 10,000 people and managing assets of US$3.5 billion (Fundación Social: 1998, p. 11).

The impact of economic growth on corporate foundations must also be taken into consideration. Unlike most other countries in the region, Colombia had enjoyed a positive rate of economic growth since the 1930s. Even during the so-called lost decade of the 1980s, Colombia's growth indicators were on the positive side. However, an economic slowdown during the second half of the 1990s had a profound impact on corporate foundations. In 1999, the biggest corporate foundations faced a crisis period, with some of them disappearing or minimally surviving. Indeed, in June 1999, the economic situation compelled the Colombian government to declare FES an "official" entity to protect the organization's existence. Fundación Social also suffered from the crisis, reducing its social programs by 70 percent. Some smaller foundations were forced to shut down as a result of the shaky economic environment.

Public/Private Responses to Social Concerns

Social-political contexts shape philanthropic foundations' response to social concerns; so does the interaction between the private and public spheres. In this section, we distinguish three modes of intervention within philanthropic practices—assistance to the poor, developmental and public governance. The three articulate the public/private logic differently. Assistance to the poor operates under the principles that Arendt characterizes as a private sphere of government: it focuses on needs of the population and it is exclusive in its orientation as long as it attends the member of the small community living around the corporation. As a response to increasing poverty in the 1980s, developmental intervention extended beyond mere assistance by opening a public space. This model aims to steer a relationship with the state, enlarging the space of deliberation to include a wider public and make the beneficiaries into subjects with negotiating capacity. In the context of the armed conflict of the 1990s and the 1991 constitutional reform, a "public governance" strategy emerged. A small number of foundations now extend their field of action toward the state and society as the target of intervention. Although different modes of interventions are associated with different periods of Colombian history, the three modes of interventions now co-exist. Indeed, the same foundation can combine different modes of intervention. The following section aims to identify the factors leading to these different modes, as well as the limits and potential for creating a space of deliberation from which social rights can be advanced.

Assistance to the Poor

In the early 1960s, Colombia was overcoming a period of intense conflict (1948–1956), generally known as *La Violencia*. The 1960s was a period of intense mobilization of trade unions[8] and social protest, with the private sector actively involved in the creation of specialized interest groups.[9] The most important corporate foundations were created in the 1960s. A weakened state and a strong division along party lines provided the entrepreneur with an opportunity to exert a more active role in social affairs. Corporate strategy focused on assisting the needs of the poor, seeking to identify "needy" people who lived near the the factory, for example, with owners deciding who met their criteria. This intervention strategy is reflected in the following statement by the director of Fundación Santodomingo, known at that time as Barranquilla Foundation:

The Foundation was created with a principal philanthropic criterion, to help those who are poorest. To help them, one had to start with education. The Barranquilla Foundation, for that was what it was called at the time, became involved in programs directed toward the education of the most desperate in Barranquilla, obviously, because it was in Barranquilla where the company was located at the time.[10]

Philanthropy is seen as a continuation of Christian community under the principle that one's fellow man is one's neighbor (Castel, 42). The prevailing representation was one of an extended family comprising both the poor and the factory owner: "The Barranquilla Foundation is always present in the civic-social programs of Barranquilla, as headquarters of the Foundation, as head of the Santo Domingo family."[11]

The neighborhood connects the factory with the poor. The factory, in a larger sense the locality, is the space that permitted an articulation of that connection and a feeling of belonging between all the parts. Barranquilla is the place where the Bavaria[12] company exists, the cradle of the Santo Domingo family, and home to the poor. It is in this concurrence of meanings that it is possible to search for the common good. Recreating an implicit social contract that unites community members on the basis of territory lessens the risk of non-affiliation.

Corporate foundations, above all, sought to provide social assistance to workers and their families, considered among the most vulnerable of target groups. The director of Corona Foundation recalls:

In the first stage (1963–88), the Foundation was almost exclusively directed to the interior of Corona, in the sense that almost the entirety of its programs were geared to the welfare of the families of the employees, to the areas where the Corona factories were situated, which were always small towns—such as Madrid, in Cundinamarca; it always becomes very important for the town. The Foundation managed scholarships for the children of employees, university credits, family wellness programs such as education programs for mothers about breastfeeding, everything from breast milk to how to deal with accidents in the house to love to the flag, literally.[13]

Corporate foundations were established in areas considered prone to communist influence and social rebellion. This is the case of Cali, the destination of many displaced by *la Violencia* and home to workers' strikes such as the 1959 sugar refineries strike. Fundación Carvajal in Cali was established in 1961 as an "instrument of social justice and Christian charity" (Valencia Llano, 1999, p. 15). Cali was also home of Fundación FES, created in 1964.

The 1960s also witnessed factory modernization with Taylor's management principles replacing previous forms of control and discipline. In the textile industry, men replaced female workers as part of this modernization process.[14] As a result of these changes, employers' philanthropic attitudes also evolved. Male workers began to receive benefits such as home construction subsidies and visits by social workers to job applicants and homeowners; women were considered male dependents, and provided with programs such as classes in embroidery, cooking, dressmaking and folk dancing (Farnsworth-Alvear, 2000, p. 225).

A similar process of modernization took place within the Fundación Social. It shut down its elementary schools for poor children, arguing that the state had responsibility for the school system. Instead, it created the National Institute of the Worker Circle with a political aim: to train young leaders from the Catholic trade union, cooperatives and Juntas de Acción Comunal (Government-sponsored community action committees) because[15] the belief was "communism will not prosper where leaders are conscious of their rights." The creation in 1964 of Projuventud and the JTC (Young Workers of Colombia) reflects the change in target population toward young leaders. *Las Marias,* numbering 160 volunteers in 1960, were replaced by specialized teachers, although not without their protest.

To sum up, assistance to the poor is characterized by a tutelary relationship between the owner and the employees, rather than on opening a public space of democratic deliberation. The representation of the factory as a big family was seen as a tool for moral rehabilitation and was motivated by paternalism and the fear of communism.

Developmental Philanthropy

In the 1980s, the number of Latin Americans living below the poverty line increased from 35 to 41 percent. The number of those living in extreme poverty rose from 15 to 18 percent (ECLAC, 1997, 28). By 1992, close to 18 million people in Colombia, 54 percent of the population, were living in poverty as measured by income, and 6.8 million (21 percent) lived at a critical level of poverty (Fresneda: 1995, 62). Processes of economic openness and structural adjustment programs in Latin America were put in place during the economic crisis of the 1980s. While structural adjustment programs primarily aimed to reduce the fiscal deficit and achieve macro-economic stability, they also had a profound impact on processes of social change in general and, more specifically, on the role nonprofit organizations play in social responsibility. Pressures to decrease public expenses by eliminating subsidies and charging for social services greatly weakened social protection. Moreover, structural adjustment required the state to delegate social responsibilities to the private sector.

Many studies have documented community solutions for providing services such as health, nutrition and child-care. This is evident in places like Lima with its estimated 1,200 community kitchens and in Santiago de Chile with its 1,383 small manufacturing workshops and grassroots economic organizations, as well as many other cases throughout Latin America.

Along with government and other CSOs, foundations began to take part in the planning, co-financing and partnership with projects aimed to include the excluded and the vulnerable, leaving aside their former simpler role of "donors" or "doers of social works" in the previous assistential model. The challenge is to create a model of social intervention that will permit the vulnerable margins of society to become participants in their own development. The development model differs from the assistance model in that a space is created in which the assisted population forms part of a wider network rather than the simple benefactor-beneficiary relationship. Gearing programs to the masses loosens the moral nexus between the benefactor and the beneficiary, although only to a certain extent in a significant amount of cases. The philanthropist still maintains him- or herself as a model of socialization: an individual's actions permit that *good* reaches the destitute. Contrasting with the private nature of the assistance model with its bond of dependency between the actors, the development model is generally based on the appropriation of technologies to help vulnerable populations further their own processes of negotiation and management of their development process. Thus, foundations became active in areas such as community and participatory development and income generation. The latter comprises half of foundation investment. Micro-enterprise programs seek to introduce independent workers, wage earners, and their families to the virtues of capitalist logic: prudence, rational calculation, access to credit, savings habits, investment and competitiveness.

In the context of a development strategy, donor and beneficiary relate to each other through the locality providing a role for local participation and negotiation, rather than through the hypothetical family structure. For example, the Fundación Social developed its Integral Local Development program that seeks "the consolidation of the poor as social subjects." The methodology includes a political dimension allowing the beneficiaries to negotiate their projects with local authorities. The Development Program for Female Heads of Household, created by FES in 1988 with the assistance of the Ford Foundation, is another example of a developmental intervention. The program included providing credit for micro-enterprises, training, personal development and social service orientation. In 1995, this program had spread to 24 cities throughout Colombia with the participation of 26 NGOs.

Under the development model, the targeted population is expanded and includes new criteria in the selection process. Categories like informal worker are added to the traditional categories of geographic proximity, inability to work, or family relationships. The Social Foundation and likeminded organizations combine parameters such as economic exclusion (poverty line, lack of basic needs and economic dependency), political marginalization (absence of a capacity to organize or interrelate) and cultural parameters to select targeted populations. Programs like that for female heads of household break with traditional schemes of working with poor women, vindicating women as active members of society and as economic actors (micro-enterprises, wage-earners) that generate income and further economic development. This program has an economic objective within an innovative model aimed to improve the economic productivity of women and incorporate important elements of gender equity/equality, self-recognition and creation of social and political networks between women.

Traditional assistance criteria are replaced by those criteria that allow the poor to be defined according to their potential as active participants in their own development. For the Social Foundation, the potential for stimulating a development process in the region where participants live is a factor for selection, as well as the criteria of poverty and exclusion. By the same token, the incorporation of an economic dimension to gender difference is translated into an element that works toward the empowerment of women.

The development model perceives the beneficiary-foundation relationship as a transitory link of learning as the beneficiary learns, develops and grows. The model attempts to create conditions through which vulnerable populations can break out of their isolated conditions and immerse themselves in the institutionalization of the state and the national economy. Generally, these communities take part in municipal development plans or are introduced in the banking system, for example.

The developmental model also defines the relationship between the corporate foundation and the state in new ways. Foundations guide the state toward social transformation, and the state has become a crucial partner for accomplishing this transformation. The Carvajal Foundation provides an example of this new relationship. The foundation lobbied the Colombian government to adopt the 1984 National Plan of Micro-enterprise Development (NPMD), which co-finances training centers that support micro entrepreneurs through credit and marketing activities. The NPMD launched a private corporation, the Corporación Mixta para el Desarrollo de la Microempresa, that seeks to strengthen microentrepreneur projects and to distribute economic resources. The implementation of the Plan is carried out mainly by the private sector, especially corporate foundations. At the time of its approval, the NPMD had US$7 million of Inter American Development Bank financing and US$3 million from national resources. In 1990, these resources doubled. Presently, there are two million small enterprises, which contribute 25 percent of GDP. The NPMD gave corporate foundations leverage in terms of financial resources, since the government co-financed half of their projects. The plan also gave foundations more decision making power by allowing them to influence the orientation and distribution of economic resources. Colombia has become a leader in micro-enterprise projects throughout Latin America as a result of the development model implemented in NPMD.

However, the developmental model also illustrates the limits of democracy within organizations of civil society. The institutional arrangements for the NPMD's implementation were far from ensuring a democratic participation of different actors. On the contrary, NPMD reinforced the advantage of corporations, already powerful groups, as compared to beneficiaries, small and medium micro-entrepreneurs. Corporate foundations are over-represented in the decision-making and policy boards advising the NPMD. They hold half of the seats on the Corporación Mixta board of directors that develops sector policy. Foundations are also members of the Asociación Nacional de Fundaciones Microempresarias, a nonprofit organization, which is an active member of the board of directors of the Corporación Mixta. There is also an over-representation on the Asociación board of directors with the largest foundations holding five of the seven seats. Foundations also had half the votes in the Technical Awarding Committee responsible for allocating resources.[16] Foundations were opposed to the creation of an organization of micro-entrepreneurs that participates at the same level as the Asociación. As one study concludes, "political empowerment was not a priority in the agenda of corporate foundations in their work with micro-entrepreneurs" (Villar, 1999).

The relationship between state and civil society—here represented by corporate foundations—raised not only the issue of private contributions to public ends but also that of public contribution to private ends. Foundations reach an important segment of small proprietors in Colombia, contributing with significant economic resources. However, foundations also benefit from government resources, a fact that explains the proliferation of foundations doing micro-enterprise development. In the case of Colombia, 20 corporate foundations have micro-enterprise development as their main activity, and most foundations include programs for small entrepreneurs among their activities. The program's success can be explained by its capacity to increase income in the poorer sectors of the economy while increasing the ties between the company, the poor and society in general. As a result, corporate foundations are gaining important social recognition. A well-known magazine (*Semana*, Dec. 3, 2001), in a section dedicated to social responsibility, mentions the case of Fundacion Santodomingo, which granted a quarter million credits worth US$28 million in the past 20 years, as well as that of Fundación Compartir, which had trained 103,000 micro entrepreneurs, and Fundación Corona with another 32,000. Being identified as a company with noble causes or altruistic activities provides a company significant benefit in terms of image vis-à-vis consumers. This admiration coincides with recent polls of public perception of trust, in which private companies outrank government and political parties: on an index of 10, the ranking is 4.98 for large companies; 3.9 for the national government and 2.77 for political parties. The latter rank is higher only than that of guerrilla and paramilitary groups (Sudarsky, n.d.).

The case of the NPMD poses important questions concerning government contributions to private actors like foundations, including the issue of state legitimacy. The state misses the opportunity for building a public discourse that allows it to recover its fragile political legitimacy, especially when an important part of this legitimacy derives from social programs. This does not mean to suggest stopping government support to corporate foundations. Legitimacy is not a zero sum relationship. The solution is to find mechanisms that acknowledge the presence and the contribution of the state to these programs. For example, not every corporate foundation's financial balance sheets are available for public scrutiny. When available, these balance sheets do not discriminate among the sources of funds nor their destinations, and beneficiaries are seldom informed of public support for these programs. Reporting about the nature of the funds would make foundations more accountable to citizens in their quality of administrators of public and not just private funds.

Public Governance

In the 1990s a small number of corporate foundations diversified toward new areas of intervention.[17] New topics included enhancing citizens' participation in public matters, promotion of civil society oversight of government programs, knowledge transfer to the social sector and facilitation of public debate between government and private sectors and also between government and insurgent groups. Several factors influenced these changes. The emphasis on privatization and deregulation supposes a reduction of the role of the state and more generally a transfer of services to the private sector in particular. The privatization of state corporations constituted a critical aspect of the Washington Consensus.

This environment opened a window of opportunity for collaboration between corporate foundations and the state because the state contracts their services. Several new laws reflect the delegation of responsibility for social programs to private parties. The Education Law 115 (1994) explicitly states that education is the shared responsibility of the family, society and the state. Establishing a mechanism of subsidies to families gives the private sector an incentive to provide services. Health sector reforms gave a major responsibility to the private sector in both financing and running the system, as stipulated in Law 100 passed in 1993.[18]

The most important reform is the Constitution of 1991, which addressed topics such as decentralization and de-concentration of functions, changes in the process of participation of civil society in public issues and new systems of financing social security. The introduction of participatory democracy within the constitutional order gave the public new spaces of participation and also made the state responsible for promoting civic organizations in national issues. The Constitution has been followed by a series of legislative acts to expand and consolidate decentralization.[19]

Within this context the public sphere takes a different turn. It is no longer a question of including marginalized populations without political mediation as in the social assistance model of the 1960s. Nor does it seem realistic that vulnerable groups, a little more than half of the population, are made actors of their own development, as attempted under the development model. Social issues in the 1990s become a problem of the entire society whose resolution determines the future of the private sector. Entrepreneurs very often recur to the maxim "a healthy company cannot reside

within a sick society" to provide a rationale for their involvement in public issues. Thus, the private sector participates actively in elaborating the
agenda of government as reflected in the document "From Business to the
National Agenda" (Consejo Gremial Nacional 1998). According to this
agenda, the responsibility of business is not limited to economic growth
and increased competitiveness. Businesses must also pay attention to "the
consolidation of democracies with high participation of civil society, a
state with efficient institutions with clear and stable rules, systems of security for citizens that resolve problems, terrorism, subversion and other
problems of violence, and thus the elimination of poverty and marginalization."(p. 13).

Through these ideas, the entire corporation is defined as socially
responsible. It is within a corporate concept of citizenship and the search
for the common good that the corporate foundation acquires meaning.
According to the president of the Corona Foundation:[20]

> In 1988 Corona put in place a program that emerged from the
> belief that a process of technological change was not sufficient to
> address processes of globalization and economic openness. What is
> also needed is to change people's mentality, culture and organiza-
> tion. A process of planned change was initiated, which in essence
> constituted the application of the principles and practices of inte-
> gral quality management . . . This process has five basic principles.
> Of those five, the fifth is to make Corona a socially responsible cor-
> poration and this is the essence of the Foundation as it was con-
> ceived . . . Therefore, what constitutes an effective organization is
> one that is socially responsible.

The responsibility is neither toward the vulnerable population, nor with
the worker and his/her family. Society becomes the purpose and raison
d'être of the foundation:[21]

> Social responsibility is like a series of concentric circles. The central
> circle is the client where the relation is based on the price, quality,
> opportunity and information. The second circle is made up of the
> members of the organization, its employees and workers. Respon-
> sibility goes beyond a just salary; it goes toward the realization of
> the worker as a human being. The third level is made up of stock-
> holders and their expectations. Without economic return they will
> abandon the firm or the country. The fourth circle is the neighbor-

ing community since we have an impact on it. The final circle is society. This is where the raison d'être of the foundation lies. It is here where Corona, as an organization and the Echavarría family carry out their responsibility before society. An organization must return what a country has given to it.

This opening of corporate foundations toward the public sphere, as in the case of Fundación Corona, presents another aspect of public/private collaboration. Although Corona opened spaces for public debate, this space restricted the quality of deliberations by using the private model of the enterprise as the paradigm to resolve the social question. In this way the rational model of the economy is extended to the management of social problems and to the public arena itself, including the relationship with the state (Burchell, 1996). More than an understanding of the public as political debate, the solution to the social question depends on improving the management of the political space as well. This point is clear in the following statement by the foundation's president:[22]

[Corona] is an organization experienced in administration. Our mission is to contribute to the social development of Colombia by improving the management of social processes. Administration has two dimensions: one is micro, how to improve the management of institutions. The other is macro: how to improve public policies where these institutions function. These institutions do not exist in a vacuum. They function according to macro public policies. How policies are designed is the key to improve institutions.

The mechanisms of social intervention do not involve the exchange of goods as does the assistance model; they are also not technologies for community development. Institutional strengthening and capacity-building form the axis guiding foundations' philanthropic activity. Thus, the Corona Foundation's board of directors defines its objectives as: "contributing to the social development of the country by improving the management of social processes through innovative programs and projects meant to facilitate access of the poorest population to the benefits generated by development" (Fundación Corona: 1996, 19). Society is viewed as a massive corporation in which the solution to the problem of development is administrative efficiency. The President of the Board of Directors of the Corona Foundation summarizes it like this: "Our country, more than poor, is badly administered" (Gutierrez: 1996, 6).

In this view, foundations have a comparative advantage over the state because of their capacity for innovation, a mechanism that also permits them to complement the state. "Functioning in their innovative capacity, the foundations find their most favorable niche because, among other factors, they have the patience, continuity and autonomy to assume risks in unexplored areas, try a new focus and methodology and initiate a process of reflection and debate, which in certain form is not viable for the State (pg. 7)." Specialized knowledge of experts and a capacity for innovation complement each other in the new strategy of social intervention.

"Know-how" replaces the donations characterizing the assistance model. Henry Gallardo, Corona Foundation's health services director, clearly summarizes the concept: "the foundation gives from what it *knows*, not from what it *has*."[23] A strategic alliance with the state and with other institutions and foundations makes it easier for innovations developed at the micro level to be replicated for society in general.

Along with this transference of know-how, the Corona Foundation lobbies for health issues in politics. Gallardo explains the rationale:

> The problem of health in Colombia is that the institutional framework generates perverse incentives . . . which implies changing this framework to generate incentives for improvement . . . we developed a series of investigations in health policy about what should be the basic principles of reforming social security in Colombia, we began with a couple of studies on the financial equilibrium of the system, if the system was financially viable or not . . . we invited the investigators and experts on the subject to a qualified audience. . . . We do not lobby in the sense of going to Congress and speaking to people of Congress, but advisory committees are established with the participation of consultants, political actors, and high level bureaucrats of the government where they contribute to the study."[24]

Not all foundations, however, adhere to this view of the public. For example, the Social Foundation emphasizes the reconstitution of the social fabric through democratic participation:[25]

> There is no sense to talk of philanthropy in Latin America. It is better to talk of social responsibility, that is, of how to create a social contract. Therefore, the political obligation is not to be "against" the State but rather how to modify the political, economic and

social relations within a country.

The Social Foundation establishes itself as an important voice in the process of participatory democracy and continued negotiations with guerrilla forces. The Foundation undertakes projects that consolidate participatory democracy through initiatives like citizen organizations to monitor elections, fight corruption and monitor human rights. The Social Foundation also jump-started the NGO "Viva la Ciudadania," one of the most popular citizen organizations. Its "Businesspeople for Peace" program, which brought together businesspeople to exchange their views over alternative solutions for ending Colombia's armed conflict in Colombia, created a space for involving business leaders in the peace process. (Fundación Social: 1998, 1999). The Social Foundation also became the Technical Secretariat of the Mandato por la Paz and participated in the political orientation of the Asamblea Permanente por la Paz.

Corporate foundations are also concerned with the peace process. The Pastrana government's (1998–2002) failed process of negotiation with guerrilla groups actively involved the wealthiest individuals and economic associations in the peace process. Main representatives of these associations participated in a negotiation table in El Caguán with FARC,[26] and meetings with the ELN in Germany in 1998 and Havana in 2001 (Rettberg: 2002). New foundations, such as Fundación Ideas para la Paz-FIP (Ideas for Peace Foundation), are being established.[27] A group of business leaders created FIP in 1999 "to work with the private sector to protect the public interest, above all. It does so in the hope of building a fairer and more equitable society" (Fundación Ideas para la Paz: 2002). Activities include the development of proposals to be used in the peace process, monitoring of the peace process, and the provision of public information on the conflict and peace process (FIP, 2002a). Some foundations have been created in response to specific problems. For example, Fundación País Libre (Foundation for a Free Country), emerged initially to support the families of kidnap victims, but then shifted to popular mobilization against kidnapping, as well as lobbying Congress for stronger legislation against kidnapping (Romero: 2000, p. 20). The attempt to solve regional problems provides an incentive for local entrepreneurs to form regional foundations and corporations. For example, Vallenpaz (Valley in Peace) was set up after the first mass kidnapping in Cali to help achieve peace through social and economic development processes in the rural communities of southwestern Colombia (Guerrero: 2003).

Private organizations also contribute by monitoring and overseeing state institutions. An example is Bogotá Cómo Vamos (How are we doing, Bogotá?), a program created by Fundación Corona, *El Tiempo*, Colombia's largest newspaper, and the Bogotá Chamber of Commerce (Cámara de Comercio de Bogotá) to oversee implementation of Bogotá's development plans (Rojas: 2004).

Conclusion

Corporate foundations are participating in the construction of a public sphere in Colombia. Their relationship with social and economic issues is not exempt from tensions and contradictions. Undoubtedly, corporations are a source of wealth and of power within the nation. Their principal function is to dominate technological change and strive toward new market challenges. Solidarity is not the result of a struggle for competitiveness and profitability. However, through the creation of the legal entity of the foundation, a small group of corporations have been able to go beyond the private aims of the company and to contribute to the creation of a space of deliberation in which debates and disagreements can arise about social issues. This involvement also inevitably strengthens the economic objectives of the corporation.

In this chapter, we have described three models of intervention by corporate foundations. While assistance to the poor is perhaps the most frequent, it is also the least public. This model eliminates the political distance between donor and beneficiary, and therefore suppresses spaces for negotiation and deliberation. Private criteria lead toward a strategy of need satisfaction. Rather than changing conditions that produce poverty, the assistance model merely strategizes about how to fulfill unmet material needs. Beneficiaries are deprived of their own voice. Therefore, the space created is not democratic, and solidarity is not likely to flourish as a result.

The developmental model contributes to the creation of a public space by steering public policy toward social ends and by constituting beneficiaries into subjects with capacity to negotiate and participate in their process of development. Notwithstanding, public space is restricted in the following ways: 1) Beneficiaries are marginalized from the process of decision-making by the corporate foundations, with no say at the programmatic level. The flow of public funds to corporate foundations actually worsens this situation because it increases the leverage capacity of the already influential corporations. This situation became clear in the case of the program of micro-entrepreneurs, who found themselves with diminished negotiating capacity vis-à-vis those of the corporate foundation. 2)

The flow of public funds toward private programs also runs the risk of delegitimizing an already weak state. The state lost an opportunity to gain legitimacy through social programs. This situation is encouraged by the lack of publicity of the sources of revenues.

As this chapter illustrates, a smaller number of corporate foundations move in broader areas of public policy, creating spaces of negotiation between the state and groups in conflict. Private foundations participate as well in designing, evaluating and monitoring social policies. Their leverage capacity allows them to successfully lobby for policies in the areas of micro-enterprise, gender, education and health. Their capacity to bring together different segments of the population has been crucial in furthering peace demonstrations, denouncing kidnapping and influencing political and economic leaders. Their privileged position in the mass media has been an important factor in denouncing corruption and gathering and circulating information. Despite this opening toward the public sphere, foundation interventions are limited by the adoption of market logic to solve collective issues that require a building of solidarity. Foundation response as measured by the extent of their involvement remains timid: only a few corporate foundations participate, and even those are restricted in their breadth and depth of influence.

The previous discussion puts into evidence two main conclusions. The first regards the need to democratize civil society in order to strengthen its potential role in broadening the public sphere. The other conclusion relates to the vulnerability of civic organizations, in this case of corporate foundations. Despite 50 years of building expertise in the social areas, recession significantly curtailed corporate foundations' contributions to social areas. This confirms the weak capacity of beneficiaries to negotiate their social rights with the state and to create lasting institutions.

References

Abel, Cristopher (1996) *Ensayos de Historia de la Salud en Colombia, 1920–1960* (Bogotá: Instituto de Estudios Políticos y Relaciones Internacionales de la Universidad Nacional y CEREC).

Abel, Christopher (1987). *Política, Iglesia y Partidos en Colombia* (Bogotá: Universidad Nacional de Colombia).

Arango, Luz Gabriela "Mujeres Obreras, Familia y Politicas Empresariales. La Historia de Fabricato," in *VIII Congreso Nacional de Historia de Colombia*, 1992.

Arendt, Hannah (1998), *The Human Condition* (The University of Chicago Press).

Arendt, Hannah (1963) *On Revolution* (New York: Viking Press).

Bailey, Michael (1999) "Fundraising in Brazil: the major implications for civil society organisations and international NGOs," *Development in Practice*, 9: 1.

Briceño Jauregui, Manuel (1997) *Del Círculo de Obreros y de la Caja Social de Ahorros a la Fundación Social: 1911–1972* (Santa Fe de Bogotá, Fundación Social).

Burchell, Graham (1996) "Liberal Government and Techniques of the Self," in Andrew Barry, Thomas Osborne and Nikolas Rose (eds) *Foucault and Political Reason* (University of Chicago Press).

Calhoun, Craig (2002) "Constitutional Patriotism and the Public Sphere: Interests, Identity, and Solidarity in the Integration of Europe," Pablo de Greiff and Ciaran Cronin (eds) *Global Justice and Transnational Politics* (Cambridge: The MIT Press).

Caro, Elvia (1999) "Visiones y Realidades de Genero en la Filantropiá Empresarial," in Cristina Rojas, Gustavo Morales "Filantropía y Carbio Social: El Caso de las Fundaciones Empresariales en Colombia," Ford Foundation, Final report, unpublished, January 12, 2000.

Casas, Maria (1995). *El Padre Campoamor y su obra: el Círculo de Obreros*. Santa Fe de Bogotá, Fundación Social.

Castel, Robert (1995) *Las metamorfosis de la cuestión social: una crónica del asalariado* (Buenos Aires, Editorial Paidós).

CEPAL (2000) *Equidad, Desarrollo, Ciudadania* (México: Vigésimo Período de Sesiones).

Consejo Gremial Nacional. *De la agenda empresarial a la agenda nacional: El sector privado frente a la tarea de reconstruir a Colombia* (Santa Fe de Bogota, Gustavo Sorzano & Asociados, September 1998).

Dinero (1998) "Envidia de la Buena" 14 September, No. 69.

Dean, Mitchel (1995) "Governing the Unemployed Self in an Active Society," *Economy and Society*, 24: 4.

Draimin, Tim (2001) "Engaging the New Social Entrepreneurism," unpublished paper.

ECLAC (1997) Economic Commission for Latin America and the Caribbean, *La Brecha de la Equidad*.

Farnsworth-Alvear, Ann *Dulcinea in the Factory. Myths, Morals, Men, and Women in Colombia's Industrial Experiment, 1905–1960* (Durham and London: Duke University Press, 2000).

Fresneda, Oscar (1995) "Los derechos sociales en Colombia: un instrumento para elevar el nivel de vida y superar la pobreza," in *Los Derechos Sociales, Economicos y Culturales en Colombia: Balance y Perspectivas* (PNUD y Consejeria Presidencial para la Politica Social).

Fundacion Corona (1996) Reporte Annual, *Politicas de Desarrollo Empresarial*.

Fundación Ideas para la Paz (2002) "Qué es la Fundación," http://www.ideaspaz .org/lafundacion/lafundacion.htm. Consulted 2003-05-08.

Fundación Ideas para la Paz (2002a) "Management Report 1999–2002," http://www.ideaspaz.org/lafundacion/management_report.pdf. Consulted 2003-05-08.

Fundación Social (1998a) *Fundación Social y Sus Empresas, 1997*, Santa Fe de Bogotá.

Fundacion Social (1999) "Contribuir a Construir la Paz y la Convivencia Social como Prioridad de la Fundacion Social," Reporte, Junio 8.

Fundacion Social (1998) "El Grupo Empresarios por la Paz Frente al Proceso de Negociacion del Conflicto Armado," mim.

Gutierrez D., Rodrigo, (1996) "La Fundacion Corona y su Concepcion de la Responsabilidad Social," in *Politicas de Desarrollo Empresarial*.

Guerrero, Rodrigo (2003) "Vallenpaz. A regional Corporation for Peace and Development in Colombia," in *ReVista Harvard Review of Latin America*, Vol. 2, Issue 3, p. 54–55. Available on http://drclas.fas.harvard.edu/publications/revista/colombia/guerrero.html

Londoño, Rocio y Restrepo, Gabriel (1995). *Diez historias de vida: "Las Marías"* (Santa Fe de Bogotá: Fundación Social).

Luna, Elba (2001) La Iniciative Filantrópica en Argentina, (Buenos Aires, GADIS, unpublished).

O'Donnell, Guillermo (1996) "Illusions about Consolidation," *Journal of Democracy, 7: 2, pgs. 34–51.*

O'Donnell, Guillermo (2001) "Reflections on Contemporary South American Democracies," *Journal of Latin American Studies*, 33, 599–609.

Peruzzotti, Enrique (2002) "Toward a New Politics: Citizenship and Rights in Contemporary Argentina," *Citizenship Studies*, 6: 1, pgs, 77–93.

Portocarrero S., Felipe, Cynthia Sanborn, Sergio Llusera and Viviana Quea (2000) *Empresas, Fundaciones y Medios: La Responsabilidad Social en el Perú* (Lima: Universidad del Pacífico).

Rettberg, Angelika (2002) "Administrando la Adversidad: Respuestas empresariales al conflicto Colombiano" (Bogotá: Universidad de los Andes, Departamento de Ciencia Política), unpublished.

Rodríguez, Cecilia de (1980) "La Política de Seguridad Social en Colombia," *El Estado y el Desarrollo* (Bogotá: Universidad de los Andes, Facultad de Economía, Centro de Estudios de Desarrollo Económico).

Roitter, Mario (1996) "La Razón Social de las Empresas. Una Investigación sobre los Vínculos entre Empresa y Sociedad en Argentina" (Buenos Aires: Centro de Estudios de Estado y Sociedad, Documento CEDES/115).

Rojas, Cristina, and Gustavo Morales (1999) *Filantropía y Cambio Social: El Caso de las Fundaciones Empresariales Filantrópicas en Colombia* (Informe presentado a la Fundación Ford, CCRP).

Rojas, Cristina (2004) "Decentralization and the Culture of Citizenship in Bogotá, Colombia," in Isabel Licha (ed) *Citizens in Charge. Managing Local Budgets in East Asia and Latin America* (Washington: Inter-American Development Bank).

Safford, Frank, and Marco Palacios (2002) *Colombia. Fragmented Land, Divided Society* (New York: Oxford University Press).

Salomon, Lester M., Helmut K. Anheir et al. (1999) *Nuevo Estudio del Sector Emergente. Resumen.* (Universidad Johns Hopkins, Instituto de Estudios Políticos, Centro de Estudios de la Sociedad Civil).

Thorp, Rosemary, and Francisco Durand (1997) "A Historical View of Business-State Relations: Colombia, Peru, and Venezuela Compared" in Sylvia Maxfield and Ben Ross Schneider, *Business and the State in Developing Countries* (Ithaca: Cornell University Press).

Valencia Llano, Alonso (1999) "Fundación Carvajal," en *Revista Credencial Historia.* Special issue on Obras Sociales: Las 10 del Siglo XX en Colombia.

Villar, Rodrigo (1999) "La Influencia de las ONG en la Política para las Microempresas en Colombia," unpublished.

Villar, Rodrigo (2001) *El Tercer Sector en Colombia. Evolución, Dimensión y Tendencias* (Bogotá: Confederación Colombiana de Organizaciones no Gubernamentales).

Warner, Michael (2002) *Publics and Counterpublics* (New York: Zone Books).

Acknowledgements

We thank the Ford Foundation for the support of the research on Colombia and a SSRCH (Canada) grant. This paper benefited from comments of Anthony D. Tillett, Cynthia Sanborn, Rodrigo Villar. We also thank Elvia Caro, Juan Carlos Jaramillo and Carmenza Saldias, who participated in the research in Colombia.

Notes

1 The Global Compact was launched at UN Headquarters in New York on 26 July 2000. Business participating in the compact embraced principles of good conduct in the areas of human rights, labor standards and the environment.

2 The study compares the nonprofit organizations in 21 countries. Five Latin American countries formed part of the comparison: Argentina, Brazil, Colombia, Mexico and Peru.

3 The Ford Foundation's study comprised four countries: Argentina, Chile, Colombia and Peru. This chapter forms part of this comparison.

4 According to the study of the John Hopkins University (1999, 6) the media of employment in the third sector is 4.8%, with countries like the Netherlands employing 12.5% and Ireland, 11.5%. Argentina employs 3.7%, Peru and Colombia, 2.4%, and Brazil, 2.2%.

5 On the history of La Obra see Manuel Briceño Jauregui (1997), Maria Casas (1995), Rocio Londoño and Gabriel Restrepo (1995) and Elvia Caro (1999).

6 Once the assets of the foundation are defined, donors renounce to these assets and to the profits produced by the foundation.

7 The empirical data were collected in a project financed by the Ford Foundation. The results appear in Cristina Rojas and Gustavo Morales (1999).

8 From 1959 to 1965 the number of people in trade unions grew from 250,000 to 700,000 (Safford and Palacios, 2002, 327).

9 The number of interest groups double between 1960 and 1980 and the number of professional association grow five times (Villar, 2001, p. 76).

10 Interview with Marciano Puche, Director Fundación Mario Santo Domingo, Barranquilla, 20-1-1999.

11 Ibidem.

12 Bavaria, a beer company and headquarters of the Fundación Mario Santodomingo, is the biggest economic conglomerate of Colombia. The conglomerate owns 87 businesses in the areas of beverages, air transportation, insurance, communication and finances.

13 Interview with Guillermo Carvajalino, director Fundación Corona, October 1998.

14 In the 1920s three quarters of the labor force in the textile industry were women. In the 1970s this proportion was reduced to 35% (Farnsworth-Alvear, 2000, p. 6).

15 Quoted in Idem.

16 The institutions participating in the board of directors are allowed to implement projects financed by the Corporation. In 1998, from the total amount of resources assigned by the *Corporación Mixta*, foundation members of the *Asociación* received 60% of the resources approved. Seven of the biggest foundations received 25% of the yearly resources.

17 The clearest cases were Fundación Corona, FES, Fundación Social and, to some extent, Restrepo Barco. With the intensification of conflict in the year 2000, this tendency is increasing, as it will be explained later.

18 According to Law 100, the health care system is divided into a subsidy regime for poor families who receive a government subsidy, and a contribution regime for persons who can afford to pay. Public and private institutions are charged with providing health services (IPS). Third sector (co-operatives or self-managed community organisations) IPSs are also considered in the provision of services under the subsidy regime.

19 The Municipal Code, Law 136 of 1994, aimed to increase participation in the local governments and the participation of users of public services in the corporate board of directors. The most important legislation is Law 60 of 1993 which regulates transfers from the national government to municipalities.

20 Interview with Guillermo Carvajalino, October 1998.

21 Ibidem.

22 Interview with Guillermo Carvajalino, October 1998.

23 Interview with Henry Gallardo, Director Health Area, Fundacion Coron, Nov. 23, 1998.

24 Ibidem.

25 Interview to José Bernardo Toro and Leonor Esguerra, Vice-presidents Fundación Social, October 1st, 1998.

26 El Caguán formed part of the de-militarized zone where conversations with the FARC (Revolutionary Armed Forced of Colombia) took place. The peace process was discontinued in January 2002.

27 It is important to mention that it is not the only position taken by business leaders in the country. As Angelika Rettberg (2002) documents, responses range from philanthropy to economic advantage-taking of the conflict and even worse to financing paramilitary groups.

8

Business and Corporate Social Responsibility: The Peruvian Case

Francisco Durand

If one were to ask executives at large Peruvian corporations if they were concerned about "social responsibility," the response would be a resounding yes—each in their own way.[1] For a long time now, Peruvian business leaders have provided charitable and humanitarian support to the people on their payrolls, in the communities in which they operate and among various other social groups, whether due to company necessities, traditions or the personal concerns of managers and owners. So, what is new in this area called Corporate Social Responsibility (CSR)? Based on a study of ten major economic power groups (EPG) or corporate conglomerates in Peru, this chapter argues that the newness here is relative, and does not involve a sudden new corporate concern for the society around it. Instead, it involves renewing and perfecting traditional business and philanthropic practices and adopting a new language about them, in response to the impulses of a changing international context and the subsequent accommodation of national institutions.

For some time now, following the decline of populism and emergence of neo-liberalism, Latin America has experienced a sort of "movement" to involve more businesses, as well as other actors—non-governmental organizations, foundations, local and regional governments and international organizations—in social responsibility initiatives. This is part of a complex process of modernizing ideas and practices that implies multiple changes and, not surprisingly, generates tensions and resistance. In this scenario not everything is rose colored, but true changes are evident. In Peru, each EPG or large conglomerate has responded in its own way to the current global challenge to be more "socially responsible." However, in our view, what has been done is still not enough.

The Peruvian case generates the following questions: How valid is what we call the "conventional approach" to CSR, that which predominates in most studies of the subject? How important is CSR to the largest Peruvian conglomerates, which are the subjects that must be "modernized"? What individual and institutional factors, internal and external, drive these new ideas and practices? What traditions and fears contain or constrain the adoption of CSR as company policies? What variations are present among cases? Finally, to what extent do current CSR practices meet the collective need to legitimize a new social pact, at a time when the private sector dominates the national economy? To answer these questions one must first determine the general state of CSR in Peru at the beginning of the 21st century, and put it in context, by inserting CSR into a wider national and international context. Then one must analyze the discourse and practices of specific Peruvian EPGs. It is important to point out that this effort is different from the study of those multinational corporations that enter a new market with ideas and practices generated elsewhere and subsequently applied in the host country.

This chapter assigns priority to the largest EPGs due to the fact that they are on the cutting edge of domestic capitalism. These groups are defined as conglomerates of companies headed by a mother company or flagship. Thanks to shared ownership and cross-participation in the boards of directors, a nucleus of Chief Executive Officers (CEOs), both owners and non-owners, leads these giant multi-firm organizations. Peru's largest EPGs have more organizational and material resources to carry out CSR than other domestic capitalists and have or should have a greater need to defend and legitimize their market position and role in society.

In response to the first question, conventional studies of CSR have contributed to the analysis of the relations between business and civil society and have produced the first empirical and conceptual advances, thus opening a new area of discussion. Notwithstanding, they tend to possess a limited vision, relating the phenomenon vaguely to the new context while failing to link CSR to scholarly business research. Basically, the conventional approach selects success stories and focuses only on "best practices," relying on information provided by the corporation itself without taking into account the opinion of "others," particularly those who suffer from social exclusion and are the primary subjects of corporate philanthropy and social responsibility practices.

Although there are important exceptions (Sulmont 2000), most studies of CSR in Peru implicitly assume the existence of a growing and positive movement toward greater elite social solidarity (Caravedo 1998 and 2000; Benavides de Burga and Guida de Gastelumendi 2001).[2] This is a Comtian positivist approach, one that speaks of advances made toward a superior stage based on the assumption that business can insert itself harmoniously within its context. Not surprisingly, this normative approach coincides with the vision held by leaders of organizations involved in promoting social responsibility, who enthusiastically speak of CSR's "development stages." To illustrate the point, it is enough to mention the role of the Organization of American States, the Inter-American Development Bank and the World Bank in supporting this movement. In a 2002 conference, CSR was seen as an "alliance for development" and the basis of a "new order for life in the 21st century."[3] These ideas have become part of a normative vision of globalization initiated at the end of the 1990s, and the main concern is to give big business a "social face."

This chapter assumes that gaps exist between CSR discourse and practice, between the individual response of large domestic conglomerates and the systemic needs to extend CSR and consolidate the new social pact. There is no need to begin with optimistic assumptions and privilege those companies that are most advanced in this practice, nor to limit our sources and perspectives to those of business. A realistic, more balanced vision admits advances have been made, recognizes that CSR is welcome and will do no harm, but must also determine its limitations, identify tensions and resistance to change, examine the gaps that exist and the curious combination of the old and the new, the national and the international. It relies on a more holistic perspective, linking CSR with the overall context in order to comprehend its "newness." CSR, as we understand it here, involves three elements: a) the internal and external ideas and social practices adopted by corporations, b) a concern for the environment and c) a sense of corporate civic responsibility, with regard to paying taxes, respecting and supporting democracy, and supporting the effort to eliminate forms of discrimination. The conventional approach—usually put forth by researchers working closely with companies—refers solely to the first two, while ours also includes the third.[4]

This chapter also tries to integrate the study of CSR studies with more extensive literature on business practice. Up to now, the latter has analyzed the relationships of EPGs with the new economic climate and with the state and political forces. Age-old labor issues have also been examined, but not the relationship between business and civil society, which is key to understand CSR and about which better theorizing and further investigation is required.[5] At the same time, CSR experts have not considered the formation of a new societal matrix under neoliberalism and the role CSR plays in this context. It is time to relate the two lines of inquiry because by doing so CSR acquires a new meaning. To achieve an understanding of this relationship, we rely on various sources that allow us to observe the context and determine how the EPGs understand and practice social responsibility. The main source of information comes from interviewing the CEOs of the ten largest EPGs in Peru and the leaders of the most important organizations that promote social responsibility. Additionally, we draw on corporate annual reports,[6] various surveys and press coverage related to CSR.

CSR as a Process of Change

CSR is understood as a set of ideas and modernization practices at large companies operating in a global context in which civil society demands are greater (including, in a significant way, the non profit organizations or third sector).[7] These ideas and practices are today more important than ever, given the fact that the private sector's structural weight has grown considerably under open markets and because the sector is in greater need to become a legitimate actor (Cannon 1994, Caravedo 1998: 40, Salmon et al. 1999, Portocarrero et al. 2000, Wilson 2000). In response to these demands, Peruvian family capitalism is attempting to modernize management and technology and have greater impact on its context, a goal that can be accomplished by renovating and extending their social practices and adapting CSR language.

In Latin America, CSR is associated with globalization, a process understood as increasing interconnectedness facilitated by the diffusion of communication technology and transport by developed countries, as well as the fall of protectionist barriers in developing countries (Stiglitz 2002: 9). In Peru, integration into the world economy began in 1990 with the Fujimori government, when external forces and their internal allies took control of the government and changed the direction of economic policies, strengthening the market and limiting the state's role. In this context, leading companies and promotional organizations (NGOs and educational institutions) emerged, financed or supported by the forces of globalization. Different actors participating in the "CSR movement" began to speak a new language and rethink private and public social policies (Sulmont 2000: 161–163).

Changes in the institutional matrix

In order to situate CSR historically, it is important to analyze changes in the social pact when Peru made the transition to a neoliberal era. In the era of populist governments, 1962–1990, the state possessed extensive regulatory powers—wages, prices, exchange rates, taxes, interest rates—and intervened in all economic sectors through state-owned companies. The state was the main institution concerned with civil society, providing education,

employment and health while acting through different promotional programs in less-developed regions and for low-income groups. The populist
social pact was based upon the assumption that the state played a proactive
social role, taking responsibility for social problems.

In this matrix market forces played a subordinate role. The private sector was directed by a relatively large number of large EPGs and a handful
of multinational corporations. Beneath this, a growing base of small and
medium-sized businesses (PYMES) as well as informal businesses quickly
developed since the 1960s. Wealth was limited by the state, but nevertheless was highly concentrated. Companies—primarily but not solely large
businesses—operated in a context marked by labor union activism, struggling to maintain relations with their workers as well as going "a little bit
further." This meant, for example, helping suppliers in rural areas or specific needy groups. It is clear that these companies were not concerned
with the general customers' needs or the environment, and even less so
with small shareholders. The large EPGs were the exclusive property of
wealthy families directed by a leader who relied upon a submissive management team, since under family capitalism personal trust was more
important than business knowledge. The country was relatively isolated
from the world market because of protectionist measures. The business
community was, in large part, bunkered in its offices due to fears of aggressive unionism.

Managers and companies established relations with society through
donations carried out discreetly, without systemic programs and through
monetary aid or in-kind payments. Requests were made through letters
sent by hospitals, churches, schools, sports teams, needy individuals, peasant communities, foundations, schools, universities and other entities.
Family foundations prevailed over company foundations. Relations with
NGOs were non-existent or distant when not hostile. This path of inter-
institutional relations is illustrated in Figure 1.

In 1990, in the midst of a deep recession and a crisis of the populist state
under the leadership of President Alberto Fujimori, the correlation of
forces shifted in favor of the market (Stein y Monge 1988, Castillo Ochoa,
Quispe and Martínez 1997). Labor unionism was severely weakened (Portocarrero and Tapia 1992). Tax and economic policies aimed at a fiscal balance, which led to the elimination of subsidies and increased tax collection
through the sales tax. In that moment the political and business class
established a close connection with international financial organizations
and multinationals, opening the economy to the world market and priva-
tizing state-owned companies (Crabtree and Thomas 1998). In this

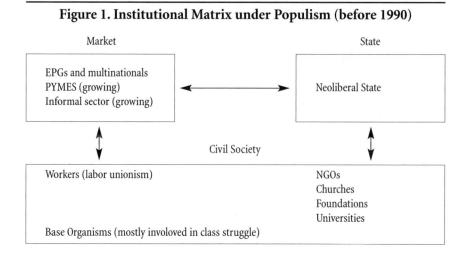

Figure 1. Institutional Matrix under Populism (before 1990)

process, illustrated in Figure 2, Peru changed its matrix, operating with a smaller State and a powerful private sector.

Under neoliberalism, the business pyramid mutated more than the base, which continued to be basically the same: more informal, but equally light in terms of resources and structural weight. A new generation of multinationals emerged, principally due to open privatization and new investments. Thus, the economy became privatized and denationalized.

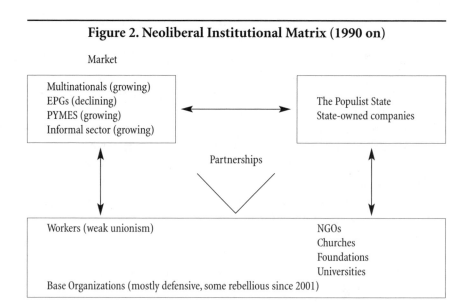

Figure 2. Neoliberal Institutional Matrix (1990 on)

Formal employment was mostly provided by the EPGs, multinationals and the state. Wealth was more concentrated than before, thanks to privatization policies and mergers. In an institutional matrix in which a strong market operated with a minimal state, the private sector's responsibility increased de facto. Now this business segment acted as the main provider of goods and services—including those that were never in private hands such as pensions, ports and airports. Direct relations with social groups and economic agents increased exponentially.

Civil society also suffered changes as unionism was debilitated and a new generation of subsistence base organizations emerged in the final crisis of populism. The poor and needy continued to send requests for help to companies. The role of NGOs, business foundations and the churches increased, becoming the most important aid providers. As time passed, the neoliberal model started to show limitations in terms of generating jobs and providing quality employment. New economic difficulties gradually became evident, including economic denationalization and corporate abuse of power, and anti-globalization social movements emerged. This new wave of more independent social movements with fewer connections to unions and parties began in 2001 and continued to manifest itself in the following years. In 2004 and 2005, CGTP, the old labor confederation, and coca farmers managed to organize national strikes and mobilizations against the new economic model (Pizarro, Trelles and Toche 2004).

In this context, domestic businesses initiated their modernization processes, assimilating new ideas and practices. Some even sought a new partnership with the state and civil society to promote CSR and to expand and improve philanthropy. Big business became a major social actor, a situation that created a systemic need to open up with civil society. Business leader Rafael Villegas has a clearer perception of the new demands that emerged from a change in the institutional matrix. He argues that, "Although we do not expect the Peruvian businessman to dedicate himself to charity, we do expect him to act with a clear understanding of the fact that the only way an economic and political system can last over time and make a country progress is through social justice. . . . If the Peruvian businessman, who at this time bears the weighty responsibility of assuming a large part of the country's development, fails to fulfill his role, we run the risk that centralism and state paternalism may take hold again. . . ." (*Presencia*, June 1995: 86).

The 1995 speech came precisely at a moment when the state had pulled back considerably from economic and social activity, and large corporations and the private sector became the engines of economic growth.

The State of CSR

In order to determine the state of CSR in Peru at the general and concrete levels, we examine information, opinions and data coming from business events, promotional organizations, and Peruvian EPGs in 2002. This was a time when CSR had really "taken off" and became part of the corporate agenda.

At the November 2002 IV Symposium on Business and Social Responsibility, organized by a major business leadership organization, Peru 2021, for instance, businessmen and national and international promoters of CSR expounded upon their ideas.[8] Several speakers spoke of how important it was to "quickly develop CSR." Promoters and business leaders considered it indispensable to "become modern businesses" and realized that they "must act and contribute to the forces of globalization." They expect to respond to a more active and critical civil society because now "reputation is essential to business and its response is achieved through CSR." They indicate that, according to a Millennium Poll, 55 percent of the world population believes that businesses should do "more than rack up earnings and fulfill legal obligations." A new climate of global competitiveness is discussed in which corporations will be capable of surviving if and only if they are "economically and socially involved."

Antamina, a new multinational mining investment in the Ancash region, is seen as an important case. This company has carried out an ambitious CSR program with peasant communities and surrounding areas. Executives at Antamina believe that mining companies today must respond to the growing demands for minerals in industrialized economies and, at the same time, to civic criticism at home and abroad, accepting responsibility for environmental damage and trying to avoid it. The response here revolves around the principle of social license. The company must have the government's blessing, respond to all international demands for environmental care and garner local support. In addition, the community must be given permission to operate as a rich and powerful intruder. This permission is obtained through CSR.

On the critical side, several NGOs and church organizations dedicated to serving the poor believe that business "creates problems" and should be responsible for "fixing" them. There is no shortage of organizations that promote CSR that contend that "CSR is still a topic for the elite," that there are "few businessmen committed to this cause" and that some large corporate groups exercise CSR in a "silent and discrete fashion."

Some Peruvian business leaders reject the criticism and find themselves at the other extreme of promoters. A traditional approach becomes evident as some express resistance toward CSR. In his closing speech, the business leader presiding over the Symposium argues that CSR "is not directly linked to business, at least not in the short term," contradicting those speakers who are in favor of more CSR. The President of Confederation of Private Business Institutions, CONFIEP, reacted similarly by arguing that there is no reason to "give in to the pressures" to "do more" socially. In CONFIEP's opinion, "CSR must be strictly voluntary," not imposed.

A survey on perceptions of CSR amongst high-ranked employees, carried out by Directo-Investigación Analítica at the request of Peru 2021, and whose results were presented at the IV Symposium, gives us a more extensive idea of CSR.[9] The majority, 92.1 percent, indicates knowing what "CSR is" and identifies those more active in the field. Answers point primarily to multinationals and large Peruvian corporate flagships. The response to "In your opinion, which Peruvian companies are socially responsible?" is as follows:

Table 1. The Companies with the Greatest Recognition Among Employees for their CSR Work. 2002

Companies (Type)	Percentage of recognition	Reason
1. Backus (Bentín)	58.8%	the most recognized
2. Minera Yanacocha (Benavides and multinational)	25.2%	the most responsible mining company
3. E. Wong (Wong Group)	15.0%	most responsible to consumers
4. Telefónica del Peru (multinational)	12.4%	
5. Coca Cola (multinational)	11.9%	good image
6. Cía. Minera Antamina (multinational)	9.3%	
7. Banco de Crédito del Peru (Romero and Brescia)	8.8%	
8. Southern Peru Copper Corp. (multinational)	8.0%	
9. Alicorp (Romero)	8.0%	
10. Citibank (multinational)	7.1%	

It is obvious that managers and white collar workers, because of their experience and information, see CSR as being performed primarily by large companies, namely multinationals and Peruvian corporate flagships. The dimensions utilized to define a company as socially responsible are first, "concern for the environment," followed by "working conditions offered to employees," "the quality of its products" and "its relationship with suppliers." These first four categories have a response frequency between 42 percent and 62 percent. The remaining three, which vary between 21 and 27 percent, refer to "social projection or community work," "ethical transparency" and "customer service and reputation or image." It becomes apparent that the CSR concept is perceived as being extensive and refers both to internal and external activities related to various stakeholders.

Regarding "what role does business play in society," 65 percent of interviewees responded "to do all this and actively help to build a better society for everyone"; 28 percent believes that there is "an intermediate point between the two" and only 6 percent responded that the role was to "generate earnings, pay taxes and generate employment." The idea of a proactive business role predominates, at least as an indication of ideological assimilation of new ideas or the need to respond more effectively to a systemic demand to reinforce the empowered role of the private sector in the nation's economy and society.

The negative side refers to ethics. Asked if "given the political corruption scandals in the country, is there any company that has disappointed you?," 75 percent replies yes and 25 percent no. The question refers to the scandals generated by videos recorded at the National Intelligence Service in which several business leaders were seen asking for favors and influences to intelligence chief Vladimiro Montesinos, or, as in the case of many media owners, receiving money (Durand 2003b, chapter 8). Two observations are important. First, companies are not identified in this case. Second, there is no reference to the question of democratization and civil rights.

When asked if "you believe that the State provides an adequate framework to promote CSR?" the consensus is overwhelmingly negative (96 percent), for various reasons: "because it is not familiar with the topic" (18 percent), because "the state does not enforce laws" (11 percent) and fails to "promote community work" (11 percent). Moreover, the government is seen as an institution that "promotes the informal sector" of the economy (10 percent) and does not provide incentives or tax advantages" (7 percent).[10]

An October 2002 IMASEN opinion survey of business opinion leaders, state officials and university leaders concerning ethics and CSR in Peru, conducted at the request of the Centro de Investigación de la Universidad del Pacífico, gives us a somehow wider and more critical idea about views on the business world, the state and civil society. With respect to "ethics, values and CSR," three groups of opinions are identifiable. There are those who believe "that the company's primary function is to maximize benefits, pay taxes and provide employment," contributing as such to the country's development. A second group of opinions consider that business "must have a more committed attitude regarding social causes," overcoming the "old paradigm of a company isolated from its social surroundings." Here we find those who believe that "there is no healthy business in a sick society." Lastly, there is a group critical to business that believes that CSR-related actions are "sporadic," and not genuinely altruistic, and that companies perform CSR because they are "concerned about projecting a favorable image of the business," meaning, CSR is basically a marketing strategy instrument. These companies, they argue, wish to appear as "good citizens" when they are not.

The different sources reveal the existence of disagreements about how to conduct and how to improve CSR based on a general consensus: social responsibility is welcomed and must be assimilated as a business principle. The importance of the debate is without question, yet it is surprising to find it circumscribed to business circles, not fully discussed in civil society or considered by national leaders as part of the country's agenda. Business sees CSR in different manners, identifying various stakeholders and recognizing they are both internal and external to the company. It is quite obvious that as long as the question of whether or not to engage in CSR is unresolved, it will be difficult to place emphasis on extending and improving it. Providing a more corporate strategic and social direction to CSR, rendering it more effective, and lastly bringing it out it into the light while forming alliances, are also on hold. Important differences are observable in different economic sectors. It is not surprising that mining is on the cutting edge due to its intrusive nature, and because it is fully immersed in the crossfire of international and local criticism. But the imperative to extend it is not so intense in other sectors. It is also surprising that the state appears to be weakly linked to the CSR concept. There is consensus on the idea that it does not promote it, yet the notion that the state "should be involved" is not welcome. CSR must be "only a matter of businesses."

In sum, although there are corporations quite advanced in these practices, and promoters willing to push it forward with enthusiasm, it is possible to sense within businesses a certain reticence, an ambiguity over whether "to do more CSR." It is also clear that the approach used to evaluate CSR is quite limited since it is carefully circumscribed to high ranking employees and employers without considering the opinion of "others"—blue collar workers, their families, the poor and the community. Finally, the concept itself is also limited because other dimensions of the debate, in particular corporate civic responsibility and the question of civil rights, are ignored.

Large Economic Power Groups and CSR

Case studies confirm general appreciations outlined above and provide greater detail. Interviews of CEOs—owners and top executives—at ten of the largest domestic[11] EPGs indicate how each faced the demands of a globalized economy and the changes in the social pact. The following factors have been identified as explaining why and how Peruvian conglomerates participate in the "social responsibility movement": a) the way corporate leaders understand CSR, which in turn depends largely on personal convictions and educational patterns, b) the economic sector where they operate and the weight of the company within it, which influences the need to develop CSR, c) the degree to which family bosses decide to reinforce managers and/or the occurrence of generational changes in family leadership after a succession crisis, d) the company's trajectory, in particular, the celebration of anniversaries that help evaluate long term trends and introduce changes, e) various external influences that point in the direction of managerial modernization and adoption of international standards typical of top companies and, finally, f) the way in which the flagship company or the EPG is perceived by "others."

Yesterday's Social Action

Traditionally, large EPGs have concentrated their social efforts on developing good labor relations—or at least this is how they explain it. Therefore, in the majority of cases, they extend social assistance to the spouses and children of employees through diverse programs. Externally, these conglomerates have also developed social assistance programs in response to letters sent by groups or needy individuals. All of the companies in question confirm having received a significant number of requests for help, indicating that "letters arrive by the hundreds every day," but few flagships study patterns or maintain records. The requests are attended discreetly according to budget considerations; aid is given either through in-kind payments or donations, depending upon the nature of each business.[12] These donations are part of a tradition that cannot be ignored because businessmen, companies and beneficiary groups insist on their preservation.

Philanthropy practiced by CEOs, whether owners or managers, also influences the decision to conduct more extensive CSR programs. We have determined that in many cases the CEO's strong religious convictions and the company's traditions or business philosophy effectively orient social actions over the long term. The former is more personal and altruistic, the latter more institutional, directly linked to the concept of social responsibility.[13] Conditions for continuity or sudden change in these ideas are greater given that many of the executives in question represent various generations of businessmen, and managers at large EPGs tend to remain at the helm for extended periods of time.

For example, the CEO of Ferreyros states that his strong social commitment stems from his status as a former member of Christian Democracy, a political party inspired in the social doctrine of the Catholic church. Likewise, the Olaechea, Benavides, Raffo and Romero groups are led by former Catholic school students. Several CEOs belong to conservative Catholic organizations, making it quite clear that religious convictions guide their actions. At Fierro, the founder, Don Ignacio Fierro, coined the phrase that "the soul of the company can be found in individuals. The company is not a trademark." For this reason, Ricardo Ruiz, the new manager, states that even if the founder of the group has died, "we are maintaining this line of thought."

Before moving on to the view that CSR involves a change process geared toward improving the company's relations with a wider context, it is important to point out that some CEOs or EPGs make tax-deductible donations as individuals or businesses. In the 1994–2000 period, for example, significant amounts were donated in this way by the Tabacalera Nacional (Fierro Group), Yanacocha (Benavides Group) and two Bentín Group companies. In addition, two CEOs, Raffo and Benavides, made donations on an individual basis, the former on a yearly basis and the latter on three separate occasions. Individual donations vary between US\$4,000 and US\$10,000, and business donations vary between US\$6,000 and US\$100,000.[14]

It is important to note that some types of corporate activities, such as those related to agribusiness, have always placed emphasis on developing social programs with their rural suppliers. In this case, poor peasants are the principal stakeholders because they control the land, produce the necessary raw materials, and private sector land acquisition is difficult. For example, a large landowner was forced to become a wine producer after land reform expropriated the Olaechea haciendas in 1970s; good relations with peasants became necessary as grape production was in the hands of the latter. Other cases, in which raw materials are supplied by cooperatives, peasant communities, small landholders or poor ranchers, followed the same pattern. Backus, the flagship beer and beverage company owned by the Bentín Group until 2002, has traditionally done this with barley producers, Gloria of the Rodríguez Group with milk-producing ranchers in southern Peru and Tabacalera Nacional of the Fierro Group with tobacco producers in various valleys. New EPGs and recently formed agribusinesses have followed the same pattern. These relations became more important following the 1968 agrarian reform. As Ruiz, CEO of the Fierro Group, says, "the question is how do you make them loyal, how do we keep them faithful." The reason behind this emphasis on poor rural stakeholders is fundamentally economic: it responds to an urgent necessity to keep supply lines open; however, it may be combined with ideas on social well-being or altruism.

Along with long-established relations with agribusiness suppliers, large EPGs generally maintain responsible labor policies, due to the existence of a well-paid, unionized "labor aristocracy." The CEOs of flagship companies all argue that they seek good relations with unions and have developed diverse social and training programs for employees over the years, the latter increasing considerably with globalization. They also point out that these patterns of good relations helped them to navigate the violent political context that dominated Peru in the 1980s and 1990s.[15] Recently, EPGs have insisted on dialogue rather than confrontation during the 1998 economic recession and with the emergence of new social movements. For example, Eduardo De Voto, manager of Gloria, says that during regional mobilizations that paralyzed the city of Arequipa in 2002, where the company has its plants, company trucks were able to circulate freely, a fact that "shows that we do not suffer from social hostilities." CSR pays off.

The New CSR

Like other businesses, Peruvian EPGs face competition from imported products and giant corporations that aggressively entered the market from 1990 on. According to Ruiz, "the situation in Peru is highly competitive, and multinationals either come to buy or bankrupt you." The 1998 economic crisis further shook several Peruvian EPGs. The current survivors are those that responded to these challenges by modernizing their operations on time. Such groups have also been subject to internal and external influences to integrate CSR based upon a belief that this is what characterizes a "leading company."

In all of these cases, furthermore, a business restructuring process emerged that implied adopting new corporate philosophies (total quality, reengineering) and adopting cutting edge technology. In three cases, companies have sought advice of outside consultants, with CSR becoming part of this modernizing package. Such efforts have led large EPGs to be more concerned about the environment and to redefine or initiate social programs with groups to which they have been traditionally related, and with other social sectors or the community at large. For this purpose, the majority of these companies has created or reinforced inter-institutional management. Three have formed foundations.

At the same time, a variety of corporate responses can be observed, some indicating a certain hesitation or fear to assume greater responsibility over or with civil society, attitudes that are contingent upon their perception of "others." CSR is clearly assimilated as a discourse, but with gap in practice, indicating a tension between the systemic needs to legitimize the new social pact and the individual responses of the top EPGs. For example, BCP, the largest bank in the country, has traditionally practiced CSR with a strong emphasis on culture—through the sponsorship of book publication and the recovery of the country's historical patrimony, principally in the area of church restoration. When BCP was subject to intense competition, this line of activity expanded. BCP has always been known for the special treatment it extends to large customers, but once the market opened up it was forced to concentrate on serving the needs of smaller customers, by reducing lines and waiting times and improving customer service. This internal restructuring process led to the acquisition of a new banking technology and the introduction of substantial improvements in customer service. Today, company documents state emphatically that "BCP's mission is to serve the customers" (BCP 2001: 43). In 1998, BCP created a specialized team to obtain the ISO 9000 certification for credit cards and mortgage operations (BCP 2001: 10). In this context of successful modernization, BCP continues to be active in philanthropic and cultural projects (i.e. large clients that receive luxury volumes on Peruvian art). It supports business events and participates in corporate alliances in the fight against drugs. BCP has also promised to contribute to the National Fund for Sports, financing the so-called "track and field seed beds" and inter-school sports at religious middle and upper class schools. These activities, which help between 50 to 250 institutions yearly, are channeled through a public relations division that seeks "to maintain BCP's image as a leading company that responsibly and sensitively supports the country's culture" (BCP 2001: 48–49). In conclusion, BCP has expanded its CSR programs in order to maintain its status as the "number one bank."

Alicorp, another giant company, has quietly incorporated CSR into its modernizing practices. The company resulted from the 1970s merger between the Romero Group and Anderson Clayton, a major agribusiness firm, with additional acquisitions in the 1990s of the bankrupt Nicolini Group and the Argentine Group La Fabril. Following these last mergers, and amidst strong competition, a profound restructuring process begun, driven by a young Alicorp manager who transformed this mega business into a managerially efficient, highly competitive and socially responsible organization. As General Manager Leslie Pierce says, "we have fought with Luchetti (a rival Chilean group) to remain in the market and we have done well." In the areas of technology, hygiene and accidents, Alicorp's plants maintain a good record. "We are in the club of the environmentally conscious," it argues with pride. "If you want to be in the major leagues, you have to have these standards," says Anthony Middlebrook, Manager of Inter-Institutional Relations. Working systems based on "Good International Practices" have been implemented along with security and hygiene norms. "Environmental technology" has been introduced at the flagship plant in Lima, obtaining various "ISOS." Along with Alicorp's main clients, which they consider to be "our strategic partners," the company has completely reorganized the territorial sales system (Alicorp 2001: 30–31). In the area of CSR, the group maintain different programs in partnership with the government and local communities, including one with 700 peasants who plant the "Durum" wheat variety. Alicorp maintains an annual donation plan and provides foodstuffs during national emergencies. The thousands of letters received every year, including requests to "give what they can," are attended "reactively." Middlebrook says that "we are conscious of the fact that we are a large company and we must help."[16] In the future, Alicorp hopes to improve its CSR program and place emphasis on education and nutrition programs, although they are still uncertain how to accomplish these goals. Alicorp places corporate emphasis on CSR but is still hesitant to publicize it because, as Middlebrook says, "in Peru success is condemned."[17]

Olaechea, a group specialized in wine production with strong competition from Chilean companies, returned to CSR almost accidentally. In the 1990s it was forced to sell Banco de Lima, meaning that the group lost its financial arm although it capitalized its operations. The idea "to return to CSR practices" at its main firm, Tacama Wines, came about in 1998, with the flooding of the Ica valley. When the question of how to help the nearby peasants arose among corporate community leaders, a local organization proposed the creation of a technological wine center. The resulting center, CTVID, is directed by Pedro Olaechea, a young and dynamic owner-businessman who enjoys the unanimous support of Tacama's Board of Directors. CTVID was created with financial support from the Spanish government, which facilitated CTVID's take-off. The center has begun planting vines on seven experimental acres, with plants provided to peasants at no cost. The idea here is to ensure a high quality grape supply with the technical support of Tacama and CTVID. Olaechea argues that, "if it is successful, Ica could become the Peruvian Napa Valley." The project is seen as "the best alternative to increase the peasants' added value." This is, he says, "our vision of social development." The company possesses a good management team and a high quality product that is competing well in the domestic market and external markets. But in order to grow they need better domestic supply of grapes. This is not altruism, he says, referring to CTVID's activities, "because we are also benefiting. . . . now that we are going to be the demand." This proposal is "both ethical and practical." Olaechea believes that "the social environment can improve" and that they are finally on the road to overcoming the black legend of hacienda owners created in 1968.

Another company, Ferreyros, the country's top importer of heavy machinery, has developed its own foundation to carry out CSR. Aside from environmental concerns and some generous donations to private universities in the 1980s under a system of tax incentives that was deactivated in 1991, the company had previously not involved itself with social programs. The concept of "volunteer work in order to do something for others," according to General Manager Oscar Espinoza, coincides with reflections made during the Group's 75th anniversary and an externally advised restructuring process. Another reform element included an increase in small shareholders participation. Due to both factors, "a reconsideration was made," and as such, "we thought that we should do something for the community." Two U.S. experts were brought in who propagated the idea that success must be linked to CSR. "In this climate," Espinoza says, "we created a program as a response to a demand for systematic aid." The decision was taken at a corporate level and Ferreyros Foundation was born. This foundation is dedicated to organizing annual student conferences entitled "CADE Estudiantil," attended by some 450 of the best university students from around the country at a cost of US$70,000 annually. This event began in 1996 and continues despite a strong recession that began in 1998. The foundation also signed agreements with provincial universities to carry out preparatory workshops, projects that "make the Ferreyros foundation recognizable" throughout the country. Nonetheless, the CADE Estudiantil is not widely publicized, due to the fact that the group follows, according to its leader, a "low profile" policy. This foundation also makes donations and maintains an active training program at the Caterpillar School, in conjunction with TECSUP, a private training center, for the purpose of "supporting clients" in their need to have qualified modern heavy machinery operators on staff. The principal stakeholders in this case are the customers. According to Pamela Abdalá, manager of FF, the students are not customers, but "credibility improves because we wish to project the image that we are a leading company that shapes leaders."

Another example of CSR is Textil San Cristóbal (TSC) in Chincha, a valley close to Lima, where the company is the town's main employer. Owner and CEO Juan Francisco Raffo, a third generation member of a family specialized in the textile industry, has changed the direction of the company's CSR focus toward the community—(principally near the plants), the workers and suppliers. This change is the result of two influences. The first is adoption of the belief that business and CSR are compatible and mutually reinforce one another, an idea which came from a relatively new member of TSC's board who was also associated with the Avina Foundation. The second is the fact that the company's current principal markets, Europe and the United States, require compliance with certain norms. As is stated in its Annual Report, TSC has been able to ". . . face, without observations, successive audits by six important customers utilizing international standards for acceptable labor practices. . . . this aspect is becoming increasingly important. . . . [in order]. . . . to minimize the risk involved in a deteriorated image. . . ." (TSC 2001: 13). It is important to point out that both of TSC's plants are certified by ISO 9000. Additionally, the company is attempting to improve perceptions related to service quality at the other end of the production chain, introducing a supplier evaluation system. TSC is carrying out a study on performance motivation with the London Consulting Group. Various projects are underway at the Chincha plant. On this big island of modernity surrounded by small town poverty, community aid projects include developing a water pump station and asphalting the highway, that is, assuming—as in the mining sector—a role that corresponds to the government. The different activities performed are not mentioned as part of TSC corporate image in the annual report. TSC also maintains a low profile.

The Gloria group has also successfully withstood the difficult test of open markets, rapidly expanding and also participating in privatization programs (Gloria 2001: 10), as well as adopting standards of "good practices." The purchase and production of milk, principally tinned, constitutes Gloria's main activity. So far this group has won the "battle of the milks" with Nestlé and Leche Holandesa, two European multinational brands. The Gloria group also has paper, cement and pharmaceutical companies. According to De Voto, the legal manager and head of CSR initiatives, the group "manages the corporate quality concept in all of its businesses," including the use of cutting edge technology at the new cooling and milk processing plants. Its principal but not sole concern is directed toward the 15,000 ranchers that provide milk on a daily basis. Similar to the Fierro group, Gloria provides technical and financial assistance in different forms to ranchers. Its truck fleet "travels throughout the country picking up milk and delivering money. The price is guaranteed, which is fundamental." The company admits there are some problems: "The work here, although the rancher complains about low prices, is seen as fundamentally social because the State does not reach where we operate."

On its 60th anniversary in 2000, Gloria contacted the London Consulting Group and adopted new ideas. The result was a new corporate code of conduct that includes "good practices with suppliers, the stakeholders and truck drivers" (Gloria 2001). In 2002, the group evaluated its different practices and social programs, attempting to organize and project these in such a way that is more clearly connected to corporate image. Gloria is a flagship company that is experiencing an interesting transition toward a CSR that, although somewhat limited by the Rodriguez family tradition of keeping a low profile, is stimulated by the necessity to modernize and become a leading company. The need to obtain a loan from the World Bank, along with suggestions from this entity related to the adoption of CSR practices, and advice from the London Consulting Group, also convinced Gloria of the need to do more socially. The group decided finally to engage in new corporate publicity, including references to its various social programs, publishing an information bulletin in November of 2002, distributed by a major newspaper. Gloria claims to have no problems with workers, although it admits to limiting themselves to "strictly complying with labor laws" which it considers is already enough because most companies do not. Gloria does not engage in programs with families. It is important to point out, however, that the group has been audited by the tax authority for allegedly making irregular donations to President Fujimori and his reelection campaign in 2000.

Wong, a young group, combines sensitivity regarding Peruvian traditions and customs with a modern business vision. The founder, Don Erasmo, has retired and the children have taken control with a sense of modernity that corresponds to a new business generation that is academically well prepared and more familiarized with global trends and the opportunities that arise, for example, in linking themselves to the Chinese economy. The supermarket chain has grown spectacularly amidst the bankruptcy of older operations and the entrance of international chains with aggressive business tactics. Wong has maintained its position as the country's number one supermarket thanks to close contact with suppliers and consumers and the loyalty of its workers. Public Relations manager Efrain Wong comments: "a business is its people. Good businesses are made with good people," and adds, "we must also give back to the community what we have reaped." For Wong, CSR revolves around a concept of "devolution." In terms of labor recruitment, Wong uses competitive criteria and relies on strong training programs. The emphasis is on excellent customer service because "we cannot expect anyone to attend to the customers' needs if they themselves have not been well attended to." When faced with competition from Disco Ahold, a Dutch multi-national, E. Wong observed, "they wanted to take our people, but not one went to the competition." External social investment at Wong includes organizing an annual parade in Lima that mobilizes thousands of individuals, including hundreds of workers, during Independence Day celebrations. This effort identifies Wong with "Peruvian culture" and is part of an ongoing war between supermarkets since it is the only national chain. Wong stores are also quite active organizing a recycling program whose proceeds support an NGO that attends to the needs of the disabled, and it also supports the Instituto de Síndrome Down (Down Syndrome Institute). Like other large EPGs, Wong receives "more than 100 letters a month" and applies the criteria of "responding according to the area of influence if it is close to a store," a practice that strengthens customer loyalty. The company recently opened several giant stores in poor neighborhoods, and Wong makes a special effort to "look good" and to be "a development pole in low income urban areas." Its principal stakeholders are the consumers rather than suppliers.

Two other EPGs studied stand out due to their multiple corporate CSR activities, although neither is completely free of problems related to civic image. The Backus Corporation, part of the Bentín Group, is the Peruvian company that shines in the area of external social investment, winning three consecutive CSR awards since 2001. Until 1980, Backus was the largest Peruvian beer company, and its industries were organized vertically. In the 1990s, Backus bought the rival Pilsen and Cuzqueña beer companies and became a monopolistic producer, hoping that loyalty to national brands would help contain international competition. INDECOPI, the regulatory body for competition, took the "solomonic" decision that a monopoly did not exist due to the presence of imported beer. In 2002, however, the Romero and Brescia Group sold their shares of Backus to Venezuelan and Colombian groups, and small shareholders, who had previously been ignored, were bought out; as a result, the Bentín family lost control of Backus. Internal and external CSR, according to Fernando

Hilbck, manager of Inter Institutional Relations at Backus, "have been practiced since the Bentíns peruvianized the brewery in 1956." He insists that "this policy has always existed, it is nothing new." To support this assertion, he points out the company's permanent support of Sporting Cristal, one of the leading soccer teams (soccer and beer have a cultural connection), in addition to continuous work with barley-producing peasants since the 1960s as well as worker illiteracy programs implemented in the 1970s. In the mid 1990s, the group began an aggressive restructuring project, investing more than US$8 million in introducing "total quality" principles (Durand 1996: 136). Following this restructuring, CSR acquired a new dimension since Backus' monopolistic condition required greater legitimacy. Hilbck says that "the social program development has been gradual, but when markets opened we established an aggressive plan." To date, Backus has done more than any other corporation, national or foreign, regarding educational matters, health, culture, sports, the environment, the arts, and other generous philanthropic donations (Backus 2002). The "strictly social" expenses correspond to 65% of the company's CSR budget, emphasis that began in the 1990s during a period of community projection. Regarding the environment, the corporation has created the Backus Pro Fauna Foundation, presided over by Elías Bentín, indicating corporate commitment at a higher level. With regards to labor issues, the Casa de Jubilados (retirement home) stands out. Requests received by mail are also attended to, but according to criteria based upon surveys used to determine needs. Backus believes that they do much but, similarly to other groups, "advertise little."

It must be noted, however, that Backus' image is marked by beer commercials that have a strong sexist and racist spin, identifying beer with blondes wearing small bikinis. A case in point is the advertisement that reads, "Do you prefer blondes or dark ones?" Regarding the extension of CSR through a more favorable tax framework, Backus executives believe that, despite limitations in the current legal framework for donations, it is preferable "not to pressure the government, because there are other issues . . . if not, resources will be distracted." The battle for control of the company in 2002 and 2003 gave way to claims by the Polar Group that Backus avoided paying taxes by overvaluing the import of ingredients in order to lower costs; this announcement affected the company's credibility, but the company hopes that the prestige associated with its longstanding social activities will help them to counteract this negative image.

Minera Yanacocha, co-owned by the Benavides de la Quintana Group and Newmont Mining, is the richest gold mine in South America. Mine exploitation began in 1992, and CSR programs were introduced as soon as social tensions arose with peasants who sold their land to the company. A dialogue was initiated in order to avoid conflict and prevent social movements.[18] Shortly thereafter, the company made significant investments in diverse internal bodies in charge of environmental care and CSR. Externally, Yanacocha's CSR programs are so extensive as to be divided into urban and rural development units. In 2002, social investment in rural development reached US$4 million, and urban development investment was approximately US$1.5 million, while investment in environmental projects exceeded US$40 million (Yanacocha 2001: 74–75). High sums are understandable given the fact that Yanacocha is a classic case of an intrusive investment that establishes a mini-state in an isolated and impoverished rural area, thus changing the economic, social and political dynamics of the region. In this scenario, positive and negative elements arise that are balanced through CSR and environmental policies. As such, Yanacocha operates on various fronts, but the most important one involves relations with the local provincial capital of Cajamarca. Cesar Humberto Cabrera, Corporate Manager in charge of social issues, admits that despite the amount invested, "the city of Cajamarca is still unhappy regardless of the fact that the mine provides 10 percent of the area's direct employment and 25 percent of the indirect employment." Notwithstanding, he claims that "there are no uprisings . . . because there is money, wages and investment." A 2000 liquid mercury spill from a truck in the Choropampa area, while traveling to the mines, allegedly contaminated a local community and generated criticism and protests. Despite the company's clean-up effort, Cajamarca's mayor and others blamed Yanacocha for the spill. In 2002, the mayor opened a new front when he argued that a new mining pit would contaminate the city's water supply. This issue led to a new round of negotiations, clarifications and public meetings. Despite new elections, the city of Cajamarca, with the support of labor unions and university students, continued to organize protest movements in 2004 and 2005. Yanacocha, like BCP and Alicorp, also had image problems when information was revealed regarding private negotiations with Montesinos to resolve problems with shareholders. Yanacocha's current Executive Director Roque Benavides was the CONFIEP president during the Fujimori government, and became well known for his non-critical support of that administration. Mining companies have also been criticized for tax privileges received during Fujimori's government, a policy that was blamed for causing a considerable decrease in tax collection (Comisión Investigadora de Delitos Económicos y Financieros 2002: 91 and ff).

Final Reflections

The study of the ten largest Peruvian EPGs indicates how and to what point this segment of private business has adopted CSR language and joined the CSR "movement." We argue that they have done so primarily as an organizational response to the challenges of globalization and the privatization of the economy generated by the adoption of neoliberalism. Any company that today claims to be "a leader" is involved in CSR practices. With the opening of the Peruvian economy and the corporate modernization process that followed, it became evident that the largest corporations must introduce cleaner technologies, emphasize safety and hygiene and provide on-going labor training programs. In addition, companies have begun to better define corporate goals, adopt codes of conduct and improve, extend or initiate social programs. In this context, family capitalism has ceded spaces to managers—a process visible at Alicorp, BCP, Ferreyros and Fierro. These companies reflect better educational standards and their more modern mind set has facilitated a quicker and more effective acceptance of CSR principles and practices. A similar trend is observed amongst new generational leaders—such as Tacama and Wong who have shown greater propensity to initiate changes.

Complementarily and to a lesser extent, the impulse for change comes from individual and collective necessity to manage business relations with the rest of Peruvian society more harmoniously. With the advent of neoliberalism, a new institutional matrix that highlights business power has emerged while the state presence has faded. CSR is a form of legitimizing the new social pact, although this does not necessarily lead to decisive changes in favor or more and better social and civic responsibility.

The general impulses toward global modernization, along with the collective responsibility related to an enhanced role of the private sector in the social matrix, have forced major domestic corporations to rethink, expand or adopt philanthropic and socially responsible policies that were previously applied in a more limited and traditional manner. Yet, the responses have not been uniform given variations of need to engage in CSR as a form of handling the social context and the existence of countertrends. In many cases, CSR has been adopted without abandoning older and more paternalistic practices; the impulse to "do more" has been contained by the fear of reactions against a society that "condemns success" or the generation of overwhelming demands from the majorities, who are mostly poor. All of these factors indicate serious corporate difficulties for establishing more harmonious relations with others in the civil society that is typical of underdeveloped economies and weak states. In several cases, philanthropic initiatives and social programs are not made public—such as in the cases of Alicorp, Ferreyros, Gloria, TN and TSC. These groups prefer to continue operating in silence, letting the groups targeted know about their generosity, but not broader public opinion. The cases reveal a paradox of practice without discourse, one that we shall try to explain below.

Another important finding related to needs or impulses to engage in CSR is that only a few EPGs have multiple stakeholders in civil society. In the majority of cases, and with the notable exceptions of Backus and Yanacocha, their social projects are limited in scope and size. Three of the ten EPGs studied have formed corporate or family foundations—Backus, Yanacocha, and Ferreyros, which is very small—and most prefer to deal directly with beneficiaries rather than through established NGOs or public sector agencies. These limitations may also be associated with the fact that CSR is relatively new in Peru, and that it takes time and effort to move in this direction. Furthermore, the state has not yet become seriously involved in the promotion of modern philanthropy or CSR initiatives, nor have tax or legal measures been adopted to enable such private efforts. All business leaders interviewed coincided in pointing to this lack of state support as a limitation. However, this problem works both ways. The testimony at Alicorp, for example, was that it is better not to attract the attention of government tax auditors if donations are made, and low propensity for fiscal responsibility by some other companies may explain lack of eagerness to demand more government involvement. In 2005, several major foundations, led by the Asociación Ancash (founded by Antamina), have taken the initiative to quietly lobby for an improved legal framework for philanthropy and CSR, an indication that they have finally realized the importance of reinforcing CSR through better legislation. This proposal comes at a time of unusual social mobilization in mining areas and some regions about the lack of corporate contribution due to tax exonerations and incentives.

This brings us to another key finding, about corporate citizenship—meaning respect for democracy and the rule of law, including labor and tax laws. While proclaiming adherence to CSR, most Peruvian EPGs, as well as multinationals operating in this country, usually prefer to keep these issues in the corporate closet. In the 1990s, during the semi-authoritarian government led by Fujimori and Montesinos, the corporate record in terms of supporting democracy and paying taxes was considerably negative. Furthermore, even today there is not a single corporation we can identify that is addressing fundamental issues of gender, age, race and cultural discrimination that are prevalent in this society. Unfortunately, those dimensions of "social responsibility" that are part of the corporate agenda in the developed world do not form part of the theory and practice of CSR in Peru. Thus, there is a gap between the broader vision of international organizations that promote CSR, and those in the corporate world that hold a narrower vision that avoids issues of a civic, legal or political nature.

The case studies indicate that the way each EPG has responded to the challenges of modernization, and the handling of the social context is varied. Factors such as the personal conviction of family bosses and managers, as well as the varied business needs that each has for practicing philanthropy and engaging in CSR, must be taken into account. The variation in business needs is largely due to characteristics of each economic sector, as mentioned below. These factors are summarized in Table 2.

Table 2. Factors that Motivate Philanthropy and CSR

Group	Personal convictions	External Influences	Needs
BCP	yes, religious	international competition	relationship with customers
Benavides	yes, religious	strategic alliances, oversight	new mining venture in rural area
Bentín	yes	international competition	monopolistic position, to secure suppliers
Ferreyros	yes, political	suppliers, consulting company	relationship with customers
Fierro	yes	international competition	to secure suppliers in rural areas
Olaechea	yes, religious	international cooperation	to secure suppliers in rural areas
Raffo	yes	international clients, consulting company	to handle the context
Rodríguez	yes, traditional	World Bank loans, consulting company	to secure suppliers, reputation
Romero	yes, religious	international competition	relationship with customers
Wong	yes	international competition	relationship with customers

The personal convictions of corporate leaders, whether religious or political or simply inspired in the way they envision their business practices, are key to explain certain practices, including the persistence of some social programs and renovation of others. Given the extraordinary concentration of power of contemporary Peruvian capitalism, the opinion and attitudes of corporate leaders are essential to understand the direction where business goes, because these individuals wield great decision-making authority and remain at the helm for long periods of time.

The peremptory need to do CSR varies greatly depending on the type of business, location and the place the companies occupy in the commodity chain, because those elements largely determine who are the strategic stakeholders. In the case of mining, the contemporary idea of social license is forcing giant mining companies to emphasize relations with nearby communities, or even an entire region where they operate. In the Peruvian case, this social involvement is especially urgent because of the governmental abandonment of most rural areas, the large number of people suffering from extreme poverty and, we may add, the recurrence of social protest. Thus, given the fact that in certain spaces companies are visible giants, and the state is weak or simply absent, corporations become a mini-state. In the case of agribusiness, or industries dependent on rural suppliers, old ways of doing social programs have not changed much because those programs are the only way "to make them loyal"—grapes for Tacama, barley for Backus, wheat for Alicorp, tobacco for TN and milk for Gloria. In the case of some manufacturing industries—(Backus, TSC), banking (BCP), and supermarket chains (Wong), the main emphasis is on consumers, who have become new stakeholders. TSC engages in CSR programs to control the possibility of international criticism since it must defend its reputation with foreign clients, who are in turn the subject of intense oversight in their country of origin. Wong is particularly aware of the importance of local consumers to stay in business. Backus provides the most advanced forms of CSR—with the exception of treatment toward small shareholders, valued only after a struggle for corporate control in 2002. Backus does social investment in part to maintain old traditions, but with greater emphasis today because its current monopolistic position accentuates the need to gain community support. Thus, the corporation has extended its varied CSR efforts.

Apart from the impact of open markets, more specific external influences explain the sudden need to get engaged in CSR. In three cases, international consultants (London Consulting Group) have introduced the concept, as a part of helping the restructuring process of several Peruvian corporations (Backus, Ferreyros, Gloria and TSC). In one case, Gloria, the need to secure international loans accelerated the process. TSC also extended CSR because clients abroad put pressure on them to behave in a socially responsible manner.

Another important finding is the difference between philanthropic donations and CSR social programs. Corporate donations are primarily relief-oriented. In this case business behaves "reactively," as one manager puts it, offering help according to the economic cycle, the overall social environment and its willingness to donate. Meanwhile, CSR social programs—for example, Ferreyros' educational initiative and its retirement home—are systematic, permanent and proactive, more organically related to the modern corporate mission, and as such cannot be suspended when variations in willingness or budget restrictions arise, as is often the case of donations in responses to letters. This is particularly important in those cases where it has become part of the company's reputation. Indeed, communicating programs to civil society reinforces responsibility.

In terms of environmental concerns today, a greater sense of responsibility has emerged, given the technological breakthroughs achieved and greater pressures coming from the state, local civil society groups and the global environmental movement. In terms of other external stakeholders, we have found significant variations among EPGs, although we can say that, despite the limitations, there is now a higher sense of responsibility toward the community at large, including groups not immediately related to the companies.

Some EPGs or their senior leaders have been closely linked to the corrupt and semi-authoritarian Fujimori government. Institutionally, the leading Peruvian EPGs—and their umbrella association, the CONFIEP—either supported the authoritarian trends of the 1990s or remained uncommitted to the struggle for democratization. This is a clear case of civic and democratic irresponsibility.

From what we have seen, fiscal responsibility among EPGs is also low. Two of the flagships have been accused of tax evasion, and several current investigations indicate a trend toward diminishing income tax collection amongst top corporations in the 1990s. A string of exonerations from tax responsibilities was obtained by large companies in the last years of the Fujimori administration, a process particularly visible in, but not limited to, the mining sector. Given the fact that large private investors have obtained numerous tax incentives, and some large corporations are not good taxpayers, their lack of interest in demanding a new system of tax deductible donations is understandable. Our research suggests that most large corporations do not want to place the tax issue on the agenda since it may reveal their tax evasion.

The critical themes outlined above, themes not considered by the conventional approach to studying CSR, merit further research, and must be an integral part of any evaluation of corporate responsibility. Why is there an unwillingness to include them? Part of the answer has to do with the finding that large corporations generally do not like public exposure, and many CEOs interviewed say that in Peru "success is condemned." Indeed, a study that asked "others"—blue collar workers, peasants, the poor, the general population—about the social and civil obligations of big business would probably demonstrate a high degree of disapproval or condemnation. Only one 1995 survey asked these questions with results that show high ambivalence—"exploiters, job creators"—a mix of admiration and hate, feelings that are stronger amongst the poor.[19] Unfortunately, this type of survey is not conducted on a regular basis, making it impossible to estimate to what extent CSR ideas and practices are changing patterns of opinion.

In order to fully understand the role of CSR in a country like Peru, we must conduct research that goes beyond the success stories, and data collected only from company sources and surveys of top managers, white collar workers and owners. The analysis of CSR must include questions of corporate citizenship as well as philanthropy or social investment, and must examine how others in society and the state perceive corporate discourse and action, including the groups that received corporate support.

At the beginning of the 21st century, the role of CSR in Peru remains heavily ideological, and it has become an important part of business discourse. Yet as this chapter shows, the CSR actually practiced by the top Peruvian EPGs is at an intermediate stage, with some important limitations to its future expansion. Attempts to exaggerate its breadth or results, as the conventional approach tends to do, suggest an unwillingness to consider the broader problems of business legitimacy and effectiveness in a context in which the power and responsibility of business have increased exponentially. Specific corporate responses to this increased role in society are better and more coordinated than in the past, but have not done enough to consolidate the new social pact that many expected to emerge with the introduction of neoliberalism.

Notes

1 All of the executives at Peruvian corporations interviewed assure that although the name of CSR is new, it has always been practiced.

2 A parallel line of inquiry is concerned with philanthropy as an individual, institutional and business practice. It explores to what extent business contributes to philanthropy or if it moves from "philanthropy to solidarity" alongside other organizations (Sanborn 2002: 4).

3 See the executive summary of the conference "The Americas Conference on Corporate Social Responsibility: Alliances for Development" (September 2002, Miami).

4 This peculiarity is due to the fact that many researchers work side by side with companies.

5 The relationship between business and civil society has rarely been studied by experts of EPGs (Peres 1998, Vásquez Huamán 2000). An early piece of work by the author (Durand 1996) discusses the social isolation of big business and the demands of modernity but does not study the question of social responsibility.

6 Interviews were also conducted with leaders promoting CRS in Peru: Avina, PERU 2021 and SASE.

7 For information on CRS and philanthropy in Latin America, see *ReVista*, Harvard University (Spring 2002).

8 The author attended the event and took notes.

9 Principally managers, executives and assistants; a total of 304.

10 A study conducted by the author on tax deductible donations indicates a drastic fall both in terms of the number of donors and the amount of donations, a process that starts with the 1991 tax reform and continuous through the decade. The 1991 reform eliminated a generous and often abused promotional system. The new system introduced limits to the amount of donations that are tax deductible and uses a complicated formula to estimate the total amount of tax deductions. According to interviews, many businesses make donations without using tax deduction mechanisms. Individual donors find the formula complicated.

11 In some cases, the owner and leader of the flagship company—Textil San Cristóbal from the Raffo Group, E. Wong from the Wong Group, P. Olaechea from the Olaechea Group—the General Manager—Alicorp of the Romero Group, BCP—a conglomerate of groups, Ferreyros of the Ferreyros Group, Tabacalera Nacional of the Fierro Group, top managers or individuals knowledgeable about CSR—Backus of the Bentín Group, Gloria of the Rodríguez Group and Yanacocha from the Benavides de la Quintana and Newmont Group.

12 Alicorp top managers claim that these are attended to according to budgetary restrictions. They also pointed out that many requests fail to specifically indicate what kind of help is needed and are usually poorly presented, an indication of problems in the demand side and unwillingness on the supply side to provide instructions. The latter might be related to the corporate fear of generating a tsunami of social demands.

13 Pedro Olaechea-Alvarez Calderón, descendant of a hacienda family and wine producers from Ica, studied in the United States. He contends that as landowners "we have always practiced it" (CRS) through a development entity in the valley. Then a revolutionary military government power came to power in 1968 and "forbade us to intervene." Additionally, the government expropriated the haciendas, putting them in the hands of cooperatives who later portioned the land among families, "atomizing the property." Since 1980, governments have favored the privatization of small plots.

14 Information collected at SUNAT. See Durand (2003c).

15 In the Fierro case, terrorists killed two employees. At Ferreyros an important terrorist leader was one of its workers, and members of the Romero and Benavides Group were abducted by guerrillas in the 1980s. Several prominent members of the business community (Delgado Parker, Hiraoka, Hotschild) were also abducted; some were injured or killed.

16 Disorganized requests and the dubious nature of some of the solicitations have complicated efforts to improve donations. To this, add the lack of legal framework for deductions.

17 It is important to point out that the Romero Group faces difficulties within the corporate community due to the relationship between the family group's leader, Dionisio Romero (also Executive Director of BCP), and Vladimiro Montesinos, President Fujimori's famously corrupt intelligence advisor, in the 1990s. Romero's meetings with Montesinos, in which he apparently sought political influence and business favors, were caught on video tape. After the scandal, Romero retired from his leadership position at Alicorp, leaving his son Dionisio Jr. at the helm while maintaining his position at BCP. This image problem has generated visible concern among Alicorp managers because it has damaged the group's reputation.

18 Conversation with anthropologist Juan Ossio, who presided over the first round of dialogue. Lima, September 2002.

19 The survey was prepared by Datum with the help of the author and published in *Business* (July 1995). The survey, taken in Lima to all social strata, showed that 38 percent of the respondents defined business people as "exploiters," 23% as "hard workers," 12 percent as "mercantilist" (rent-seekers) and only 4 percent as "visionaries." Negative feelings were even stronger in low-income social sectors. For comments, see Durand (2003a: 199–201).

References

Aguero, Felipe. 2002. "Business Social Responsibility in Latin America: Argentina, Brazil, Chile, Colombia, Mexico and Peru. A Preliminary Report." School of International Studies, University of Miami, (May).

Alicorp. 2001. "Memoria anual 2001." Alicorp.

Backus. 2002. *Generación 2000*. Año 4, vol. 14.

Banco de Crédito del Perú-BCP. 2001. "Memoria anual 2001." Lima: BCP.

Benavides de Burga, Marcela y Guida de Gastelumendi. 2001. "Responsabilidad social empresarial: un compromiso." Lima: Cuadernos del CIUP-SASE y PERU 2021.

Campodónico, Humberto. 1999. "Las reformas estructurales en el sector minero peruano y las características de la inversión 1992–2008." Santiago de Chile, Naciones Unidas, Comisión Económica para América Latina y el Caribe, Serie Reformas Económicas no. 24.

Cannon, Tom. 1994. *La responsabilidad social de la empresas: respuesta a los nuevos retos sociales, económicos, éticos y ambientales*. London: Financial Times-Folio.

Caravedo, Baltazar. 1998. *Perú: empresas responsables*. Lima: SASE-Servicios para el Desarrollo y PERU 2021.

Caravedo, Baltazar 2000. *Lo social y la empresa a fines de siglo: responsabilidad social empresarial, avances y logros*. Lima: SASE-Servicios para el Desarrollo y PERU 2021.

Castillo Ochoa, Manuel y Andrés Quispe Martínez. 1997. *El Estado post-ajuste: institucionalidad, Estado, actores y conflictos empresariales*. Lima: Centro de Estudios y Promoción del Desarrollo-DESCO.

Centro de Investigación de la Universidad del Pacífico-CIUP. 2002. "La opinión pública y los grupos de poder económico: una aproximación cualitativa sobre ética, valores y responsabilidad social." Lima (octubre).

Congreso de la República del Perú. 2002. *Balance de la inversión privada y la privatización*. Lima: Fondo Editorial del Congreso de la República del Perú.

Crabtree, John y Jim Thomas, eds. 1999. *El Perú de Fujimori*. Lima: Instituto de Estudios Peruanos y Centro de Investigación de la Universidad del Pacífico.

Dammert Ego Aguirre, Manuel. 2001. *El Estado mafioso*. Lima: Editorial El Virrey.

Directo. 2002. "Percepciones de empleados sobre responsabilidad social empresarial." Investigación Analítica (noviembre)

Durand, Francisco. 1996. *Incertidumbre y soledad: reflexiones de los grandes empresarios de América Latina*. Lima: Fundación F. Ebert.

Durand, Francisco. 2003a. *Empresa & sociedad en el espejo*. Lima: Biblioteca Business.

Durand, Francisco. 2003b. *Riqueza económica y pobreza política*. Lima: Fondo Editorial de la Pontificia Universidad Católica del Perú.

Durand, Francisco. "Donaciones, impuestos y responsabilidad social," in F. Porto-carrero and C. Sanborn eds. *Estudios sobre filantropía, responsabilidad social y voluntariado en el Perú.* Lima: Centro de Investigaciones de la Universidad del Pacífico.

Ferreyros. 2001. "Memoria anual 2001." Lima: Ferreyros.

Gloria. 2001. "Memoria anual 2001." Lima: Gloria.

Peres, Wilson, ed. 1998. *Grandes empresas y grupos industriales latinoamericanos.* Mexico: CEPAL y Siglo XXI.

Pizarro, Rosa, Laura Trelles y Eduardo Toche. 2004. "La protesta social durante el toledismo." En DESCO-Centro de Estudios y Promoción del Desarrollo. *Peru Hoy: los mils días de Toledo.* pp. 30–99. Lima: DESCO.

Portocarrero, Felipe *et al.* 2000. *Empresas, fundaciones y medios: la responsabilidad social en el Perú.* Lima: Centro de Investigación de la Universidad del Pacífico.

Portocarrero, Gonzalo y Rafael Tapia. 1992. *Trabajadores y sindicalismo y política en el Perú de hoy.* Lima: ADEC-ATC, Asociación Laboral para el Desarrollo.

Portocarrero, Felipe y Cynthia Sanborn, eds. 2003. *De la caridad a la solidaridad: filantropía y voluntariado en el Perú.* Lima: Centro de Investigaciones de la Universidad del Pacífico.

Salamon, Lester M. *et al.* 1999. *La sociedad civil global.* Madrid: Fundación BBVA.

Sanborn, Cynthia. 2002. "From Charity to Solidarity? Latin American Philan-thropy in Changing Times." *ReVista* (Spring), pp. 3–7.

Sociedad Nacional de Industrias-SNI. 2003. "Propuesta: reactivación del sub-sector vitivinícola." SNI (febrero).

Stein, Steve y Carlos Monge. 1988. *La crisis del Estado patrimonial en el Perú.* Lima: Instituto de Estudios Peruanos y Universidad de Miami.

Stiglitz, Joseph E. 2002. *Globalization and its Discontents.* New York: W.W. Norton & Company.

Sulmont, Denis. 2000. "La responsabilidad social en el Perú." En Denis Sulmont y Enrique Vásquez, eds. *Modernización empresarial en el Perú.* pp. 123–182. Lima: Red para el Desarrollo de las Ciencias Sociales en el Perú.

Tabacalera Nacional-TN. S/f. "Impacto socioeconómico del cultivo del tabaco, la agroindustria y la industria manufacturera de cigarrillos." Lima: TN.

Textil San Cristóbal-TSC. 2001. "Memoria anual 2001." Lima: TSC.

Vásquez Huamán, Enrique. 2000. *Estrategias del poder: grupos económicos en el Perú.* Lima: Centro de Investigación de la Universidad del Pacífico.

Wilson, Ian. 1999. *The New Rules of Corporate Conduct: Rewriting the Social Char-ter.* Westport, Connecticut: Quorum Books.

Yanacocha. 2001. "Yanacocha: su compromiso con Cajamarca: balance social 1992–2001." Lima: Minera Yanacocha SRL.

9

Corporate Social Action in a Context of Crisis: Reflections on the Argentine Case

Mario M. Roitter and Marcelo Camerlo

Corporations have become the focus of attention in the contemporary social agenda. Their economic role and the social impact of their activities as a whole open up a much needed debate about the relationship between corporation and society, a debate that until now has oscillated between praise and denunciation—a black-or-white issue. This chapter seeks to contribute to a better understanding of some of the debated issues, focusing on "corporate social action," social interventions that corporations carry out of their own volition.

That companies carry out community action is nothing new. However, what has changed in the last decade, taking into account the diverse cultural and historical contexts that have flourished? In Argentina, for example, the question of "corporate social responsibility" became more relevant in the 1990s, with larger corporations taking the lead. A modest amount of academic production—in reality, closer to consultancies than independent research—has tracked these shifts. However, this research has primarily examined the implementation of corporate social responsibility and how it could be improved, emphasizing the need to underline the positive effects of these corporate actions as a way to fuel their development. As this type of social practice became increasingly common in the framework of transformation processes throughout Latin America, the concept of corporate social responsibility was heavily influenced by the postulates of the so-called Washington Consensus.[1] Thus, a new balance was configured that involved a reframing of the public realm beyond the role of the state. The public and private spheres became more intimately connected.

The December 2001 Argentine crisis caused a political, social and economic shock, an expression of "death foretold" for a type of economic model and a concept of society that inherently entails an exponential increase of poverty and inequality. The Argentine crisis, and other similar processes in Latin America, has as one of its consequences the need to revise the premises and certainties of the "single discourse" that predominated in the 1990s. And, in that context, it also seems advisable to revise the model of corporate social action devised in that decade, as well as the conceptual frameworks used to study and analyze it.

This chapter seeks to explore the specific strategies, scope and influence of corporate social enterprise in the present Argentine context, thus contributing to the discussion and elaboration of new conceptual frameworks. Up until now, the specific nature of these practices has rarely been examined as part of the literature on corporate philanthropy, and this lack of analysis hinders the application of models designed for other contexts. More pertinent analytical tools must be developed in order to engage in effective corporate philanthropy. Our inquiries will hinge on a simple but fundamental distinction: we shall call *corporate social action* (CSA) the explicit interventions of a company in the social sphere, while we propose to designate the particular forms of CSA in different historical and cultural frameworks as *approaches*.

The first section of this chapter deals with the hypothesis that the notion of "corporate social responsibility" formulated in Argentina during the 1990s is in itself a particular form of corporate social participation—which we shall call *modern approach*—and corresponds to a certain context of social transformation that took place in those years. In the second section, we show that the 2001 Argentine crisis demonstrated the deficiencies of the *modern approach*. There are two distinct sources of these deficiencies. The first involved intrinsic factors, including limitations of certain types of interventions such as the "teach them how to fish" method, the lack of connection between what is said and what is done, and the over-reliance on good will as a motivating factor. The second source of deficiency in the modern approach stems from Argentina's particular circumstances, with growing complexity in its social situation, the eclipse of the state's role in issues of development and social change, the presence of certain structural economic features and the corporate leadership profile shaped by the processes of privatization and globalization.

In the third section, we broach the need to have more suitable conceptual frames to understand CSA in a context of underdevelopment. Three analytical guidelines are suggested to direct the debate: a) the tension between the voluntary and mandatory dimensions of the links between corporation and society, b) CSA potential to become an instrument for social development, and c) its inescapable character as *social asset*. We believe that one of the current key issues is the need for a debate about volunteering, self-regulation and regulation.

We are well aware that an in-depth discussion of these questions far exceeds this chapter's scope. However, these factors must be considered as an integral part of updating the discussion of corporate social actions and placing it into a more solid academic context.

The Modern Approach of Corporate Social Action

We believe that the idea of "corporate social responsibility" coined in Argentina in the 1990s was a peculiar formulation *of* and intervention *in* the society from the perspective of the corporate world, the aforementioned *modern approach*, corresponding to a certain context of structural transformation in the political, social and economic spheres. Therefore, we will characterize that context, the new corporate practices and the main features of that *approach*.

Argentine society underwent a deep and swift transformation in the 1990s, characterized by a process of reforms that, in one way or another, affected all of Latin America. This transformation redefined the public and private roles in the economy, as well as a shift of the relative power of the social actors. Policies like privatization, open markets and deregulation had a noticeable impact in economic and political terms. And this cannot be considered just a byproduct but an effect intrinsic to the aims, modes and scope of these processes. It was actually a plan to produce "[…] a reorganization of social hierarchies. To alter the balance between the public and private spheres means to change the distribution of material and symbolic resources which have an impact on the shape of political life … shifting from openness and visibility into a domain more reluctant to access and revision … Privatization describes a direction of change, though it lacks a specific origin or destination … the same forces promoting privatizations in order to cut down on bureaucracy and waste also promote cuts on social expenditure," which caused the systematic trend toward privatization to produce a regressive redistribution of wealth (Starr, 1993: 34).

Fueled by these reforms, the Argentine economic structure changed dramatically, affecting the dimension, nature and mode of relations between the public and private realms. In this context, the corporations became not only the driving economic force, but the very center of the social arena, following the dominant international trend.

This rise and transformation of the private brought also about revalorization of nonprofit private organizations, in addition to the significant growth many corporations enjoyed in the 90s. These private organizations have played a growing role in recent years as suppliers of social services to the community—either acting on their own, allied to other corporations or through actions coordinated with the state.

Many of the most important local companies were taken over by foreign investors, causing a significant turnover of the who's who in the business world. Privatization of state owned companies—which in turn produced an important increment of direct foreign investment—contributed to this turnover. So did large-scale purchase of stocks in traditional local companies, heirs to the industrial substitution of imports which, on the whole, had been created in the 70s and 80s. The main changes took place in the most dynamic sectors, such as the exploitation of natural resources and service companies mostly unaffected by foreign competition. Thus, the entrepreneurial map underwent a massive transformation. Within the course of a few years, the largest companies came under private control, mostly foreign.[2] This globalization process—experienced in its own particular way all over Latin America—brings about a significant change of the social actors and their relationships to society, as well as cultural transformations that include the introduction of a focus on corporate social responsibility and a more intensive discussion of its diverse dimensions and scope.

The Convertibility Law[3]—establishing peso-US dollar equivalency—completely modified the macroeconomic context. Until that moment, the prevalent view was that under high inflation, entrepreneurial strategies favored mostly short-term options over those that demanded sustained efforts. In particular, the trend was to give low priority to initiatives toward the community beyond charitable philanthropy (Thompson, 1992).

In this scenario of stability, the so-called structural reforms helped the country's economy to break away from its long process of stagnation, significantly increasing corporate size[4] and profits. However, these reforms also had the negative side-effects typical of such quick and profound restructuring: high unemployment, fragmentation and social polarization. This, in turn, gave rise to new social demands the large corporations could hardly ignore.

Corporation Practices[5]

In an expanding market with large sectors of the Argentine society experimenting a sensation of sustained progress, some economic indexes such as the per-capita income seemed to indicate a country emerging from underdevelopment. In this boom environment, the corporations leading this economic transformation began to occupy a place of recognition in the social sphere through their own activities and those of their foundations.

Although the corporations acted in various ways in this new scenario, many researchers[6] agree that a large percentage of the corporations seemed to share a concern about the social environment surrounding their business activities well into the 1990s, although to varying degrees. No one disputed the convenience of reaching out in that direction; the debate centered on the search for suitable and effective means of social intervention and, in some cases, the need to find fresh approaches for social enterprise on the part of companies and corporate foundations.

The mass media helped focus attention on CSA issues, playing a key role in promotion and diffusion, granting awards for the best initiatives,[7] forums, institutions like the Foundations Group (GDF)[8] and chambers of commerce and other promotional institutions linked to the business world.

Most of these new initiatives shared a key element: the importance assigned by these companies to nonprofit organizations. For the most innovative companies, investment in the community in partnership with these organizations has turned out to be, as in the case of other countries, an excellent device to broaden the results of their actions, to help sustainability and to acquire a positive and prestigious image.

Although the presentation of the empirical data exceeds the possibilities of this chapter, we consider it important to provide some elements for a better understanding of the scope of CSA in Argentina. A survey carried out in the late 1990s by Gallup, under the direction of Universidad de San Andrés, pointed out that half of the 147 companies polled made contributions to social organizations either directly or through their foundations. They also found explicit policies and guidelines for the selection criteria: 70% claimed to have defined fields of social action and 60% had defined a certain profile of recipient. Both claims reveal a certain degree of formalization of these practices. In turn, a survey published by *Mercado* magazine indicated that out of 355 companies with the highest sales volume in the local market, 43.7% had undertaken social projects and 17.5% intended to do so in the near future.

As for the role of corporate foundations, companies tend to consider their creation as the fulfillment of the need to organize and systematize their philanthropic activities by carrying out these functions outside the corporate structure. However, only about 10% of the corporations have chosen this means to participate in the social area.[9] Regarding the actions of this type of institutions, Table 1 shows foundations' expenditure levels during the 90s. However, the figures in that table do not represent accurate averages, since the access to information about each foundation was not the same or covered all the years of the period; they are mere indicators of the scope and relative importance of corporate foundations.

Table 1. Corporate Foundations in Argentina
Reference values for the 1990–1999 period[a] US Dollars

Foundation	Total Expenditure USD	% Donation / Total Expenditure	Activity Sector
Perez Companc	52,189,185	67.9	Oil/Finance
Renault	5,878,607	15.8	Automotive
Bunge y Born[c]	4,833,840	35.0	Food
IRSA	4,298,135	90.9	Construction
Fortabat Amalia	3,945,046	85.9	Cement
YPF	3,347,318	24.0	Oil
Hermanos Rocca-Techint	3,280,816	70.3	Steel
BankBoston	3,000,099	24.0	Finance
Banco Mayo[b]	2,925,532	4.8	Finance
Banco Galicia	2,200,529	58.8	Finance
Banco Patricios[b]	1,278,402	61.3	Finance
OSDE	1,005,068	0.0	Health
Jorge Macri	897,904	61.8	Food
Roberto Noble – Diario Clarín	804,959	18.0	Communications
Banco Nación	752,419	6.0	Finance
Arcor	737,785	94.8	Food
Banco Crédito Argentino	636,359	5.3	Finance
Acindar	619,780	33.2	Steel
Bagley-Mosoteguy[c]	566,000	38.7	Food
Bemberg	443,381	95.3	Beer
Bco Roberts[b]	385,669	29.7	Finance
Avon para la mujer	349,993	12.7	Cosmetics
Telefónica de Argentina[d]	319,980	10.9	Telecommunications
Astra	311,460	5.4	Oil
ESSO	293,180	84.6	Oil
T.I.A.[b]	257,979	88.4	Commerce
Bco Francés	256,744	83.4	Finance
Konex	256,628	0.0	Commerce
T.I.M.[b]	251,000	1.2	Health
Cargill	248,624	13.9	Food
Bayer	235,349	0.0	Pharmaceutical
Lloyds Bank	199,759	94.2	Finance
Terrabusi[b]	152,000	100.0	Food
Banco Ciudad de Buenos Aires	150,235	26.4	Finance
G. Ramos- Ambito Financiero	132,553	0.0	Communications
Peñaflor[b]	114,125	46.0	Beverages
Roemmers	106,000	0.0	Pharmaceutical
Aluar	84,665	2.8	Aluminum
TOTAL	**97,147,187**	**32.1**	

a.   As the source did not have all the figures for the period, these averages should be considered only as reference values and not accurate percentages.
b.   No activity during the second half of the decade.
c.   When the companies changed hands, they became family foundations.
d.   The figure corresponds to 1999; this foundation had no activities until that year.
Source: Available yearly balance sheets presented by the Foundations at the Inspección General de Justicia-Ministero de Justicia.

Their level of expenditure is in some senses significant, reaching almost a hundred million dollars,[10] a figure that may be considered relevant especially when compared with some of the expenditures of government programs implemented during the same period. For example, the government's entire food program for destitute sectors of the population amounted to roughly 350 million dollars.[11] However, one company alone accounted for slightly more than half of all corporate foundation spending: the Pérez Companc Foundation,[12] with 53%. Thus, there is a noticeable gap between the values corresponding to the large foundations and all the others. The ten largest foundations account for 88% of the yearly expenditures registered by these 39 organizations. Such heterogeneity makes it very difficult to establish indicators of their activities at an aggregate level. However, many of these foundations are of the so-called *operative* type, those foundations whose activities focus on their own programs instead of funding third party programs. Indeed, Table 1 shows that the ratio between donations and total expenditure reaches an average of 32.1% and that nearly half the foundations are below that level. This means that in the case of Argentine corporate foundations one should not take for granted they are donor institutions since, in most cases, that is not their main activity. Also, the figures in Table 1 do not necessarily imply that the parent corporations may not have made independent donations on their own.

Another feature that may help characterize these foundations is the fact that 61% were created before 1990, and at that time 86% corresponded to large local companies. During the '90s, half of the new foundations[13] were created by transnational corporations of foreign origin, a fact that also mirrors the changes in the sources of capital that took place in the largest companies in Argentina.

As for their recent evolution, no conclusive trends can be observed, though it is evident that the funds administered by corporate foundations since 1998 have somehow diminished. The crisis in the Argentine economy and changes in corporate ownership caused eight of these foundations to cease their activities or at least, not to have declared any relevant activity since 1995. An additional two corporate foundations have become family foundations.

We can see that CSA has relevance for large corporations, acquiring a significant level of development. However, we should inquire into the actual dimensions of CSA. This is a pertinent question because of the general lack of information about outcome in terms of the magnitude of the social problems being addressed through corporate social action. This investment in social programs may lead to the belief that corporations in effect are able solve problems that the state cannot or will not or that, in the best of cases, offers only partial solutions. However, what happens in fact with corporate actions is quite different. Only certain problems or a reduced number of clients or beneficiaries can be addressed, as should be expected since the very nature of CSA implies a narrow scope and small scale.

Does that make corporate social action irrelevant? We think not, since CSA may make a big difference for the NGOs involved in a certain field, as well as for the communities directly benefiting from these actions. In particular, NGOs that have managed to establish a partnership with a corporation may find the association essential for tapping into available resources and a wide network of contacts. The same advantage applies to the neighboring communities around company sites or the specific targets of company programs: undoubtedly these actions can help solve their problems.

Yet, although these actions may be beneficial, they will have little impact if they do not involve the company in the mid-term in a process of collaboration that steadily leads to a commitment of its central capabilities, rather than just the donation of specific resources such as money or supplies. When process is taken into account, the CSA may gradually evolve from a mere *philanthropic* perspective (donations) toward a *transactional* perspective (whereby both parties exchange resources and benefits) that will eventually lead to an *integrative* one, in which all the participants manage to align their strategies and produce new value.[14]

In other words, CSA is a healthy practice that may generate small-scale innovative actions that may later be replicated on a larger scale. The discourse underlying the specific CSA actions and the accompanying implicit social model are the issues at stake. The issue here is not just the specific practices but when these corporate actions are seen as a vicarious mode of wealth redistribution.

The CSA *Modern Approach*

What we call the *modern approach* to CSA basically uses the following criteria as guidelines for corporate social action:

From sporadic to permanent action. When corporate social actions start to be perceived as intrinsic to corporate practices, rather than just being viewed as circumstantial activities, they become a standard characteristic of all large or internationally known corporations. As a result, corporate social action is in turn demanded from within and from outside the company.

Social expectations about CSA pervade the corporations themselves, spreading among the staff and the executive levels.

From charity to strategy. The *modern approach* is characterized by a professionalization of corporate social activity. The slogan "from charity to strategy" is emblematic of the changes in the way projects are formulated and implemented, as well as in the definition of the appropriate areas of concentration and alliances with other organizations.

These concerns and initiatives are manifesting themselves in large corporations all over the world. By the mid-90s, the U.S. organization, the Conference Board, claimed that strategic planning of donations had become the most suitable way to face pressures—particularly when resources are scarce—by integrating economic aims with more effective actions toward the community. So-called *strategic philanthropy* proposes that corporate social action should: integrate different corporate areas, have specialized staff, apply evaluation and follow-up mechanisms, favor the involvement of the staff as a whole, be proactive and promote strategic alliances with other actors (Alperson, 1995).

Another indication of the growing trend to professionalism is the emergence of a large number of training opportunities for staff dealing with community related activities as well as for people involved in volunteer work and for the officials of corporate foundations.[15]

From "the fish" to "the fishing rod." In the *modern approach* to CSA, the purpose of community related activities is perceived and understood in a distinct manner, using a strategic model. Methods used in the modern approach attempt to go beyond mere assistance practices, always scorned though ever present, to provide the recipients with resources to strengthen their own abilities. The slogan that illustrates this position is "Don't give fish but teach them to catch fish."

Increasing emphasis on promotion of more active recipients reflects a number of trends and notions that have become widely accepted in the last years, such as empowerment, self-sustainability or social assets, all polysemic terms hard to translate into Spanish that have become part of a common lexicon because of their frequent use and diffusion by diverse agencies, foundations and academic centers from the United States. These buzzwords all stress the importance of developing the intrinsic capabilities of groups and communities chosen as beneficiaries of both private and public actions.

Particular characteristics of large corporations. Although it is usually said that in order to promote community-oriented activities you do not need large amounts of money, experience demonstrates that social actions have become the domain of large corporations. A strong correlation exists between the growing size of a company and its likelihood of undertaking community actions, as evidenced through international experience. (Roitter, 1995). Factors such as higher exposure to public opinion, bonds between this type of action and communication strategies, the need to accrue skills to face a steadily growing social demand and the influence of progressively stronger presence and pressure of some NGOs help account for this correlation.

Consequently, the *modern approach* to CSA appears linked to a new model of intervention put forward by and for large companies whose operations are framed in very different contexts and in an increasingly competitive environment with a great deal of exposure to public opinion resulting from the global scale of their operations.

Corporate community involvement, especially by transnational companies, is often explained away by seeing it as a public relations strategy to defend itself against certain accusations such as questionable environmental practices, unfair treatment of minorities, subcontractor exploitation of child labor and other issues brought into the limelight mostly by advocacy or watchdog organizations in developed countries.[16]

The "good neighbor" goodwill. The features of the so-called *modern approach* to CSA could be summed up in what many corporations consider an attribute of their "good neighborliness." This idea of the corporate role supposes a volunteer-like intervention in the concerns of the community based on a self-perception of the corporation as yet another—but better endowed—actor in the geographic area shared with the communities where the corporations have located their productive or trading activities.

This "good neighbor" intent, often adopted by companies in the case of Argentina, expresses the search for an adequate integration to their social environment as well as a disposition to "give back to the community part of what has been received." We might say that the value of this approach is based on the fact that it offers a twofold connection in community-oriented actions, operating both as *explanatory and operative criteria* guidelines for the CSA.

On one hand, it provides a conceptual framework: the neighborly notion refers to a shared social space where the corporation is an actor among others, with equally shared responsibilities. The ideas of common good and solidarity, far from being residual or secondary facets of eventual altruistic initiatives, become the basic foundation for daily behavior. On the other hand, in the operative dimension, it leads to the articulation of concrete modalities and areas of intervention: some areas are the neighbor's ground, and others are not; and the same goes for certain issues, behavior patterns or attitudes. In this way, applying this notion enables the corporation to define what, in terms of good neighborliness, it is that they should do, how, when, where, for and with whom.

When corporations understand "good neighborliness" as an intrinsic component of their identity—and not only as an isolated and sporadic trait of certain sectors or persons—they are able to link their social activities to their business strategy.

To sum up, in the *modern approach* to CSA, corporate actions explicitly meant to intervene in the social sphere appear as a permanent function of large or transnational corporations. These corporate actions involve strategies intended to go beyond charity, that is, aimed at promoting and strengthening communities and organizations linked to them by means of two metaphors that operate as guidelines: the *good neighbor* figure and *teaching how to fish.*

Debated Models

In this second part of the chapter, we argue that the 2001 Argentine crisis exposed some of the problems of the *modern approach* to CSA, and of CSA as a whole. We therefore propose a debate on phenomena derived from intrinsic traits of such an approach, as well as the broader meaning these actions have as a discourse about the social sphere.

Corporate Practices in a Context of Crisis

The economic, social and political crisis that had been brewing in Argentina since 1998 exploded toward the end of 2001 with a profound impact on relevant sectors of public opinion. The large corporations—most particularly the banks—became one of the main targets of criticism and social unrest.[17] In this context, many companies—both those who had systematic social programs and those who only carried out sporadic initiatives—had to reformulate their programs and give priority to traditional charitable practices or set them in motion, respectively. One way or another, what up to that moment might have been understood as the progressive consolidation of the *modern approach* to CSA had to be altered because of overwhelming pressures.

Unlike what usually happens in business-cycle slumps, companies did not cutback on their social expenditures because of the dimension of the crisis. However, the corporate funds made no noticeable difference on Argentina's deteriorated set of social indexes.

One factor in keeping corporate philanthropy going and shifting it back toward the charitable model was the will of the corporate employees. Directly or indirectly affected by the magnitude of the social catastrophe unleashed, they undertook spontaneous solidarity initiatives which in most cases had a favorable echo in the corporate leadership, who encouraged or even supported them. Although these actions were mostly money and food collections and distribution, in many instances they had effects well beyond the immediate circumstances that may result in more ambitious and integral practices, as well as in the channeling of their concerns through volunteer programs.[18]

We believe the multiplication of this sort of program is due to a number of factors. First, for the global corporations, volunteering is a CSA practice close to the heart of their culture. Second, it allows CSA to be linked with other business objectives such as management policies and motivation of human resources. Finally, we view it as a mechanism to fortify the corporate position in the public eye.[19]

Some Overlooked Factors

We think that beyond the consequences of the Argentine crisis, the *modern approach* has effectively proven to suffer from certain limitations. In order to better understand these limitations, we should consider both intrinsic traits and some specific characteristics of Argentine context that might have influenced CSA methods of operation here. What follows is an attempt to identify these two types of factors.

Intrinsic Limitations of the *Modern Approach* to CSA

In the first place, the application of the "teaching how to fish" metaphor is a somewhat restricted guideline for decision-making in issues concerning corporate social action. This representation of what is "good for the poor" is not quite pertinent in countries where poverty and marginality involve large portions of the population and are structural components of the problem. In this context, the "fishing rods" are almost useless since what we lack is fish. On the other hand, this metaphor may contain a patronizing view of the social phenomena since it presupposes that the company *knows better* what sort of tools the community needs for its development. For example, training programs focus mostly on what the corporation considers "pertinent" rather than on what the community and the individual members can create and adopt as tools for their development.

And yet, it seems unreasonable to expect that each individual company may or should shoulder the social and economic dynamics to which it belongs, and their consequences. In this kind of context, one must also take into account that it is unrealistic to propose effective solutions that may go beyond mere charity without considering the long-term structural problems affecting society. This restriction may not be easy to lift, and yet it must be taken into account to avoid a reductionist notion of the social responsibility of the corporation, limiting it only to the community-oriented initiatives. Thus, we might remember here that the problem of the unequal distribution of wealth in Argentina and all over Latin America should be approached from other perspectives, since CSA cannot ever be considered an effective alternative mechanism to improve the distribution of the fruits of progress.

So-called *terminology inflation* is a second factor limiting the '90s approach. By terminology inflation, we mean not only the proliferation of overlapping terms to define the same practice (strategic philanthropy, social entrepreneurial investment, corporate social responsibility) but more specifically, a gap between practice and discourse, that is, between notions, models and proposals on one hand and concrete behaviors on the other. Very few companies have managed to live up to the attributes of the *modern approach* with their social programs, though most claim to have adopted it.[20]

Thus, while the *modern approach* is well-known and accepted, putting it into practice seems to be a gradual idea; the issue of whether the gap is due to the inertia inherent in all changes or to the poor implementation of the new notions is open to debate. It is also an open question, as most public opinion seems to think, that all the talk about empowerment or the modern approach is nothing more than a circumstantial public relations strategy. In terms of the public message, we ought to question the pretense of novelty and the far-from-proven discourse about SCA that sees it as a model of efficacy compared to the archaic and wasteful ways of the state. Implicit or explicit scorn for state actions on the part of the private sector—whether by NGOs or corporate actors—tends to overlook or not take into account the constant renovation of state philanthropic actions attempted by many civil servants, thus overestimating the impact of private philanthropy. Instead, some of the corporate social actions seem to be far from that idealized image of "the new and effective." This is particularly true when either discourse or actual practices turn citizens, who have rights by the mere virtue of being citizens, into clients or beneficiaries of the donor's generosity.[21] When citizens' rights are not acknowledged, philanthropic actions are nothing but charity. That is why many of the men and women committed to social practices in corporations and foundations strive to adopt actions that help to consolidate the rights of the citizens, an emphasis that necessarily leads these citizens to include in their discourse a revalorization of the public sphere.

Local Factors Influencing CSA

Among specific local factors, we might mention:

Growing complexity of the social situation. Argentina has been affected by the overall crisis of an economic and social model. Signs of this crisis began to emerge as early as 1998, because of the country's inability to compensate for the social effects triggered by the opening, deregulation and privatization processes. Although these policies led to a 4-year period of growth and modernization, they lacked the necessary actions to spread these advantages to a large sector of the population. Thus, during that period, unemployment, poverty and inequality increased to levels never before seen in the Argentina.[22] What happened here belies the widespread common cliché claiming that "you can't distribute wealth without producing it," abundantly proven by the events of the early 1990s in Argentina and the recent history of other instances of swift growth in Latin America demonstrating that distribution of the fruits of technical advances and the so-called structural reforms are not a spontaneous product of the dynamics of the free market.[23]

Lack of state institutionality. The role played by the state in terms of social responsibility is somewhat ambiguous. Citizenship often involves little more than the mere formality of casting a ballot (O'Donnell, 1997). Corporations face a peculiar dualism in the face of this weakening of the public sphere and the consequent hegemony of the private sectors. On one hand, the private sectors appear as the center of contemporary social life, a sort of hero of modern times (Weil, 1992). On the other hand, however, the sector is ever more suspect because of its accumulated power, more so in underdeveloped countries where it is accompanied by the parallel powerlessness of state regulation. We have seen that the business sector contributes significant amounts to social issues, and undoubtedly these contributions increased in the 1990s. However, neither the quantity nor the extent and rationale seem to justify the great value suggested by the dominant discourses.

Structural economic factors. There are also a set of factors produced by the direction and the extent of development of the economic base of countries such as Argentina. These factors—that could be called structural in their nature, though the jargon may sound outdated—affect CSAs, causing them to present a profile quite different from the typical model in more diversified and integrated economies. Here, we might mention that the *density of the productive structure*, that is to say, the number and quality of up stream/down stream links among corporations, influence the opportunities to develop, expand and spread alliances between NGOs and business. When an NGO and a company agree on a joint initiative or program, the company usually appeals to their suppliers or trading channels. The denser the productive network, the more chances to establish relevant and sustainable initiatives. In Argentina and most other Latin American countries, these productive networks are fewer than in developed countries, where the *modern approach* to CSA appears more consolidated.

The *spatial concentration level of the productive activities* of the country should also be considered. Again, we can say that the higher the concentration, the fewer the opportunities of interaction between companies and communities. One of the problems in Argentina is the extreme concentration of business in the Buenos Aires metropolitan area, something that reduces, or even prevents the establishment of the links described with the *good neighbor* metaphor. On the contrary, wherever you find a large company in a medium or small community, the links tend to multiply, promoting local development.

Lead economic actors and behavior dynamics. In Argentina, the large companies, predominantly those of foreign origin, led the way in the establishment of CSA in the 1990s. This, in turn, shaped a number of specific characteristics in the application and theoretical foundation of the prevalent model of social action.

In many underdeveloped countries, many multinational corporations do more business in exports than in the local market, a market that also tends to be rather limited. Therefore, local consumers are not a priority for these corporations. This is a severe limitation to one of the main motivations of the *modern approach*: the appeal to consumers' preference for companies engaged in CSA. Concerns related to legitimacy and prevention of potential conflict become the more relevant, and these are not always enough to support a sustained effort in community actions.[24]

Compared to Brazil, for example, Argentina does not have a significant number of "world class" national companies, in terms of size and participation in international markets. Experience shows that these "world class" companies are the ones with the largest social programs. Luis Pagani, president of Arcor, one of the few multinational corporations from Argentina, considers that the lack of local businessmen in the most significant areas of our economy creates an added cost since as "a local entrepreneur, besides managing his company, (he) is involved in community concerns with his ideas and drive."[25] Though admittedly the manager of a foreign corporation may take active part in community matters, he or she can hardly be qualified to play a leading role in key issues regarding the economic and social development of the host country. For instance, a local businessman may be particularly interested in the amount of public and private investment in science and technology, something that could be irrelevant for the management of a multinational as these functions are usually based at company headquarters.

Another factor concerns the origin of investment capital, an issue that seems to influence the modality, magnitude and degree of commitment of the corporations to the community. In this regard, a study by David Logan[26] argues that most transnational corporations tend to apply the motto "earn abroad and spend at home," focusing most of their donations close to their home countries, even in sophisticated and extensive markets like those of Europe.

As a last factor, we should mention the impact on CSA of the systematic turnover of CEOs in a large number of multinational corporations. This turnover results in time lags while the new management catches up with local conditions and builds up its relationships with local social institutions. Once these bonds have been put into place, the CEOs may be assigned to another destination, thus beginning the process anew. However, this phenomenon becomes less relevant as corporations begin to create institutionalized links with their social environment.

Challenges of the Crisis

Although the above-mentioned factors should be taken into account when analyzing CSA conditions in Argentina, we believe that CSA has provided one of the possible answers to the poverty and exclusion affecting the country, transcending mere manifestations of a crisis and becoming structural in essence. This is undoubtedly a significant development, one that should be recognized and promoted. It has been accompanied by a search for new modalities of social intervention characterized by an increasing participation of civil society in public affairs and a growing concern—as yet lacking satisfactory answers—to redefine and strengthen the state's role in view of the problems plaguing our society. The new conditions created by this crisis have also produced a fertile atmosphere conducive to thinking and searching for new alternatives, a powerful motivation to turn criticism into challenges that may consolidate achievements and take on new demands.

In this spirit, the next point introduces experiences and advances attained by CSA as useful references to ponder the new approaches on the matter.

Rethinking the Nature of Corporate Social Action

Corporate involvement in the contemporary local and Latin American scene takes several forms.

CSA actors are conscious of the search for alternatives and modifications of position, making it possible to find experiences, proposals and formulations that may be considered attempts to redefine CSA. We attempt here to look beyond the current scenario and frame CSA within the broader context affecting Argentina and conditioning the type of practices carried out by the different social actors. We have thus identified three guidelines to analyze CSA: a) the tension between the voluntary and mandatory dimensions made evident by the debate about the links between the social and economic spheres, b) CSA potential to become a tool for social development and c) its undeniable value as "social asset." We believe that these three guidelines may contribute to the discussion of more integrative *approach* to face the current Argentine society's demands and challenges. CSA is a result of willingness, consensus and demand.

Corporate social action must stem from the will to undertake this type of action. The notion that community-oriented activities go "beyond" any mandatory regulation is a trait that has been clearly pointed out by most academic studies on this matter: "to become a socially responsible company is a decision the corporation must embrace willingly. Each corporation should come to it because they wish to, not because it is a market demand or mandatory by law or has become the fashion" (Chacón, 2001).

Nevertheless, in a final analysis, other factors come into play that exceed and condition the mere expression of will. We refer here to formal and informal mechanisms, such as agreements and pressure applied by other organizations and civil society institutions and the existence of international standards and regulations set by legal framework. To better understand the nature of CSA we must establish a distinction among three areas or levels of action that jointly suppose a coherent program including willing, consensual and mandatory actions. These three areas of CSA are:

a) The *area of individual self-regulation*, in which CSA stems from company initiatives to carry out community-oriented activities.

When these actions are sustained over time, as more proactive corporations do, they develop internal self-regulatory mechanisms, including formulation of criteria to direct and shape their actions and to add a degree of formalization and institutionalization aimed at fulfilling certain *social expectations*. This is what is generally meant by the ideas widely adopted in the '90s, stressing the willing and individual components, although as integral parts of corporate behavior. These ideas, prevalent in the region and the world, could be expressed by the often quoted definition put forward by the Business for Social Responsibility (BSR) organization: corporate social responsibility is the action of "operating a business in such a way that it will consistently fulfill or exceed the ethical, legal, commercial and public expectations placed on the corporation" (IAPG, 2001). However, this definition merely emphasizes the voluntary component of CSA without mentioning a very important aspect: *expectations* are representations of the social sphere constructed around the specific conditions of each particular country. If we include legal aspects among these conditions, as BSR has done, we would find that, in countries with low institutional density and quality, to comply with the law is in itself a way to *exceed* the expectations placed on the company. And clearly, this is not the line of our argument. To comply with existing norms cannot be considered voluntary behavior, and the idea of *exceeding expectations* may only materialize when they are very low.

b) The *area of inter-organizational self-regulation*. In this instance, CSA emerges as the product of consensus reached among organizations. Unlike the previous area, the process of CSA institutionalization does not arise individually, but involves the participation of several actors, such as other companies, quality certification agencies, nonprofit organizations or even state institutions like municipalities or specific departments. The consensus reached may be formalized, for example, in strategic alliances, written commitments, agreements or codes of ethics. In this way, although it is still a voluntary activity not subject to external regulatory pressure, sustaining and fulfilling it is in itself a form of commitment, since it arises from a process of consensus.

The issue of corporative self-regulation, particularly in regard to multinational companies and their global challenges, has recently been the focus of literature in the United States.[27] However, most of the available academic production refers to individual cases, which is not enough to grasp what is actually happening. Some of the academic production includes very persuasive papers meant to induce CEOs to adopt these new practices. Other critical essays condemn corporate social activities as mere public relations instruments to benefit the corporation (Haufler, 2001). As Jessica Mathews points out in her introduction to Haufler's book, when we approach these issues, we must take into account the advisability and viability of policies in which the private sector has a hand in the management and regulation of the world economy. This consideration necessarily implies a debate on the control mechanisms of accountability the corporations should adopt in this instance, as well as the legitimacy and balance of power needed in the globalization process.

While we agree with some of the concerns raised by these authors, we believe it is necessary also to ask ourselves: What regional and world forces could drive a change of multinational corporation practices in the underdeveloped countries? Would large corporations be interested in raising standards of social responsibility in those countries whose appeal is precisely loose state regulation mechanisms? Is there a conflict between these regulatory mechanisms and the traditional norms based on legal imperatives? Is this proposal just an expression of the power acquired by corporations to shape policies only for their own sake? Isn't this just a naive way to step into the vacuum left by the weakness of governments? Would this be a pragmatic way to check and influence corporate behavior more flexibly and effectively than legal norms can? Doesn't their voluntary character imply a low degree of effectiveness? How could civil society, and in particular NGOs exert any influence on such manifestly unequal negotiations? Could this be a viable method in only certain regions or should it be applied globally? Are corporate commitments trustworthy when society lacks enforcement power? How transparent should self-regulatory mechanisms be for public opinion to accept the legitimacy of non-democratic forms of regulation?

The list of questions opened by the debate on the challenges of self-regulation is far longer than the answers we can find today. However, it might be interesting to pursue these issues and assess the validity of the options proposed to minimize the "collateral damage" caused by the current globalization processes. This is indeed an inescapable task if we believe that globalization should be more than just profit and gain for a few corporations and nations, as is the case until now.

c) The *area of regulation* and corporate social action. In this instance, some aspects of CSA lose their voluntary nature and become legal mandates. At this level, undertaking certain activities in the social sphere is a requirement of the legal framework, and therefore meeting these demands is not a matter of voluntary choice for the corporation. We see here a peculiar situation, since the external mandates cancel out voluntarism. Meeting norms like paying taxes or fulfilling the conditions of concession contracts for privatized public services, implementation of environmentally friendly production systems or respecting regulations on employee working hours and compliance with anti-monopoly laws, are not optional actions like CSA. So, what are we talking about here? We propose that corporations adopt a proactive attitude toward the legal conditions that frame their activities following, for example, the recommendations of the Green Book of the European Communities Commission (2001). Although this document emphasizes the voluntary nature of corporate social action, it also claims that CSA requires a legal basis clearly defined and respected, adding that "in countries lacking such normative, efforts should be focused on the creation of an adequate legislative or government set of rules in order to provide a uniform framework to base the development of socially responsible practices."

In other words, CSA acquires legitimacy when it takes place in a quality institutional context that may become a guarantee and frame of reference for social expectations. Also, we should always keep in sight the permanent interaction and evolution of these three areas on which CSA is founded. In this sense, a good illustration is what happened with the voluntary/individual, self-regulated/consensual and legal spheres in environmental conservation and protection issues. What used to be voluntary has gradually acquired a self-regulating character among organizations and is now becoming mandatory. Thus, some aspects and contents of what is today part of CSA may steadily evolve, change and broaden in scope.

In conclusion, we consider that each of these three areas presents specific dynamics and features articulating particular forms of behavior, contents and aims. In the case of self-regulation, these features depend on the internal capabilities of the corporation. So-called strategic philanthropy illustrates many of these components, such as focus on subject areas, establishment of specialized offices or departments, hiring professional staff, and strategic articulation of the social function with all the other corporate functions. In the case of inter-organizational self-regulation, these features refer to different sorts of links, such as joint programs, pacts and agreements, codes of ethics, standards of reference and rankings. According to the predominant consensual character of this area, the efficacy of these institutions depends largely on the degree of acceptance and recognition they attain in a given community, and on the respect and efficiency of the regulatory framework.

In the second place, we consider that the features and dynamics peculiar to each area grow stronger in their interaction with each other. The area of *individual self-regulation* is characteristic of innovative leader corporations, which develop their programs far ahead of the average behavior of the business sector. Thus, they contribute to the renovation of CSA and become a spur and a model for the rest of the social actors. In turn, *inter-organizational self-regulation*, as the mechanism applied by inter-sector collaboration, expresses the capability of a community to join individual efforts in pursuit of collective social goods.

In the third place, we claim that the characteristics acquired by each of these areas and the quality of their interactions are shaped and influenced by the surrounding contextual conditions. We refer here to *state regulation*, the threshold of minimal mandatory demands expressing the advances each society has made on the matter, though it includes also other conditioning factors mentioned above. These conditions are the structural economic parameters and the profile of the leading economic actors. Taken as a whole, all these factors are essential to study and understand the peculiar situation of a society such as Argentina, where you may find, for instance, low levels of efficiency in state regulation mechanisms, a strong presence of the area of individual self-regulation—only in the case of large corporations, and a weak, but steadily growing development in the area of inter-sectors and inter-organizational self-regulation.

CSA as a Potential Tool for Social Development

CSA is potentially capable of becoming a tool for social development and can integrate the set of state and social institutions working—or eventually able to work—toward this aim. This function of CSA is demanded, and in some cases, promoted, by different sectors of society, including some actors of the business and corporate scene.

The prevalent formulations of the '90s emphasized, together with the voluntary component, the need to align the social practices with the corporation's business aims.[28] However, just as in the case of voluntarism, concentration of efforts only in the development of the internal capabilities of the company to implement a more professional program of community actions without a complementary discussion about their potential impact on society is clearly insufficient in contexts where the social situation is highly precarious. The degree of exclusion and fragmentation of Latin American societies—together with the crumbling of traditional security and social containment policies—make up a situation in which both modalities of intervention, assistencialism (the "handing out fish" model) and individual skill-building (the "teach them how to fish" model) show evident limitations.

It is precisely within this contextual frame that CSA in Latin America has become the object of scrutiny and concern for many authors and organizations in our region.[29] Taking these contributions into account, we must stress the double reference to the postulate that the corporation is "a key component for social and economic development." On one hand, these postulates seem to conceive social actions as a tool for the promotion and creation of skills and well-being for society at large and/or for the common good. On the other hand, promotion and creation of skills and well-being requires a social change, that is, an explicit effort to change the current situation and revise now generalized practices of social action, particularly those of the large corporations. It is not just a matter of increasing activities, resources or number of programs; nor of any particular kind of development. It is an evolution involving a degree of social transformation centered in more inclusive and equitable policies for the entire population.

In the first case, the differences with the previous approach involve: a) the purpose of social actions—more than just providing "fishing skills," b) the concept of the limits of responsibility, as its scope extends to both the internal and external facets of business strategy and, c) the operative modality, as it is no longer relegated to just one of the company areas but becomes the very aim of the corporation. Although the ideas of change and evolution are part of the previous approach, in the second case, they seem to serve exclusively internal improvements for the corporation, such as products and procedures, staff commitment and the search for excellence in the implemented programs.

What we propose here is a shift in focus from within the corporation to its environment and vice versa, perhaps linking this focus to the ideas of economic, social and environmental sustainability. In other words, we propose a wider and more far-reaching horizon of activities. As we shall see next, this extended scope and responsibilities of corporate social action has its counterpart in a greater involvement of the other social sectors, making crucial the presence of a state with regulatory powers, a necessary condition for transforming private well-being into public well-being.

CSA as Concern for All of Society

CSA is a practice that should involve all businesses, not just the large corporations. And even more, CSA affects all the social actors, since, depending on their capabilities, they may influence entrepreneurial actions both to express and support demands for regulation of corporate practices, as well as contribute their own resources for joint actions. In this way, the modality of CSA in a given community, considered as the result of the interaction of the different actors there, becomes a *social asset*, the product of a given society. In our opinion, viewing corporate social action primarily as the initiative and territory of large companies would greatly reduce the CSA field. This view gradually has become an issue of contention, with voices arguing for the need to recognize the participation of actors other than the large corporations.[30] In turn, we consider that the responsibility of corporate social action should extend in two directions: toward the business sector at large and toward all the existing social actors.

When we say "all the companies," we mean that small and medium businesses cannot be excluded from the debates about CSA, as they were in the 1990s. Nowadays, many of these companies are the protagonists of encouraging experiences of bonding with their surrounding communities, despite the efforts and resources invested in their commercial survival.[31] When extending responsibility to the business community as a whole, we face a great challenge: that all companies engage in these activities does not mean they must all apply the same modalities, but tailor them according to their capabilities. This means similar responsibility and commitment, but different ways of carrying out this responsibility and commitment. However, the inclusion of all members of the business community in CSA does overlook the fact that large corporations have a greater impact resulting from the role they play in contemporary social affairs and the resources at their disposal.

In terms of reaching out toward other social actors, consumers play a key role. They may influence corporate social behavior both as individuals and through their organizations. The more these consumers take into account corporate social action in their purchase decisions, the more efforts corporations will make to engage in actions that may reinforce approval of their company and loyalty to their products or services.

Consumers, mass media and NGOs can all recognize and reward or punish corporate performance in different ways. The challenge is how to do this, finding and formulating diverse ways to influence CSA, according to the conditions and situation of each country. In Argentina and the rest of Latin America, there are few watchdog organizations to monitor corporate behavior and exert pressure for the socially useful investment of recourses.

Finally, when we accept the necessary or even inevitable involvement of all the social actors, CSA becomes a true *social asset*. CSA is not the private turf of some corporations, nor is it a closed practice that arises spontaneously or can be imposed only from outside. Rather, CSA contents and modalities result from a collective process of elaboration. The involvement of all the social sectors implies participation, proposals, negotiations and regulations that lead to the construction of socially responsible corporate social actions. And of course, it is an open construct, subject to constant adjustment. Thus the relevance of participation, of being aware and assuming this dimension as a collective endeavor.

A Closure and an Opening

In a context ridden by growing unfulfilled social needs like that of Argentina, it might sound absurd to put forward more ambitious proposals. We think otherwise. Although the available corporate resources for social undertakings are far less than potential state investment, corporate behavior may have a huge impact on society both directly and indirectly through the promotion of socially-oriented actions and discourse. We hope the proposals presented in this chapter will arouse debate and contribute to the development of a more systematic and integral view of the issue of corporate social action, leading to the adoption of approaches consistent with the peculiarities of each country.

In view of these considerations, we must make a clear distinction between what is a responsible social action and what is not. To that effect, the imperative is to involve all sectors of society in an open and wide debate around certain core issues and questions we have tried to outline here.

Because we are dealing with a process of social construction, the contents to be discussed, as well as enlisting a wide spectrum of participating actors, are crucial.

We believe some of the considerations presented in this article may lead to new research directions and actions. To that effect, we may ask some questions: What are the limits framing corporate social actions? What are the present and desired attributes in the fields of individual self-regulation, collective self-regulation and traditional regulation? What kind of interactions operate between voluntary self-regulation and mandatory regulation and how can we add to their synergy? What is the specific potential of CSA in Argentina for it to become a tool for social development? How can these actions be formulated, and what would be their eventual impact on other social and state areas? How can we promote and strengthen the participation of the different social actors? What are the different dimensions and channels used by corporations to influence society?

Corporate involvement in social issues demands not only a discussion of the best ways to implement a given program or initiative, but also a searching look into their impact on the social sphere and how they may support a mode of development to confront the challenges of globalization so that the rights of the citizens may be protected and promoted in the broadest sense.

Notes

1 See: Williamson (1993).

2 A survey of large Argentine corporations by the National Institute for Statistics and Census points out that while in 1993 280 out of the 500 largest companies were national and 220 foreign, in 2000 this ratio had shifted to 314 foreign and 186 domestic.

3 This norm established the peso-US dollar equivalence, but was also accompanied by a fast process of privatizations, deregulation of the trading and labor markets and a even wider opening to international trade.

4 Among others, the whole system of food distribution and long-term consumer goods concentrated in a few large corporations.

5 To develop this issue we have used as empirical evidence the results of the survey of the operations Balance presented at the Inspección General de Justicia by 45 corporate foundations in different years of the 1990s. We have also used the studies carried out by: Allen, et al. (2000); CEDES (1999) and Universidad de San Andrés-Gallup Argentina (1998).

6 Besides those already mentioned, see IAPG (2000); Roitter (1996); Luna (1995).

7 Such the case of the Ciudadanía Empresaria award. see www.amchamar.com.ar.

8 GDF affiliates the donor foundations in Argentina, see www.gdf.org.ar.

9 Universidad de San Andrés and Gallup Institute Argentina (1998).

10 This value corresponded to about 100 millon pesos in the currency rate of the period. Nowadays it would represent about US$35 million.

11 See: Informe de Gasto Social Nr. 4: Estructura y Evolución del Gasto Social Focalizado: 1997–2002. Sistema de Información, Monitoreo y evaluación de Programas sociales (SIEMPRO). Presidencia de la Nación. Buenos Aires, August 2002.

12 One should take into account that this foundation keeps an extremely low informative profile, making it difficult to ascertain what is the destination of this high expenditure, as well as regarding their assets, which reach more than a billion pesos. This foundation shows high variability in their annual expenditure. In the first half of the 1990s their budget was roughly 10 millon pesos, while in the second half it reached almost 150 millons. There is no evidence that this level of expenditure has continued in recent years, but we may safely assume it must have decreased noticeably as a sizable part was invested in the building of a university and other building initiatives.

13 There is no information about some foundations created after 1999, or when the source lacked data. Among these, we should mention the following foundations: Aguas Argentinas, Andreani, Diario La Nación, Ingenio Ledesma, Instituto C&A, Luncheon Tickets, Majdalani.

14 See: Austin (2000).

15 A most relevant contribution is the *Social Enterprise Knowledge Network* (SEKN) program, with members from academic centers of the Americas and Spain, whose aim is to produce knowledge about the existing alliances between NGOs and corporations and similar issues, in particular, case studies to help integrate these subjects in the postgrade business curriculum (See: www.sekn.org).

16 There is a great deal of bibliography on this subject, broaching it from different perspectives. Among others: Schwartz and Gibb (2000), Grayson and Hodges (2002) and Lozano (1999) present it as a challenge, while Werner and Weiss (2003) and Klein (2000), with a critical look, consider it a problem intrinsic to global corporations.

17 This perception had precedents before the crisis broke out. For instance, in the mid-2001 a survey by Gallup-Argentina showed that the level of confidence in the large companies had dropped from 36% in 1994 to 19%.

18 At present, 35 companies support this type of programs. Most of them operate in a global scale and started these programs in the last two years .

19 Another factor that may favor this CSA modality is the lower relative costs of these initiatives, specially when the company is now paying for volunteer time and it isn't part of the operative programs or grants undertaken by the company or the corporate foundation. This may seem to be something low cost and high value; however, one should not overrate this type of approach as it may trigger unwanted effects in the long run.

20 This problem does not seem to be exclusive to Argentina and Latin America. A recent study has found that even in the United States, the strategic philanthropy model has hardly taken root (Marx, 1999).

21 See: Paoli (2002).

22 The National Institute of Statistics and Census (INDEC) revealed that in 1990–1999, the gap between the income of the poorest 10% and the richest 10% of the population widened to 57%. The wealthy earn 23.7 times more than the poor. Added to the unequal income distribution are factors such as the impoverishment of large sections of the population and the growing vulnerability of the middle class, resulting in a stready rise of social exclusion for a larger number of people.

23 See: Reich (1991) and Rifkin (1996).

24 Some industries, like oil and chemical companies, may be an exception to this rule, because their potential threat as environmental hazards drives them to undertake programs to demonstrate their commitment to ecological concerns.

25 From the interview in *Tres Puntos* magazine, June 2001.

26 See: Cannon (1994).

27 See: Haufler (2001), Parker (2002).

28 This correspondence is clearly expressed, for example, in the definition presented by James Austin (2000) in his evolutive model of multi-sector collaboration, or Allen, Coduras and Husted (2000: 58), for whom "the corporation's strategy is the sum of their business strategy and their social practices."

29 See: Martinelli (1997); Portorcarrero, Sanborn, Llusera and Quea (2000); Teixido, Chavarri and Castro (2002).

30 See: Green Book, European Community, paragraphs 23 and 89; Fundación SES (2001).

31 See: Balián de Tagtachian (1998).

References

Allen, David, Coduras, Alicia and Husted, Bryan, 2000. "¿Qué hacen las empresas por la sociedad," Revista Mercado, Buenos Aires. (April).

Alperson, Myra, 1995. *Corporate Giving Strategies That Add Business Value, A Research Report,* The Conference Board, New York.

Austin, James, 2000. *The Collaboration Challenge.* Harvard Business School. Josey Bass Publisher, San Francisco.

Balian de Tagtachian, Beatriz, 1998. *Pobreza y filantropía empresarial,* www.gdf.org.ar.

Business for Social Responsibility, 2000. *Corporate Social Responsibility: A Guide to Better Business Practices.* San Francisco.

Cannon, Tom, 1994. *La Responsabilidad de la Empresa,* Ed. Folio, Barcelona.

CEDES, 1999, *Actividades hacia la comunidad de las grandes empresas,* report prepared for the U.S. Chamber of Commerce in Argentina, mimeograph, Buenos Aires.

Chacón, Castro, 2001. *Libro Verde de la responsabilidad social de las empresas,* www.grupcies.com.

Comisión de las Comunidades Europeas, 2001. *Libro Verde: Fomentar un marco europeo para la responsabilidad social de las empresas,* Brussels.

Council on Foundations, 1996. *Measuring the Value of Corporate Citizenship,* Washington.

Fundación SES, 2001. *Responsabilidad Social Empresaria. Aportes a la emergencia de una nueva cultura empresarial.* Fundación SES, Buenos Aires.

Grayson, David and Hodges, Adrian, 2002. *Everybody's Business,* DK Publishing, New York.

IAPG (Instituto Argentino del Petróleo y del Gas), 2001. *Actividades Comunitarias de la Industria del Petróleo y del Gas,* Buenos Aires.

Instituto Nacional de Estadísticas y Censos, 2002. *Las Grandes Empresas en Argentina,* INDEC, Buenos Aires.

Klein, Naomi, 2000. *No Logo,* Random House Limited, Toronto.

Kosacoff, Bernardo; Porta, Fernando; Stengel, Alejandro, 2001. "Construcción de una empresa regional en un marco de transformación institucional: la experiencia de los años noventa," in *Globalizar desde Latinoamérica. El caso Arcor,* McGraw-Hill Interamericana, Colombia.

Haufler, Virginia, 2001. *A Public Role for the Private Sector. Industry Self-Regulation in a Global Economy.* Carnegie Endowment for International Peace, Washington D.C.

Luna, Elba (editor), 1995. *Fondos privados, fines públicos. El empresariado y el financiamiento de la iniciativa social en América Latina,* GADIS, Fundación Juan Minetti, Fundación Banco Mayo, Fundación Ford, Espacio Editorial, Buenos Aires.

Lozano, Joseph, 1999. *Etica y Empresa.* Editorial Trotta, Madrid.

Martinelli, Carlos, 1997. *Empresa-Cidadà: Uma visào innovadora para uma açào transformadora,* GIFE-Paz e Terra, Sao Paulo.

Marx, Jerry, 1999. "Corporate Philanthropy: What is the Strategy?" *Nonprofit and Voluntary Sector Quarterly,* vol. 28, no. 2, June.

O'Donnell, Guillermo, 1997. "Acerca del Estado, la democratización y algunos problemas conceptuales," in *Contrapuntos, Ensayos sobre autoritarismo y democratización,* Paidós, Buenos Aires.

Osorio, Jorge, 2000. "Ciudadanía Empresaria y Responsabilidad Social," en *Revista Filantropía y Responsabilidad Social,* PROhumana, año 1, no. 2, April–June, Chile.

Paladino, Marcelo and Mohan, Anupama, 2002. *Tendencias de la Responsabilidad Social Empresaria en Argentina,* Universidad Austral, Buenos Aires.

Paoli, Maria Celia, 2002. "Empresas e responsabilidade social: os enredamentos da cidadnia no Brasil," in Boaventura de Souza Santos (editor): *Democratizar a democracia: os caminhos da democracia participativa*, Ed. Civilizaçao Brasileira, Rio de Janeiro.

Parker, Christine, 2002. *Open Corporation: Effective Self-Regulation and Democracy*, Cambridge University Press.

Portocarrero S., Felipe; Sanborn, Cynthia; Llusera, Sergio; Quea, Viviana, 2000. *Empresas, fundaciones y medios: la responsabilidad social en el Perú*, Biblioteca en Responsabilidad Social, Universidad del Pacífico, Lima.

Reich, Robert, 1991. *The Work of Nations,* Random House Inc. New York.

Rifkin, Jeremy, 1996. *El fin del Trabajo*, Paidós, Buenos Aires.

Roitter, Mario, 1995. El Mercado de la Beneficencia, in Thompson, Andrés (Editor) *Público y Privado Las Organizaciones sin fines de lucro en Argentina*. Ed. UNICEF/Losada, Buenos Aires.

Roitter, M., 1996. *La Razón Social de las Empresas. Una investigación sobre los vínculos entre empresa y sociedad en Argentina*, Documento Cedes, Buenos Aires.

Schwartz, Peter and Gibb, Blari, 2000. *Cuando las buenas compañías se portan mal. Responsabilidad y riesgos en una era de globalización*, Ed. Granica, Barcelona.

Teixido, Soledad; Chavarri, Reinalina and Castro, Andrea, 2002. *Responsabilidad Social. 12 casos empresariales en Chile*, Fundación PROhumana, Chile.

Thompson, Andrés, 1992. "Sin Fines de Lucro," Separata Boletín Informativo Techint no. 272, Buenos Aires, Oct.–Dec.

Universidad de San Andrés and Instituto Gallup de la Argentina, 1998. *Estudio de Filantropía Empresaria*, Universidad de San Andrés, Buenos Aires; Instituto Gallup de la Argentina, Buenos Aires.

Weil, Pascale, 1992. *La comunicación Global. Comunicación institucional y de gestión*, Ed. Paidós, Barcelona.

Werner, Klaus and Weiss, Hans, 2003. "El libro negro de las marcas." Editorial Sudamericana, Buenos Aires.

Williamson, John, 1993. *Democracy and the Washington Consensus*, Institute for International Economics, Washington D.C.

SECTION

III

FOUNDATIONS AND FRAMEWORKS: BUILDING AN ENABLING ENVIRONMENT

10

Private Resources for Public Ends: Grantmakers in Brazil, Ecuador and Mexico

Shari Turitz and David Winder

During the last two decades, the spotlight has moved onto the civil society sector as a key agent of development and social change in Latin America. An increasing number of civil society organizations are taking on the challenges of shaping societies that are more democratic, have lower levels of corruption and guarantee citizens their basic human, social and economic rights. There has been little information available, however, about the presence of professional philanthropic institutions in the region that are channeling grants to local civil society organizations. The research described below constitutes a start in developing our understanding of the role these local grantmaking foundations play. As civil society leaders, policymakers, donors and scholars continue to struggle with ways to sustainably finance civil society organizations, the need for further information about these local philanthropic organizations will be essential.

Since its founding in 1986, The Synergos Institute has built a body of knowledge on grantmaking foundations throughout the developing world. Synergos has used that information to construct a capacity-building program that has worked to build and strengthen grantmaking organizations globally. In 1999, Synergos received a grant from the Tinker Foundation to work with its partners (Centro Mexicano Para la Filantropía (Mexican Center for Philanthropy, CEMEFI) in Mexico, Grupo de Institutos, Fundações e Empresas (Group of Institutes, Foundations and Businesses, GIFE) in Brazil and Fundación Esquel-Ecuador (Esquel Foundation, Ecuador) to begin to quantify the emergence of institutionalized philanthropy in Mexico, Brazil and Ecuador, offering a basis for extrapolating lessons for the region.

The research on grantmaking organizations resulted in information that advances the field of academic research on philanthropy in Latin

America. The studies highlighted the fact that grantmaking foundations are a relatively new and growing phenomenon, and to the surprise of many, that the majority of resources mobilized by these organizations are local not international. Also surprising was that most of the organizations have endowments, though they tend to be small.

In addition, in all three countries, grantmaking organizations have very low visibility, and in some cases, a low level of transparency. These organizations tend to operate in economically or politically important regions of their countries, and most favor education in their grantmaking programs. Lastly, while grantmaking is historically associated with Christian charity, the more recently incorporated grantmakers are not affiliated with the Church and are more often associated with the civil society and business sectors.

The following chapter draws on findings from the three studies commissioned by Synergos during 2000 and 2001.[1] The chapter is divided into three parts. The first briefly describes the methodology and objectives of the study. The second explores the particular characteristics of local grantmaking foundations in Brazil, Ecuador and Mexico. The third provides a comparative analysis, extracting lessons for the region, and the concluding section addresses challenges and makes recommendations for promoting the growth and development of these vital civil society resource organizations.

Methodology and Objectives of the Study

Research undertaken by Synergos, in partnership with GIFE, CEMEFI and Fundación Esquel, sought to identify local philanthropic organizations engaged in grantmaking and to learn more about the role they are playing in their respective societies. The studies did not attempt to capture all funding available for local civil society organizations but instead to capture the development of institutionalized philanthropy as a way to gauge the growth of a local, professional philanthropic sector. In that way, Synergos did not include corporate giving programs where those were not organized as a separate legal entity, nor did the study include international foundations (i.e., Ford Foundation, Kellogg Foundation and Avina Inc.) which are extremely important in the region today, though their presence over time is not guaranteed.

While the work of these actors is essential, it was our belief that a professional, locally-based sector is important for strategically and permanently investing in the development of civil society organizations and, in partnership with government, working toward the resolution of persistent poverty problems. As so little information is available about these local professional institutions, Synergos endeavored to learn more.

Researchers carried out extensive national scans to uncover all existing grantmaking organizations in the three countries. They consulted databases of foundations and NGOs, membership rolls of local associations and, through their interviews, asked grantmakers to identify others they were familiar with. While an attempt was made to be exhaustive, for a variety of reasons, including reluctance on the part of foundations to disclose financial information, the studies do not cover the entire grantmaking sector.

As grantmakers are not a well-defined sector in the three countries, arriving at a common set of criteria to determine which organizations to include was essential. The criteria used for selection were that the organizations:

1. *Make grants to nonprofit organizations or individuals.* This could not be part of a commercial activity, but had to benefit nonprofit organizations or individuals. (To be included in this study, at least 5% of program budgets had to be dedicated to grantmaking.)

2. *Were private, non-governmental.* They could not be part of either a government or business entity.

3. *Were independent and not-for-profit.* The foundation/organization had to be independently incorporated and had to be able to make its own decisions. (Corporate giving programs were not included.)

4. *Were locally owned, governed and operated (i.e., by nationals of the country).* The foundation had to be indigenous to the country, though some portion of its income could be mobilized externally.

For each organization, the researchers obtained data on the: history of the organization; sources of funding; permanent assets such as endowment, real estate and earned income; areas of grantmaking and target populations for grants; types of grant recipients; and non-grant services provided.

The research sought to generate information on grantmaking organizations in each country for a number of audiences, including policymakers, practitioners in the philanthropic sector and academics. Synergos hoped the studies would contribute to strengthening the emerging grantmaking sector by increasing its visibility, both locally and internationally; identifying its capacity building needs; identifying best practices that could be documented and shared with other organizations locally and internationally; and linking donor organizations to potential local partners.

Grantmaking Foundations in Brazil, Ecuador and Mexico

Brazil

The Brazilian study is the first attempt to identify those national organizations that are making grants for public benefit in Brazil. It provides many valuable insights into the origins and nature of these organizations and their capacity to mobilize and distribute resources and suggests ways to increase their role and impact. The findings are based on a universe of 31 grantmaking foundations.

The results of the survey show that this emerging group of organizations, (64% if which were created after 1980 and 79% in the case of corporate foundations), is providing vital resources to the nonprofit sector, thereby lessening their dependence on international sources of funding. In 1999, they channeled $120 million reals (approximately US$69.5 million in 1999) in grants, in addition to managing projects and programs in partnership with a wide range of organizations, both governmental and nongovernmental.

A noticeable feature of the grantmaker sector is the central role played by private corporations. Sixty-one percent of grantmakers were formed by corporations, the remainder being created by wealthy families or individuals or by civil society organizations. The data analysis highlights important differences between corporate and non-corporate foundations.[2] The most important is that corporate foundations channel a much higher percentage of their budget to programs and projects they manage directly (42% as against 14%). This means that nonprofit organizations seeking grant support depend most heavily on non-corporate grantmakers. In explaining why corporate grantmakers give fewer grants the author concludes that "organizations identified as 'grantmakers' tend not to distinguish between donations to third parties and resources invested in their own programs and projects: companies and businessmen consider as 'donations' all those resources they apply to the social sector."[3] Another consideration is that the majority of the organizations surveyed "prefer not to be seen as grantmakers because it would lead to an increase in the number of grant requests over and above their capacity to respond."[4] They also consider that the term "donor" implies a paternalistic and ineffective form of social action.

The study shows that over three-quarters of all foundations operate their own programs in addition to giving grants. One striking feature of the Brazilian context is that these programs are frequently operated in partnership with other nonprofits, government programs, community associations or corporations. Through such partnerships, which take many forms and also include donations, foundations test pilot programs, replicate successful initiatives and transfer business skills.

It is significant that education is given a high priority by Brazilian foundations, constituting a programmatic priority for 81% of foundations.[5] The author suggests that this is largely because education is a popular cause with the public, represents a low risk and fits national priorities, making it possible to leverage government resources.

The Brazilian study shows that corporate grantmakers are playing a key role in the creation of a new professional culture of grantmaking and have introduced concepts and practices from the business sector into the management of their organizations. They have created a new type of organization that differs from the traditional model of a "classic" grantmaker and reflects a new concept of business social responsibility, favoring a more proactive involvement of business in the social arena.

Interestingly, only one of the foundations studied has opted to develop credit programs as a means of channeling funds to community-based organizations. This appears to be the result of a conscious decision to leave this particular type of assistance to a network of NGOs specializing in providing this service.

The newness of the sector poses a series of challenges to Brazilian grantmakers, such as the dependency on one or few sources of funding; the inexistence of a capital base of any significant size and the consequent limits to their financial autonomy; and the lack of policies and instruments to ensure organizational transparency. Not surprisingly, corporate foundations are in a stronger position than non-corporate foundations regarding independence from international funding. They mainly rely on a regular flow of funds from their parent companies, usually in the form of annual transfers, the amount of which is often linked to annual profits. It is noticeable that only 32% of foundations have assets that produce income (i.e. endowments, company shares and real estate). Only half of these are endowment funds and only 4% of foundation income comes from returns on endowment investment.

The author points to a number of possible explanations for the limited role played by endowments in Brazilian foundations including the lack of an 'endowment culture,' the pressure on foundations to respond to demands for resources from civil society, the lack of fiscal incentives and the young nature of most foundations which have not yet had time to build an endowment.[6]

While the grantmaking sector in Brazil is small, many of the organizations included in it are powerful and well organized. The national association of foundations, GIFE, plays an important role in advocating for the overall foundation sector (both grantmaking and operating), including pressing for a more favorable and clear legal and fiscal environment. Corporate social responsibility and social investment have become powerful concepts in Brazil and several strong associations are networking and providing information to businesses interested in increasing their social engagement. These efforts, coupled with a new government encouraging development partnerships, will certainly result in an increase in grantmaking organizations in the future.

Ecuador
In Ecuador the grantmaking foundation sector is relatively new and has yet to establish a strong and clear separate identity in Ecuadorian society. Its development broadly mirrors that of the non governmental sector as a whole.

Grantmaking foundations, like NGOs, experienced their major growth spurt in the past twenty years. This came about in part as a response to the increasing poverty and inequity in the country resulting from a widening economic crisis and the inability of the state to respond adequately. This period has seen the emergence of a corporate foundation sector—led by a few large national corporations—supporting a range of programs in health, education, training and micro-credit.

This study was the first attempt to document the foundation sector in the country. It identified 21 organizations that met the survey criteria.

Eighty percent of the foundations are based in the capital city of Quito, along what is known as the *sierra,* or mountainous region. The fact that Quito is the seat of the national government and, therefore, the headquarters of agencies of international cooperation helps to explain this concentration. But cultural factors seem to offer an even deeper explanation. In the *sierra,* collective action and the creation of civil society organizations have been favored as a way of addressing acute social and economic problems. Most of these Quito-based foundations work nationally, also channeling grants to the coastal region.

Grantmaking foundations are a relatively new phenomenon in Ecuador, with 65% created during the past 20 years. This is explained by a change in the model of state development (with the public sector increasingly relying on civil society to carry out social development activities) and by the increasing desire of international cooperation to channel their aid through non-governmental organizations. All six corporate grantmakers were incorporated during this period as well.

Grantmakers in Ecuador also tend to have a hybrid character, channeling grants, operating programs, projects and/or institutions and offering credit on a non-commercial basis. Ninety-five percent of the foundations directly implement their own programs. In other words, the majority of foundations are principally operating foundations, although they also channel grants. Grantmakers feel that operating programs help them to better control the application of funds. It also gives the foundations the freedom to raise additional funds as many of the operating programs generate income. The survey showed that income generation activities include the operation of training centers, cooperatives, consultancies, health centers and tourism services.

Not surprisingly the emphasis on program operation is reflected in high overhead costs. Over 50% of the foundations have administrative/operating costs of over 25% of their total budget.

Ecuadorian foundations give grants in a wide range of fields with education, community development, institutional development and health favored by most. The high investment in education and training reflects a response to the poor national public school system and the priority corporate foundations place on increasing the skills of the future work force.

Most foundations face a constant challenge in raising the funds required to respond to the program demands placed upon them. To address this problem and guarantee a regular flow of funds, 60% of the foundations are building endowments. However, in no case do these endowments exceed US$3 million and, therefore, do not yet represent a significant source of income.

One unexpected finding was that foundations receive most of their funding (69%) from local sources. Not surprisingly, the percentage rises to 82% in the case of corporate foundations, as they receive regular injections of funds from their parent company. The high percentage of local funding reflects the foundations' success in developing a diversity of income generating programs rather than a well-honed capacity to raise contributions from the local elite.

Despite the success in raising funds locally, many foundations still rely heavily on grants from international organizations, including official development assistance (ODA) agencies, international foundations and corporations. Corporate grantmakers, which depend much less on international funding, only receive international funding from ODA agencies and foreign corporations. Non-corporate foundations, on the other hand, by necessity show a more diversified strategy and try to access all possible sources of international funding.

The study estimates that Ecuadorian foundations have a total annual budget in excess of US$36 million of which approximately US$15 million is channeled as grants. This figure, while not conclusive because some organizations did not have or did not want to share their financial information, highlights the important role these institutions play in a country like Ecuador, where 60% of the population lives in poverty.

One feature of foundation disbursement strategy that sets Ecuadorian foundations apart from their counterparts in Brazil and Mexico is the use of credit facilities. Half of Ecuadorian foundations give both grants and loans. The reasons cited for the use of loans is that it ensures that their relatively limited resources are able to assist a greater number of organizations and communities and that it obliges the beneficiaries to make efficient use of their resources.

The study provides us with a useful first assessment of a relatively young universe of grantmaking foundations, working toward creating improved systems of financial sustainability that will enable them to respond effectively to the challenges of increasing poverty and environmental degradation. There are many positive signs, including efforts underway to build an association of foundations, the Ecuadorian Consortium for Social Responsibility (Consorcio Ecuatoriano de Responsabilidad Social), that will work toward increasing the accountability and effectiveness of its members and obtaining improved tax provisions for foundations. The fact that half of the foundations already issue public information on how to request grants and loans and that 90% of foundations have annual external audits constitutes a good beginning.

Mexico

The research conducted in Mexico, as in Brazil and Ecuador, was the first attempt to identify grantmaking foundations as a separate sector. It surveyed a total of 74 grantmaking entities (identified as donor institutions) meeting the established criteria. The resultant data profiled a diverse, dynamic and evolving sector that is playing an increasingly important role in channeling funds to a range of grassroots development programs, building partnerships across sectors and having an impact on social policy both at the local and national levels.

The study found that the behavior, grantmaking practices and fundraising strategies of the foundations that were surveyed depended in part on their date of creation and in part on whether they were corporate, community or private foundations. The author classifies grantmaking foundations into three generations, each with distinct characteristics.

First, those from the *charitable generation* (end of the 19th century to the 1930s) were founded on interpretations of Christian charity and tend to have a low profile and channel most of their support to charitable organizations. (Ten grantmakers were founded during this period.) The second generation, or *transitional generation* (1940s to 1960s), coincides with a period of economic growth in Mexico. (Eight grantmakers were founded during this period.). Grantmakers in the transitional generation tend to be more proactive in their approach to social issues than the previous generation, and they reach a more diverse group of beneficiaries. They are also more concerned about the professional development of their staff. They tend to rely on support from volunteers and have developed limited links with other sectors of the society.

The third generation, or *development generation* (1960s to present), is characterized by an increased participation of civil society in the public sphere and a noticeable increase in the emergence of grantmaking foundations—particularly of community and corporate foundations. Organizations from this generation (56 in total) show an interest in making their activities and staff more professional. Most of their support goes to communities and they place high value on the creation of strategic alliances with other social actors.

Underlying this concept of collaboration is a new paradigm of development that emphasizes the responsible participation of all social actors. This trend has been particularly pronounced since 1985 when the strong civil society response to the disastrous earthquake which shook Mexico City resulted in the emergence of a number of grantmaking foundations. This post-85 period saw the emergence of two new groups of actors: *corporate foundations,* who gave greater emphasis to the concept of efficiency and effectiveness in their grantmaking, and *community foundations,* that have been developing concepts of co-responsibility and citizen participation. (See Appendix I for more information about Mexican Community Foundations.) This generation is characterized by increased hiring of salaried employees and attention to their professional development in areas such as fundraising and project design and attention to endowment building. Foundations of this generation are also more likely to seek to exercise a leadership role in the formulation of social development policy.

The figure of the "hybrid" grantmaker also appears in Mexico. Even when many Mexican organizations are moving toward the model of a "pure" grantmaker (that is, professional organizations specialized in the mobilization, administration and channeling of private resources for public ends), most add the operation of programs, projects and/or institutions to their grantmaking activity. However 76% of foundations described themselves as "primarily grantmaking."

As in the cases of Brazil and Ecuador, the study found that foundations rely primarily on local sources to fund their grants and operations. This is an indication of the strength of local philanthropy. Local sources provide 79% of foundation resources.

Apart from a few fortunate foundations that have endowments from their original benefactor or foreign and domestic government sources, most of the 64% of the Mexican grantmakers that have made a start toward building endowments are not yet at the stage where they produce significant dividends.

The Mexican grantmaking community has made considerable strides in developing networks for collaboration and the sharing of learning and experience. The Centro Mexicano para la Filantropía (Mexico Center for Philanthropy) has supported the creation of sectoral affinity groups in which regular interaction takes place.

An interesting trend among Mexican foundations is their success in building partnerships across sectors with a view to mobilizing increased resources and deepening program impact. For example, the Fundación del Empresariado Chihuahuense (The Chihuahua Businessman's Foundation, FECHAC) raised over US$26 million between 1994 and 2000 through an agreement with the state government that instituted a small payroll tax for this purpose. These resources have been channeled as grants to NGOs and community-based organizations to fund programs in the fields of education, social welfare and health.

Another trend is for community foundations and other non-corporate foundations to seek the involvement of corporate representatives and wealthy individuals on their boards of directors as a means of accessing new skills, in addition to resources.

Mexico has developed a rich diversity of donor institutions. They have displayed strong innovation in both the mobilization and application of resources. With the transition from one-party rule in 2000, Mexico has seen increased openness to collaboration between civil society and government. This represents a new opportunity for the creation of development partnerships that can leverage resources and knowledge, building collaborations that address persistent poverty problems.

Uncovering Trends and De-bunking Myths: Grantmaking Foundations in Brazil, Ecuador and Mexico

The grantmaking sector has evolved in different ways in each country as a result of diverse historical, political and socio-economic factors. There are, however, interesting trends that emerge across countries, highlighting particular sectoral characteristics and institutional forms. These trends help to distill information about a growing philanthropic force in the region while de-bunking myths and shedding light on the sector's potential as well as its challenges.

Sectoral Characteristics:

Grantmaking foundations are a relatively new phenomenon and were founded by diverse actors
Grantmaking foundations, as a sub-sector of civil society, are a relatively recent phenomenon in all three countries. While some organizations were founded in the first half of the 20th century, most grantmakers were created after 1980, paralleling two important trends: an increased role of civil society organizations in national development and an increased role of the private sector in tackling persistent social and economic problems. Since 1980, the majority of the founders of grantmaking organizations have been either civil society or business leaders. And in all three countries, most corporate foundations were created since 1980, reflecting an increased awareness on the part of business of their need to institutionalize and professionalize their social actions.

In Brazil, 64% of grantmakers were created after 1980—with 48% in the 1990s. The majority of those created since 1990 are linked to the private sector. In Ecuador this figure increases to 65% since 1980. In Mexico the figures are even more striking, with 70% of grantmaking foundations founded after 1985 during the *development generation*.

Table 1. Who Created the Foundations*

	Brazil (total: 31)	Ecuador[7] (total: 21)	Mexico (total: 74)
National civil society leaders and organizations	19.4%	55%	31%
Private individuals/families	19.4%	40%	34%
Business leaders/corporations	61.3%	30%	23%
Religious leaders/and organizations	12.9%	10%	4%
International organizations		0%	
Government			8%

(*) Data from: Andrés P. Falconer, Brazil

There Is a Significant and Growing Community of Grantmaking Foundations

In all three studies, researchers confronted a common misperception that there were few national grantmakers in their countries and that those that existed were charity-focused. The studies, in fact, uncovered a significant number of grantmaking foundations—126 in total with 31 in Brazil, 21 in Ecuador and 74 in Mexico. Together these organizations channel over US$138.5 million annually,[8] mainly to nonprofit organizations.

For a sector that was presumed almost nonexistent, these figures were surprisingly high. If compared to the number of grantmaking foundations in more developed countries (approximately 56,000 in the US[9]; 1,650 in Canada,[10] and 1,579 in Japan),[11] the figure is still quite modest and represents a challenge for a region with a growing nonprofit sector and persistent social, economic and environmental challenges demanding new institutional sources of income.

Significant Impediments Exist to Creating a Sectoral Consciousness

A common identity among grantmaking organizations will contribute significantly to their ability to professionalize and increase their role, encouraging the growth of existing organizations and the birth of new ones. While there have been some interesting strides of late in defining a common identity, there are several impediments that need to be overcome.

Grantmaking foundations in Brazil, Ecuador and Mexico show an identity and character different from their peers in the developed world, particularly the United States. First, they do not define themselves as grantmakers—that is, through their activity of making grants. Instead they tend to define themselves based on their area of program activity (such as environment, health or education). This might be related, in part, to the negative connotation the word *"donación"* (grant) has in both Spanish and Portuguese. Grantmaking organizations increasingly seek to differentiate themselves from traditional, charitable initiatives to which the word *"donación"* and *"donante"* (grant and grantmaker) have historically been associated. In the three countries, grantmaking foundations tend to reject the concepts of charity and dependence and are striving to professionalize their activities. To demonstrate this they have adopted new terminology such as "social investment" and "transformative philanthropy" to describe their social action.

In addition, the word "foundation" does not necessarily define an organization as a grantmaker. In all three countries, "foundation" can mean an organization that operates programs or one that gives grants.

Lastly, exacerbating a lack of common identity is the fact that in all three countries, grantmakers can incorporate as one of several different legal entities (e.g. foundation, institute, civil association, institute of private assistance). The lack of a clearly defined legal framework for grantmakers makes it more difficult for these functionally similar organizations to forge bonds, learn from and strengthen one another.

Underscoring this issue is the fact that different words were used to describe these organizations in the three studies themselves. In both Brazil and Ecuador, in the absence of a local language equivalent, researchers opted to use the English word, *grantmakers*. In Mexico, the researcher decided upon donor institutions (*instituciones donantes*).

In all three countries, however, there is a growing awareness of the specific character and role of these organizations, resulting in the emergence of networks of foundations under the umbrella of the Group of Institutes, Foundations and Businesses in Brazil; the Mexican Center for Philanthropy in Mexico; and the Ecuadorian Consortium for Social Responsibility. These associations are promoting a sense of common identity and working to strengthen existing grantmakers and to promote new ones.

Corporate Philanthropy Is an Expanding Sector

Corporations and corporate leaders are an increasingly influential force within the grantmaking sector in all three countries. The introduction of corporations to the social arena in the last two decades has brought about important changes including, in some cases, the professionalization of the nonprofit sector through the introduction of modern business practices in the management of nonprofit organizations and the adoption of new concepts, such as social investment and strategic alliances.

Brazil shows the highest number of corporate grantmakers: 61.3% of the organizations identified were created by private corporations. In contrast, the study revealed that most grantmakers in Mexico and Ecuador were founded by private individuals or civil society leaders (or a combination of both). The studies found that 30% of the Ecuadorian foundations had been created by business and that number decreases to 23% in Mexico.

These numbers are not surprising. Compared to other Latin American countries, Brazil's private sector has been the most dynamic in embracing its role as a social actor. In Ecuador and Mexico, this tendency to participate is still evolving and has not yet reached a point of maturation.

According to a recent paper prepared by Brazil's leading corporate social responsibility organization, Instituto Ethos de Empresas e Responsabilidade Social (The Ethics Institute for Business Social Responsibility), among the reasons for greater corporate responsibility in Brazil are: the increasing recognition of the complexity of social problems and the intensification of urban violence in Brazil; recognized limits of government action and the perceived growing need to build partnerships; a strong Brazilian third sector and a demanding Brazilian consumer; and the dissemination of a culture of quality in business management where corporate social responsibility is an important factor.[12]

Foundations Tend to Concentrate In or Around the Most Important Cities or Regions

The studies showed that most grantmakers are located in or around the most important cities or regions, either in economic or political terms. In Brazil, 77% of the grantmaking foundations are located in the Southeast, particularly the city of São Paulo. In Mexico, 71% are based in Mexico City, and in Ecuador 80% can be found in Quito.

This initial reading might lead us to conclude that grantmakers favor locating around the most developed or prosperous areas. But in Ecuador, Guayaquil and not Quito stands out as the most important city in terms of size and commercial activity. And the north of Mexico (particularly the border region), and not the state of Mexico, shows the most rapid levels of economic growth in the country.

One explanation for this concentration of grantmakers in certain major cities or regions is the existence of higher levels of connectivity or association "*asociatividad*" among citizens.

This is the case in Ecuador, where the concentration of grantmakers is based primarily on cultural factors that privilege, in the mountainous region around Quito, a tendency toward collective action and the creation of civil society organizations. In the case of Mexico, the high concentration of grantmakers in the capital city is mostly explained by the presence of a more enabling environment, in terms of access to funds, contacts and opportunities for professional growth. In Brazil, the concentration of grantmakers in the Southeast is based on the existence of a more vigorous social investment culture, linked to the presence of national networks of foundations and business associations.

Few Fiscal Incentives Exist for the Grantmaking Sector in Brazil and Ecuador with More in Mexico

The fiscal environment is especially unfavorable to grantmakers in Ecuador and challenging for those in Brazil. Even when the law recognizes a growing space for civil society organizations, there is an absence of deliberate policies to stimulate the grantmaking and philanthropic organizations. Mexico, however, has made some strides in this area, possibly contributing to the larger number of grantmakers found there.

Brazilian law does not allow individuals to deduct donations made to social projects (except those made to national, state and municipal Councils for the Rights of Children and Adolescents and for cultural projects that are part of the National Program of Cultural Support). There are also no fiscal incentives for the use of bequests in the creation of foundations.

In Ecuador there are no special regulations or fiscal policies for grantmakers. Grantmakers must pay income tax (whenever they generate income as a result of the sale of a service) as well as the value added tax. In addition, Ecuadorian law does not allow individuals to deduct donations to grantmaking foundations from their personal income taxes.

In Mexico, grantmakers receive national and international fiscal incentives. They include incentives at the federal and state levels found in the Mexican Income Tax Law (*Ley del Impuesto Sobre la Renta*). These fiscal incentives take the form of exemptions, subsidies and tax deductions. In some cases, grantmakers also benefit from the loan of buildings, the donation of vehicles and furniture. In addition, there are international incentives found in the agreement between Mexico and the United States to avoid double taxation, signed in 1993, which provides that United States citizens and corporations can make tax-deductible donations to authorized Mexican nonprofit institutions. Grantmakers are also exempt from income tax and can issue receipts for tax purposes. It is important to highlight that the issuance of these receipts can only be made by "*authorized organizations*"—that is, those that have been certified by the government as transparent and healthy organizations. Close to 89% of the Mexican grantmakers fall in this category.

Institutional Characteristics

Most organizations combine grantmaking with direct operations
Unlike the United States and Canada, there are few "pure" grantmakers in the three countries—organizations whose sole activity is the channeling of resources through a competitive grantmaking process. Foundations tend to have a hybrid character, adding the operation of programs, projects and/or institutions to their grantmaking activity.

There are several reasons sighted for this "hybrid" character of the grantmakers. One reason is distrust on the part of foundations of nonprofit organizations and in particular their capacity to efficiently manage philanthropic resources. Another reason cited is the perception, mentioned earlier, that grantmaking is charity and therefore does not attack the root causes of societal problems. Another is the desire on the part, especially of businesspeople, to create their own programs utilizing business methods and a more entrepreneurial approach.

The Brazilian researcher created the following model to capture the unique nature of grantmakers. While developed for Brazil, the model also captures the types of foundations found in Ecuador and Mexico. The model attempts to illustrate both the way that these foundations vary along a spectrum according to whether they aggressively seek out programs and projects or are reactive to requests (proactive vs. reactive) and whether the foundations are open to funding proposals presented to them or closed to that possibility (open vs. closed).

In Brazil, 77% of foundations carry out programs and projects in addition to making grants. Brazilian corporate grantmakers channel fewer resources in the form of grants than non-corporate foundations (30% and 75% respectively). This highlights their preference for the direct operation of programs as their main strategy for social investment. The majority of Brazilian grantmakers fall on the pro-active side of Table 1, varying in their openness to proposals from civil society organizations.

In Mexico, in contrast, foundations channel 50% of their income in the form of grants or scholarships: 76% of the foundations (particularly those created in the past decade) recognize grantmaking as their main activity and only 24% also operate their own programs and projects. More than their counterparts in Brazil and Ecuador, Mexican grantmakers tend to approximate the model of a "classic grantmaker" found in more developed countries. This greater emphasis on grantmaking could be a result of proximity to the United States and the influence of the U.S. philanthropic tradition where the vast majority fall into the "classic grantmaker" category.

The study found, however, that Mexican foundations vary in the way they make grants from "closed" grantmakers that tend to provide grants to a "family" of institutions on an almost permanent basis, to the more "open" grantmakers that have a transparent and responsive grantmaking program. As noted later, transparency among foundations in Mexico is a persistent challenge, while the newest foundations—especially corporate and community foundations—tend to be more open.

Even more than Brazil, the hybrid character of Ecuadorian grantmakers is predominant, with 95% of the grantmaking foundations operating programs and projects and managing their own institutions in addition to channeling grants. The majority of Ecuadorian grantmakers would be solidly in the hybrid category both being proactive in their activities and receptive to proposal from civil society organizations (Ecuadorian grantmakers approve 36% of the proposals they receive). Unique to Ecuador is that in addition to grants, credit on a non-commercial basis represents an important part of the resources channeled by 50% of the foundations studied.

Foundations Are Successful in Mobilizing Most of Their Funds from Local Sources

The studies conclusively showed that grantmakers receive most of their funding from local sources (the majority from corporate contributions, earned income fees, grants or contracts from the government, donations from individuals and income from endowments). This breaks one of the most entrenched myths of the sector: that grantmakers are mere channels for international funding. Local funding is greatest among corporate grantmakers, who receive the vast majority of their resources from their local parent corporations. In both Brazil and Ecuador, approximately 68% of the resources mobilized by grantmakers come from local sources, while in Mexico, 79% of the funds received by foundations come from local sources.

International funding—from official development assistance and foundations—is more prevalent among non-corporate grantmakers. But there are important differences between the three countries. In the case of Brazil, international funding represents more than half of the resources received by these organizations. In Ecuador the picture is totally different. Even while international funding is higher among non-corporate foundations, local funding still accounts for 68% of their resources (mostly from income generating activities).

Table 2. Sources of Funding*

	Brazil	Mexico[13]	Ecuador
Local sources	69%	79%	68%
International sources	31%	9%	32%

(*) Data from: Andrés P. Falconer, Brazil, Boris Cornejo, Ecuador, Alejandro Natal, Mexico

Most Foundations Lack Significant Endowments

Endowments do not represent a significant source of income for grantmaking foundations in the three countries. In Brazil, only five organizations

(16%) have endowments, with another five having other types of permanent assets such real estate. In Ecuador, 60% of the foundations have an endowment, but these do not exceed US$3 million and are not an important source of income. This is also true for Mexico, where 64% of the foundations have an endowment although with very few exceptions, endowments do not exceed US$3 million.

The studies introduced factors that explain this key departure from grantmaking foundations in developed countries. Five reasons mentioned include: the young nature of the grantmaking sector; the absence of sufficient fiscal incentives; the lack of an "endowment culture" among foundations and society at large; the perception that endowments are *"frozen resources"* that do not contribute to urgently needed social investment; and the lack of foundation staff capacity in raising endowment funds. While these developing countries clearly also struggle with resource constraints in addressing myriad social problems, researchers did not point to a lack of national resources as a key factor in limiting endowment growth.

This should not lead one to conclude that endowments are not important for grantmakers. Increasingly, foundations are seeking to increase their capital base through the creation or strengthening of their endowments.

Table 3. Endowment

	Brazil	Ecuador[14]	Mexico
Foundations with endowments and other permanent assets	32.3%	60%	64%
Foundations with no endowments and other permanent assets	67.7%	25%	36%

(*) Data from: Andrés P. Falconer, Brazil, Boris Cornejo, Ecuador, Alejandro Natal, Mexico

Support for Education Is a Priority for Most Grantmakers

In all three countries, education is the primary focus of grantmaker investment. This is not surprising as throughout Latin America education stands out as a priority area, both for governments and civil society organizations alike, as they struggle to improve development indicators and quality of life.

Disaggregated by country, Brazilian grantmakers prioritize education, with 81% having that as the focus of their investing. The Brazilian study speculates that, besides being compatible with the country's social agenda, investment in the education of children and adolescents represents a low risk strategy for the funder and a high pay-off in terms of public acceptance.

In Ecuador, the researcher posits that the focus on education might also be a response to the perceived inadequacy of public investments in the education sector. In addition, the precarious financial situation of grant-makers, where they are often also raising funds for programs and endowments, leads many to work in those fields for which foreign and domestic funding is most available. The Mexican study also explores this hypothesis but concludes that foundations seem to be genuinely responding to the demand coming from the nonprofit sector for funds in education and not responding to the needs of outside donors.

The Vast Majority of Grantmaking Foundations are Private, Secular Organizations

In the three countries, the origins of the grantmaking sector can be traced to the strong presence of the Catholic Church through the creation of institutions that provided resources and services to poor and marginalized groups. Based on different interpretations of Christian charity, these institutions flourished during the end of the 19th and the beginning of the 20th centuries and, in many cases, preceded the existence of a social security system.

During the 20th century the dominance of the Church in social action was complemented by an increased role for government and then, toward the end of the 20th century (after 1970), the emergence of strong civil society organizations and an active business sector. While the liberalized Catholic Church under Vatican II played a major role in the development of civil society in the 1970s, and influenced many corporate leaders to become involved in social action, most organizations that emerged did not directly affiliate with the Church. As a result, it is not surprising that in the three countries studied, civil society leaders, private individuals and corporations appear as the most frequent founders of grantmaking foundations today.

This presents an important difference with the older grantmakers that were either created by or closely related to the Catholic Church. Today only a small percentage of foundations are officially linked to religious groups (three in Mexico, four in Brazil and five in Ecuador). While the traditions of the Catholic Church, both in its charity orientation of the 19th and early 20th century as well as its more social justice orientation of the 1960s, certainly influenced the development of many of these grantmakers, they do not align themselves with the Church, nor credit the Church for their founding. It is important to mention that while the Church plays a smaller role in institutionalized philanthropy in the region, much individual giving is still made to churches and church-based organizations, emphasizing the continued strong affiliation between philanthropy and the Catholic Church in Latin America.

Many Foundations Lack Transparency in Their Operations

As mentioned, grantmaking foundations are seeking to become more professional. One of the ways in which they can do this is by increasing the transparency of their operations, particularly in terms of their grantmaking criteria.

The study found that this is an area in which most foundations still need to build capacity. In Mexico and Brazil, only 30% and 32% of foundations respectively publish guidelines for grant applications, while in Ecuador this number increases to 50%. In addition, in Mexico financial audits are often not made public and few foundations share their financial statements with the public. As a result of the political changes in Mexico in 2000, particularly community and corporate foundations are demonstrating a greater willingness to publish reports of their activities and are seeking to become more transparent in their operations.

There are several explanations for this apparent low rate of accountability. The grantmaking sector is young and still developing in Latin America. Many have small budgets and low capacity and are unaware of the need to incorporate mechanisms of transparency and communication in their operations. Others fear that due to the tremendous need for local philanthropic resources, increasing the transparency and visibility of their foundation will result in an inundation of grant requests, exceeding the foundation's ability to respond. In Mexico there are additional historical reasons for the lack of transparency. Mexican foundations have emphasized the need for independence and autonomy and have been unwilling to disclose information for fear of government intervention.

Grantmakers Play Important "Bridging" Roles in Society

In all three countries, the majority of grantmakers see their role as bridging organizations and use their unique position in society to build alliances with civil society organizations, other foundations, government and the private sector. In Ecuador most grantmakers see their role as strengthening the civil society sector and several of the large grantmaking foundations, such as Fundación Esquel, have been leaders in creating spaces for dialogue on social and political challenges facing Ecuador. In Brazil all organizations studied practice partnership-building in some form, many adopting a type of proactive grantmaking referred to as creating *parcerias* (partnerships) where foundations "co-invest" with the recipient organization, other businesses or government. In Brazil, the grantmaking sector is particularly powerful because of its strong connection to the private sector and the sector has used that power to advocate for more enabling social policies for civil society.

In Mexico, grantmakers, especially those in the 3rd generation, are able to create "spaces of trust" where diverse sectors that formerly were unable to work jointly are coming together. This is a particularly important role as distrust and polarization between government, civil society and business persists in Mexico despite the recent political transition.

Conclusions and Recommendations

Grantmaking foundations are a growing phenomenon in Latin America. Their growth can be largely attributed to both a developing civil society sector seeking to create local financing mechanisms and to the increased social role being played by the private sector. While grantmaking has formerly been strongly associated with charity, new social actors are revolutionizing the practice and creating a new variant of a grantmaking foundation that is more professional and takes a more proactive role, often carrying out its own programs.

Despite rapid growth over the past two decades, the sector still faces several challenges. The majority of grantmakers are organizationally and financially fragile. While there is a move toward professionalism, their capacity to raise and manage resources is limited, and most foundations rely on a few sources of income. Though almost half of the organizations studied have endowments, their small size presents a challenge to the sector. Latin American grantmakers will need to explore ways to diversify income and reduce expectations that endowments will offer financial stability in the short term. Although foundations have made great strides in reducing their dependence on international funding, there is also a need to mobilize more resources from private individuals locally.

While the evidence in not conclusive, it seems likely that fiscal incentives contributed to the growth of grantmaking foundations in Mexico where the fiscal framework is the most enabling. It also appears that the limited fiscal incentives in Brazil resulted in increased support for particular causes for which individuals and corporations could receive tax deductions (children, youth and culture). Government policymakers and civil society leaders need to analyze the relative benefits of encouraging, through new fiscal incentives, the development of a local grantmaking sector as those incentives imply a shift of resources from the public sector to private organizations. At a minimum, however, there should be more clarity about the incentives that exist, perverse disincentives such as high levels of bureaucracy and the complexity of current regulations should be corrected, and more effort should be made to understand and publicize the incentives that are available, encouraging individuals and businesses to access those benefits.

The lack of a clear identity for grantmaking foundations also contributes to their organizational, and potentially financial, fragility. Without an ability to articulate a common identity, organizing the sector will be difficult and grantmakers will remain obscure. Poor visibility will make de-bunking myths of the past difficult and will continue to hinder the sector's growth. As so much can be learned by connecting with similar organizations, the more grantmakers can identify with one another, the faster their organizational capacity will increase. Associations of foundations can play an important role in building a sectoral consciousness, bringing these organizations together for capacity-building and assisting them in achieving a clearer and more enabling legal environment.

While grantmakers are making great strides in this area, professionalism continues to be a challenge. Boards of directors are not being used to maximum advantage and many foundations have high overhead costs that reduce the impact of their programs. Steps to keep overhead costs low are essential for maintaining a good public image for the sector. Few foundations have rigorous evaluation systems, limiting their ability to measure impact and use the results to raise more resources. A self-regulating mechanism for grantmaking foundations would help tremendously to set a standard for quality among grantmakers, confronting the myths of inefficiency and paternalism.

Studies such as the one carried out by Synergos are essential for promoting the sector and identifying sectoral leaders. Further research, especially on the impact of grantmakers, would help greatly to increase knowledge and awareness of the role of the sector. It could encourage local leaders to start grantmaking foundations and identify ways of enhancing the capacity of the sector.

The power of grantmaking foundations is that they have the ability to support the actions and desires of empowered local communities that diagnose and present solutions to their own problems. While the hybrid nature of foundations in the countries studied has resulted in proactive, impactful and creative philanthropic models, the question of whether the present sector is sufficiently responsive to local needs is an important one. As underscored by Brazilian researcher, "If there is not agreement between [grantmaker] priorities and social demands, private philanthropy runs the risk of contributing to the reproduction of inequality and maintaining exclusivity, contrary to its discourse."[15] If the Brazilian foundation sector is not willing to provide significant strategic financial support to the more than 200,000 civil society organizations, there remains the difficult question of who will.

In places like Brazil, Ecuador and Mexico, the practice of grantmaking needs to be encouraged and strengthened to guarantee a local resource base for the third sector as its takes on new challenges and responds to new demands.

Notes

1 Andres Falconer and Roberto Vilela. *Recursos Privados para Fins Públicos: As Grantmakers Brasileiras*, 2001; Boris Cornejo Castro. *Recursos Privados para Fines Públicos: Los Grantmakers en el Ecuador*, 2001; Alejandro Natal with Patricia Greaves and Sergio García. *Recursos Privados para Fines Públicos: Las Instituciones Donantes Mexicanas*, 2002.

2 In this chapter we have at times referred to the grantmaking organizations studied as simply "foundations." When we refer to "foundations," unless otherwise specified, we are referring to grantmaking organizations. This should not be confused with the Spanish or Portuguese translation, *fundación* or *fundacão* where the word does not necessarily refer to a grantmaking entity.

3 Falconer, Andres and Vilela, Roberto. *Recursos Pivados para Fins Públicos: As Grantmakers Brasileiras*, 2001. p. 64.

4 Ibid. p. 66.

5 After education, arts and culture and community development were of greatest priority to 42% of foundations.

6 Ibid. p. 55.

7 Because of the mixed nature of the founding groups in Ecuador, the percentages do not add to 100%.

8 The figure of US$138.5 million includes donations made by *Nacional Monte de Piedad* in Mexico, which itself channels over US$22 million annually, over 40% of annual giving in Mexico.

9 The Foundation Center press release, June 2002 with data from the year 2000.

10 Philanthropic Foundations of Canada website, data from the year 2002.

11 Japan Foundation Center data from studies conducted of grantmakers since 1987.

12 Medeiros Peliano, Anna Maria T., Nathalie Beghin and Valdemar de Oliviera Neto. *Philanthropy for Equity: The Brazilian Case.* Prepared for the Global Equity Initiative project developed by the John F. Kennedy School of Government, Harvard University, 2003.

13 Due to a lack of culture of transparency, the origin of 10% of the income of Mexican grantmakers was not made available.

14 15% of Ecuadorian foundations did not specify whether they had endowments.

15 Falconer p. 68.

References

Adoum, Alejandra with Venza, Angela. *The Esquel Ecuador Foundation (Fundación Esquel-Ecuador): A Case Study.* Series on Foundation Building. New York: Synergos Institute, 1997.

CIVICUS. *Sustaining Civil Society: Strategies for resource mobilization.* Edited by Leslie M. Fox and S. Bruce Schearer. Washington: CIVICUS, 1997.

Comunidade Solidária. *Série Marco Legal—Terceiro Setor: Uma agenda para Reforma do Marco Legal.* Anna Cynthia Oliveira, Consultora. Rio de Janeiro: International Center for Not-for-Profit Law (ICNL), 1997.

Conclusiones y Propuestas de la Mesa de Diálogo entre las Organizaciones de la Sociedad Civil y el Equipo de Transición en las Áreas Social y Política del Presidente Vicente Fox Quesada. CEMEFI, 2000.

Cornejo Castro, Boris. *Recursos privados para fines públicos: Los grantmakers en el Ecuador.* Quito: Fundación Esquel, 2001.

Cornejo Castro, Boris and Venza, Angela. *Responsabilidad Social: Una Empresa de Todos.* Quito: Fundación Esquel, 1998.

Directorio de Instituciones Filantrópicas, 2000, CEMEFI.

Dulany, Peggy. *Toward a New Paradigm for Civil Society Leadership: The Art of Bridging Gaps.* Keynote address at the W.K. Kellogg Salzburg Seminar on Non-Governmental Organizations: Leadership and Civil Society, 1997.

Dupree, A. Scott, and Winder, David. *Foundation Building Sourcebook: A Practitioners Guide Based on Experience from Africa, Asia and Latin America.* New York: Synergos Institute, 2000.

Falconer, Andres and Vilela, Roberto. *Recursos privados para fins públicos: As grantmakers brasileiras,* São Paulo, Brazil: Ed. Peirópolis—GIFE, Grupo de Institutos, Fundações e Empresas, 2001.

Fernandes, Ruben César. *Privado porém público: O terceiro setor na America Latina.* Rio de Janeiro: Relume Dumará/Civicus, 1994.

GIFE. *Investimento social privado no Brasil—Perfil e catálogo dos associados GIFE.* São Paulo, 2001.

Investigación sobre las Fundaciones en México. Centro Mexicano para la Filantropía. México, 1993.

Landim, Leilah. *Defining the Nonprofit Sector: Brazil. Working Papers of the Johns Hopkins Comparative Nonprofit Sector Project, no. 9,* edited by Lester M. Salamon and Helmut K. Anheier. Baltimore: The Johns Hopkins Institute for Policy Studies, 1993.

Medeiros Peliano, Anna Maria T., Nathalie Beghin, and Valdemar de Oliviera Neto. *Philanthropy for Equity: The Brazilian Case.* Prepared for the Global Equity Initiative project developed by the John F. Kennedy School of Government, Harvard University, 2003.

Natal, Alejandro with Greaves, Patricia and Garcia, Sergio. *Recursos privados para fines públicos: Las instituciones donantes mexicanas.* México: CEMEFI—Centro Mexicano para la Filantropía, 2002.

Salamon, Lester M. and Helmut K. Anheier. *The Third World's Third Sector in Comparative Perspective. Working Papers of the Johns Hopkins Comparative Nonprofit Sector Project, no. 24,* edited by Salamon, Lester M. and Helmut K. Anheier. Baltimore: The Johns Hopkins Institute for Policy Studies, 1997.

Salamon, Lester M.; Anheier, Helmut K.; List, Regina; Toepler, Stefan; Sokolowski, S. Wojciech and Associates. *Global Civil Society: Dimensions of the nonprofit sector.* Baltimore: Johns Hopkins Center for Civil Society Studies, 1999.

Salamon, Lester M.; Anheier, Helmut K.; List, Regina; Toepler, Stefan; Sokolowski, S. Wojciech y colaboradores. *La Sociedad Civil Global: Las dimensiones del sector no lucrativo.* Traductor: Marcos Azcárate. Madrid: Fundación BBVA, 1999.

Schearer, S. Bruce. *The Role of Philanthropy in International Development.* Paper prepared for conference on Human Centered Development: the Role of Foundations, FLOs and NGOs in Bellagio, Italy, 1995.

Schearer, S. Bruce, and Tomlinson, John. The Emerging Nature of Civil Society in Latin America and the Caribbean: An Overview. New York: Synergos Institute, 1997.

Synergos Institute. *Seminario: Fundaciones Latinoamericanas para el desarrollo de la sociedad civil—México, Centro América, El Caribe y la Región Andina.* Cali, Colombia, Abril, 1997.

Synergos Institute and GIFE. *Seminário: Recursos privados para fins públicos—Fortalecendo fundações e institutos no Cone Sul—Informe final.* São Paulo: Synergos Institute/GIFE, 1998.

Szazi, Eduardo. *Terceiro Setor: Regulação no Brasil.* São Paulo: GIFE/Peirópolis, 2000.

Valencia, Enrique and Winder, David. *El Desarrollo: Una tarea en común: Diálogos Sociedad Civil-Gobierno Brasil, Colombia, México.* Ed. Indicadores, Desarrollo y Análisis (IDEA), A.C.; Red Observatorio Social and The Synergos Institute. México: Amaroma Ediciones, 1997.

Various authors. CSROs *and Development in Asia Series.* New York, The Synergos Institute.

Various authors. *Foundation Case Study Series.* New York, The Synergos Institute.

Verduzco, Gustavo, List, Regina, y Salamon, Lester M. *Perfil del sector no lucrativo en México.* Baltimore: CEMEFI and The Johns Hopkins University, Institute for Policy Studies, Center for Civil Society Studies

Williams, Maurice J. *The Emerging Nature of Civil Society's Contribution to Development: The Role of Official Development Assistance.* Report on conference. Co-published by The Synergos Institute and Overseas Development Council (ODC), 1995.

Winder, David. *Civil Society Resource Organizations (CSROs) and development in Southeast Asia: A Summary of Findings.* New York: Synergos Institute, 1998.

Workshop Report: *Innovative Endowment Building and Investment for Grantmaking Organizations.* Southern African Grantmakers' Association and The Synergos Institute. Johannesburg, South Africa, June, 2000.

Appendix I

The Emergence of Community Foundations in Mexico

In Mexico, the emergence and rapid growth of the community foundation sector has been one of the most notable developments within the civil society sector in recent years. Since 1996, over 20 new community foundations have been formed and are currently operating in all regions of Mexico. These organizations are heterogeneous in that they have emerged through the initiative and efforts of diverse actors. For example, the first community foundation (to be referred to as such), the Oaxaca Community Foundation, was created in 1996 with considerable support from the international foundation community. Since then, by and large, the impetus and inputs needed to create community foundations in Mexico have come from local initiative. Typically, the equation has involved a core group of actors from the local private sector and the social development sector convening and agreeing to collaborate to establish a completely new and permanent source of resources of development in their community.

The government has also played a valuable role in stimulating and supporting the growth of this movement. Current Mexican President Vicente Fox, while Governor of the State of Guanajuato, provided support, both financial and in terms of leadership, that facilitated the establishment of new community foundations in Irapuato, Leon, Celaya and San Miguel de Allende. In addition, the state government of Chihuahua was instrumental in creating the regulatory framework necessary to establish the Fundacion del Empresariado Chihuahuense, A.C., currently the biggest community foundation in Mexico.

What is a Community Foundation in Mexico?

No formal regulatory designation exists specifically for the Community Foundation in Mexico. Within Mexican legal and fiscal regulatory structures, they are typically represented within the fiscal code by one of the three designations established by the federal government of nonprofit, benevolent institutions: AC: Civil Association; IAP: Institutional of Private Assistance; or IBC: Institution of Private Benevolence. Nevertheless, the Mexican Community Foundations Group, a sectoral affinity group coordinated by the Centro Mexicano para la Filantropía, A.C. (CEMEFI) has elaborated a definition that states the following: a community foundation is "an independent and autonomous organization, private and not-for profit, dedicated to attending to the critical needs of the community and elevating the quality of life in a specific and delimited geographic area."

The following breaks downs this definition into more detail. Mexican community foundations are expected to:

- **Be independent and autonomous:** Mexican community foundations are not tied to a specific person, institution, business or government entity. They represent the issues, needs and interests of the community, through a diverse and representative leadership body, the board of directors or *consejo directivo*. Decisions made within the community foundation reflect the expression and interests of its beneficiary population: the community.

- **Be private and not-for-profit:** Mexican community foundations are not public institutions and are not motivated by the generation of a private economic benefit.

- **Address the critical needs of the community:** Community foundations in Mexico can and do have varied programmatic goals and objectives. This is due to the fact that the community foundation is created to respond directly to the priority needs within the community. This requires identifying the priority needs within the community, which the community foundation does through community outreach, diagnostic processes and by relying on strong leadership representing the diversity within the community.

- **Improve quality of life:** The goal of every Mexican community foundation is to improve the quality of life or the health and welfare of the citizens of the community.

- **Stay within a determined geographic area:** Each Mexican community foundation is born from and responds to the needs of a specific geographical area within Mexico. This is a critical component of its identity. The leadership, funding and administration of the community foundation is fundamentally tied to the reality that it is a local institution in every respect.

What do Mexican community foundations do?

Community foundations are, at their institutional core, grantmaking institutions. That is, they mobilize financial resources, primarily from the local community, for the purposes of making direct investments in the institutions within the community working directly with the priority beneficiary populations as they are identified by the foundation. In this sense, they are "patrons of social change and development."

A recent survey of a subset of the most established Mexican community foundations found that, in 2002, Mexican community foundations gave $US7.49 million dollars in grants to local institutions through over 1,400 individual grants. Their permanent endowments, an important indicator of sustainability, range from zero to $4.4 million US dollars with the average endowment being US$602,030.

As part of their role as local institutions, Mexican community foundations are committed to facilitating and encouraging local philanthropy within their communities as a means of both sustaining their own operations and leveraging new funds for local priority needs. Their success and sustainability depend largely on their ability to mobilize resources from the local community. Nevertheless, the sample of the Mexican community foundations surveyed demonstrates that over 75% of the Mexican community foundation funds (annual operating budget) are raised from local sources, including private donors, corporate donations, service fees, investment income and funds from the government. Mexican community foundations still raise a substantial portion (24%) of their operating budgets from international sources, with private international foundations accounting for 28% of the community foundations' total operating budgets.

Summary Results from Survey of 15 Mexican Community Foundations:

Average staff size:	10 paid staff, 39 volunteers
Average annual operating budget:	US$730,715
Total amount (US$) given in grants in 2002:	US$7,497,010
Number of grants given:	1,493
Composition of operating expenses:	
Grants:	41%
Programs:	35%
Services:	1%
Administration/operations:	15%
Other (including investment in endowment):	8%
Composition of revenue sources:	
Domestic:	76%
International:	24%

11

Too Much or Too Little? The Role of Tax Incentives in Promoting Philanthropy

Ignacio Irarrázaval and Julio Guzmán

Tax incentives in several Latin American countries of Latin America aim to promote philanthropy and the nonprofit sector. The purpose of this chapter is fourfold:

- Define the main types of these tax incentives;
- Present the rationale and concerns about philanthropy tax incentives;
- Describe the empirical reality of tax incentive use and effects;
- Recommend how to strengthen philanthropic tax incentives.

Our analyses are based on studies of the tax incentive systems in effect in Argentina, Brazil, Colombia, Chile, Peru, and Mexico.

What Types of Tax Incentives Are Used?

Various policy instruments may be implemented to promote nonprofit institutions: direct fiscal contributions, funds open to competition, subsidies, or tax incentives. The last category is one of the policy options available to promote philanthropy.

To understand different types of tax incentives, a distinction must be made between tax exemptions and tax benefits (also known as tax privileges). Exemption releases nonprofits from the obligation to pay a certain tax and is generally applied to institutions that engage in actions for the common good or for providing material aid to low-income individuals in areas such as education, culture and science. In this case, the beneficiary of the exemption is the nonprofit itself. The following taxes, among others, may be open to exemption:

- Income Tax (tax on personal income, rents from investments, etc.)

- Value Added Tax (general sales tax)
- Death duties or estate tax
- Land tax (net worth, real estate)
- Industrial and commercial licenses
- Customs duties
- Social security

In addition, the difference should be clarified between legal exemption and simple administrative release from payment of the tax concerned. In the latter case, the benefit depends on the discretionary decision of the fiscal authorities in response to individual applications received, at times causing arbitrary or inconsistent decisions to be adopted.

Tax benefits, in turn, provide an incentive for donating and in most countries, are linked to the purpose of the donation. According to international literature, there are two ways of applying tax benefits to donations:

- Tax credits
  Part or all of the donation becomes a tax credit against taxes payable in a given period, thus reducing the amount that the taxpayer would have to pay. Tax credits grant taxpayers the same tax preference for a contribution in the same amount and are thus more equitable from the standpoint of tax policy.

- Tax deductions
  The consideration of part or all of the donation as a tax-deductible expense allows partial reduction of taxable income and results in a lower tax payment. The cost of the donation would be substantially lower for donors taxed at high tax rates.

Why Tax Incentives for Nonprofit Institutions?

Nonprofits play a significant role by providing public goods and services that neither the public sector nor other institutions are able to supply, especially when consumer demand is heterogeneous. As a result, a minority of nonprofits supply such goods and services or deal with other than the usual causes or issues. Nonprofits also enjoy comparative advantages to understand the demands of their beneficiaries, because of closer relationships and experience. The government, on the other hand, is restricted by having to show everyone the same treatment, providing standardized services regulated by slower than normal procedures. In addition, nonprofits have a capability to mobilize volunteers, which enables citizens to take part in developing and applying policies and actions in the public interest. Finally, another distinctive feature of nonprofits are their capacity for innovation. Unlike the government, they do not necessarily have to prove the results of their actions or use standard methods. Now let us turn to the rationale for specific types of incentives described in the previous section.

- *Why income tax exemptions?*
  From the standpoint of economics and tax equity, income tax exemptions for nonprofits are justified, since their income should not be considered taxable, for they do not pursue profit and are forbidden to distribute profits among their directors. This implies that tax exemptions should be based on the use rather than the origin of income. In practical terms, this implies that nonprofit commercial activities ought to be taxable with Value Added Tax (VAT) and all other taxes payable on similar commercial activities conducted by private enterprises, thus respecting the origin of the funds obtained and fair competition with the other organizations.

  From a sociopolitical standpoint, tax exemptions are justified because of the role that nonprofits play in a pluralist society. Through tax exemptions, the state allows the generation of manifold goods and services that would go undeveloped if the government directly managed the funds collected. The mere incentive to donate is a product of these exemptions, together with donor involvement in a cause in the public interest. As previously mentioned, the state is restricted to relying on the preferences of the majorities, inevitably leading to the existence of a minority dissatisfied with the supply of certain goods and services. In such cases, tax exemptions support the organization of nonprofits engaged in supplying such minority groups with goods not provided in sufficient quantity by the state or in raising awareness of special causes.

  Exemptions also help strengthen civil society by allowing more resources to become available irrespective of the political preferences of the groups in power at a given time.

  Although the administration in office may be able to allocate funds to certain activities, it may not be disposed to do so. Thus, exemptions allow citizens to express their preferences in the allocation of at least part of the public funds.

- *Why tax benefits on donations?*
  The previous arguments in the context of pluralism and independence from the current administration are also valid, in theory, to justify benefits on donations. Three other benefits, however, may also be mentioned.

(1) Imperfections in the donation market
The natural imperfections of the "market" for donations justify promoting tax benefits. If only one donation mechanism were available among private organizations, donations would be less than the social optimum. Donors tend to behave in an opportunistic manner, and if they assume others will also make donations, they eventually donate less than they originally would have. For this reason, the act of donating *per se* is worth subsidizing. In this context, benefits are justified because they stimulate the level of private donations, raising them closer to the social optimum.

(2) Resource "additionality" as a result of incentives
The effectiveness of incentives as a mechanism to raise the level of private donations depends on the response of individuals to tax incentives. If donations grow more than the loss of tax income or tax expenditure (also known as fiscal waiver), then incentives create an "additionality" of resources. Thus, the introduction of tax incentives on donations becomes a treasury-efficient instrument of fiscal policy, increasing the total amount of funds for social purposes. The use of tax incentives to encourage giving assumes that the decision to give (together with the amount given) is dependent on the "price" of the gift. If there are tax incentives on donations, the marginal price per *peso* (or dollar) donated is less than one, for only a fraction of the total amount donated is an out-of-pocket expense for the donor. Thus, the introduction of tax incentives lowers the "price" of donors' donations.

(3) Exclusion from the tax base
Similar to the case of tax incentives, expenditure on donations cannot be properly classified as part of what should be considered consumption, and therefore should not be taxed. The basic theoretical argument holds that deductions intended as tax incentives help to correct the tax base or the amount of taxes so that it will reflect what is considered to be the ideal tax structure. In other words, donations ought not to be taxed because they do not increase the wealth of the donors or produce profit.

• *What concerns are there about tax incentives?*

Public finance specialists express several concerns about tax incentives. The promotion of philanthropy through tax incentives is a more complex approach, engendering side effects in the tax system itself. These side effects make it difficult to measure tax expenditure and opportunity costs associated with public goods not provided by the fiscal cost of tax incentives.[1]

One of the most common arguments in the debate on the relevance of tax incentives for nonprofits is the contention that the state is the sole agent entitled to define social priorities, by virtue of the ability to represent the will of the people apparently vested in the administration currently in office. However, the counterargument suggests that the state has no monopoly on the definition of what is "public."[2] In fact, in a pluralist society, it is both possible and desirable that governmental efforts in the area of social policies be combined with the effort and innovation of private enterprise in the same area.

Tax benefits have also been criticized because of their lack of resource additionality, although often the total amount of donations is greater than the amount of funds that the state gives up as a result of the benefits.

Although the decision to give may not be influenced by economic factors since giving is often an altruistic act inherent in human nature, the decision regarding funds' destination, as well as donor perception of individual nonprofits, do respond to nonprofit incentives and stimuli. In other words, the market for "donations" is a true market, in which nonprofits compete to attract the largest possible number of donors. As a result, institutionally weaker nonprofits generally attract fewer resources in the form of donations, thus letting resources concentrate in a few better-known and more firmly established nonprofits.

Another criticism of the use of tax incentives is the lack of adequate supervisory mechanisms to monitor the proper use of such incentives. In Latin American countries, for instance, no system of accounting or compiling ongoing information has been developed on the amounts involved in tax incentives, nor are there any registers or databases to support true and effective follow-up on nonprofit work.

In conclusion, while various economic and sociopolitical arguments support tax incentives, whether as exemptions for nonprofits or tax benefits on donations, there are concerns about the use of this instrument. The heaviest criticisms arise in the economic literature, which questions the distortions that might take place in the tax system and the scant empirical evidence that private donations increase beyond tax expenditure.

What Is the Tax Treatment of Nonprofits in Latin America?

First, let us look at the general situation with tax systems in Latin America.

Several authors suggest that the establishment of efficient and effective tax systems in developing countries is a major challenge. The structure of economy very often prevents collecting certain forms of tax; tax authorities have limited collection capability, and poor data quality is an acknowledged fact. In practical terms, this all suggests that tax policies in underdeveloped countries are not rational (Tanzi and Zee, 2000). According to Tanzi and Zee, developing countries, in most cases, tend to set up tax systems that are viable in terms of collection capability, irrespective of being modern and efficient. This implies setting numerous low taxes, fairly low utilization of taxes on income, and reliance on taxes on foreign trade and on consumption. In brief, tax policy in developing countries seems to pursue the possible rather than the optimum.

According to International Monetary Fund figures, taxation in developing countries equals about 18% of Gross Domestic Product (GDP), with not much difference among countries. In contrast, tax burdens exceed 35% of GDP in the Organisation for Economic Co-operation and Development (OECD) countries and in North America. As for tax income structure in some Latin American countries, income taxes or direct taxes account for a fairly low share of GDP. Direct taxes in the OECD account for more than 14% of GDP, while in Latin America, they account for as little as 6%. Almost all Latin American countries collect 70–80% of their tax income through indirect taxes. Most Latin American countries have set up Value Added Tax, in most cases under an invoicing and credit procedure, which has brought about a significant degree of modernization and increased collection efficiency. Simultaneously, however, complete economic sectors have been left out of the system, while different tax rates apply to different products. Though politically attractive, such options often end by causing difficulties in system administration.

Thus, one concern about the design of an incentive system favoring nonprofits is that it not be allowed to encourage tax evasion, which in Latin America amounts to between 25% and 39% of total potential collection. Similarly, the literature on public finance generally agrees that the definition of "special regimes," whether sectoral or regional, will affect the collection efficiency of the system.

Tax Expenditure

The notion of tax expenditure may be described as tax exemptions, subsidies and incentives that are not necessary for determining the calculation base of a given tax or that escape the standard tax calculation. In other words, provisions and deductions that incorporate a given tax in measurement of net income must be distinguished from standards that move away from the notion of net income. These measures provide an incentive, special exemption or encouragement to a specific group of taxpayers or a given economic activity. In the case of income tax, personal deductions and other necessary expenses,[3] the process of going from gross income to net income to net taxable income is not tax expenditure; situations of this nature are "normal," whereas others conform to special situations.

Most Latin American countries fail to carry a register of tax expenditure, a substantial limitation to public finance in those countries, because this constitutes a form of public spending not subject to scrutiny or budgetary control. This matter ought to be systematized in order to be able to assess the cost to the state of this kind of expenditure and in particular to compare fiscal effort to promote nonprofits with other areas or sectors.

In this context, a study conducted by the Argentine Ministry of Economic Affairs estimated tax income foregone in 1999 due to tax waivers and promotion régimes. The same study found 32 items identified in Argentina as a tax expenditure with an effect of some significance on tax collection. Tax expenditure for the social area in 1997 accounted for an estimated 1.6% of GDP, while explicit social expenditure accounted for 19.3% of GDP. Another estimate for 2000, this time included all tax expenditure[4] or close to 14% of projected national taxes. In Chile, in turn, an estimate made by the Ministry of Finance points out that tax expenditure appears to account for 4.4% of GDP, or 20% of the total potential collection; of this figure, nearly 80% of tax expenditure goes to benefit the savings-investment sector and the real estate sector. These figures show that tax incentives signify an alternative cost for the nation. Notwithstanding, most of such incentives fail to address the purposes of nonprofits.

More specifically, as illustrated by a study by Irarrázaval (2001), it is possible to illustrate in particular the effect of fiscal waiver on three tax benefits that operate like a tax credit for donors.[5] In this case, these tax incentives are addressed to nonprofits, which are most substantial in the case of Chile.

Table 1. Estimated Tax Expenditure Associated with Incentives such as Tax Credit

Chile	1997	1998	1999
Total Fiscal Waiver (US$) MUS?	31.8	23.1	28.0
% Fiscal waiver on income tax collection	0.20	0.29	0.38
% Fiscal waiver on corporate tax collection	2.00	1.61	1.62
% Fiscal waiver on total income tax collection	1.97	0.97	0.98
% Fiscal waiver on total net tax income	0.29	0.22	0.24
% Fiscal waiver in relation to GDP	0.05	0.03	0.04

Source: Irarrázaval, I (2001)

As the table shows, in 1999, the fiscal waiver associated with the three incentives operating as tax credits totaled less that 1% of the sum collected for income tax. In turn, this represented 0.24% of the total collected for net tax income. The same amount, in terms of GDP, was about 0.05%, reflecting the very small amounts involved, especially considering that only about 2,000 taxpayers, natural and juristic persons, registered tax credits on the annual returns they filed. This means that only about 0.1% of Chilean taxpayers actually utilized these incentives. In Chile, 95% of the fiscal waiver associated with the three incentives under examination arises from corporate tax, while a minimal fraction arises from the use of benefits by natural persons. Secondly, incentives benefiting nonprofits account for only 25% of the total funds mobilized in the form of tax credits, the balance being incentives for the production sector.[6]

Tax Exemptions and Benefits

As we examine main Latin American trends in nonprofit tax treatment, we seek to provide a synthetic, detailed description that must necessarily rely on certain assumptions in order to compare situations.

To make the classification of exemptions more appropriate and synthetic, the following distinctions are used:

Procedure for obtaining exemption:

- Automatic (Legal Exemption). Exemption obtained by right upon accreditation as a nonprofit organization.
- Discretionary (Administrative Waiver). Additional procedure required, exemption granted by competent authority.

Scope of exemption:

- Specific purposes. The exemption covers nonprofits conducting activities in certain areas described under the law, such as social assistance, education, and other forms of activity.
- Full. Covers all areas where the organization operates.

Table 2. Tax Exemptions for Nonprofits

	Income Earnings Tax		Value Added Tax		Other Taxes		
	Form	Scope	Form	Scope	Imports/for trade	Estate	Real Estate
Argentina	Discretionary	Specific	Automatic	Specific	—	—	—
Brazil	Automatic	Full	Automatic	Full	Discretionary/ Specific	—	Automatic/ Specific
Chile	Discretionary	Full	—	No special exemption	Discretionary/ Specific	Specific	Automatic/ Specific
Colombia	Automatic	Specific	—	No special exemption	—	—	—
Mexico	Discretionary	Specific	Discretionary	Specific	—	—	—
Peru	Automatic	Specific	Discretionary	Specific Partial	Discretionary/ Specific	—	No exemption
Venezuela	Discretionary	Specific	—	—	Discretionary/ Specific	—	—

Source: Prepared by the authors, based on information cited in References
Note: Blank boxes mean there is no information available.

As Table 2 shows, all the countries studied provide an income tax exemption favoring nonprofits. In general, as described in the case of Brazil, exemptions apply to all nonprofits that distribute no portion of their assets or income, apply their resources totally to achieving institutional objectives, and keep their accounting up-to-date. Argentine legislation, however, sets limits to compensation paid to the officers of the institution. Social assistance and education are the most frequent specific purposes for nonprofits. Countries report several types of barriers to prevent or restrict the use of such exemptions, including, in Argentina,[7] the establishment of a general register of organizations qualified for exemption, which sets forth various conditions for permissible exemptions, which has meant excessive delay due to defective administration. In Chile, exemptions must be applied for to the President of the Republic, which makes them even more discretionary. Finally, in Mexico, while the available exemptions are quite generous in practice, the kind of activities potentially entitled to exemption is quite limited.

For VAT, as Table 2 shows, the trend is unclear. In most cases, the procedure is discretionary but restricted to the specific purposes of the organization. By way of illustration, this form of incentive is in effect in Mexico, although in practice so very precisely limited that it is virtually inaccessible. The situation is different in Peru, where international nonprofits may apply for reimbursement of the general sales tax on purchases made in the country. In this context, a degree of regression is observed in Argentina, where certain activities that used to be tax exempt are now subject to taxation.

On the other hand, exemptions favoring nonprofits can be found in respect of less important taxes such as taxes on foreign trade. In such cases, the general rule is that the procedure is discretionary and the exemption is tied to the purposes of the institution. Finally, it is common to find that exemption from local taxes, such as real estate tax, license to operate, or commercial license is granted to nonprofits more automatically.

Some legislatures are more generous than others in their tax treatment of nonprofits. This is the case in Brazil, where nonprofits active in education and social assistance are free and clear of federal, state and municipal taxes. In addition, Brazil grants a legal exemption on social security contributions to nonprofits in social assistance. This situation is unique among the countries under examination.

Table 3 refers to tax benefits available to individuals who make donations to nonprofits. Again, for purposes of simplifying the comparison, benefits are classified as to procedure, scope, and limitations.

Lastly, Table 4 summarizes the situation in terms of tax benefits available to juridical persons making donations to nonprofits. Again the information is classified according to procedure, scope and limitations.

Interestingly, with a few minor exceptions, tax benefits available to natural and to juristic persons are quite similar. The most serious barrier to the use of such benefits is the procedure for accrediting the donation through certificates acknowledged by the tax authorities. In Mexico, for instance, the law makes a differentiation among institutions that give assistance by providing that authorized institutions may issue receipts to donors, which are then deductible from income tax, whereas civil organizations require a discretionary permit from the Department of Finance, which is issued only to associations that have no individually designated beneficiaries. In other words, to accredit donations, civil institutions must go through a twofold process. Similarly, in Colombia, fiscal authorities often demonstrate excessive zeal and formality in overseeing certificate issuance by recipients of donations.

Table 3. Tax Benefits to Natural Persons Making Donations to NPIs

	Deductible as Expense			Tax Credit		
	Form	Scope	Limit	Form	Scope	Limit
Argentina	Automatic	Specific: Health Education Research	5%–35% of net earnings for the period	—	—	—
Brazil	Discretionary	Specific: Culture Education	—	Discretionary	Specific: Culture	12% of tax
Chile	—	—	50% of donation that is not credit is deductible as expense	Discretionary	Specific: Culture Education	50% of donation, limit 2% of net taxable income
Colombia	Automatic	Specific: Health Education Culture Religion Sports Environment Social	30% of net income. No limit for higher education, 125% for sports, culture & research	Automatic	Specific: Higher education (study grants)	60% of donation, limit 30% of basic income tax
Mexico	Discretionary (for "authorized" recipients)	Specific:	No limits	—	—	—
Peru	—	—	—	Discretionary	Specific: Culture Education	30% of donation, limit 10% of taxes payable
Venezuela	Automatic	Universal	1%–10% of net income	—	—	—

Source: Prepared by the authors based on information cited in References.
Note: Blank boxes mean that no information was available

The scope allowed for donations, especially in some countries where the tax threshold affecting the donation varies, depends on the area of non-profit activity. In Colombia, for example, deductions as a general rule may not exceed 30% of the donor's net taxable income, yet some areas are open to preferential treatment, such as sports, where deductions may be as high

Table 4. Tax Benefits for Juristic Persons Making Donations to Nonprofits

	Deductible as Expense			Tax Credit		
	Form	Scope	Limit	Form	Scope	Limit
Argentina	Automatic	Specific: Health Education Research	35% of tax rate	—	—	—
Brazil	Discretionary	Specific: Education Culture Sports		Discretionary	Specific: Culture	—
Chile	Automatic	Specific: Health Education Culture Seniors Social Assistance	2%–10% of net taxable income	Discretionary	Specific: Health Higher Education and education	5o% of donation, limit 2% of net taxable income
Colombia	Automatic	Specific: Health Education Culture Environment Social	30% of net income, no limit on higher education, 125% for sports, culture & research	Automatic	Specific: Higher education (study grants)	60% of donation, limit 30% of basic income tax
Mexico	Discretionary	Specific: (for "authorized" recipients)	No limits	—	—	—
Peru	—	—	—	Discretionary	Specific: Culture Education	30% of donation, limit 10% of taxes payable

Source: Prepared by the authors based on information cited in References.
Note: Blank boxes mean that no information was available.

as 125%, with no ceiling for donations. This fact leads to inequitable motivations to donate, for there will be more interest in promoting some areas to the detriment of others, which might also have a social impact.

Information in the above tables and some isolated data from other Latin American countries obtained from the papers reviewed indicate some common trends in tax treatment of nonprofits in the seven countries under study.

Exemptions

As mentioned above, the most important taxes in terms of collection are income tax and Value Added Tax. Exemption trends are as follows:

- All the countries examined contemplate exemptions from income tax or tax on earnings, provided the amount of such exceptions is applied to the purposes of the institution and not distributed among its officers.

- Notwithstanding, in most of the countries (four out of seven) the benefit is obtained through a special, more or less complicated procedure. In three countries, the benefit is obtained automatically, by the act of qualifying as a nonprofit institution.

- Irrespective of the way the benefit is obtained, in most countries (five out of seven), it is granted to nonprofits in accordance with their objectives and purposes. In three countries the benefit is granted comprehensively, regardless of the nonprofit's area of work.

Value Added Tax

- In general, exemption from Value Added Tax is found to be more restrictive than exemption from income tax, with no clear trend among the countries examined. In any event, the available information reveals that comprehensive exemption is in force in Brazil only, as all other countries limit the exemption to the purposes of the institution.

Other taxes

- Two other taxes are frequently found to qualify for exemption in the case of nonprofits. One is the import tax, as most of the countries offer to exempt nonprofits in accordance with their particular ends. In addition, exemption from income tax or property tax is often found in Latin America, and is usually granted automatically. This tax is frequently collected for local or state benefit.

- Also at the local level, exemption from payment for municipal, commercial, or industrial licenses is granted practically automatically in most cases.

Tax benefits for natural persons who make donations

- Table 3 shows that in the countries reviewed where tax benefits are available for natural persons who make donations to non-profits, the benefit most frequently takes the form of expense deduction.

- These deductions are usually offered for specific purposes that the state is interested in enhancing, sometimes restricting the benefit to those specific areas alone. As a result, a discretionary situation arises together with lack of uniformity among nonprofits, some of which will receive substantial benefits simply by operating in the recognized area, while others will not.

- Benefits in the form of tax credits generally need to go through an additional administrative procedure. In Chile, nonprofit projects that receive donations must have prior approval from the appropriate authorities. Similarly, accrediting the donation in order to utilize the benefit is also a complex process. Issuing donation certificates is a complicated procedure and requires further auditing, all of which may discourage use of the privilege.

- Practically in all instances of tax benefits, limits have been set that act as boundaries to the extent to which benefits arising from tax incentives may be applied. These limits are set according to the amount of the donation or a percentage of the tax payable or of the taxpayer's net income. With a few exceptions, the limits that define these thresholds are quite low, the percentage of income or of payable tax being more restrictive than the percentage of the value of the donation.

Tax benefits for juristic persons making a donation

- Practically no differences are found between the tax treatment given to donations made by natural or juristic persons. Again, Table 4 shows that expense deduction is a more frequent form of benefit than tax credit.

- Generally speaking, based on the information reported, corporations in Argentina, Chile, and Colombia perceive that their donations will be more strictly audited.

- Twofold accreditation is also generally found in the countries examined: once before a judicial institution to register the nonprofit, and once before the administrative authority to gain access to various tax benefits.

Thus, it may be concluded that a variety of tax incentives is available in Latin America covering diverse areas, but that apart from empirical ignorance of their uses, numerous implicit and explicit obstacles keep them from being used.

Recommendations for Philanthropic Tax Incentives

Are new incentives needed?

In debating the importance of tax incentives in promoting philanthropy and nonprofits, an overview of the context where this debate takes place is useful.

Civil society exists in the context of the country as a whole, so no matter how important the benefits nonprofits bring to society, the tax context in which nonprofits function does not exist in isolation from the rest of the economic and taxation system and therefore, both need to be consistent. Tax incentives must therefore agree with the policies for fiscal and macroeconomic balance in the various countries. In this context, tax consistency should also be considered. The fiscal literature of international organizations insists that it is advisable to have a simple tax system with a minimum amount of distortion. Promotion of nonprofits through tax incentives is often criticized because of its complexity. Several authors suggest that a complex tax system with numerous exemptions and differentiated treatments introduces unnecessary (public) costs associated with oversight and (private) costs of filing tax returns, its very complexity requiring the aid of accounting experts and advisers. In addition, in most cases, the opportunity costs associated with intangible public goods are not known. These issues are particularly significant in Latin America, where, in the view of various public finance experts,[8] tax systems are already troublesome and inefficient enough.

Empirical evidence about the effect of tax incentives is inconclusive, in part due to a lack of information. The results of various studies concerning developed nations differ widely, especially owing to differences in data and estimation methods applied, although they agree as to the positive effect of tax incentives on the level of donations made, especially in the group of taxpayers faced with marginally higher tax rates.[9] In other words, there is agreement that at least funds for nonprofits increase, but there is little evidence on cases of net additionality.[10] In Chile, one of the few Latin American countries with quantitative information available in this context, it has not been possible to prove net additionality, though some indications suggest that tax incentives have augmented the total funds available to nonprofits.[11]

The tax context in Latin America also should be borne in mind. Shome (2001) points out that the main changes in tax structure in the region have been reductions of the income tax rate for individuals and organizations, while Pita (2001) shows that the trends in income taxes have been rate reduction, less dispersion, increased integration of taxes (both personal and corporate), fewer exemptions, fewer tax incentives, and less use of differential rates. Moreover, during the past decade, countries have focused on collecting excise taxes such as VAT in order to simplify current tax structures.

Finally, the economic context of the region is worth reviewing. According to the Preliminary Balance-Sheet of the Economies of Latin America (ECLAC 2002), the Latin American economies completed half a decade of low growth, with –0.3% growth of per capita GDP since 1998. It should also be recalled, however, that the region is showing signs of incipient recovery as from the second quarter of 2002, and a 2.1–2.2% growth projection for 2003. In this recessive context, fiscal policy also lost degrees of freedom in most of the countries of the region, in most cases with rising fiscal deficit partly accounted for by reduction of income. Thus, many countries applied a fiscal policy designed to face sustainability problems of public indebtedness, which brought additional contraction and measures were taken in some countries to enhance collection or raise taxes. Such was the case in Argentina, where an export tax was created; Uruguay increased social security funding; and Venezuela raised the rate of VAT. All of this took place in a context of 9.1% unemployment, the highest figure for the decade, added to the incipient resurgence of inflation.

The foregoing leads us necessarily to suggest that tax incentives are not "the" basic or fundamental strategy for promoting philanthropy and donations. This means that it is not advisable to consider tax reform for that purpose; it is relevant, however, to consider ways to reduce current obstacles to efficient use of existing mechanisms. To this end, the myth around the fiscal cost of incentives to nonprofits will need dispelling. As shown by the above figures, such cost is lower that the cost of other incentives. Nor can the issue be ignored, since it has been viewed and perceived for years by donors as a major instrument to encourage donations. In Peru,[12] for instance, lack of a favorable tax framework was given as the main reason why entrepreneurs abstained from entering into major philanthropic ventures. In Argentina,[13] too, higher deduction ceilings on donations to nonprofits are viewed as helping to "strengthen the social sector." Therefore, the most advisable course should be to retain such existing incentives so as to create no major distortions in the tax system and make an effort to give effective encouragement to the use and operation of existing incentives.

How can we strengthen existing incentive systems?
With unclear evidence about the overall effect of tax incentives and the fact that the Latin American economy is currently going through a period of low and unstable growth, it is neither possible nor advisable to suggest introducing major changes in tax policy to promote philanthropy.

Notwithstanding, examining current legislation affecting nonprofits in these countries, the diversity and multiplicity of provisions becomes apparent and it will be observed that the decisions of the administrative authorities often overrule construction of the law beyond what the legislators intended. Other data suggest that the use made of tax benefits is rather limited. Indeed, in Brazil,[14] according to an IPEA study, only 8% of the corporations in the southeast area of the country took advantage of federal tax exemptions; similarly, only 4% of these corporations utilized state and municipal fiscal incentives. In Chile, in 1999, only 2,157 taxpayers applied for recognition of a credit filed with their annual income tax returns, which is a minimal percentage of the total taxpayers in the country.

In this context, the state can contribute to make the whole process of utilizing tax incentives easier by formally recognizing philanthropy, its role in society and subsequent benefits, to put incentives in the context of public policy, rather than as a gift to just another pressure group. Of immediate concern, therefore, is how to make appropriate and expeditious use of existing incentives, rather than the need to increase or modify current mechanisms. For this reason, we present the following strategic ideas intended to empower the use of incentives without introducing major changes into the present institutions.

- Disclosure and public scrutiny
  The tax structure and available tax benefits must contribute to nonprofits' transparency, for they receive funds that involve fiscal waiver for the state. In general, this is a very weak issue in most countries, since there is little information on the activities of these institutions or the funds they manage. In this context, progress might be made toward a more efficient information system that would furnish reports on nonprofit management and funding, based on essential standardized information. Where organizations are required to submit monthly reports on economic and productive management, nonprofits should deliver at least one management and financial report each year, particularly if they are empowered to receive tax incentives. In addition, information should be developed on the amounts of fiscal waiver associated with donors. The government

can account for the fiscal waiver in the public sector budget, enabling taxpayers to compare the opportunity cost or the effort made in favor of nonprofits with other areas enjoying similar treatment such as small- and medium-scale mining and agriculture.

One way to cooperate would be by official consolidation of provisions, usually scattered over a wide variety of legal texts of varying importance.

- Promoting donations and philanthropy in general
  If nonprofits are known to contribute goods to society, not only benefits to vulnerable groups but also public goods like pluralism and diversity, responsibility for promoting "production" of these goods is shared by all actors in society. Just as the state promotes private investment and the private sector funds the public sector by paying taxes, both sectors may be thought of as promoting nonprofits. In this connection, it is worth recalling that "in developing countries, the tax administration is the tax police,"[15] meaning that it is not enough for legislators to seek to promote nonprofit activity by means of tax incentives; the important thing will be the attitude of the tax administration. Unless it gets involved, it will not matter how generous the law is or how restrictive its enforcement. It is interesting to note how in some developed countries such as Canada, the tax authorities themselves take care to promote the use of tax incentives to NPIs through instructions, mechanisms, and a web page. This means recognizing implicitly that the society takes an interest in such institutions. Specifically, meetings might be encouraged among tax experts in each country to examine implementation of a policy beyond the present administration. Similarly, potential donors might be linked to the same tax authorities to dispel any possible apprehensions of the former.

- Certifying donations
  Accrediting donations can be a problem for both donor and beneficiary. The view in many Latin American countries is that making use of tax incentives will cause a closer scrutiny of the donor by the tax authorities. Therefore, beneficiaries are often ignorant of the regulations and details of the operation, and are content with receiving the donation without taking care to accredit it. The donation certificate should entail the same legal and formal requirements as any other public instrument allowing expenses to be deducted and acknowledged by the tax authority. If the tax authorities acknowledge sales

slips, invoices and other instruments as documents actually certifying expenses, without necessarily having to check the authenticity of each, since the issuing organization or institution is duly empowered to do so, then the donation certificate should be an instrument with an approved format and acknowledged *ex ante* by the tax authority. The problem of excessive red tape required to accredit donations is stressed by foundations in Argentina and Colombia.

e. More flexibility in the temporary use of deduction and credit benefits

If the legislator has defined certain deduction and credit thresholds for certain purposes, the most sensible course would be for it to be fully utilized. In terms of flexibility, it seems advisable to be able to transfer to succeeding years any portion of the donation exceeding the established threshold. The amount of the donation is associated with a complete or indivisible project or initiative, so it seems advisable for the beneficiary to be assured of receiving the full amount committed by the donor, irrespective of the latter's year-end balance sheet. This issue was suggested by experience in Chile and has been implemented in Argentine legislation.

f. Homogeneous, non-discriminatory tax structure

Given the diversity of areas where nonprofits operate, the variety of benefits available in each, and the fact that for most nonprofits, there is a lengthy list of justifications for their existence, it becomes difficult, indeed practically impossible, to assess which of those areas is more important for the country's development, from a socioeconomic or cultural standpoint. This implies that tax treatment of nonprofits should be the same, that is, with no distinction of the purposes they serve, since this mechanism is not intended to privilege one area over another. A different situation arises if the state seeks to empower one area over another for reasons of greater affinity with its policy priorities, in which case other forms might be resorted to, such as direct fiscal contribution, differentiated funds open to competition, or special subsidies for beneficiaries.

Along the lines of simplification, it may be noted that double accreditation is required in several countries. On the one hand, the institution must accredit itself in juridical terms, while on the other it must apply for and obtain preferential tax status. In our view, this seemingly makes no sense, since upon seeking institutional accreditation as nonprofitmaking and meeting specific information requirements, certain tax benefits should be in order. On the other hand, along the lines of making criteria homogeneous, it seems logical to allow the same privileges to donors as natural or as juristic persons, particularly when countries are perceived to be trying to advance toward integrated tax systems.

Philanthropy experts in Argentina, Colombia, Chile, Mexico, Peru and Venezuela have repeatedly mentioned the issue of different tax treatment of various nonprofit areas.

- Tax benefits

  In the authors' opinion, it is advisable to elect the form of tax credit rather than tax deduction, because the former is more transparent and equitable. The optimum procedure would be for credits to apply automatically to donors, with no need for specific accreditation or assessment of every eligible donation, much less an assessment of the beneficiary each time it is the recipient of a donation.

  However, an optimum level cannot be set for tax credit ceilings, since that will depend basically on the fiscal balance strategy in effect in each country and on the desired level of incentives.Tax benefits should be designed to increase nonprofit funding beyond the associated fiscal waiver.

Notes

1 Notwithstanding the above, such authors as J.G. Simon (1987) have reviewed every one of those donations, presenting background information that fails to validate them.

2 See Viveros (1997).

3 E.g. non-taxable minimum, family dependents, expenses to produce rents, and others.

4 Includes fiscal cost of tax expenditure in social and economic sectors.

5 Law on Donations for Cultural Purposes, Law on Donations for Higher Education, Law on Donations for Educational Purposes. The Law on Sports and Games enacted in 2001 is not included.

6 E.g. Credit for Forestry Development, Credit for Investment, Southern Law, etc.

7 Since the enactment of AFIP General resolution 729/99.

8 Comments by J. Vial JKSG and R. Bird, Harvard Law School at the seminar on October 20, 2001.

9 For example, Price Waterhouse separated the effect of tax incentives on the number of individuals deciding to donate and the total amount donated by each, distinguishing among income brackets. A more significant effect was found among persons with higher incomes.

10 See for example, Auten G., Clarfeber C. and Schmalback D (2000; Cordes (1999); Barret K., McQuirk A., and Stenberg A. (1997); Randolph J. (1997).

11 See Irarrázaval, I. (2001).

12 C. Sanborn, "Philanthropy and Corporate Social Responsibility in Peru," paper presented in a workshop at Harvard University in 1998.

13 *La Nación*, editorial, 30/1/01, Buenos Aires, Argentina.

14 Information contributed by Sonia de Avelar in her presentation at the Workshop on Brazil, "Philanthropy and the emerging *ciudadania empresarial*," David Rockefeller Center for Latin American Studies, Harvard University, October 2001.

15 See M. Bird and B. Casanegra, Improving Tax Administration in Developing Countries. IMF.

References

Arthur Andersen (2001) Latin American Guide 2001.

Cerny, M. (1999) Taxation and transition: Nonprofit organizations in a market economy. Tax Notes International. Sept. 27.

ECLAC (1998) *El Pacto Fiscal: Fortalezas, Debilidades, Desafíos*. UN, Santiago.

ECLAC (2002) *Balance Preliminar de las Economías de América Latina y el Caribe*. Santiago.

David Rockefeller Center for Latin American Studies: Web Page: *Filantropía y Cambio Social, Cambridge, MA. http://www.fas.harvard.edu/~drclas/pages /initiatives/philanthropy/philanthropy.html*.

Falcao, J. and Cuenca, C. (1999) *Mudanca Social e Reforma Legal: Estudos para uma nova legislacao do Terceiro Sector*. Comunidade Solidaria. Rio de Janeiro

ICNL The Tax treatment of Nongovernmental Organizations—A survey of best practices from around the world. *www.icnl.org/*.

Irarrazaval, I. and Gúzman, J. (2000) *El rol de los incentivos tributarios para las instituciones sin fines de lucro: Análisis de la experiencia internacional*. Estudios Públicos no. 77. Santiago.

Irarrazaval, I. (2001) "Diagnóstico de Incentivos Tributarios como Fuente de Financiamiento de las Organizaciones de la Sociedad Civil." FOCUS study for Ministerio Secretaría General de Gobierno—Chile.

Itriago, M.A. and Itriago, A.L. (2000) "Estímulos tributarios a la Filantropía en Venezuela." Working draft presented at Taller: Reforma Legal, Filantropía y Cambio Social en América Latina.

Jorratt, M. (1996) "Evaluación de la capacidad recaudatoria del Sistema Tributario y de la Evasión Tributaria." Working paper for Conferencia Técnica del Centro Interamericano de Administradores Tributarios.

Jaramillo, J.C. et al. (1999) *Entidades sin ánimo de lucro: Régimen Tributario Especial*. Legis Editores S.A. Colombia.

Oliveira, A.C. (1997) *Marco Regulador de las Organizaciones de la Sociedad Civil en Sudamerica*. InterAmerican Development Bank—UNDP, Washington.

Oliveira, A.C. (1999) *Fliantropia e incentivos fiscais as doacoes*. In: Falcao, J. and Cuenca, C. (1999).

Pita, C. (2001) "Los Sistemas tributarios latinoamericanos y la adecuación de la imposición de la renta a un contexto de globalización." Paper: Seminario Política Fiscal en América Latina.

Price Waterhouse & Caplin & Dryslade (1997) Impact of Tax Restructuring on Tax-Exempt Organizations. Working paper for Council of Foundations and Independent Sector.

Salamon, L.M. (1997) *The International Guide to Nonprofit Law*. Nueva York, John Willey & sons.

Salamon, L.M.; Hems, L., & Chinnok, K. (2000) "The Nonprofit Sector: For What and for Whom?" Working Papers of the Johns Hopkins Comparative Nonprofit Sector Project no. 37. Baltimore.

Salamon, L.M.; Sokolowski, W; & Anheier, H. (2000) Social Origins of Civil Society: An Overview. Working Papers of the Johns Hopkins Comparative Nonprofit Sector Project no. 38. Baltimore.

Simon, J.G. (1987) "The tax treatment of nonprofit organizations: A review of Federal and State Policies." In: *The Nonprofit Sector: A Research Handbook*. Editor W. Powell. Yale University Press.

Shome, P. (2001) "La Tributación en América Latina: Tendencias estructurales e impacto de la administración." Paper: Seminario Política Fiscal en América Latina.

Messineo, A. (1999) Taxation of Non Profit Organizations: Argentina. Cahiers de droit fiscal International—International Fiscal Association—1999 Eilat Congress.

Ministerio de Economia-Argentina (2000) *Estimación de los Gastos Tributarios en los Sectores Sociales. www.mecon.gov.ar.*

Ministerio de Hacienda—Budget Department (2002) Report on public finance.

Tanzi, V. and Zee, H. (2000) "Tax Policy for Emerging Markets: Developing Countries." IMF Working Paper WP/00/35. Washington.

Viveros, F. (1997) "Sobre el Régimen Fiscal de las Organizaciones de Servicio Público o como, en realidad Fortalecer la Sociedad Civil." Simposio virtual sobre el Marco Regulador de las Organizaciones No Gubernamentales. Introductory document, room 2. *www.vita.org/technet/ong/paper4.htm.*

Weisbrod, B. (1991) "Tax policy toward nonprofit organizations: An eleven country survey." Voluntas vol. 2 no. 1.

12

Creating a Favorable Environment for Philanthropy and Civil Society: The Case of Brazil

Eduardo Szazi

It is clear that the process of strengthening the Third Sector in Brazil will be accomplished through the "appropriation" of the entities by society. This ownership is based on a new consciousness that organizations belong to the citizens, not so much in the heritage sense, as in the sense that individuals believe in the causes for which they advocate. Social responsibility is growing in Brazil, gaining an ever stronger presence in the media, in academic production and in the daily discussions of common citizens and business leaders.

The process of reform was a political learning experience, as much for the government as it was for civil society. The process of legislative reform within the Third Sector in Brazil between the years 1997 and 2001, has been dramatic, conceived in partnership between representatives of organizations of civil society and the federal government to confront the growing social demands regarding ethics in the management of public goods and causes and to strengthen instruments for citizen participation in the definition and implementation of public policy.

Before the Reform: The Political and Institutional Context

An extensive process of institutional reform emerged in Brazil with the beginning of the political opening in the 1970s and re-democratization in the 1980s. A cornerstone of this reform was the 1988 Federal Constitution, which guaranteed citizens broad freedom of association and prohibited state interference in the functioning of independent non-governmental associations.

The Constitution, which regulates the social order, guaranteed the participation of civil society in the formulation and management of diverse public issues such as social security, health, education, culture, environment, indigenous populations and the protection of children, adolescents and the elderly.

After more than 20 years of political oppression, these new guarantees led to the flourishing of tens of thousands of new civil society organizations[1] and to a new public policy management model based on advisory councils in which an equal number of representatives of civil society and the government began to define governmental actions and programs, managing growing and sizeable amounts of resources kept in earmarked funds.[2]

Civil society participation extended beyond public policymaking to direct involvement in social programs for the benefit of the neediest sectors of the population. Examples of this commitment were the campaign against hunger led by sociologist Herbert de Souza (Betinho) and the campaigns for environmental and consumer rights. Since 1988, nonprofit organizations have received a steadily increasing quantity of public resources, funding services in diverse areas of activities throughout the entire country. Despite these clear advances, however, not all was wine and roses.

In 1991, the Brazilian president began to be investigated for corrupt practices involving the fraudulent allocation of public resources to nonexistent aid organizations. The investigations at the behest of civil society organizations led to the president's impeachment and removal from office. A democratically elected president's removal from power because of corruption, within the context of institutional regulation, demonstrated that Brazilian society had committed itself to ethics in the management of the public good. It is important to note that the impeachment as a political episode involved civil society organizations that received public resources for the purpose of funding their social assistance activities, as well as the government. This demonstrated that the commitment to ethics in the management of public goods transcended the limits of government to embrace all those institutions that managed resources under the banner of "the social good" or, in other words, Third Sector organizations.

The impeachment made it clear that the system in charge of certifying the public interest of civil society organizations needed to be improved. A new paradigm of governance and accountability had to be developed. The citizenry needed to be shown that civil society organizations were trustworthy instruments for the promotion of the much-needed reforms and that these institutions were capable of adequately managing the resources allocated to them, be they public or private. Moreover, it was necessary that the discrediting shadow of corruption not be allowed to limit the resurgence of one of the most effective forms of individual participation in public life: non-governmental organizations—NGOs.

In order to prove their trustworthiness in competently administering development projects, several organizations began to collaborate in the creation of umbrella organizations regulated by strong ethical principles and with the clear intention of actively participating in the definition of public policy through legislative reforms and other means. Some of these organizations played an important role in the reform of third sector legislation.

Principal Actors In the Reform

Brazil's redemocratization made the appearance of thousands of civil society organizations possible. Recent research (Landim, 1993) identifies nearly 220,000 nonprofit entities in the country, many created during the decade of the 1980s.

During the 1990s, most new institutions focused on providing charity, but some umbrella or associative Third Sector organizations entities did emerge. These new organizations were dedicated not to direct assistance, but to the formulation of public policy. They drew their strength by operating in association with other groups working toward the same goals.

The associative groups adopted a structure similar to that of the labor movement, with a number of entities at the local, regional (federations) and national (confederations) level. However, we believe that in adopting this structure, certain weaknesses developed that are rooted in a corporativist model that sought to protect the organizations' own interests. This model did not conform to the role of the third sector, which is based more on the principle of building a better society for all. Therefore, although these entities gained nationwide representation, we do not see in them the political representativity necessary to play a significant role in the legal reform process.

In 1991, the Brazilian Association of Non-Governmental Organizations (ABONG) was created, with the goal of bringing NGOs together around a common agenda that focused on strengthening the activities of civil society and its influence on public policy.

In 1995, after some years of informal existence, the Group of Institutes, Foundations and Businesses (GIFE) was officially created. As the first association of Brazilian grantmakers, its mission was to contribute to the promotion of Brazilian sustainable development through the strengthening of institutions' political and institutional structures, as well as to provide support for the strategic activities of institutions, corporate foundations and other private entities that carry out voluntary and systematic social investment in the public good.

The same year, the federal government also set up the Advisory Council of Comunidade Solidária, initially made up of 10 cabinet ministers and 21 civil society representatives. In 1996, this council started acting in support of the following directives:

1) Strengthening civil society through promotion of voluntarism, the reformulation of legislation of governance between the state and civil society and the contribution to Brazilian Third Sector definition and self-knowledge through an information network.

2) Adoption of innovative social development initiatives through partnerships between the state and civil society.

3) Maintenance of a systematic, high-level political dialogue between the principal governmental and nongovernmental protagonists within the social sector, focused on a strategy for the social development of the country (Comunidade Solidária, 2002: 10).

The Reform Process

Defining the Agenda

1   In 1997, the Advisory Council of Comunidade Solidária began a process of dialogue with representatives of civil society organizations and the government with the intention and for the purpose of promoting reform in legislation related to the Third Sector. This reform initiative was viewed as necessary by its supporters based on the fact that, having been conceived during the decade of the 1930s, the laws of governance pertaining to the Third Sector were not able to adequately encompass the numerous and varied activities of civil society organizations. Nor were they capable of regulating the new roles such organizations had come to assume, i.e., the efficient management of the public and private resources that were invested in them, and the necessary publicity and social control required and demanded of them by post-impeachment Brazilian society.

2   The general political goal of the reform process was to contribute to the construction of a national strategic position around and based on a minimal agenda of priorities, measures, tools and procedures for the recognition and actions of Third Sector entities.

The first phase of the process consisted in the identification of nearly 300 organizations of civil society representative of the diverse segments of the Third Sector, according to categories of origin, field of activity, philosophical position, dimension and representation. These organizations were subsequently consulted through questionnaires addressing a score of diverse legal issues. In addition, personal interviews were conducted with a number of the specialists and participants in the Third Sector directly involved with these issues.

A preliminary document was sent out for comments and critiques to nearly 60 interlocutors from civil society and the government, containing 63 problems and more than 100 suggested and formulated proposals for solutions. The document was once again revised after the feedback process, identifying five proposals for general consensus[3]—concerning the Third Sector's strategic role, its scope, transparency and responsibility, as well as its relationship with the state—and eight proposals for specific consensus[4]—dealing with administrative registers and files, contracts with public authorities, mechanisms for self-regulation, institutional mechanisms for responsibility, donations, voluntarism, labor relations and information about the Third Sector.

The position paper served as the guideline for discussions by the 20-member working group created in late 1997 to study the points of consensus and to prepare legal reform proposals. Ten members came from different governmental ministries with involvement in these issues; the other ten represented civil society organizations.[5] The meetings took place in Brasília at the Palácio do Planalto (The White House), the headquarters of the federal executive branch, and were developed over an eight-month period.

The First Controversy: Who Should Benefit?

In 1997, Brazilian civil society organizations still lived in the shadow of the presidential impeachment. In the wake of the investigation, some of the congressmen who took part in the government coalition were identified as having created ghost philanthropic entities to obtain public funds and use them for their own benefit. In addition, the system for establishing "public service," created in 1935, demonstrated its inability to adequately sift out public interest entities The public became outraged when it was discovered that that elite recreational clubs and entities with clear commercial goals had been disguised as social interest nongovernmental entities in order to obtain public funding.[6]

The old classification system considered "public service" organizations to be only those not-for-profit entities dedicated to education and social assistance. Official recognition was carried out through the granting of titles and registers that distinguished the entities that could take advantage of the tax exemptions and receive public funding. The process was slow and bureaucratic and it was not uncommon that winning exemptions depended on political patronage.

Civil society organizations hoped to change this system, broadening the spectrum of recognized activities of social interest, reducing bureaucracy and, in so doing, making the system more socially effective and efficient.

However, there was a problem: over the course of the more than seventy years during which the old regime was in power, a number of hospitals and educational institutions had obtained "public service" status, but in practice functioned as purely commercial entities, charging their clients for most services rendered. From the perspective of the assessors, these entities should not have been recognized as members of the Third Sector because they did not apply their resources with a universalistic public-sector logic that permits substandard levels of sufficiency, but with a private-sector logic, selective and with a system of payment upon completion of services rendered.

Yet excluding those entities with more commercial profiles would imply the revocation of acquired rights—which is prohibited by the federal constitution—and would subject the new legislation to a barrage of judicial actions, weakening the reform process.

Therefore, by virtue of this institutional barrier, the working group opted to create a new classificatory system, without modifying the previous one and consequently without altering existing acquired rights. Within this new system only those private entities of public interest would be admitted—that is, participants in that still diffuse—and why not say it—somewhat confused concept of the Third Sector. But which entities would be classified as Third Sector?

Governmental representatives maintained that institutions of learning and hospitals that were not free should remain outside the new regulatory system, based on the fact that the government identified these groups years ago as beneficiaries of a loophole in previous regulations that had granted them millions of dollars in tax breaks.[7] Civil society representatives were divided over the issue: some supported the government's initiative, while others fought against the change, fearing that the withdrawal a constitutional exemption could precipitate a move toward the reduction of tax advantages for nonprofit entities. In the end, the plan continued with the exclusion of educational and health institutions that were not free from the new classificatory model, although subsequently, this exclusion nearly led to the rejection of the proposal in the National Congress because of pressure from congressmen connected to these institutions.

The working group then assumed the arduous task of listing the entities that comprised—for legal purposes—the so called Third Sector, narrowly defined as being made up of those legally recognized private institutions receiving resources, be they private or public, for investment in public interest causes (Fernandes 1994, 21).

As the first criteria, the working group identified the entities according to their mission and, from that, defined as beneficiaries of the new regulations those institutions dedicated to the promotion of social assistance; the promotion of culture; the defense and conservation of historic and artistic heritage; the free promotion of education and health; the promotion of food and nutritional security; the defense, preservation and conservation of the natural environment and the promotion of sustainable development; the promotion of voluntarism; the promotion of economic and social development and the fight against poverty; not-for-profit experimentation with new socially-productive models and of alternative systems for production, commerce, employment and credit; the promotion of established rights, the formulation of new rights and free legal assistance in areas of complementary interest; the promotion of ethics, peace, citizenship, human rights, democracy and other universal values; studies and research, the development of alternative technologies and the production and dissemination of information and technical and scientific knowledge related to the above mentioned activities.

It should be noted that the requisite of being free existed only for educational and health institutions, due to the reasons already discussed, leaving all other organizations the ability to charge for their services. There is a reason for this distinction. Recent research demonstrates that in Brazil the Third Sector spent nearly 10.9 billion *Reals* in operational costs in 1995, corresponding to 1.5% of the gross domestic product for that year. A significant part of those resources (61.1%) was generated by the entities themselves; the government contributed 12.8% and private donors the remaining 26.1%, figures that are arrived at by adding monetary and in-kind donations together with the value of voluntary work (Landim 1999, 47).

The draft of the new legislation, a considerable improvement over the previous regulatory system which only provided the concession of recognition to entities that directly carry out educational and social assistance programs, was based on the GIFE proposal, extending certification to civil society organizations that make donations or render intermediary support services to those organizations that carry out these programs. The new legislation took into consideration, in a an unmistakable form, the relevance of grantmaking entities within the Brazilian social context.

The working group went even further—in relation to existing legislation of other countries—with the provision that, not withstanding possible action in the above listed areas, organizations would not be able to be certified if they originated in the public sector—and are therefore not civil society organizations. Others excluded from certification were for-profit entities, special interest groups and those organizations subject to their own distinct legal system.[8]

Acting in favor of the potential beneficiaries outside of an organization's membership group, the working group clearly excluded from new certification entities that were associative in name only or were of mutual benefit, since these entities conducted activities principally for the benefit of their own associates, favoring their interests over those of the public. (Szazi 2001: 28).

The Second Controversy: The Recognition Process

Working group members were aware that these new definitions would not be sufficient to guarantee public interest, especially taking into account government inability to fiscally monitor the organizations.

Governmental representatives therefore built upon the standards for public service organizations, recommending the creation of an extensive list of bureaucratic obligations, with copies of numerous documents, declarations, biographical summaries and multiple years of annual reporting in order to obtain certification. Civil society representatives widely rejected these bureaucratic requisites, advocating in their place a simple and rapid process with some social control. The disagreements about the regulation represented a clash of cultures: on one side, the state as inspector and regulator, perhaps with some residual dependency on authoritarian practices left over from the years of the dictatorship, and on the other side, a citizenry that wished to live in freedom.

The controversy was resolved when it became apparent that mere control over documentation was not sufficient to restrict the creation of loopholes and that that bureaucratic difficulties did not impede favoritism since it was generally acknowledged that an increase in bureaucratic difficulties leads to greater risk of traffic of influence (Ferrarezi, 2001:07).

In addition, the debate took into account the fact that the Brazilian constitution guarantees non-interference by the state in the functioning of associations that can be freely created, independent of governmental approval. Therefore, the state could not indiscriminately impose a new form of management upon civil society organizations. To conform to the constitutional mandate, the civil society organizations would have to choose to submit to guidelines, and thus, voluntary support for the new classificatory model was essential.

Since the new regulatory system depended on voluntary compliance, the procedure could not be complex and bureaucratic, as such difficulties would deter organizations from joining the new system, thereby impeding the Third Sector from growing and achieving its goals. Civil society representatives lobbied effectively; the draft law made provisions for a simple certification process, based on standard commonly held documents easily available to all entities.[9]

Nevertheless, organizations needed to build into their social statutes mechanisms to guarantee quality of management, efficiency in the application of resources and social control of the entity's activities. In attempting to address these concerns, another controversy arose—that of accountability.

The Third Controversy: Accountability

From the beginning, the GIFE supported the need for transparency in the origin and application of the entities' resources, particularly given the fact that grantmakers do not seek public sector funding, have an identified source of funding (normally from business sources) and do not base their financial strategy on a broad base of contributors. The proposal, even though well received by government intermediaries, experienced a certain degree of resistance from the representatives of some civil society organizations. Because of privileged contacts with international sources, many organizational representatives were not willing to make their financing strategy public, since in doing so, they would run the risk of creating competition for such resources.

The difference in the financing model implied a change in the process of accounting and the resolution of conflicts of interest. While elected directors of grantmaking entities are paid by their supporting entities or have their remuneration defined by them, the leaders of "independent" entities are paid through consulting contracts by the very entities that they direct. These entities often determine directors' payment, even those under a system of "exchange" of decisions (in which A defines the contracting of B and B defines the contracting of A).

The need for internal controls to avoid conflicts of interest in the decision making process and the publication of deliberations is today, although not clearly stated, the principal barrier to support for the adoption of the new classificatory system.

In addressing the issue of accountability, the debates were helping to form the consensus that civil society organizations should not be given the luxury of badly administering the resources at their disposal. Appropriate administration was considered particularly necessary in these cases since the organizations' working funds were raised for the benefit of the causes advocated by these organizations. Entities acted as overseers of the investments of their sponsors, who did not invest their resources *in* the organization, but *through it*. Given this dynamic, a mechanism had to be established to guarantee that the resources provided be properly administered and invested in the cause for which they were intended.

As already discussed, the reform process for the legal framework was supported by the belief in the need for institutionalization of mechanisms of transparency and responsibility capable of envisioning the creation of systems of self regulation for the Third Sector. Within this system, primary control should be held by civil society, with secondary power in the hands of the public sector. One level of control would not necessarily imply the rejection of the other, but would require the ability of a number of different actors to simultaneously exercise control over organizations' social activities.

The first task focused on the identification of common practices of external control and their incorporation into the new model of accountability advocated for by the law.

The first traditional tool to be incorporated into the proposal was that of an elected fiscal advisory council. Although very well known within the Third Sector, such advisory councils were not legally mandated and therefore not common practice, as were those for which the social statutes made concessions. This lack of standardization meant that councils were on several occasions not elected and, even if elections did occur, advisory bodies were composed of people connected to administrators through friendship or family ties, thus compromising its independence for purposes of evaluation and control.

The second tool adopted was an independent audit. Although ultimately integrated into the proposal, much debate preceded its adoption. The government initially proposed a mandatory external audit of all entities with an annual budget of more than 300,000 *reals* (at the time equivalent to almost US$250,000). From the point of view of civil society representatives, such an obligatory process was absurd since it would involve higher expenditures through fees, thus draining resources from socially beneficial causes and diverting them into the coffers of private businesses. The final proposal incorporated into the law adopted external audits only for entities receiving public resources in excess of 600,000 *reals* ($US500,000).

In addition to these traditional mechanisms, the working group reached an agreement—not without heated debates—that certain information should be accessible to any citizen, whether or not they were direct beneficiaries of or contributors to any entity. This access included the right to know which entities are certified and to obtain information about their activities and copies of their financial reports. It was argued that citizens had these rights because Third Sector causes were public by nature, therefore inevitably affecting the general public. Moreover, citizens with concrete evidence of error or fraud would have the right to anonymously request authorities to initiate auditing proceedings that could lead to many procedural outcomes, including revocation of title and initiation of criminal proceedings against the directors of the entity, if serious crimes were indeed discovered. Upon adopting this directive, the working group surpassed even international standards for allocating to the general citizenry formal inspection power over certified entities, making public and broadening the base of social controls capable of monitoring these organizations.

As a condition for exercising this power, the law required that organizations newly certified under these regulations establish a permanent system for the promotion of information about their activities[10] and the effective dissemination of their reports of activities, balance sheets and proof of fulfillment of Social Security obligations , thus obliging the entities to make these documents available for examination to any member of the general public. The new law does not define the specific way in which entities must disseminate this information; it speaks only to the effectiveness of the process. As a result, each organization may define the methods that best meet its specific needs, according to its own means of communication and financial abilities.[11]

In addition to these three instruments of control for use by members of civil society—the fiscal advisory council, the independent audit and the monitoring control of individual citizens—the working group debated the issue of governmental oversight. In the heat of these discussions, public sector representatives assumed a disproportional moralizing fervor, seeking to impose restrictions of the most random nature,[12] restrictions which in no way would contribute to the development of the Third Sector.

To deal with resistance from this public sector, civil society representatives initiated closer and more direct contacts between the two opposing sides through meetings, telephone conferences and e-mails in the hope of reaching an agreement regarding basic points. Civil society representatives negotiated as a block with government representatives, always responding with alternative proposals that were in keeping with the spirit of the draft document. The strategy of these civil society representatives was non-confrontational, framed as the presentation of an objection and a firm suggestion, with objective arguments, and without any overt emotional appeal such as "We are NGOs" or "We are doing what the government should be doing." This strategy was effective, resulting in a much less bureaucratic and restrictive proposal than the previous one. The revised proposal provided for governmental control on three levels: the Public Ministry,[13] which held responsibility for oversight of cases involving disclosures by associations, as well as all those involving foundations; the Secretary of Federal Revenue, which was in charge of applying the same instruments and criteria used in oversight of other legal entities, and the Ministry or public entity that distributed the resources to the entity, which held the contractual power to review accounts.

However, accountability alone was not sufficient, since even a resource invested correctly can by used poorly. To meet society's best interests, it is not sufficient not to steal; resources must be invested efficiently. Taking into account this distinction, governance became the next focal point of the debates.

The Fourth Controversy: Governance

As was the case with many other countries, Brazil adopted the principle that elected leaders of civil society could not be paid, based on the fact that they performed such activities voluntarily. For many practitioners within the Third Sector, this system was considered harmful, since the vast majority of social initiatives occur due to a handful of middle class individuals who feel "driven" to dedicate themselves to bettering a given social situation. Moreover, such initiatives are often directed either by leaders who, having other forms of sustenance, can dedicate all of their day to management of the entity or, needing to "earn their bread," can only donate a few hours, during their free time. Given the alternatives—the majority of which are inadequate for engaging participants from the lower middle and lower classes—a distorted practice of professionalization has spread throughout Brazil. In this system, the true leaders of the entities are contracted as professionals, leaving the organizational board of directors full of "front" people, who lend their names to the advisory boards of such entities, individuals who are normally recruited among the friends and family of the real directors. This procedure, and the way that it works, has caused serious harm to the image of civil society organizations and to the quality of governance, which in practice, has transformed the entities into the fiefdoms of a few individuals. Although initiated and imbued with the best of intentions, these organizations were run like a family business with close knit and exclusive ties.

To break with this practice, legal authorization for the remuneration of directors had to be granted, and a system set up to impede those same individuals from abusing their decision making power, fixing their own payment or conducting business with personal relations for their own advantage.

During their working sessions, group representatives debated the role of legislation in the implementation of a model of governance that would be adequate for meeting the public's social expectations. Is the law capable of introducing good management practices? Moreover, would it be an instrument capable of separating the "good" civil society organizations from the "rest"? And, finally, would joining the new system imply that an organization was "good" and not adhering to it, imply that it was "bad"? Would it indeed separate the wheat from the chaff?

The working group agreed that the answer to these questions was affirmative. Drawing its inspiration from legislation regulating publicly traded companies, the group decided that certified organizations' commercial activities should be traded in the stock exchange, that the organizations should establish within their directives detailed rules regarding conflicts of interest, and that they should impose severe sanctions on controlling shareholders and administrators who conduct business for their own personal benefit and to the detriment of the interests of the company and its minority shareholders.[14]

While there was consensus regarding the introduction of rules related to conflicts of interest, government and civil society representatives disagreed about the remuneration of organizational directors, with government representatives wanting to maintain the tradition of voluntary leadership.

Civil society representatives based their argument on the premise that the construction of solid regulations regarding conflict of interests would put an end to the reason behind the prohibition on paid employment for directors. The regulations would include imposing restrictions on accruement of personal gains and the establishment of regulations within NGOs concerning the management of public funds.

Other disagreements emerged. The governmental proposal simply prohibited the conducting of commercial or financial business between an organization and its directors, its founders and relatives up to twice-removed and businesses in which these individuals held a stake of more than 10%. Civil society, on the other hand, proposed the adoption of a tool for the resolution of conflicts of interest similar to that used in the U.S. system, in which business between related parts is permitted, as long as such activities are made explicit to the council director and are declared in the minutes; that the interested parties do not participate in the making of decisions related to the activities; and, in certain cases, that they not even be present at a meeting, in order not to make other leaders feel uncomfortable. Despite the efforts of civil society representatives, the government proposal prevailed in the final text,[15] reinforced by a requirement that prohibits the conducting of business with any relative up to three times removed.

Seeking to strengthen the quality of governance, the working group proposed that entities must take into consideration as part of their decision making process the principles set forth in the federal constitution for public resource management: legality, impartiality, morality, efficiency and dissemination of mission. The presumption was that investors—private or public—expect resources to be appropriately invested. In addition, these concepts were already well studied within Brazilian law and had been upheld numerous times by the courts. Therefore, controversies over their interpretation could be avoided, preventing possible squabbles over terms not yet clearly defined, such as "competence," "managerial responsibility" or "transparency."

A Fifth Controversy: Fiscal Incentives for Donations

In Brazil, few fiscal incentives exist for donating to social projects. Only large businesses that adopt a more complex system of filing their income taxes can deduct as operational expenses their donations to entities considered of "public utility," and these businesses are limited to a total deduction of 2% of their gross operational profits. Individual donors enjoy no fiscal advantages for making donations to such entities.

This situation demanded the creation of new legislation for incentives for making donations. The working group began by examining a legal proposal that allowed for an increase in the limit of donations from businesses from 2% to 5%, extending the right to all companies regardless of size. It also raised again the issue of deductibility of individual donations up to the limit of 10% of owed income taxes. However, the initiative was blocked by an institutional limitation, since according to existing tax laws, the head of the executive branch maintains the personal prerogative to present projects related to the concession of fiscal incentives to the legislature. Nevertheless, the group worked on a legal proposal which—along with a proposal that dealt with other issues already discussed—was presented to the president of the Republic, whose role it was to present it to the National Congress.

The Results of the Reform

The First Phase: 1997–1999

The working group presented both projects to the president after extensive meetings between June 1997 and May 1998. However, the government's economic division shelved the fiscal incentives project, leaving only the remaining one to be sent to the Congress.

Despite this setback, the result of the reform process was on the balance not insignificant, since many new laws were introduced, substantially reforming the legal framework of the Brazilian Third Sector.

The first law approved (passed in 1998) defined voluntary work and established that volunteers were not employees of civil society organizations, eliminating the risk of any labor and Social Security responsibility for participating entities. The working group, although it supported the measure, could not take credit for it since Congressional review of this proposal was already underway before the group's creation.

The principal legal reform, passed in 1999, dealt with the certification of private not-for-profit companies as legal entities, in the form of Civil Society Organizations of Public Interest (SCIPs), and the establishment of the supporting Term of Partnership. This new so-called Law of the Third Sector was considered innovative in its recognition of the public benefit mission of civil society organizations and of the new areas of their activity that previously had received no legal backing. It imposed mechanisms of social control and of responsibility in the use of state resources, fostering partnerships between the state and OSCIPs with the creation of a new legal instrument for cooperation, the Term of Partnership.

The new law was published in the legal registry with little fanfare on the part of the government, which spent several more months finishing the edits to the regulatory decree (3.100, of 30.06.1999) and adapting it to the structure of the Ministry of Justice, the body that would be legally responsible for the certification of entities. The government left publicity about the new law in the hands of the Third Sector. Since the law was focused on governance issues and did not offer any fiscal incentives, initial support was relatively insignificant. The process, aggravated by the lack of information, resulted in an overwhelming number of court denials of certification requests: only eight out of 131 requests were approved in 1999).[16]

The reform process needed to deepen through greater mobilization on the part of the not-for-profit sector—including publicizing the law's benefits and encouragement of organizational adherence—and the introduction of new laws that would provide OSCIPs with a broader array of advantages that would outweigh the restrictive aspects of the rigid rules on social and governmental control and governance.

The Second Phase: 2000–2002

Despite the fact the working group was already formally disbanded, it continued to act in the second phase of the reform process—this time, with a new strategy. The group sought to obtain for the OSCIP's, at the very least, the benefits that had already been secured over the years for "public interest" entities. The group introduced such modifications by attaching them to legislative incentives packages for similar issues being developed in the executive and legislative branches. Provisional measures[17] were extremely helpful in this regard.

Beginning in 2000, several laws strengthened the reform process:

- The period of time for acquiring the certification as an OSCIP and of Public Utility was extended until March of 2004.
- Donations made by businesses to entities certified as OSCIPs, could be deducted as an operational expense up to the limit of 2% of gross operational profits.
- Customs was authorized to donate seized goods to OSCIPs, as is already taking place with organizations which hold a Declaration of Public Utility.
- The issue of fiscal tax incentives arises for OSCIPs that pay their directors. Since the publication of this Provisional Measure, OSCIPs that opt to pay their directors can be exempt from income taxes and receive deductible donations from donor businesses, thus providing a fiscal tax incentive.

- OSCIPs became able to receive donations of movable goods from the state.

Based on these wide-ranging and beneficial laws concerning the Third Sector, another set of laws specifically pertaining to entities that work in the field of micro-credit was introduced:

A new legal entity, Credit Societies for Microenterprises (SCM), allows the participation of private initiatives in the micro-credit sector.

- Micro-credit OSCIP's are now exempt from current laws regulating interest rates (which limit interest rates to 12% a year), permitting market level interest rates and sustainability.

- SCM's are now able to borrow from the National Financing system; they can have a broad nationwide presence, and can be controlled by an OSCIP. Micro-credit service offices can also be created by financial institutions under a recent Federal Reserve Board resolution .

- A Micro-credit Gateway seeks to gather and disseminate information regarding microenterprises in one central Internet clearing house (www.portaldomicrocredito.org.br). A joint project of Sebrae/SP and the Committee for the Promotion and Strengthening of Micro-credit, the Gateway is administered by the Brazilian Association for the Development of Micro-credit (ABDM) with daily updates by the Third Sector Information Network (RITS, www.rits.org.br). The committee, the ABDM and the Gateway grew out of the first round of discussions.

- The development of a booklet *Introdução ao microcrédito* was developed in partnership with the Federal Savings Bank, the Ceape Network and Sebrae.

The adoption of new measures and improvement of the set of incentives offered to entities certified as OSCIP, as well as the better dissemination of information through Third Sector-sponsored websites, publications, courses and events, led to a growth in the number of approved certifications and a reduction in the number of denials, as can be observed in the table below published by the federal government on the Ministry of Justice's official website.

The number of entities certified (814) seems small in relationship to the pool of 220,000 entities previously cited. The fact is that it is indeed small, as is the number of entities labeled as being of public utility at the federal level in more than 67 years enforcing law 91 of 1935 (7,200). However, in comparing the rates of growth, we see that the adoption of the model of OSCIP resulted in a much higher rate (an average of 203 per year) than

Table 1. Total Number of Requests for Certification as OSCIPs
12/03/2002

	Certification of OSCIPs				
	1999	2000	2001	2002	Total
Approved	8	83	252	471	814
Denied	123	231	110	68	532
Total	131	314	362	539	1346

that of federal "public utility" (on average, 107 per year) and that, according to the publications on certifications in the official press, the number of requests for certification as an OSCIP has already surpassed those of federal "public utility."

We believe that the process of strengthening the Third Sector in Brazil will be accomplished through the "appropriation" of the entities by society. This ownership is based on a new consciousness that organizations belong to the citizens, not so much in the heritage sense, as in the sense that individuals believe in the causes for which they advocate. Social responsibility is growing in Brazil, gaining an ever stronger presence in the media, in academic production and in the daily discussions of common citizens and business leaders.

The law fulfills an important role in this "appropriation" through the establishment of mechanisms that foster private social investment through fiscal incentives, expand and improve standards for governance and social control, and impose new ethics for management. In establishing and maintaining these new norms, the law actively contributes to the increased consciousness-raising of the actors involved in the definition, financing and control of civil society organizations, making the process of promoting these organizations irreversible.

The set of laws approved over the course of recent years clearly demonstrates that any residual lack of credibility in the Third Sector resulting from the 1991 impeachment process had been overcome. It also demonstrates that the federal government has come to view partnerships with civil society in a much better light, seeing them as a method for confronting national social problems—although statistical data to demonstrate the level of growth of resources is not yet available. Within the private sector, the resources invested in social causes through OSCs continue to grow from year to year[18] as is reflected in the growing prominence of social reports and balance sheets in large businesses' financial reporting.

Conclusion

The process of reform was a political learning experience, as much for the government as it was for civil society. And it was not an easy one. It was not easy for the governmental representatives, who had to meet with members of civil society to define together that which, in their autocratic tradition, had previously been defined entirely by the state. It was not easy for civil society organizations either. From one moment to another, they had to go from being critics of the law to supporting it, and in doing so, had to confront all of the complexity of conceiving something that was new and in harmony with a legal system that had existed since 1500. Moreover, the new legislation needed to be able to address the concerns of a society of 170 million inhabitants and 220,000 not-for-profit organizations.

Legal reform is a process that is continually nurtured by new perceptions, opinions and examples, a process that turns it into a constant never ending task. Both the federal government and associative organizations have difficulties in grasping and understanding all of civil society's demands, due to the simple fact that the mass media is imperfect and that it is utopian to imagine that all of the society's myriad opinions and expectations can be conveyed in a form that is simultaneously systematic and organized. However, the conundrum of effective communication should not lead to paralysis in the practitioner's search for a new model, even if this new model is an imperfect one. If perfect democracy does not exist, neither can there exist a perfect legislative process.

For civil society this is a painful conclusion, which calls into question the axiom that civil society organizations represent the interests of civil society. In truth, these organizations represent only segments of these interests that, although working toward public benefit, will never be necessarily unanimous in agreement and, therefore, never immune to criticism. For the pessimists, the low level of support for Law number 9.790 of 1999 was a testament to the rejection of the new legal model. For the optimists, it was proof that that the relationship between the media and civil society organizations needed to be improved or refined, since the lack of support was, pure and simple, rooted in the public's lack of knowledge about the new law and the failure of organizations to understand that society had changed and needed a new standard for the administration of the public interest. Participating organizations observe that it was neither one nor the other of these issues, nor was it both at the same time; the problem resided in the difficulty in communicating with and building a consensus among their own members.

Legislative reform also required a greater theoretical and scientific foundation than organizational representatives had at their disposal at that time. If possible, more systematized international experiences should be brought to the analysis in such a way that, on the one hand, practitioners would not waste their time and energy reinventing the wheel and, on the other, would not attempt to implement experiences that either had notoriously bad results or had already been discarded in other countries. Representatives in the process also must have the complete support of their organizations, with an internal network for research and discussion, thus providing them with the data and advice needed to advance their proposals at the negotiating table in a consistent manner.

The participation of civil society is highly relevant in the debate and the formulation of the new legal framework. Not only is the importance of the participation of civil society in the actual process undeniable, it is necessary that more permanent channels of communication between organizations and the government be implemented so that they may continually and actively participate in the debates that affect the Third Sector. Such channels should not be limited to the executive branch, as occurred in this first phase of reform, but should be extended to the legislative and judicial branches as well. The expansion of such channels is necessary since the strengthening of communication with the Congress is essential for participating in emerging debates. Active participation in the debates is equally important in regard to dealing with the judiciary, since numerous laws can have different interpretations when applied to the evaluation of a dispute and certain concepts need not be considered by the law, since they are the product of jurisprudential process.

There is still much to be done in Brazil. It is necessary to expand fiscal incentives, which play a large role in increasing private capital flows for projects of social benefit. It is also necessary to strengthen the structure that fosters the participation of civil society in the public policy advisory councils created by the 1988 Constitution, so as to make them effective agents of social change and environmental protection. Finally, it is necessary to create a database capable of equipping parliamentarians, judges and promoters of justice with reliable information about the Third Sector to influence them in their activities related to the creation, application and control of the new laws and, also, to serve as a reference for researchers and those interested in civil society organizations.

Finally, it is necessary to strengthen the foundational principles with the production of the quality of knowledge necessary to make institutional articulation of this kind possible and to create, expand and occupy the spaces available so that legal reforms of these kinds may be introduced. These reforms, in turn, will serve as the basis for the evolution of these foundational ideas and continue to nurture the ongoing cycle of social refinement and laws that drive the reform process forward.

Notes

1 According to Wanderlei Guilherme dos Santos' study based on the survey of the registration of associations in the cities of São Paulo and Rio de Janeiro, between 1920 and 1986, 6,460 associations were created in São Paulo, 4,424 (68%) of which were formed between 1970 and 1986. The trend found in Rio de Janeiro was similar. Of the 5,755 associations established between 1946 and 1987, nearly 65% (3,731 entities) were created between 1971 and 1987. According to Lester Salomon and Helmut Anhier, "between 1978 and 1991, the number of organizations registered/listed in the Federal Registry increased from 76,000 to 190,000, on the average of approximately 9,000 new organizations per year."

2 Among the funds cited are: on the local, state and federal level, the Funds for the Rights of Children and Adolescents and, on the federal level, the National Fund for the Environment, the Fund for Support for Workers, the Fund for the Guarantee of Service Time and the Fund for the Protection of Associated Rights.

3 They are: 1) the strengthening of the third sector, which include not-for-profit civil society entities of public interest, representing today a strategic national orientation by virtue of their capacity to generate projects, assume responsibilities, undertake initiatives and mobilize the resources necessary for the social development of the country; 2) the strengthening of the Third Sector demands with legal framework be reformulated; 3) the reformulation of the legal basis of the Third Sector demands the construction of a broader understanding about the coverage/breadth of the meaning of the Third Sector; 4) the expansion and strengthening of the Third Sector is the responsibility ,in the first place, of the very society, which should institute mechanisms of transparency and responsibility capable of the construction of its self-regulation and 5) the reformulation of the legal framework of the Third Sector which demands that the establishment of rights be accompanied through the sharing of responsibilities of Third Sector entities with those of the State when they involve state resources.

4 They are: 1) The establishment of the identity of the third sector presupposes adequate classification of the organizations of which they are part, guaranteeing recognition of their specificities and making possible more efficient partnerships between Third Sector organizations and the state; the procedures for institutional recognition of Third Sector institutions must be revised and simplified in such a way as to reduce operational costs and to streamline and

make more effective the relationship between the state and civil society; 2) Legislation related to contracts and agreements must be revised , aiming to identify more adequate mechanisms of relation between the state and the Third Sector when involving state resources; 3) Mechanisms for the self-regulation of civil society must be created, aiming to guarantee publicity and transparency, efficiency and effectiveness in the functioning of Third Sector organizations; 4) More suitable mechanisms for responsibility must be implemented, aiming to guarantee that resources of state origin administered by organizations of the Third Sector are well invested and effectively targeted to meet the public's interest; 5) Feasible conditions for Third Sector financing must be achieved to reach a permanent flow of resources capable of guaranteeing the functioning of their organizations; 6) A legal framework must be created for the regulation of voluntary service; 7) Alternatives must be identified to permit Third Sector entities to establish labor contracts for fixed periods of time, without damaging the fundamental rights of the employed, but recognizing the special condition of the employer with public and not-for-profit goals; 8) It is necessary to foster the creation of information systems about the Third Sector which are accessible to the public.

5 Working group civil society representatives included Alexandre Fonseca (Rotary), Eduardo Szazi (GIFE), Humberto Mafra (Fórum Brasileiro de ONGs e Movimentos Sociais para o Meio Ambiente e Desenvolvimento), Jorge Eduardo Durão (Federação dos Órgãos para Assistência Social e Educacional—FASE e ABONG), Sérgio Carvalho (Cruzada do Menor), Silvio Santa Anna (Fundação Esquel), the Advisors of Comunidade Solidária, José Paulo Cavalcanti Filho, Miguel Darcy, Rubem César Fernandes and Pedro Moreira Salles.

6 At the time the newspapers made a big deal of the fact that The Tennis Club of Brasília (Academia de Tênis de Brasília), a club with the strictest of access, and a Golden Cross, and a well known vendor of health spa memberships was registered as a public service organization.

7 Education and welfare institutions that obtain the title of public utility can also claim a certificate of philanthropic purposes that exempts them from the quota paid by employers toward social security. As hospitals, schools and universities are usually large employers, this exoneration represents an enormous tax benefit which, according to the federal government, implies a loss of 200 million reals yearly.

8 They are: commercial societies; labor unions, class-based and professional associations; institutions that are religiously-oriented or geared toward the dissemination of a particular creed, cult, devotional or confessional practices and visions; partisan organizations and their like, including their foundations; entities of mutual benefit with the intention/goal of providing goods or services to a restricted circle of associates or members; health plans and the like; private medical institutions (hospitals) that are not free and their sponsors; private schools dedicated to formal education/teaching/training that is

not free and its sponsors; cooperatives of any type or genre; public foundations, private foundations or associations created by public entities or public foundations.

9 Copy of the social statute, minutes of the election of the directors, tax identification card, balance sheets, and income tax returns from the past year.

10 The list is available on the web page of the Brazilian Ministry of Justice (www.mj.gov.br).

11 We can observe an increasing dissemination of data among web pages, in special reports, newspapers and other internal means of communication and forms of mass media, from social balance sheets (annual reports) of sponsoring businesses to billboards on the façades of the organizations' offices.

12 We cite the proposals of requests for the curriculum vitae of directors as an indication of the level of involvement in investigations and/or juridical processes of various natures. Additional requested documents included photocopies of income tax declarations/statements, audits, lists of contractors and donors, with their respective costs, etc.

13 In Brazil, the attorney general has a constitutional responsibility to defend the legal order, the democratic system, as well as the social and individual interests of those who cannot defend themselves. Based on the Civil Code, the AG also has the power to supervise and provide council to foundations.

14 In reference to this particular issue, this author sees a strong parallel between public companies and civil society organizations, in that both base their strategies for growth and the financing of their operations on attracting popular savings, offering in return a benefit for the administration of the investor: in the case of companies, personal profit and in the case of NGOs, social profit. Poorly administered, both cause harm that transcends individual financial losses caused to investors, since the performance of individual entities can damage the image of the entire sector and contribute to a decrease in the level of investments made in other organizations with similar profiles.

15 The debates over this issue illustrate the difficulties inherent in the process of political articulation. For example, governmental representatives were not won over through the vote. They needed to be convinced. If they did not accept the proposal put forth by civil society representatives, they would simply impose theirs, since, according to the argument made by one of the governmental intermediaries/representatives "they can make the law by themselves; if they were consulting, it was to broaden the debate, but, in no way whatsoever, did they need the majority of the working group."

16 According to the official statistics found on the site http://www.mj.gov.br/snj/oscip.htm, most recently consulted on 3/03/2003.

17 In accordance with the federal constitution, the president of the Republic, in situations of relevance or extreme importance and urgency can adopt

provisional measures by force of law, measures that are then passed on to Congress, which has thirty days to consider them.

18 Members of the GIFE annually increase the level of investment they make from year to year, forecasting for 2003 a total of one billion reals in resources for social projects.

References

Conselho da Comunidade Solidária. *Seis anos de interlocução política: metodologia, resultados e avaliação de 1996–2002.* Conselho da Comunidade Solidária: Brasília, 2002, p. 10.

Fernandes, R.C. *Privado porém público—o Terceiro Setor na América Latina.* Rio de Janeiro: Relume-Dumará, 1994.

Ferrarezi, E. *El nuevo marco legal Del Tercer Sector em Brasil.* in Revista del CLAD Reforma y Democracia, no. 20, Venezuela, June 2001.

Landim, L. *Para além do mercado e do Estado? Filantropia e cidadania no Brasil.* Rio de Janeiro: ISER, 1993.

Landim, L. and Beres, N. *Ocupações, despesas e recursos: as organizações sem fins lucrativos no Brasil.* Rio de Janeiro: Nau, 1999, p. 47.

Salamon, L. and Anheier, H.K. *The Emerging Sector: An Overview,* Manchester/New York: Manchester University Press, 1996, pp. 105–6.

Santos, W.G. *Razões da disordem,* Rio de Janeiro: Rocco, 1993, p. 80–9.

Szazi, E. *Terceiro Setor: Regulação no Brasil.* 2a. Ed. São Paulo: Peirópolis, 2001.

13

Enabling Environments for Philanthropy and Civil Society: The Chilean Case

Gonzalo de la Maza

What is an enabling environment for linking philanthropy, civil society and social change? In a recent article, volume editor Cynthia Sanborn wondered how realistic it was to think of philanthropy going "from charity to solidarity," establishing affirmative links with poor communities, defending basic rights and struggling against inequality.[1] If that is difficult to imagine, this chapter gives it another twist and asks: What would be an enabling environment for that kind of philanthropy, and for strengthening civil society in general?

By posing the question about social change, this chapter introduces the idea of substantive directions for philanthropy. This means not just encouraging philanthropy and civil society in general, but in particular, orienting them toward tackling poverty, inequality and injustice. It is quite possible for philanthropy to grow and at the same time to inhibit social change rather than foster it. Indeed, as mentioned at the outset of this book, in Latin America the connotations of the term are associated with paternalism and social control by those in power. Something similar happens with civil society: it is not a homogeneous set of organizations and kind-hearted, progressive individuals, but rather reproduces within itself the contradictions and conflicts of the actors that compose it. And although both philanthropic practices and civil society actions are emerging phenomena in the region today, their significance is not single but rather involves various distinct projects. This enhances the importance of examining the real potential that both have for achieving societies that are fairer, more democratic and better developed.

If social change is the substantive goal, how can we define it in a non-arbitrary way? This chapter does so in the context of goals widely accepted by society. In the Chilean case, such goals include a society that is democratic, integrated, economically developed and sustainable. Therefore, an "enabling environment" would be one that favors philanthropic practices and actions by Chilean civil society in the pursuit of such goals, not just for the sake of developing those activities *per se*. Given the author's own experience, this chapter will deal in more detail with civil society and to a lesser extent with philanthropy in its narrower sense.[2]

This kind of philanthropy can be defined in practice as the involvement of individuals and corporations in the tasks of expanding democracy and producing more public goods. An enabling environment for this should encourage people to increase their time and dedication to volunteering, to make larger contributions in money to solidarity causes, and to expand their own sense of co-responsibility for resolving social problems, rather than looking to the state for everything. As for corporations, the above should take the form of larger monetary contributions to nonprofit causes and the enhancement of corporate social responsibility. In brief, an enabling environment for social change-oriented philanthropy should encourage increased and diversified volunteering, more corporate and individual social responsibility, and growing resources from the private sector for tasks in the public good.

As for civil society, the environment would be enabling when it promotes the emergence of a more organized and diverse civil society, the variables of which may be described as follows: (a) reinforcement of civil society organizations (encouraging internally stronger organizations, more closely linked to one another, more democratic and more efficient); (b) assurance and encouragement of pluralism, diversity and inclusion of civil society (freedom of organization and of speech, affirmative action in favor of the underprivileged, and equitable access to economic and institutional resources); (c) assurance of, and encouragement to, new actors (equitable access to economic and institutional resources, respect for organizational autonomy, public support for what organizations do); and (d) development of mechanisms for accountability, social control, civic awareness, respect for existing powers (government, large-scale economic corporations, and mass media).[3]

Discussion about the creation of enabling environments for philanthropy and civil society is normally restricted to legal and financial reforms. This chapter argues that the debate should be expanded. The evidence suggests that legal and tax mechanisms, though important, are neither a radical impediment to, nor a magic wand for, increased philanthropic action per se. Corporations donate even without tax exemptions, exemptions are not always utilized, and civil society organizations adopt legality in a highly instrumental way. To promote philanthropy, structural variables must first be considered, including prevailing socio-economic trends and conditions, as well as the cultural setting. Aside from legal and the tax frameworks, the institutional environment must take into consideration the state's institutional and political capabilities that may play a part in amending such conditions, favorably or otherwise. This chapter focuses primarily on this latter set of issues.

The following diagram represents what an enabling environment might look like:

Structural variables
- Socioeconomic trends
- Cultural guidelines

↓

Enabling environment
- Institutional framework
- Public policies
- Legislation
- Funding mechanisms / tax framework

↑

Expected impacts
- Philanthropy: focus on public issues, volume and diversity of volunteer action, social responsibility, and private resources
- Civil society: organization, diversity, opening, and capacity for social control

More specifically, this chapter discusses the role of public policies—especially government action—in creating and developing an enabling environment for strengthening civil society and developing philanthropy in Chile during the '90s. Government action in this case continues to be significant for defining social dynamics. Substantive questions include: To what extent have public policies implemented since 1990 contributed to creating positive environments for the development of philanthropy and a civil society aimed at social change? Are public policies really effective for achieving such goals? What obstacles do they face, for example, for amending structural variables?

The Chilean case appears particularly appropriate for observing public policies, for these policies underwent reactivation from 1990 onward, as a result of the social and political mobilization that began in 1983. Transition period governments have always cited the strengthening of civil society as a guiding principle, although under various names such as social participation, the third sector and nonprofit institutions. Furthermore, data show that a substantial amount of public funds have gone to the execution of social programs by private actors.

In Chile, the state's main thrust has been innovation in government policies and programs. The legal framework has been amended only partially, the institutional framework even less. Tax mechanisms set up in the '80s remain virtually unchanged. Thus, the Chilean case will serve to reflect on the potential of government programs to create enabling environments.

The Context of the '90s: Economic Dynamism, Active Social Policy, and Social Precariousness

Recovery of democratic institutions in Chile took place in 1990, in the framework of a political arrangement negotiated between the Armed Forces, which controlled the state since 1973, and the new forces responsible for administration of the government—a broad coalition of political parties that had won a plebiscite in late 1988. This negotiation included keeping the Constitution of 1980 unchanged except for a few minor reforms agreed upon in 1989.[4] In economic matters, major policies continue in place to ensure control of inflation and opening of the economy to the foreign sector, based on mobilization of large-scale private capital. These policies have resulted in sustained economic growth, though very unequal in its social implications.[5] The government, meanwhile, adopted a more active social policy, mainly in terms of substantial investment in basic social infrastructure (education, health, housing, and public works). This stage came to an end in 1997; the rate of growth dropped, unemployment rose, discontent was expressed in political terms, and social disorganization deepened.

The institutional transition failed to obtain a consistent social base, since it concentrated on social control, governance, and keeping up economic growth. Deactivation of social movements, the political and legal limitations of the transition, together with a rising degree of privatization in social and economic relations, gradually weakened the social and political agreement that made the transition possible. Gradually, the society has become mercantilist and social inequities deeper, in terms of inequitable access to opportunities for social mobility. Economic growth brought with it a set of opportunities, which, however, mainly serve those who owned resources to take advantage of them prior to their advent: such resources concentrate in Chile's central area, in wealthy urban communities, in adult males with more education, and in the members of existing social networks. Economic results, together with reactivated public policies, longer working hours and over-indebtedness, resulted in increased income and gradual reduction of poverty, according to measurements of income and basic needs.[6]

Recent measurements show that the structure of income distribution in Chile does not greatly differ from other countries of Latin America, except as regards the top income decile, where an extraordinarily high proportion of income and opportunities concentrate.[7] That is why in the Chilean case it is important to distinguish clearly between the evolution of poverty and of inequality, and to recognize that while both trends became consolidated since 1987, in the latter there has actually been a regression. In the context of this chapter, one may then say that philanthropy aiming for social change should contribute to moderating the strong trend toward inequality and income concentration found in Chilean society, a hazard for democracy and social integration.[8]

The contribution of public policies has been crucial for raising the incomes of the poorest. The state, however, has not had the tools necessary to alter inequality of opportunities nor to redirect the economic model that causes it and blocks the prospects of 40 percent of the low-income population. Social public expenditure has doubled in absolute terms since 1990, has risen by a little more than 2 percentage points of GDP, and accounts for three-fourths of total public expenditure.[9] How is it possible that in spite of these efforts of the public sector, the increasingly inequitable structure of Chilean society remains unaltered? The rigidity of income distribution is linked to the fact that only public expenditure is redistributing, while the main sources of income tend to be concentrating. It is difficult for social expenditure to increase without growth of total public expenditure, which appears politically unfeasible in the short term, although the Chilean state is one of the smallest in size among the countries where the so-called "free-market economy" prevails.[10] The redistributing function of public expenditure is limited by the fact that it accounts for only one-fifth of total expenditure in the economy. Hence the paradox that while state monetary outlay accounts for 72 percent of total income for the poorest decile of the population, the position of this decile in terms of income distribution is improved by only 0.1 percent.[11]

The above leads us to suggest that promotion of philanthropy cannot be sought at the expense of the state's basic tasks, but must necessarily be thought of as supplement, complement or expansion of these tasks. The same may be said of strengthening civil society: in the Chilean case, this cannot be conceived simply as a "transfer of power" from the government, for that power is quite limited in size. Next to the democratizing agenda of state institutions as such, what must be considered is utilization of public policies as an element for strengthening civil society, so that the latter can act with more autonomy, influence the public agenda, and act as counterweight to the immense concentration of economic, political, and communicational power in the hands of a reduced sector of the population.

The democratic transition can show major achievements in the social area, which have nonetheless failed to translate into stable social participation and integration. Nor have these achievements found expression in major collective mobilizations or political demands, but instead have taken the form of fear and insecurity, political disaffection, and the weakening of collective and community links. People tend to withdraw into privacy and their home life, distrust "the others," and have few instruments with which to develop shared projects. The social link deteriorates. A high degree of mistrust is observed, with precarious associations, growing instrumental use of social relationships, and weaker cohesion within the family.[12]

The profound economic and social transformations caused changes in sociability and social relationships. From a period of adjustment, when an excluding and concentrating neo-liberal model was adopted, the step was taken to one of growth sustained by the same model, with the addition of government action in the social area with a view to palliating its more acute implications. Although income levels rose and the supply of social policy improved, this failed to cause stable social integration and participation. The economic inclusion arising from the current model is precarious, uncertain, partial, and profoundly inequitable. On the political plane, the limitations of the transition, the reduced role of the government, and the "authoritarian enclaves" prevent significant changes and real participation. Under these circumstances, the challenge of creating an enabling environment for civil society is, overall, a challenge to integrate, create bonds, times and spaces for the construction of collective projects.[13]

The Policies of the Transition Period

How have public policies influenced the context described above? How capable have they proved to be in creating enabling environments for the development of a civil society and a philanthropy that will in turn have an impact on the challenges described? This chapter distinguishes between the approaches and overall practices of public policy—particularly in the social area—and initiatives specifically aimed at the nonprofit sector and civil society organizations. These latter initiatives are just a fraction of the extensive government strategies that impinge more decisively on social dynamics. This section will discuss such general strategies and policies and the next section will deal with actions addressed specifically to the non-profit sector, philanthropy and civil society.

Initially, the formula used to describe the objective of government action was "growth with equity." This term was intended to denote the governmental wish to keep up the economic model that was showing such substantial dynamism since the mid-eighties. It also signified that corrections were to be injected into that growth and were expected to help to overcome some of the sources of inequity found in Chilean society. It was a question of adapting the formula coined by ECLAC, but replacing "development" with "growth" and having "equity" mean in practice "reduction of poverty."

The suggested formula ensured governance during the transition period and gained the commitment of dominating actors who, though politically in the opposition, nonetheless benefited directly from the economic policy. It also helped to control possible social unrest arising from unsatisfied demands accumulated during the lengthy dictatorship. To this end, the tools of social policy were utilized and the so-called "consensus policy" was encouraged. In legislation, therefore, only what was supported from the beginning by the right-wing opposition was promoted, that is, matters that had previously been the object of negotiation outside the legislature. Social mobilization was not resorted to in order to establish new correlations of strength and so, although a quiet setting was thus ensured for the transition, the levels of democratic policy were weakened and social participation was left without space of any importance.[14]

Continuity and Innovations in Traditional Social Policies

Traditional social policies, such as health care, housing, education and social security, underwent major change in Chile, outstanding in the Latin American context. Yet here too, elements of continuity combined with change and marked the institutional, political and financial environment for Chilean civil society. Among the trends established during the military régime—reduced funding, focalization, diminished concentration, municipalization and privatization—the first of these, public expenditure, was significantly increased, and focalization was modified, by refining procedures and adding new "priority groups." New programs were set up, though generally without altering the social policy institutions designed by the military dictatorship. Budget increases were significant in all areas and have continued over time.[15]

The main objectives of major social policies implemented under the Concertación administrations did not include creating enabling environments for developing philanthropy and strengthening civil society. The spaces opened to participation by various kinds of civil organizations mostly seek co-financing of programs and policies (housing, health, later education), thus subsidizing the shortfall in public resources. Another major form of linkage between government action and private units is outsourcing, whereby the government plans the action and allocates the resources, while the private sector executes programs and projects. Main outsourced services have been managed by corporations, though some nonprofit organizations (educational supporters, housing programs, capacity-building for labor) have also participated. Where both forms of organization concur, no form of incentive exists to foster consolidation of the nonprofit sector as service operator. Rather, competition is encouraged between corporations and nonprofit agencies (NGOs, municipalities, sometimes social organizations) with a view to obtaining the most cost-effective equation for the administration.

In the case of health care, the mixed system set up in 1981 was retained, in which the private sector captures the higher-income sectors (about 25%), while the public sector provides health care for the majority, including handling of catastrophic diseases, services for senior citizens and, generally, all the "nonprofitable" sides of health care. At the same time, neither the subdivision of Servicio Nacional de Salud (National Health Service) into 27 self-managed regional services, nor municipal management of primary health care was reversed. Despite a substantial injection of funds, the public system suffers from chronic lack of funding, which has led to considering overall health-sector reform linking public and private sectors in a different way.

As for links with the community, the Programa de Promoción de la Salud (Health Promotion Program) began in 1992 and for a time the Consejos Locales de Salud y de Desarrollo de los Hospitales (Local Health and Hospital Development Councils) were promoted, both programs that allowed support to be obtained for hospital management and preventive health care. Their action is based on volunteer work, financial and material contributions and community organizations. However, there is no link between these initiatives and the current discussion of health reform, nor any share in defining policy directions.[16]

In education, too, private and public establishments under municipal management continue to exist side by side, the latter receiving the lower-income population and students rejected by the private system. The private system comprises a paid private sector (7% of all students) and a subsidized private sector, which operates with funds contributed by the state. This latter sector includes nonprofit corporations (mostly of religious origin) and a growing profit making corporate sector, which receives the government subsidy. The subsidized private sector as well as the municipal sector have benefited from increased school subsidies and from implementation of various programs for improving the quality of education, and also from government funds for construction of infrastructure to allow primary schools to operate on a full-day basis. Subsidy management makes no distinction between the profit and nonprofit sectors.[17]

Tools for encouraging donations from private business are available only for education and a substantial amount of funds has been mobilized for primary and higher education. In the former case (Law on Donations for Educational Purposes), this has meant not only the involvement of corporations in educational projects but also support for municipal schools. In the latter case, donations have concentrated mainly on private universities catering for high-income sectors, run by conservative religious groups. This has indirectly resulted in increasingly inequitable supply of education (with resources that the state fails to receive) and concentration of power, which is detrimental to the diversification of Chilean civil society. In juridical terms, universities are nonprofit organizations; in practice, however, most of them belong to corporations that operate them for profit.[18]

In housing, public policy aims to supply the largest number of "housing solutions" for homeless groups, thus reducing the immense housing deficit prevailing at the end of the military régime. This strengthened the prior alliance with the real estate industry, which has a vast "captive market." Public policy moves within the bounds set by private control of land and subsidizes the demand of the poorest population, who ensure the profitability of the real estate business.[19] Financing through housing subsidies began during the military régime, in order to stimulate private supply of "housing solutions" for the poor. This objective was retained during the transition period, though with increased resources and more efficient management. The role assigned to nonprofit organizations was reduced to technical assistance projects and organizing the demand of certain slum-dwellers. Today, a handful of NGOs are devoted to housing and urban development. The beneficiary population has been organized in various "committees," a non-permanent form of institution mainly designed to enable beneficiaries to meet the required amount of prior savings and financial contribution to obtain their "housing solutions," and for street paving.

One negative result of the housing policy—directly stemming from the success of its unilateral, sectoral approach—is the massive emergence of "the poor with a roof," or extensive peripheral housing developments with no access to services, conceived as "low-cost housing condominiums" lacking legislation to operate properly, with immense problems of community life and day-to-day living.[20]

A Change of Paradigm: Policies for Children

Another sector that receives continuing government subsidy, but with a different outlook, is care of children at social risk. During the dictatorship, a sector of traditional institutions was organized for what were then termed "children from irregularly constituted homes," involving a subsidy per child inmate of such institutions. In 1990, the Chilean government signed the International Convention of the Rights of Children and began an overall redefinition of policies for that sector, seeking to make them consistent with the approach proposed in the Convention. This meant aiming to reduce the duration of each child's stay in the institution (indirectly fostered by the existing form of subsidy) and promoting innovative programs in the hands of nonprofit institutions sharing the same approach based on rights. Simultaneously, a profound legal reform of the sector was promoted, including institutions (Servicio Nacional de Menores or agency for children), laws governing protection of the rights of children and a law on juvenile criminal liability. An office was recently set up in the purview of the Ministry of Planning (MIDEPLAN) to coordinate policies addressed to children. As application of the provisions under the International Convention is reviewed from time to time, the government has reported extensively on its own actions, while the non-governmental sector has also set up its own networks for monitoring and reporting to the appropriate United Nations agency.

The sector of policies for children shows the transformation of a traditional sector with the participation of civil society and with financing mechanisms to make it possible. At the same time, such participation is not limited to executing programs but also establishes levels of political interlocution that have had an effect on legal reform projects. In spite of subsisting unresolved problems, the sector has a consistent body of doctrine and law, with a framework of long-term policies (national and regional plans for children) and funding mechanisms not dependent solely on projects open to competition. Directed exclusively to the nonprofit sector, this sector of policies for children has also developed organs for consultation and political negotiation. Though program execution continues to be outsourced, the framework in this case is radically different. Paradoxically, one of the problems to be resolved is corporate defense of institutions developed under a subsidy policy designed for "outsourcing services," but lacking the present legal and political frameworks.[21]

Private philanthropy focuses mainly on childhood issues, especially in the form of assistance and based on traditional Christian charity values. NGOs basing their efforts on the paradigm of children's rights have had many problems with obtaining funds from the corporate sector. No specific incentives have been established for this sector.

Outsourcing Services without Strengthening Civil Society: Capacity-building and Productive Development
Capacity-building for labor has been emphasized considerably throughout this period through various mechanisms, all of them outsourced rather than carried out directly by the government. The most widely used mechanism is a tax privilege, whereby corporations may discount a certain amount of their taxable profits if applied to worker training. The mechanism has expanded over time, though it is still far from reaching the limit of its possibilities as many corporations fail to take full advantage of it. Although the government has introduced various innovations intended to extend use of the privilege and coverage of capacity-building of labor, this tax privilege has not in general been used to develop the nonprofit sector; nonprofit organizations may not utilize the privilege nor has the emergence of "social corporations" or other forms of nonprofit organizations been fostered in the area.[22]

Other capacity-building programs financed directly by the state are addressed to unemployed young people (through the Servicio de Capacitación y Empleo or Capacity-Building and Employment Agency—SENCE) and the Fondo de Solidaridad e Inversión Social or Fund for Solidarity and Social Investment—FOSIS. Though many NGOs have had successful experience in this field, the form always used by the government to finance such courses from time to time is a commonly used bidding format. This method prevents working in the medium and long term, and consolidation of civil society organizations, for they are subject to the same rules as any consulting firm specializing precisely in submitting projects and setting up *ad hoc* teams to run them, with no territorial projection or over time. Since mid-decade, however, a coalition of nonprofit institutions in Santiago specializing in the area (FORJAR) obtained approval in Congress for an allocation of resources for several years to fund more long-lasting projects than those promoted by public agencies. This experience has not been repeated.[23]

As for productive development programs, the government has resorted to novel ways to stimulate corporate innovation through association. These are known as PROFOS (short for Proyectos de Fomento or Development Projects), in which the state subsidizes hiring a manager to develop innovation projects that involve a number of businesses, grouped by product, location or other form of productive linkage. A 1996 proposal to apply this mechanism to the nonprofit sector, followed by an attempt by a coalition of NGOs (REDESOL) to negotiate the proposal for application to a project of a productive nature. None of these attempts succeeded. Paradoxically, the Chilean government fosters association among habitual competitors—businesses—and competition among the actors traditionally associated with cooperation, the NGOs.[24]

A Comment on Modes of Financing

Public modes of financing used in traditional social sectors, especially subsidy and allowance, have proved adequate to reinforce the participation of private actors in areas of national activity that the state seeks to privilege. This was done in the past with such fields as health care, forestry development, export promotion, financial brokerage for loans to micro-sized business, road-building concessions and private participation in education. Rather than being utilized in favor of civil society and philanthropy, public modes of financing have been used very pointedly in favor of private enterprise, following in the steps of the military administration, which began implementation of these mechanisms. The Chilean government is experienced in outsourcing and transferring funds to private agents, by subsidizing them extensively, an experience that has increased in the context of public expenditure in the social area. To create favorable conditions for the nonprofit sector and civil society would mean a higher political priority on the government agenda, as well as a clearer understanding of the functions to be performed by the sector in social development. So far the nonprofit sector has been conceived mainly as part of a set of private agents that cooperate with the exercise of state functions, at a lower cost. Recently, the situation began to change with the implementation of the Plan for Strengthening Civil Society (2001), though it is too early yet to assess its results.

New Social Institutions

Since 1990, new institutions have been created that specialize in the social area, with innovative programs marking the difference from the "traditional" areas emphasized by the former military administration. These institutions are defined for certain groups of the population that are considered vulnerable and for whom no programs or policies had been formulated. With a multisectoral character, these institutions were grouped under a new ministry, MIDEPLAN (former Planning Bureau), created for the purpose. Initially, specialized institutions were organized for youth, women, native peoples and population in extreme poverty. Agencies for seniors and for the disabled were added later.[25]

The general impact of the innovating institutions has been fairly low. They have not succeeded in linking effectively among themselves and with traditional social policy, which continues to follow a sector approach because of the lack of a social authority at the ministerial level and the lack of a definite institutional integration within the public sector.[26] Nonetheless, these innovating institutions introduced into the administration a concern for actors not taken into account previously, thus expanding the governmental agenda to include these new actors as active participants. Perhaps the greatest achievements in this context belong to SERNAM (National Department of Women), which attained ministerial status, obtained recognition by the Convention for the Elimination of all Forms of Discrimination against Women, and governmental approval for a National Equal Opportunity Plan, with appropriate regional plans, as well as negotiated commitments with other government agencies. Paradoxically, SERNAM lacks financing instruments to propel the equal opportunity agenda among civil society organizations.

These new institutions keep up more permanent contacts with civil organizations in their respective sectors and have set up countless points of participation at various levels of policy implementation. However, the format based on projects of brief duration allocated by competition reduces such participation to a merely instrumental dimension (obtaining the project) and fails to allow a more permanent type of association to be built. The goals, periods, modes and products expected from the participating bodies become technocratic or, even worse, clientelist, to the extent that they are subordinate to the agenda of the institution. The multiplication of specialized institutions that call upon civil society in an independent manner, causes fragmented and ephemeral associations. Thus the crucial issue is not the creation, but rather the design and implementation, of institutions, with varying experiences in that regard.[27]

All the above institutions operate under the system of bids and competition for projects, mostly addressed to nonprofit organizations, on a professional or membership basis. As a result, multiple public funds have emerged to finance small projects through manifold "financing windows." For their part, civil society organizations provide a significant amount of funding that is complementary to government support, since in most cases such projects entail a substantial share of co-financing from the executing institutions.

From the standpoint of funding, these state institutions may be said to have contributed to the subsistence of a set of social organizations of various types, which at one time or another were in charge of executing the projects. The system has nonetheless showed numerous limitations for developing an autonomous civil society with more capabilities: the small overall amount committed, continuous changes in terms and conditions of competitions, short project duration, instrumental nature of participation, and multiplicity of "windows." As for philanthropy, these projects as a rule fail to consider it among their priorities, except to require community contributions and count on volunteer work as a non-valued component of the projects financed.[28]

This situation seems to indicate that focused programs can also play a role in the structuring of associations, especially in poor sectors, since that is where governmental activity is concentrated. Such programs are in fact structures of incentives for the poor, stressing bonds with the government at this "last link in the chain" of public policies. Figures from the Report on Human Development for 2000 show that there are more than 80,000 associations of various kinds in Chile (not counting religious institutions) and describe such association as fragmented, unlinked to networks and scarcely influential on the direction of public policies. Indeed, social programs addressed to priority groups, as well as other government agencies, such as Chiledeportes (sports and games) and Instituto de Desarrollo Agropecuario (agriculture and livestock), do in fact influence associations among groups of the poor, yet in a way that fails to reinforce their sustainability or to develop greater capabilities. Given that this is the sector that grew most during the '90s in budgetary terms and that its relationship with popular groups is direct, it is understandable that despite deficient institutional design, its contribution to the development of civil society might be different.

Environmental protection is a special case. This is a completely new area of action in Chile, with low-profile public institutions (Comisión Nacional del Medio Ambiente [CONAMA] or National Environment Commission) that face strong pressure from big business interests. *Vis-à-*

vis major environmental controversies (hydropower plants, production mega projects), the state has played a subordinate role. Even so, an institutional mechanism for participation was set up, linked to environmental impact studies that corporations must submit to develop their projects. This experience served as the base for the draft law on bases for participation, currently in preparation (see below). A key element is the constant, well-organized activity of the environmentalist movement within Chilean civil society, encompassing various networks and organizations, with well-maintained international links and financial support.[29]

Regarding funding, CONAMA has utilized the usual mechanism of competition for small-scale projects for grassroots organizations, with low impact and high dispersion. However, the Fondo de las Américas (Fund of the Americas), established in 1995, was endowed from the conversion of Chile's bilateral debt with the United States and devoted to environmental issues. This fund is wholly allocated to non-governmental nonprofit organizations and managed by a mixed council elected among non-governmental and government-designated executors (with a majority of the former). The fund is a concrete transfer of public resources for autonomous management of civil organizations, which has caused an interesting mobilization of additional resources. It inspired the present proposal for a Mixed Fund for Strengthening Civil Society (see below). In spite of this, however, once available funds were exhausted, the Chilean government failed to support a second debt reconversion agreement or to allocate other resources to continue the Fondo de las Américas, which closed in 2004.

Policies for Civil Society

This section deals with government programs and policies specifically addressed to the relation between government and civil society as an objective of government action. Major definitions and positions that were structured have evolved during the period.

The '90s

The policy of "social agreements" arrived at between 1990 and 1993, mainly between big business and the union movement, concerned such issues as the minimum wage. Even more important, the policy confirmed the political worth of negotiation and agreement over and above union controversy. These agreements let the union movement defer its specific demands in favor of political governance in exchange for a few concessions in terms of wages, layoffs and compensations. However, the agreements failed to amend the Labor Code enacted by the dictatorship. This Labor Code had caused "considerable deregulation of labor activities, reduction of the protective nature of the right to work, loss of power among union organizations and reduction of the scope of collective bargaining."[30] In practice, the commitment to the political process restricted its autonomy, and widened the distance between leaders and union membership.

Regarding urban popular organizations, the decade began with democratization of the juntas de vecinos or neighborhood organizations, a territorial form of organization that developed under military intervention. Active mobilization arose around the neighborhood groups, which was achieved during the '80s, although not linked to the broad and diverse fabric of social organizations arising during the same period. Although a conglomerate of neighborhood organizations (and Community Unions of Neighborhood Organizations) have lasted in part until the present time, the organizational existence of the neighborhood organizations began to decay significantly in the '90s. A 1996 law aimed at regulating the neighborhood organizations, in fact, weakened them by allowing several to be organized per neighborhood unit, and by failing to address the issue of financing and spaces for participation.[31] The government also set up the Division of Social Organizations, in the Ministry known as Secretaría General de Gobierno, as the link with territorial social organizations.

Another major step among explicit initiatives addressing civil society was the organization of a Liaison Bureau between government and NGOs in the purview of the Social Division of MIDEPLAN. This bureau organized a Consultative NGO-Government Committee, chaired by the minister and composed of leaders of various networks, specific institutions, foundations linked to political parties, and other "personalities."[32] The Asociación Chilena de Organismos No Gubernamentales (ACCION) (Chilean Association of Non-Governmental Organizations) was established during this period, grouping more than one hundred NGOs active in development promotion. For the first few years, the debate focused on directions for nascent government programs and an enactment of a "Model Charter for NGOs" was obtained. This charter provides a preapproved format that simplifies (saving time and expense) the juridical establishment of NGOs as Nonprofit Corporations. This had not been possible during the dictatorship because approval was required from the president himself. The charter fails to resolve the substance of the problem, which stems from provisions in the Chilean Civil Code enacted in the 19th century, but does make operation easier. Other and wider proposals from NGOs were disregarded.[33]

From 1994 onward, the second Concertación administration emphasized the implementation of a national and intersectoral program involving civil society and aiming at overcoming poverty. An Interministerial Social Committee was established and persons representing the various sectors of civil society were called to form the Consejo Nacional para la Superación de la Pobreza (CNSP) (National Council for Overcoming Poverty).[34] Business leaders, religious, NGOs, health care institutions and others formed part of the council, with regional and provincial affiliates organized in 15 locations across the country. Two years later, however, the Program for Overcoming Poverty was reformulated; as a result, CNSP action caused controversy, internally with representatives of big business and externally with the then-members of the Interministerial Social Committee, who were subsequently replaced.[35]

In 1996 MIDEPLAN again undertook to define a policy for the nonprofit sector, basically its share in "the design, execution, and assessment of social policies."[36] These suggestions were discussed by a new group known as Comité Consultivo de Políticas Sociales (Consultative Committee on Social Policies), and at regional meetings, and were approved by the Committee of Social Ministers. As a result of this process, a Plan de Acción para el Fortalecimiento de la Sociedad Civil y de las Organizaciones Privadas sin Fines de Lucro y con Fines Lucrativos (Action Plan for Strengthening Civil Society and Private Nonprofit and Profitmaking Organizations). The plan was never implemented, however, because the administration was near the end of its term and the new authorities would once more alter the governmental directions.

After the Year 2000

During the presidential campaign of incumbent President Ricardo Lagos, an agreement was signed with persons connected with the NGO world, seeking to innovate public policies in favor of public recognition and support to civil society organizations, amending the legal frameworks for the latter. The direction followed by the Lagos administration (in office until 2006) was based on the diagnosis that citizen participation had weakened, this being the "unfinished business" of the transition period, that is to say, a lagging component of the democratic process. The grounds for such a policy fail to examine critically the characteristics of the economic and political process, but rather add to it a specific public policy that to date had been non-existent.

The three instruments principally utilized are: summons to the Consejo Ciudadano para el Fortalecimiento de la Sociedad Civil (Citizen Council for Strengthening Civil Society), issue of the Instructivo Presidencial de Participación Ciudadana (Presidential Instructions on Citizen Participation), and preparation of a Draft Law on citizen participation in public policy. The Citizen Council called on representatives of NGOs, health care institutions, leaders of groups of neighborhood organizations, corporate foundations, study centers and foundations linked to political parties. It issued a December 2000 report on its work that made proposals in four areas: legal framework, funding, volunteering and public policies. The administration took up these proposals to a considerable extent in March 2001 in the Plan for Strengthening Civil Society. The Plan was implemented with financing from the Inter American Development Bank, which provides funds for development of volunteer work, public dissemination and studies on legal issues. The presidential Instructions on Citizen Participation were issued at the same time, providing for the commitment of 16 ministries to engage citizen participation in their policies and programs. The Ministry Secretaría General de Gobierno (SEGEGOB) was put in charge of monitoring performance of such commitments. The first compliance report was issued in January 2003.

As a supplementary measure, the Mixed Fund for Strengthening Civil Society Organizations was established in 2002 as an instrument seeking to organize public funds made available to these organizations, while promoting capacity-building and institutional reinforcement. This fund, designed to attract other public and private contributions, partly meets the 1996 CNSP proposal in regards to the collection of the various scattered public funds transferred to civil organizations for their own development. It began with a fairly reduced amount of funds, focusing mainly on capacity-building.[37] Consultative bodies with non-governmental participation contributed to the development of this policy at all levels and ensured a form of management marked by transparency. SEGEGOB, in turn, keeps up ongoing dialogs with NGO networks, and representatives of national groups of neighborhood organizations.

The formulation of the Law on Citizen Participation in Public Policy, which had begun during the previous administration, was continued by the Lagos Administration under the Division of Government Modernization in the purview of the Ministry Secretaría General de la Presidencia (SECPRES). At first this proposal contemplated citizen participation at the decision-making level, as well as the information and proposal level, covering the central, decentralized, regional and local levels of government. Eventually, however, the proposal became limited to only the central level of public policy, proposing levels and instruments that do not involve other legal reforms, and establishing "the obligation to regulate and comply thoroughly with public policy at the information, consultation, and proposal levels," excluding participation at decision-making level. It further includes participation of officials in management of institutions and contains a mechanism for defense and protection of the rights and interests of civil society as regards citizen participation, entrusted to the citizen defense functions, which is still in the process of creation.[38]

Changes in Financing Laws on Private Donations

During 2003, the Lagos administration faced harsh accusations of public corruption, including use of public funds for political campaigns. This led to negotiations between government and opposition resulting in the swift passing (the bill was rated as of "extreme urgency") of a law providing for tax privileges for corporations donating funds for political campaigns, further guaranteeing donor anonymity. The bill also extended the tax privilege to private donations in the areas of poverty and disability. These two areas were thus added to the existing ones of education, culture, and sports. There was provision for an entitlement ceiling and also for a mixed fund in which 30% of every donation is to be deposited. This fund, to be managed by representatives of both government and civil society, is intended to provide resources to institutions unable to obtain them from private donations; in other words, its object is partial redistribution of private donations under tax privilege, which in the past had shown a marked tendency to concentrate in a very small number of beneficiaries. In addition, the law sets out a register of institutions described as being of "public interest" that may also benefit from such funding.

The current law has raised a number of objections from various segments of civil society. NGO networks object to being included in a law mainly designed for political funding, to keeping theme restrictions considered arbitrary for obtaining donations entitled to privilege (the themes are not even consistent with government priorities), and to the fact that the tax privilege does not extend to individuals, but is restricted to corporations paying second category tax. In turn, the more publicly visible philanthropic foundations have come down forcefully on the establishment of the Mixed Fund, since it takes away part of the donated funds, also objecting to the ceiling established, the greater controls and penalties contemplated on wrongful use of donations, and the restriction of donations to corporations. The foundations also contend that the practical effect of the law has been a drastic drop in donations, especially those intended for cultural activities, adding to corporate reluctance to make donations. Corporations, together with members of Congress belonging to the right-wing opposition, have been holding formal talks aiming to amend the law.

Despite the absence of a favorable legal framework, the large-scale corporations have lately begun to show an interest in so-called "corporate social responsibility." Major efforts along these lines originated in foreign-based corporations established in Chile, operating in various countries under their corporate policies. Following the execution of trade agreements with the European Union, the trend has also been taken up by Chilean corporations exporting to Europe. The behavior pattern usually takes the form of a foundation directly linked to the corporation, which takes action related to the business or otherwise, usually in neighborhoods close to the industrial facilities. Some of the factories that have gone through more serious difficulties with the public have made various efforts of this kind to improve their public image.

Few such foundations, however, have been set up to make donations to NGOs and other organizations, as is usual in the northern hemisphere. Fundación Minera Escondida and Fundación Carmen Goudie are among the few that do make such donations. Two major endowments that helped to fund non-governmental projects were Fundación San José de La Dehesa, organized by a religious congregation to undertake housing projects, and Fundación Andes in various other areas. The resources of both are exhausted and their activities have come to an end.

Despite the uncoordinated nature of its sector policies, the Chilean government has developed permanent and specific actions to organize interlocution with at least a fraction of civil society. These actions lack continuity in both their objectives and their institutional referents, passing from the social area "against poverty" (MIDEPLAN) to the political area (SEGEGOB). These actions are also disconnected from those conducted in relation with organized labor and business, conceptualized as "social concertation," institutionally located in the Ministry of Labor, and without influence on definition of the public sector budget. In 2000, the strengthening of civil society became a transverse objective of public policy, including mainly NGOs, health care institutions, neighborhood organizations and centers linked to political parties. Application of this policy received financial and political support from the Inter-American Development Bank, taking the form of programs for the development of civil society and initiatives focusing on increasing civil society participation in public policies.

Fiscal support of private donations by way of tax exemptions and privileges has not been consistent with government priorities in poverty sectors, making fragmentary progress based on legislation on specific issues. The recent law on donations, designed to extend the range of privileges, systematizing and unifying previous legislation, was made subordinate to a law on donations for political purposes and has raised considerable criticism, allowing the expectation of prompt amendment.

Although it is too early yet to assess the policy aimed at strengthening citizen participation, it may be observed that the executive branch of the Chilean government is advancing in various sectors, in regards to incorporating citizen participation mechanisms, in the form of institutional commitments with political support from the president and embodied in a draft law. The latter shows continuity with the previous effort to modernize the civil service, where the main progress to date has been to increase available public information, simplify procedures, improve access to public utilities, all of it conceptualized as better customer/user service. Overall policy consistency is still to be seen, in terms of extension to civil society, institutionalized participation, impact on sectoral policies and concrete mechanisms for strengthening civil society and promoting philanthropy.

Conclusions

It is impossible to think of creating enabling environments for philanthropy and civil society without making reference to the severe structural limitations affecting both. In societies marked by severe inequality, as in Latin America in general and Chile in particular, the reproduction of socioeconomic gaps raises a particularly high barrier against social change. Another major challenge involves the social and cultural implications of the dominant, neo-liberal economic model, which deepens social fragmentation and weakens the bonds of solidarity among individuals, even where the model is successful as regards to promoting economic growth, as is the case in Chile. The functions of governmental coordination, together with the ability to ensure universal application of certain basic rights, are challenged by this context, which requires developing new approaches to public policy.

In Chile, as in much of the region, emphasis has been placed on the need to amend the legal and tax frameworks for philanthropy and civil society. Yet it is also possible to apply other instruments of public policy to the same end. Following substantial reduction of the state, activating and strengthening public policy may be seen as a prerequisite for necessary changes in legislation and taxation. These changes cannot be viewed solely as the means to stimulate philanthropy and civil society in general, because that could also contribute to reproducing inequalities. In Chile, for example, the promotion of private donations for education demonstrates that such a mechanism can be effective in terms of mobilizing resources, but can have contradictory effects from the standpoint of social equity and change. Something similar happens with the transfer of social programs to private hands by outsourcing, unless appropriate institutional frameworks are built for that purpose.

Chilean social policy shows interesting results with its ability to innovate in focused programs, increase available resources, and go from a palliative strategy to one of social investment. The effects of such activation of social policies, however, are cut short by excessive sector emphasis and dismemberment of the public sector itself, together with an excessively instrumental relationship with civil society. Promotion of philanthropy and civil society is a substantive objective that should form an integral part of policy, from design to implementation and assessment. It is important to establish stable and legitimized mechanisms for institutional participation, and to ensure policy continuity and assessment of results in this area. Public policy potential is not exhausted by developing programs or increasing available resources; the institutional framework in which it moves is also fundamental.

Policy initiatives can materialize the possibilities provided under the legal and tax framework. For example, in promoting capacity-building for labor by means of tax privileges, as well as through corporate association, the Chilean government has consistently unified both issues. However, it has not done so to promote civil society, which up to now has been viewed mainly as executing outsourced programs. The case of policies for children has developed in a positive fashion: the legal framework was reformed to make sure that the rights of children are guaranteed and consistent with international provisions, thus assuming non-transferable government responsibility. At the same time, policies were enacted to favor ongoing involvement of civil society organizations in actions included in that legal framework. Outsourcing functions in that area are backed by mechanisms that are insufficient but sustainable in regard to funding, while the non-governmental sector possesses national and international links favorable to such potential.

Legal reform may prove a fairly lengthy and difficult path to travel, given that well-consolidated or fundamental legal texts must be amended and favorable political consensus, to the extent that giving up power is involved, is not necessarily assured. The same applies to the tax framework, which faces reasonable opposition from those responsible for public finance, since extending tax privileges in Chile cannot involve fiscal waivers. The bill on donations was finally passed after considerable political pressure, and even then various civil society organizations considered the measure insufficient and poorly designed.

Utilization of active public policies can begin even before such legal reforms are implemented, and can serve to promote those same reforms. It is possible to induce reinterpretations of provisions and procedures, administrative amendments (as in the case of the Model Charter for NGOs), institutional amendments (new social policy institutions, the role of SEGEGOB), and introduce external elements (IDB loan). The potential of such changes will depend on their being inserted in a strategy that does not renounce more permanent institutional amendment.

An enabling environment is not composed only of a specific policy or program to "promote civil society," however important that may be. Consistency of the entire strategy of public policies is of the essence, because the ability of the government to influence the overall trends of society is at stake. In Chile, the constant budgetary expansion for sector policies (especially health care and education) multiplied links between civil society and government in areas of general interest. A "policy for strengthening civil society" must grant priority to these areas or risk losing importance. The various aspects of such a policy must be synchronized to build an enabling environment. A consistent policy would also have to influence the links between focused programs and poor groups excluded from society. A government concentrating resources in the social area and assigning them to poor sectors needs to "read" the implications of its actions in the forming of associations at the popular level, which does not depend solely on the "motivations" or the "political culture" of the poor. The same may be said about promoting private philanthropy in such issues. Until now the incentives have not been allocated to privilege the poor and excluded sectors. On the contrary, some of them have reinforced inequalities and resource concentration.

The present trend across the continent to outsource services and program execution with private actors is not sufficient to cause the advent of a philanthropy at the service of social change, and aiming to strengthen civil society. To avoid falling into social defenselessness and exclusion, outsourcing should be preceded by the establishment of legal frameworks based on ample consensus and effective systems for regulation and accountability. A particularly important area is strengthening the nonprofit sector that provides services, as part of civil society. The requirements of these organizations differ from those of private organizations or consulting firms active in the social area, and egalitarian treatment is favorable to the latter. A distinction must also be made between member-ship organizations (such as grassroots institutions) and organizations spe-cializing in providing professional services. In fact, the Chilean government has successfully applied its policies to develop other areas of economic and social activity, but the business sector has put bounds to such action, even in the social area. Strategies designed to promote corpo-rate association or subsidizing productive operations might be successfully applied to the nonprofit sector and civil society.

Among mechanisms intended to transfer resources for private execu-tion of programs, a distinction has to be made between programs that help reinforce and promote sustainability of civil organizations, and programs emphasizing competition among organizations to obtain better operating costs. In some areas, subsidies and allowances are supplemented with pri-vate funds, mobilized by solid and committed nonprofit institutions, expanding the area of services where they conduct activities. While bids and competition for projects also mobilize private funds, they are deficient in sustainability and seem to have a rather negative institutional effect on the profile of civil society organizations. The pioneering experience of Fondo de las Américas shows that certain forms of financing may be extended to mixed-management funds, but it has been cancelled. The area of co-determination of budgetary frameworks and transfers based on results has not been explored.

The present international framework that grants economic and social rights and sets out provisions for state compliance may prove to be a fac-tor in support of civil society, by establishing standards and mobilizing cooperation in the form of resources, together with ensuring more numer-ous and better mechanisms for civil society participation in social pro-grams and policies. International non-governmental networks also operate as a major pressure element *vis-à-vis* financing and political bod-ies, enhancing the capability for influence in sectors of civil society. Inno-vations in Chilean public policy regarding the environment and children, for example, are evidence of the foregoing.

The kind of effects that certain directions taken by public policy are having on philanthropy and civil society need to be examined more pro-foundly and in greater detail. Policy options adopted normally involve tradeoffs among actors and priorities. Research should be directed not so much to register or identify legislation, tax mechanisms, or programs and funds implemented, but to the specific implications that each one holds for civil society and philanthropy, an issue where evidence is still scant. The decentralizing trend currently in progress shows that initiatives should not be contemplated solely from the standpoint of central government, but should also include local and regional experience, together with the regulatory frameworks through which innovative changes are taking place in the link between the public institutional framework, philanthropy and civil society at local and regional level.

Notes

1 "Reducing the tremendous gap between rich and poor should be the major challenge of the next wave of philanthropy. But is this not a fundamental contradiction? Can those who most benefit from the unequal distribution of wealth and other resources really be expected to reverse that situation?" Cynthia Sanborn: "From Charity to Solidarity? Giving and Volunteering in the Americas," *ReVista, Harvard Review on Latin America,* Spring 2002, p. 7.

2 This choice leaves out two very important arguments that we lack space enough to develop here: one is that in fact philanthropy and civil society ought to guarantee pluralism in society and avoid being bound by he need for consensus (this is the "American" argument), the other contends that a struggle for political projects underlies such concepts, as Evelina Dagnino suggests in "On Confluence and Contradictions," Paper presented at LASA 2003, p. 4 ff. Let us just say that our view is not opposed to these arguments, but rather —without disregarding such situation—seeks to develop a possible base for a public policy in favor of such practices.

3 Here we adapt the criteria established for a "healthy civil society," defined as one capable simultaneously of acting autonomously, cooperating, opposing, and controlling the action of large-scale political, economic, and communicational powers. See: Robert O. Bothwell: "Indicators of a Healthy Civil Society," in . . . *Beyond the Price and the Market,* p. 251ff.

4 The Constitution of 1980 not only contains clearly authoritarian features and grants great power and autonomy to the Armed Forces, adopts a neo-Liberal economy, and restricts the role of the Executive and the Legislature, it also includes protection mechanisms that make it very difficult to reform. In fact, the three administrations of the Concertación de Partidos por la Democracia have not succeeded in doing so.

5 Whereas growth took place at an average of 6.3% absolute and 4.7% per capita between 1989 and 2000, employment rose by only 1.7% (0.8% from '94); productivity increased by 5.6% yearly, while real remunerations grew by only 3.6% on average. Official figures in: *Indicadores Económicos y Sociales,* at www.mideplan.cl.

6 In 1990, 38.6% of individuals received monthly incomes below the so-called "poverty line." In 2003, the figure was over 18%, still higher than it was thirty years earlier, in 1973, when it included 17% of Chileans, following two decades of economic stagnation.

7 Patricio Meller. "Pobreza y Distribución de Ingreso en Chile (Década de los Noventa), in P. Drake and I. Jaksic, eds., *El Modelo Chileno: Democracia y Desarrollo en los Noventa* (Santiago, 1999). Inequality of income distribution is held to be exceeded only by Brazil, in the continent.

8 This also seems to be strongly felt among the Chilean population; according to recent data, "Chileans make a distinction between these principles (equity and equality) and consider both essential. The former, because its absence affects and destroys individuals. The latter, because its absence affects and destroys the nation as a community." M. A. Garretón and G. Cumsille: "Las percepciones de la Desigualdad en Chile." *Proposiciones*, no. 34, Santiago de Chile, 2002, p. 75.

9 República de Chile, Informe Nacional de seguimiento de los compromisos asumidos en la Cumbre Mundial de Desarrollo Social. Copemhague 1995. Mimeo, Santiago de Chile, 2000.

10 According to the Heritage Foundation, among the 14 "freest" economies, government consumption in Chile is the lowest in percentage of GDP (8%), third in expenditure (24%) and fourth in weight of State-owned companies (2.94% of GDP) See: Genaro Arriagada: "Chile: el más pequeño estado entre las 'Economías Libres.'" In www.asuntospublicos.cl Informe no. 284. Enero 2003.

11 It should be recalled, in addition, that users are increasingly paying for part of public services: 50% in health, close to 40% in housing, and 10% in education, with a tendency to increase by way of shared financing. Claudio Sanhueza: "El Copago en las Políticas Sociales." Unpublished.

12 Citizen awareness is marked by mistrust and insecurity. a feeling of lack of power and control over one's own life, and fear. In the words of UNDP, other insecurities underlie the fear, "those provoked by the weakening of the social bond, the community feeling, finally the very notion of order." Public space is weakened because of a perception of "lack of recognition and representation of public institutions, precisely those responsible for creating the bonds that make for modern citizenship." UNDP: "Desarrollo Humano en Chile 1998. Las Paradojas de la Modernización." Santiago, 1998.

13 We have developed elsewhere an idea first suggested by Pedro Güell: "If dissociation persists between what determines me and I cannot control, and what I can control but is immaterial, the prospects of change are nullified. They depend on finding a time and a space where different links can be developed, and that means going beyond the neo-Liberal character associated with globalization, together with subordinate, unregulated insertion stimulated by structural adjustment policies. It means addressing the construction of alternatives." G. de la Maza: "Hacia la Globalización." In: R. Alvayay y J. Salinas, eds.: *Iniciativas Locales Ciudadanas hacia un Chile Democrático*. Santiago de Chile, 2003.

14 See in this connection M. A. Garretón: *La Sociedad que Vivi(re)mos*, Santiago de Chile, 2000, p. 143ff.

15 The largest increase between 1989 and 2000 took place in programs for priority groups (11.7% per annum), the amount of which came to equal the housing budget (which grew by only 3.9% per annum). Education increased by 9.3% per annum, and health by 8.1% per annum. www.mideplan.cl.

16 Alejandra Valdés: "Resumen del Diagnóstico. La Participación Social y Ciudadanía en Salud," Instituto de Asuntos Públicos Universidad de Chile. Informe Preliminar, octubre 2002. More information on the health care policy in G. de la Maza: "Más pero no Mejor. El problema de la calidad de vida." In: O. Muñoz and C. Stefoni, eds. *El Período del Presidente Frei Ruiz Tagle*, Santiago de Chile, 2003 pp. 299–332.

17 In 2003, a bill was under discussion by Congress on the full-length school day, to which regulations have been added for both disclosure of the use made of resources and requirements that private subsidized schools accept students "at social risk."

18 "In the course of 2002, a total of 69 universities and professional institutes received donations: 38% went to four private universities and INACAP, a professional institute owned by *Confederación de la Producción y el Comercio* (Production and Trade Confederation); the universities are Los Andes, owned by Opus Dei; del desarrollo, owned by a group of UDI (main right-wing political party inspired by Pinochet); Adolfo Ibáñez, owned by the Ibáñez Group; and Andrés Bello, belonging to the Saieh Group." Genaro Arriagada: "La actual crisis política." In: www.asuntospublicos.cl; Informe 286, enero 2003.

19 This fact increases segregation in cities. Also the inordinate and inorganic growth of intermediate towns and reproduction in rural areas of precarious urban development models (slums or poblaciones).

20 Such condominiums are thought to provide "housing solutions" rather than "problems," so that they are not included either in governmental or municipal policy, in spite of the fact that most of the "new social problems" to which the population attaches priority—insecurity, crime, drug traffic and abuse, juvenile unemployment, neighborhood conflicts, etc.—are generated there. One million persons are estimated to live under such conditions in Santiago alone. A good characterization of emerging sociability is given in the movie *El Chacotero Sentimental.* See also J.C. Skewer: "El Diseño Espacial de los Campamentos y su Desmantelamiento por las Políticas de Vivienda." In: *Proposiciones*, no. 34, Santiago de Chile, 2002. pp. 233–245.

21 Other current problems are the low amount of subsidy, the resistance of the section of the judiciary in charge of "juvenile justice," as well as the political resistance that the approach based on rights still arouses in the right-wing opposition. See, in this context, "Corporación OPCION," *Cambio de Mirada*, no. 1, Santiago de Chile, 1998.

22 Only a few business corporations have structured intermediary bodies for capacity-building of labor (OTIR), by collecting the funds from the tax privilege at the end of each year and keeping them from being wasted in terms of utilization.

23 In fact, this occurrence is considered "exceptional" and was obtained after intense lobbying directly in Congress, based on good positioning of the organizations concerned.

24 The proposal is in: Consejo Nacional para la Superación de la Pobreza, *La pobreza en Chile: un desafío de equidad e integración social*, Santiago de Chile, 1996, p. 232.

25 The Chilean Agency for International Cooperation was also in the purview of MIDEPLAN until it was transferred to the Ministry of Foreign Affairs.

26 In the late nineties the government announced the closing of MIDEPLAN, which has not so far taken place. Other institutions, i.e. the National Institute of Youth, the National Commission for Indigenous Development, and the Agency for International Cooperation, have also undergone severe internal crises.

27 The territorial approach to policies, which permits coordinating institutions and actors of various kinds on the same territory, is still very new in Chile, though it is making headway hand in hand with the process of decentralization and strengthening regional and local actors. It was tried by FOSIS in the late nineties, but discontinued to give priority to emergency employment programs. See. FOSIS: "Memoria de Aprendizaje," Santiago de Chile, 2000.

28 "Regarding funds open to competition for social projects and initiatives, emphasis is laid on supporting government work rather than funding civil society organizations . . . a new culture should be promoted to manage government funds and programs focusing on creating strategic alliances among public and private actors, to expand the coverage and improve the quality of the work done by civil society institutions." Consejo Ciudadano: "Informe Final," p. 32. Another author adds: "The central problem in Investment Funds is the unilateral way they relate to civil society organizations, focusing on project financing and neglecting other forms of mutually beneficial relationships . . . A broader concept should embrace functions of determination, production, and financing initiatives in association with social organizations." F. Salamanca; "Nuevas Formas de Co-provisión entre Estado y Sociedad Civil," In: *Proposiciones*, no. 34, Santiago de Chile, 2002, p. 273.

29 This is "reinforced by a style of public management based on creating and expanding spaces, e.g. the democratically elected *Consejo de Desarrollo Sustentable* (Council for Sustainable Development). Other interesting instances of citizen participation at directive level of public agencies have failed for political reasons, as in the case of the *Comisión Nacional de Desarrollo Indígena* and the Board of Directors of *Televisión Nacional*." Consejo Ciudadano: "Informe Final," p. 16.

30 Jaime Ruiz Tagle: "Desafíos del Sindicalismo Chileno frente a la Flexibilización del Mercado del Trabajo." In: *Revista de Economía y Trabajo*, no. 1, Santiago 1993. Elsewhere we show that union membership rose between 1988 and 1992, then fell steadily for the next decade. Also, unions are getting smaller, collective bargaining is less and less frequent, and union inactivity more extended. See: G. de la Maza, "Los Movimientos Sociales en la Democratización de Chile" In: P. Drake and I. Jaksic, *El Modelo Chileno*, Santiago de Chile, 1999.

31 For more information, see G. de la Maza, "Los Movimientos…," *op. cit.*

32 All Concertación administrations have resorted to setting up Councils and Commissions of a consultative nature, inviting their members in a personal (not institutional) capacity, and bringing together representations of widely different nature This fact has worked strongly against forming consensus among the members of such commissions.

33 See ACCION, "Preocupaciones inmediatas de los ONG en su relación con el Estado." In: *Cooperación al Desarrollo* no. 12, Santiago de Chile, 1994.

34 See the contents of the presidential decree creating the Council, in: CNSP, *op. cit.*, p. 7.

35 The CSNP stopped operating as such, its Technical Committee was inactivated together with a considerable number of its regional affiliates. Given the new circumstances, Fundación Nacional para la Superación de la Pobreza (FNSP) was founded and is still in existence, managing some programs with public funding. More details in D. Raczynski and C. Serrano: "Viejos Nuevos Problemas en la Lucha contra la Pobreza en Chile." In: O. Muñoz and C. Stefoni, *op. cit.* p. 355ff.

36 MIDEPLAN, "Bases de una Política de Estado para el Tercer Sector." Santiago de Chile, 1998.

37 This initiative has brought face to face the more "restricted" view of development of civil society organizations and the "broader" view of redesigning public policies and links between government and civil society. The proposal by the Mixed Financing Fund and the comments of civil organizations, at www.participacionciudadana.cl.

38 SECPRES, *Proyecto de Reforma y Modernización del Estado, Propuesta de Ley de Bases de Participación Ciudadana en la Gestión Pública*, Santiago de Chile, January 2002, p. 5. In: www.participacionciudadana.cl.

14

Self Regulation and the Legitimacy of Civil Society: Ideas for Action

Rodrigo Villar

"And who supervises the NGOs?" queried a Colombian daily.[1] Soon thereafter, Colombia's most widely circulated weekly newsmagazine entitled one of its main articles, "NGOs: heroes or villains?"[2] These headlines reflect an intensification of public scrutiny of the activities of civil society organizations (CSOs)—including private foundations, professional NGOs and grassroots organizations—that is developing throughout Latin America. With this scrutiny, the uncritical acceptance of the virtues of CSOs could be a thing of the past. The wide variety of contributions made by donors and civil society activists toward the resolution of increasing problems of poverty, social exclusion and environmental destruction, continues to be acknowledged. However, as these organizations grow in number, visibility and influence in the public arena, their role and legitimacy are being examined more closely and realistically. The sector is increasingly asked to render an account of its results, political responsibility and public transparency. This current demand for "accountability" poses a great challenge for CSOs, but it can also be a great opportunity to redefine the future and identity of the sector and to expand its legitimacy.

The development of self-regulation mechanisms and the promotion of more transparent and accountable CSOs could contribute to strengthening their legitimacy. This, in turn, would create a more favorable operating environment, increasing support for these organizations. Several influential voices have begun to express themselves on this issue. For example, in January 2005 Alberto Nuñez, Vice-chairman of the Employers' Confederation of the Mexican Republic (Coparmex), addressed an open letter to President Vicente Fox in the Coparmex magazine, proposing that he "believe and support, with true political will, the serious and representative institutions of civil society," adding ". . . however, demanding transparency and a rendering of accounts, not only in economic terms, but far beyond, in their governing bodies, their code of ethics and values and, most importantly, in the measurement of their achievements in the use of the resources provided to fulfill a mission" (Nuñez, A. 2003).

In keeping with this trend of promoting transparency and public responsibility, Ford Foundation President Susan Beresford made an important call to establish ethical and professional standards in the field of philanthropy. At the first meeting of associations of Latin American foundations in November 2002 in São Paulo, she emphasized that the sector itself should carry out this task, rather than have it externally imposed by state regulation. "If the people of our profession do nothing to establish ethical practices, state regulators outside this profession will do it for us, and they may impose more standards and a greater rigidity than we need or wish for" (2002: 3).

Existing public trust toward CSOs cannot be assumed; and the option of greater state regulation of CSOs if trust declines is far from automatic. However, as stated previously, the development of collective mechanisms for self-regulation may play a key role in creating an enabling environment for these organizations, in which legitimacy and public trust will prevail and which will, at the same time, contribute toward limiting excessive state regulation.

Certain umbrella associations and some networks in Latin America have been developing such mechanisms for self-regulation. However, the systemized and shared knowledge of this topic in the region is limited, and self-regulation strategies have not yet been evaluated to see how they expand legitimacy and generate public trust. There is a lack of mapping of the type of mechanisms used in self-regulation and about collective processes for their development. If the demands for accountability of CSOs keep growing over the next few years, public education on self-regulation should be included in a future work agenda, since it is one of the principle mechanisms dealing with this phenomenon of greater accountability. In this case, both collective education among umbrella associations in developing these mechanisms and dialogue between associations and researchers involved in this issue will help to convert the demand for accountability into a strategic opportunity to make progress in the development of this sector's legitimacy and identity.

This chapter seeks to discuss the relationship between legitimacy, accountability and self-regulation, illustrating through examples the progress made on these topics in Latin America, and proposing ideas for a social education and research agenda on these topics. These are some initial thoughts and questions that identify the issues that must be studied in-depth in the future. If we agree that legitimacy, accountability and self-regulation are the main challenge for CSOs, we must seek operative solutions.

The chapter first puts forth a few hypotheses on possible reasons for the demand for accountability. It then explores issues of legitimacy and accountability for CSOs, and continues with a section dedicated to analyzing the possibilities and limitations of state regulation and of self-regulation in terms of such accountability. A fourth section illustrates the progress made by the region's umbrella organizations in establishing an ethical objective and collective self-regulation mechanisms. The importance of social education is also analyzed as a requirement for achieving any progress in self-regulation processes. A final section emphasizes the need for "downward accountability" and the role that donors might play promoting this. The chapter concludes with ideas for a future agenda on the topic.[3]

Why the Increased Scrutiny of CSOs?

The growing scrutiny of CSOs in Latin America seems to have different origins. The investigation of the reasons for such scrutiny could help us to understand who is asking for accountability, the type of demands being made, and why these demands have arisen. The inquiry into the reasons for the scrutiny can also help provide information about the type of answers that CSOs themselves are developing in response to these demands. Nonetheless, little investigation on this topic has been carried out regionally beyond the pioneer article of Oliveira's (1999). While this chapter speculates somewhat about the future, it also poses some hypotheses on why this demand for accountability is growing.

First, doubts about what Adil Najam calls the "myth of infallibility" of the CSO (Najam, A. 1996: 339–340) have demonstrated that values such as democracy, equity, inclusion, participation and interest in public issues are not inherent to the sector's organizations. He also shows that the virtues frequently attached to its organizations—such as working with the poor, being flexible and innovative and producing social capital—cannot be generalized, even though they are present in a considerable number of these organizations. This has led to a more realistic analysis of the sector and more critical examination of its potentials.

For example, the last World Bank report on poverty emphasizes this idea of not generalizing about CSOs. After showing the potential of these organizations to develop anti-poverty programs and to mobilize poor communities, the report issues a word of warning: "Sometimes, NGOs reflect the political system in which they prosper, or the local groups of interest, and in this regard they may not serve the interests of the poor as well as they should. NGOs are not a panacea and it is important that they become responsible for their actions, particularly with the poor groups which they allege to represent" (World Bank 2001: 111).

Second, CSOs have assumed new roles in venues for political dialogue, often projected as vehicles for democratization. However, questions about these organizations' "representativity" and their ability to speak on behalf of others is increasingly subject to further debate both by the detractors of the organizations and some of the alleged represented parties.

The 1990s were a period in which the growth, visibility and public presence of CSOs in Latin America grew significantly (Toro, O.L. and Vila Moret, E. 2000). In some cases, this presence challenged or queried existing power structures. Therefore, some sectors have used as a weapon the strategy of discrediting some CSOs by calling them "non-representative" and demanding accountability.

This is the case of human rights organizations in Colombia, and led thirty of them to began the campaign "We live to defend life" in late 2004. The campaign seeks to defend the work of human rights organizations and counteract public accusations deprecating the task of the human rights defenders in the country (*El Espectador*, 2002). Funding sources and the alliances with sector organizations are changing. At present, governments, international banking institutions and private industry provide greater support. Each of these sources entails new demands for sector accountability.

Finally, cases of corruption, scandals, failures and bankruptcy existing in the sector's organizations are often quite visible, a fact that deteriorates public trust and increases the demands for accountability.

If such hypotheses are true, the sources of demand for accountability and reasons for criticizing CSOs would be many and often contradictory. In order to deal with these varied demands, a deeper understanding is needed of the complexity of CSOs' target audiences and priorities in establishing accountability. This chapter offers some elements that may contribute toward navigating in the midst of this complexity.

Legitimacy and Accountability: Diverse Audiences and Sources

CSOs' legitimacy and the confidence they arouse in the public are these organizations' greatest assets and an essential resource for their survival. This legitimacy is closely related to the issue of accountability, if we understand "accountability" as making individuals or organizations responsible before others, for the fulfillment of their promises and actions (Brown, D. and Fox, J. 1998: 439, and Brown 2005, this volume).

The relational character of accountability implies that organizations become responsible for their actions before certain groups and audiences. This relation is not static but, on the contrary, implies permanent action to generate trust, legitimacy and support toward the organization, derived from the credibility and effectiveness of its actions. In addition to being a transparent information process, accountability may be understood as a key strategy in building the identity and legitimacy of CSOs, as well as a constant public clarification of their promises and continued search for public support.

In the case of CSOs, which are mainly guided by voluntarily selected social missions or actions, the criterion of responsibility is derived from such actions. These organizations' legitimacy is obtained by "explaining and accepting the responsibility for developing the assigned mission according to the agreed expectations."[4]

However, the question as to whom CSOs should give an account of what they do to obtain further legitimacy, is a rather complex and critical one when deciding the strategies of any organization in this sector. This is especially true if one takes into account the variety of stakeholders in these organizations and the difficulties of assessing the public value created by their programs (Moore, M. 2002: 3).

CSOs may render account to their boards, founders, employees, members, donors, funding agencies, governments, beneficiaries, allies or to the public in general, but each of these audiences require different levels of responsibility, just as the CSO has a particular interest with each of the audiences to maintain or expand legitimacy. Given that these audiences do not always coincide in the demands, CSOs must make strategic decisions about who has priority among the audiences. The tension is even greater if consideration is given to the weight of third parties in CSO financing.

Unlike the case of private companies, which derive their financial support and social legitimacy from the buyers and direct beneficiaries of their products, CSOs receive an important portion of their resources and support from third parties. Such third parties may be individual donors, corporate donors, national and international foundations, volunteers or governments that transfer these resources trusting in their social return. But in addition, as Mark Moore points out (2002), legitimacy and support are not only obtained from material contributors. Government agencies that provide legal status or public records offices, tax authorities that supervise the use of tax exemptions, auditors, accrediting organizations, peers, the media and, of course, those who benefit from the activities of these organizations are also essential in creating a favorable environment of trust toward the CSO. This group of authorities needs more than just a "flow of resources," but also the support and "flow of good will or enthusiasm for the CSO" (Moore, M. 2002: 15). "The greater the legitimacy of an organization in the eyes of the world, the better its probabilities of obtaining resources, attracting volunteers and enjoying the deference and trust to relatively operate in the world. It is important to take into account that the sources of legitimacy and support are all the stakeholders and not only the beneficiaries or the donors" (Ibid: 13). As we will see in the last section of this chapter, third parties—particularly philanthropic donors—can play a catalytic role in promoting accountability. This extends beyond accountability to the third parties to those that CSOs are supposed to serve.

Different sources of legitimacy of CSOs

In addition to the different audiences, the CSOs have several sources of legitimacy. David Brown, in recent work carried out with a group of researchers and social activists interested in this subject, proposed four categories (Brown, D. et al. 2001: 64–65), as follows:

- *Moral legitimacy:* Based on moral values that may have sufficient acceptance and strength to legitimize the action of the CSOs.

- *Technical legitimacy:* Derived from the knowledge, experience, competence or information of the organizations involved in the task of incidence.

- *Political legitimacy:* Derived from the democratic representativity, the transparency and the process of rendering accounts to the "grassroots communities" or to the constituents on behalf of whom they speak and act. This type of legitimacy involves the decision-making process, the form and manner in which the members of the organizations participate in the articulation and follow-up of activities.

- *Legal legitimacy:* Based on meeting the legal standards and expectations, both internal (existence of responsible boards of directors, reports to the public, transparent handling of accounts), and external, based on complying with the law or the policies established by those institutions based on which incidence processes are articulated.

The work of Brown and his colleagues is particularly interesting because it not only acknowledges the existence of different sources of legitimacy but—like the different audiences and groups interested in the process— makes several demands in relation to the sources of legitimacy and the use of different standards to assess the legitimacy of an organization (Brown, D. et al. 2001: 72). This diversity of demands could be a source of conflict for CSOs and requires that they develop strategies to meet the different demands or prioritize the sources and groups with which they wish to build their legitimacy (Brown, D. 2002: 72–74).

Functions of the CSO and the sources of legitimacy

Sector organizations serve various functions, which influence their type of management structure, the sources they may use to obtain legitimacy and the accountability criteria that may be used. When CSOs render services and work toward the population's welfare, technical and professional criteria are essential in the type of responsibility the organization assumes toward its beneficiaries. However, if the organizations work with groups to jointly establish strategies for social mobilization, influence public policies or promote transformations in public awareness or in institutional coalitions, the technical-professional criterion is insufficient; political and moral legitimacy must also exist to channel the responsibility of the organization (Brown, D. and Moore, M. 2000: 12).

A CSO that provides services can, in certain cases, keep the beneficiaries outside the organization and become responsible before them, basically for the quality of the services it renders and for the efficiency of its programs. However, a CSO that works and receives funds on behalf of certain groups, aims to represent them or influence policies in their name, needs to expand its governing and accountability structure before such groups. In these cases, it is important for the organization to somehow involve the grassroots community with which it works in the decision-making process, rather than treating them solely as clients or beneficiaries outside the organization. Organizations that work with grassroots communities and not with clients must prioritize mechanisms such as consultation, exchange of information, direct participation in the formal decision-making process, assembly and negotiation for the development of shared agendas or concerted program agreements (Brown, D. and Moore, M. 2000: 13–14). CSOs that intend to exercise an influence on public policies do not necessarily have to be associations controlled by its members to be legitimate, but they do have to be responsible for what they do before whom they allege to represent in order to guarantee their legitimacy (Edwards, M. and Hulme, D. 1996: 14). We will take a further look at this subject later.

Accountability: Between State Regulation and Self-Regulation

As we have observed, the subject of public responsibility and CSO legitimacy is a complex issue since it involves different audiences and different forms of responsibility, according to the different sector functions and different means for accountability. In view of the increase in the demand for "accountability" from the CSO, the challenge is to develop mechanisms in response to this demand. Such mechanisms can range from adequate state regulation by the state to the development of self-regulation mechanisms in each organization, subgroups of organizations or in the sector in general. Each of the mechanisms can contribute to develop specific aspects of public responsibility but none of them can individually assume the number of new challenges.

State regulation, for example, may contribute to the development of legal and bureaucratic "accountability" or conformity of the organizations to the existing laws and procedures. For example, if the law obliges each organization to submit an annual public report with information on its social mission, programs, sources and use of the funds, this could contribute to the transparency of the sector. Governmental demand for this type of publicity can be based on the CSO's use of public funds received directly from the government (transfers, subsidies and governmental contracts) and the public (donations from citizens and companies), as well as indirect public funds obtained from tax incentives on donations, from nonprofit organizations and from relevant government tax waivers. The advantage of state regulation, in terms of publicity, is to make these procedures inclusive to all the organizations of the sector as a whole. Their true scope will depend on the ability of the state to enforce such criterion of public information and of the demand of the population for its fulfillment.

It is of great interest to analyze the potential of legislation in Brazil to promote greater "legal accountability" for the Organizations of Civil Society of Public Interest (OCSPI) to expand CSO legitimacy. After extensive consultations among CSOs and deliberations among governmental officials and representatives of civil society,[5] new legislation was proposed to include the OCSPI. The law enacted as a result of this process (Law 9790 of March 23, 1999) establishes provisions concerning the conditions for organizations to voluntarily propose themselves and qualify as a member of the OCSPI. It also imposes mechanisms for social control and public responsibility in the handling of public funds and creates a new instrument that facilitates cooperation and the transfer of funds in the alliances between the government and the OCSPI, the "termo de parcería" (Szazi, E. 2003, and this volume).

In order to avoid excessive state regulation and to promote mechanisms guaranteeing these organizations' transparency and public responsibility, several civil society representatives of those who participated in the deliberations about the new legislation proposed that priority be given to the control by the citizenry over the OCSPI instead of control by the state. They therefore proposed the chosen mechanisms of tax advice, independent audits and a novel citizens' watchdog power. This 1999 law establishes that any Brazilian citizen, whether (s)he is a beneficiary of or contributor to the organization, can request financial and program information from any OCSPI. In the event of the existence of substantiated evidence of fraud or embezzlement, citizens may request authorities to carry out the pertinent investigation (Szazi, E. 2003 and this volume).

While this legal course can contribute to develop the legitimacy of the CSOs in terms of their dynamics, other considerations such as democratic political responsibility (answering to grassroots organizations and the use of participation mechanisms), moral responsibility (the development of standards, code of ethics), as well as technical professional responsibility (mechanisms for accreditation, assessments of performance and the results), can be further developed through self-regulation, in which "the rules are drawn-up, managed and enforced by the same persons whose behavior must be regulated" (Oliveira, A.C. 1998: 3). The potential of self-regulation, in terms of generating trust, legitimacy and public support, is enormous. Its limitations are determined by the number of organizations that actually obey the rules they create. The second- and third-level umbrella organizations, the networks, the forums of organizations, the spaces for encounters, etc. may play a key role in establishing these rules for its associates as a whole, in the form of valuation horizons, code of ethics, standards and coalitions for the development of coordinated programs.

In building public legitimacy and an enabling environment for CSOs, the development of self-regulation mechanisms can become an essential tool to generate public trust and counteract the pressures of excessive state intervention in CSO regulation. The greater the trust of the public in CSO governance systems and in their self-regulation mechanisms—in addition to CSO capacity to seriously deal with social problems—the less the pressure for government regulation. According to Oliveira, "The CSOs are interested in securing the confidence of society in general, obtaining a positive and responsible image, showing themselves as active upholders of democratic values, sensitive to the target public and based on this, to prove that it is unnecessary for the State to excessively regulate the performance of our organizations"(1999: 3).

Umbrella Organizations and Collective Processes

Self-regulation strategies can be developed at different levels, ranging from those adopted by individual organizations in their bylaws and the strengthening boards of directors to assume greater responsibility to those collective actions in which the networks of associations representing CSO subgroups adopt resolutions among their members on standards, code of ethics, rules of conduct and other shared standards to regulate the collective conduct of the members.

In a period like today's, in which competition for funds among sector organizations is growing and organizational survival often trumps its social mission, it is important to think beyond the limits of individual organizations and create joint structures and networks, as well as to strengthen the capacity of the organizations to articulately face the acute problems of poverty, equity, democracy, exclusion and not just to survive in the competitive world of the "social enterprises."

However, given the diversity of segments or subgroups of CSOs represented by associations, federations or confederations of related CSOs (NGOs, foundations, neighbor councils, cooperatives, etc.) or divided into subjects (early childhood, environment, grassroots development, etc.), and the lack of organizations that represent the sector as a whole, Oliveira is right when she says that "the self-regulation of the sector cannot only be conceived as a phenomenon that will multiply due to the variety of segments and groups of entities gathered under the respective umbrellas" (1999: 11). The "umbrella" organizations can act as a catalyst in the building of civic values and shared rules among their members and in the establishment of standards of collective responsibility for their fulfillment.

In Latin America, the subject of self-regulation is being introduced with increasing force by different umbrella organizations and CSO networks such as national associations of NGOs,[6] national associations of foundations and donors,[7] national organizations for the promotion of social entrepreneurial responsibility,[8] or regional networks.[9] These associations and networks are playing an important role in coordinating actions, representing subgroups of third-sector organizations and promoting concerted self-regulation processes. Systematic study of their progress would be of great value not only for each one of them, but also for other CSO associations that aim to incorporate these issues in their agendas. We describe some of their progress below in order to demonstrate the importance of the issues that are being raised and the importance of more systematic investigation in the future.

Building common agendas and the clarification of the promise

The visions of CSOs are historical-political products and are not derived a priori from their structure and operating method (being an NGO, non-profit organization or CSO). What can be expected from these organizations as a whole depends on the concerted action processes that will enable them to channel their activities under common or shared agendas and the capacity to carry out what they agree to do. The building of common identities and consequently of the shared promises that are the basis for future accountability is an essential task of the umbrella associations and the networks. "Both associations and networks are necessarily political beings," as we are reminded by the director of Brazil's Group of Institutes, Foundations and Companies (GIFE) in her article on the role of the associations of foundations. "We cannot become integrators, supporters of social transformations, ahead in our reflections, promoters and shapers, without assuming a political stance. . . . It is politics in the sense that it is not neutral, that it is strategic and defends a course of action: that of social transformation based on the belief in a fairer society" (Raposo, R. 2003: 25).

Based on these shared standards, these organizations of organizations may become catalysts for collective coordinated action and self-regulation by developing standards for their members, accreditation mechanisms and codes of ethics.

A good example of this process for negotiating expectations and ideas is the process initiated by the Colombian Confederation of NGOs in the year 2000, the result of which is the "Programmatic Agreement for Peace." The Confederation is a fourth-level organization that gathers 12 regional federations, 8 networks and 10 national associations of NGOs, grouping together more than 1,000 NGOs with a wide variety of topics and ideologies. The program agreement was a common political instrument among the different organizations, built collectively by the members of the Confederation and voluntarily assumed by its organizations. It is an agreement for "civil society organizations to channel their objectives outwards (in society) and not inwards, not to fragment but to articulate society," to "provide answers to politicians, military servicemen, businessmen and government officials about the NGOs," and to show "the political stance of the CCONG and its confederates, how they conceive democracy, the organization, institutions, human rights, their duties within the network, the building of public interest, productivity, national and international alliances, etc." (CCONG, 2002: 5–6).

This "Program Agreement for Peace" proposes that a central role be played by the NGOs in the building of a social government of laws set forth in the Constitution of 1991 and places human rights as the ethical goal of the actions of the NGOs. Based on these guidelines, NGOs can build their identity within the context of the CSOs, to project themselves as social actors to the population, to establish relationship guidelines with the government, private enterprise and funding agencies and to maintain their autonomy and identity while developing actions within a context of collaboration between sectors. It is also an agreement that sets the bases to establish the political responsibility assumed by the members of the Confederation and the criteria for the accountability of its organizations.

Examples such as that of the Colombian Confederation of NGOs show us ways in which to establish a collective identity and a sociopolitical orientation of an important subgroup of the Third Sector, as well as to establish the bases for what we could call "strategic accountability." The latter refers to CSOs' more general impact and their overall contribution to social change and to the solution of complex societal problems. This last type of responsibility does not belong to the organizations individually but to the group of actors and organization networks that decide to act collectively to produce sustainable social changes (Edwards, M. and Hulme, D. 1996: 8–11).

One further step in creating the conditions for strategic accountability is currently being worked on by RedEAmérica, a thematic network of 53 corporate foundations and corporations operating in twelve countries in the Americas. In a similar fashion to the Colombian Confederation, RedEAmérica established its collective vision of what it means to fund and support grassroots development in a series of documents shared by the members of the network.[10] Within this framework, RedEAmérica is now working on developing a set of evaluation indicators for measuring the strategic goals they seek to achieve in promoting grassroots development: developing collective capacities at level of grassroots organizations, promoting social capital, alleviating poverty and strengthening democracy.[11] Those indicators would be the standards for evaluating whether the members of RedEAmérica are delivering the promises they set for themselves.

Umbrella organizations and codes of ethics
Another mechanism used by some of the "umbrella" associations is the code of ethics. The case of GIFE is very interesting since it represents the dilemmas faced and the importance of developing clear concepts to achieve an "ethical" philanthropy, particularly within a context such as that in which GIFE was created, in which justified suspicions existed about the

value and nature of its philanthropy. In the aforementioned document on associations of foundations, GIFE's director explains that in the case of this organization, "it was no coincidence that the first official decision of GIFE was to approve a code of ethics," since this association originated within a context in the history of Brazil, in which the complaints of corruption against President Collor de Mello were widespread, and involved several philanthropic organizations (Raposo, R. 2003: 4–5).

To prove that it was possible to provide an "ethical philanthropy" and channel private resources in benefit of the public required a code of conduct that would clearly explain that the association members would "give priority to public interest over private interest" (Raposo, R. 2003: 6). Consequently, the ethics code spelled out GIFE members' commitments to the principles that guide associates in their interactions with their supporters or donors, with their beneficiaries and allies, with similar entities, with public power and how professionals who belonged to GIFE should conduct themselves (GIFE. Code of Conduct: 1–2).

Seeking to emphasize public issues, private resources for social investment in public issues (philanthropy) were distinguished from those private resources for social investment in which private interests prevail, such as the many resources used in social entrepreneurial responsibility programs (Raposo, R. 2003: 24). The code establishes that: "Social investment practices have a different nature and must not be confused or used as a tool to market tangible and intangible goods (profit making), by the financing company, such as for example, marketing, sales promotion or sponsorship. . ." (GIFE, Code of ethics: 1).

In this regard, GIFE is making an important ethical distinction with many implications, in terms of emphasizing benefits for the communities and public welfare over the benefits of the donors and companies, when they use their resources for social investment.

The Brazilian Association of NGOs (ABONG) and the Colombian Confederation of NGOs (CCONG) have each recently developed their declaration of principles. The former published its statement in 2000, while the latter approved its declaration in a 1998 meeting. In the case of the CCONG, each of its members signed his or her acceptance of this declaration, which establishes organizations' duties toward society, confederated NGOs, other NGOs, CSOs, the State and international cooperation (CCONG 1998). In addition to the program principles that guide the actions of the association, the declaration of the ABONG establishes guidelines for relationships with the State, international cooperation, other NGOs, etc. (ABONG 2000). Both declarations explicitly mention commitment to transparency, prevalence of public interest over private interest and commitment to efficient management of their resources.

However, neither declaration establishes sanctioning mechanisms in the event of noncompliance nor strategies to settle any conflicts of interest nor reporting procedures in case of the violation of any of the principles adopted by their members. According to Anna Cynthia Oliveira, it seems that these codes of conduct and the declaration of principles continue to be, in terms of self-regulation strategies, "shy, localized and under-disseminated measures. The codes are an internal issue of these networks, that have no echo in society and are ignored by the State"(1999: 3–4).

CSOs and the Promotion of Self-regulation in Other Sectors

It is interesting and somewhat paradoxical that in Latin America, CSOs have made more progress in promoting mechanisms to make others responsible for their actions (particularly governments) and in promoting the self-regulation of other sectors (particularly companies) than in promoting self-regulation of the nonprofit sector itself. A wide variety of associations and social control strategies work to keep the state "accountable," a theme we will not delve into at this point.[12] However, company promotion of standards and criteria for self-assessment is a more recent phenomenon; we would like to mention some paradigmatic models such as the Ethos Institute and the Abrinq Foundation in Brazil and the Mexican Center for Philanthropy (CEMEFI).

A pioneer example in Latin America of entrepreneurial self-regulation undertaken by a CSO is that of the Abrinq Foundation for Children and Adolescent Rights. In 1995, this Foundation began its Children's Friend Company Program, mobilizing more than 2,000 companies and sponsoring ten agreements among producers' groups. Through this program, the Abrinq Foundation promoted commitments by companies for the eradication of child labor and support to children's programs (Abrinq Foundation, 2003a). Each company involved signs an agreement in which it agrees not to employ children, not to enter into contracts with suppliers that use child labor, to support the children of employees to attend school, to invest in children's social programs and to donate an equivalent of 1% of the Income Tax to the Children and Adolescents Rights Fund. This process is accredited by the Abrinq Foundation and renewed annually, once the commitments assumed by the company are verified, either directly or through an auditor. Once accreditation has been obtained, the company may use the Abrinq seal "Children's Friend Company Program" (Abrinq Foundation 2003b).

The ETHOS Institute has developed a strategy to produce social responsibility standards by providing companies with a backup service in the assessment and planning of social responsibility strategies. It thus uses a tool called the Ethos Indicators of Social Responsibility, with quantitative and qualitative indicators in the areas of values and transparency, including relationships with the company's internal public, with the environment, the suppliers, the consumers, the community and the government and society. Company-generated information is analyzed by the Ethos Institute, which carries out a comparative diagnosis with leading companies in the area of social responsibility, offering recommendations to each company for strengthening its weak areas (Ethos Institute 2001). Unlike the Abrinq Foundation, the Ethos Institute does not certify companies nor grant them distinctions of any kind. Its role is to create standards and to support companies to achieve them.

In 2001, CEMEFI began awarding its Distinction of Social Responsibility to those companies that meet minimum standards in the categories of corporate ethics, company care and preservation, quality of life in the company and involvement of the company with the community. CEMEFI decides the awards—initially based on each company's self-assessment of the company in the four mentioned areas, using the indicators provided by CEMEFI. Then, CEMEFI reviews and verifies the information with those responsible for the areas in each company. Based on this information, CEMEFI awards the Emblem/Distinction to the selected companies in a public ceremony. The recipients may used the Distinction in their publicity and printed material throughout its valid period. The companies may be awarded the Emblem/Distinction once again by following the same process every year (CEMEFI, 2003).

Certification and promotion of standards by CSOs in the business sector have led to the development of mechanisms, procedures and significant results that could produce good skills to develop self-regulation strategies for CSOs themselves.

Self-regulation and the collective learning process

The development of rules and standards for self-regulation, as Anna Cynthia Oliveira points out, constitutes a "political and learning process that is not achieved in the short-term" in which "guidelines must be launched, small and large workshops to discuss them must be implemented, different means of consultation used, joint design and preparation workshops promoted, until the consolidation of a body of rules and standards—which upon approval by the vote of the affiliates in the assembly and having met all the statutory formalities, may thereafter become a true obligatory code for all members" (1999: 12–13).

In developing collective self-regulating mechanisms, the social learning process and co-production of rules, standards and mechanisms are as important as the outcome, given that each of the members of the participating organizations needs to conform to these norms, which carry significant weight in the adoption of institutional decisions. Members of umbrella organizations are required to participate in the process and adopt it, "make it their own." Moreover, the process serves to inform the public interested in CSOs to understand the self-regulation mechanisms and learn to use them. A document drawn up by the organization representing the U.S. nonprofit sector points out, "Our experience confirms that the establishment of ethical standards begins by a commitment to a process, which is more important than any code or standard. The adoption of ethical standards of behavior requires the inclusion of all the individuals and entities affected by the work of the organization" (Independent Sector, 2002: 8).

The previously mentioned examples of CCONG and GIFE, as well as the preparation of a new law for OCSPI codes of conduct in Brazil, evolved from highly participatory processes among their members. Likewise, dissemination and public education campaigns were key in promoting accreditation standards and mechanisms among the different companies. In both types of strategies, the incorporation of behavioral rules, regulations and standards implies the need for social education. At the same time, such social learning requires participation processes, as well as educational and communication processes to produce meaningful institutional and cultural changes.

Together with these social learning processes, it is also important to establish and disseminate supervisory mechanisms and sanctions for breach of the standards proposed in the self-regulation processes. "The adopted standards will be of no value without the corresponding supervisory mechanisms. And these mechanisms can be understood at two levels: monitoring exercised by the association of CSOs itself and that which may be exercised by the target-population and society in general, linking the advertising of such standards to the dissemination of reports by each affiliate" (Oliveira, 1999: 13). Annual renewal and the use of auditors/supervisors in the accreditation programs of the Abrinq Foundation and CEMEFI are good examples of the initially proposed monitoring mechanisms. In addition, Brazilian legislation on OCSPI (mentioned above) provides a good example of the type of monitoring that both the public and beneficiaries may exercise. The frequent absence of institutional channels or power of these two groups to be informed and demand accountability from CSOs constitutes a central point that must be debated and developed in a work plan on CSO legitimacy and "accountability." This subject will be developed in the following section, emphasizing the importance of "downward accountability."

The Importance of "Downward Accountability"

Since CSOs pursue objectives of public interest and receive funds and support on behalf of third parties, the public and the end-beneficiaries of CSO activities should receive privileged treatment in the accountability process, allowing them opportunities to exercise influence over the projects and programs with which they will be involved (Oliveira, A.C. 1999: 5).

In practice, however, the issue of transparency and to whom accounts should be rendered does not solely depend on a moral obligation, but also on a relationship of power. Relations with CSOs demonstrate great asymmetry in the capacity of different audiences to enforce standards. This asymmetry partially stems from the fact that CSOs generally obtain funding from sources other than their beneficiaries, as discussed in the introductory section of this chapter. Grassroots organizations and direct or indirect beneficiaries of the CSOs, as well as the general public, often have less enforcement power and less capacity to demand accountability from organizations than CSO donors and contractors. Some organizations have counteracted this asymmetry of "upward accountability" with an explicit strategy to empower these groups with the aim of empowering them to meet their demands ("downward accountability"), thus directly responding to the weakest links in the chain. Nonetheless, on many other occasions, the claims of groups who should be answered are ignored, since these groups often lack sufficient power and mechanisms to take advantage of accountability (Brown, D. and Moore, M. 2000: 8).

Nowadays, as several Latin American governments, the international banking system and companies begin to incorporate CSOs into their agendas, tensions concerning demands for accountability shall most surely surface in CSO decision-making. When these tensions emerge, it will be paramount not to sacrifice the civic roots and the responsibility toward the grassroots organizations (downward accountability) to obtain funds from governments, financing institutions and private firms (upward accountability).

Inequity within the third sector and the challenge of democratization

The previously mentioned asymmetry in accountability is not only related to differences in power between the actors outside the sector (government, international agencies, private companies) but also to the inequity in the voice and capacity of organizations within the sector. The voice, participation and capacity of organizations are not equally distributed within society or among sector organizations. Acknowledging this asymmetry implies proposing the sector's democratization as a challenge, taking into account that imbalance in social participation may have a negative impact on democracy and social development (Verba, Sidney; Schlozman, Kay Lehman and Brady, Henry, E. 1999).

A current phenomenon that makes this asymmetry even more complex is the assumption on the part of the government, the international donor community and even a number of organizations within the sector itself that organizations providing services and the most professional of organizations are the ones that can best serve the poorest and "represent" their causes adequately. Grassroots organizations of the most underprivileged, those that seek their social mobilization and promote collective efforts, as well as organizations fomenting political dialogue carry less weight in the current agenda. In some circles, there is more talk about clients than about social bases, more about providing services than about promoting citizenry, more about meeting needs than about guaranteeing rights, more about implementing projects than about boosting social reforms, more about strengthening organizations than about promoting movements in relation to relevant social problems (Fowler, A. 2000: 643).

Direct provision of services to the most underprivileged sectors has its importance, but the support provided to organization and the mobilization of these sectors, as well as the strengthening of the voice of the excluded individuals themselves and of their ability to influence the public agenda, is essential from a perspective of democracy and social change. It is important to supplement the work carried out on behalf of the underprivileged with the work with the underprivileged. The professionalization of organizational life at the expense of the growth of membership and of widespread social participation must be prevented. Emphasis must be placed on reconnecting civil organizations with social movements and the general public to prevent what some authors have discovered to be a trend in some countries: the fact that civil society's organizations and particularly the NGOs, are presently closer to the powerful and farther away from the excluded (Hulme, D. and Edwards, M. 1997).

Within this context and considering the potential democratizing role of CSOs, it is important to face the challenge of creating skills and mechanisms to truly guarantee the possibilities of "downward accountability." To this effect, poor communities and excluded groups must be empowered and develop collective action skills in order to participate in problem-solving and coordinate with the different agents and institutions the orientation of policies and social programs to the community's benefit (Narayan, Deepa et al. 2000: 165). CSOs face an important challenge in the incorporation of the voice of the poor and excluded in the strategies of overall development programs. They must ensure the participation of such communities in the deliberation of public issues so that public institutions and CSOs can meet the demands of grassroots organizations, creating mechanisms to render accounts to these communities concerning programs implemented for and with them.[13]

Donors and philanthropies could have a catalytic role in promoting this downward accountability. As far as we know, there are no examples of this type of accountability promoted by donors. However, RedEAmérica is designing its funding system with this in mind. The concept of empowerment and incorporation of the voices of the poor permeate RedEAmérica's approach. Network members fund and support projects as a learning tool for strengthening the capacities of poor people to participate in the public decisions that shape their lives. This community-driven development approach implies that the voices of the poor are included in the design and implementation of any project funded and supported by a RedEAmérica member.

RedEAmérica is now creating the Grassroots Development Fund for channeling resources from donors to grassroots organizations through members of the network. As a way to continue the incorporation of downward accountability, donors would have two types of reports in the current design of the Grassroots Development Fund. The first would be a set of grassroots development indicators defined by RedEAmérica, while the other would consist of a client evaluation of the service provided by the network member to the grassroots organizations. With this type of evaluation, RedEAmérica's members and the donor community are creating the conditions for the incorporation of the voices of the poor in the complete cycle of projects. In doing so, the network is promoting the downward accountability that must guide grassroots development.

Conclusions

The greatest asset of CSOs, their legitimacy and public trust, is increasingly being subjected to scrutiny in Latin America. Developing strategies to face this environment of increasing scrutiny is essential for CSOs to expand their legitimacy and to create favorable environments for their operation. Together with public policies and laws, there are other strategies that can favor the development of public trust in CSOs. One of these strategies is the development of collective mechanisms for self-regulation. Such mechanisms can contribute considerably to meet the current demand for accountability from the CSOs and the expansion of their legitimacy. At the same time, the development of such mechanisms can become a method through which to transform this challenge of greater "accountability," providing an opportunity to convey the visions and guidelines of subgroups of CSOs, and further project their identity and responsibilities before the public.

The question of the legitimacy and accountability of CSOs is, however, a complex issue that requires strategic decisions by each organization and by the organizations that represent subgroups of such organizations. The diversity of sources of legitimacy, the multiple audiences that can claim further accountability from CSOs, as well as the different standards used to do so, obliges CSOs to clearly establish their priorities in terms of to whom and how to respond to the different and often conflicting demands for accountability.

Additional stress in the exercising of accountability comes from the fact that CSOs—particularly those of public interest or that render services to third persons—receive the majority of their resources from persons or institutions other than the beneficiaries themselves. Those providing resources usually have more power to demand accountability than those who receive the services. This asymmetry in power is often translated into a prioritization of "upward accountability" strategies over "downward accountability" strategies. In order to avoid sacrificing civic roots, public responsibility and the importance of the links of the CSO with their grassroots communities, it is important to develop "downward accountability" strategies, including the involvement of grassroots communities in the orientation of programs and in their accountability.

The development of self-regulation mechanisms begins to be present in some of the CSO umbrella organizations in Latin America. Experience is already accumulating in the use of different strategies. However, the research, processing and education shared by these organizations about the type of mechanisms used, their development and the results of their use are minimal. This type of education—combined with a better understanding of the origins of the current demands for accountability, the main characteristics of these demands and the kind of arguments being used to request further accountability from CSOs—can significantly contribute to the development of this subject in the region and to the design of mechanisms that will help expand the sector's legitimacy.

An important work plan for this sector must include measurement of the level of trust in the region's CSOs. Any significant work plan should also examine factors such as the agents that demand a further investigation of these organizations, the segments of CSOs from which greater accountability is requested and the responses of the umbrella organizations and networks of CSOs to these challenges. This is a plan that opens up a venue for collaboration among researchers and leaders of CSOs, particularly the umbrella organizations and networks, given the potential education that may be obtained from a combination of empirical investigations, the development of concepts and exchange of experiences.

Notes

1 *El Pais.* "And who supervises the NGOs?" October 10, 2002.

2 *Semana.* "The NGOs—heroes or villains?" November 18, 2002.

3 A preliminary version of this document was presented in the Seminar on Philanthropy, Social Responsibility and Citizenry, organized by the Kellogg Foundation and CEDES in Antigua, Guatemala, on April 3–5, 2001.

4 See report: Building on Strength: Improving Governance and Accountability in Canada's Voluntary Sector. Panel on Accountability and Governance in the Voluntary Sector. Final Report. February 1999. (http://www.web.net/vsr-trsb/pagvs/Building on Strength.htm). pp. 10–11.

5 The main "umbrella" organizations of the country were one of the agents of civil society that participated in this process. Grupo de Institutos, Fundaciones y Empresas—GIFE (Group of Institutes, Foundations and Companies), the Brazilian Association of NGOs (ABONG), the Brazilian Forum of NGOs and a mixed organization with representatives of the government and civil society, Comunidad Solidaria, who played a key role in this process (Szazi, E. 2003).

6 Among them, the Brazilian Association of NGOs (ABONG); the Chilean Association of NGOs, ACCION; the Colombian Confederation of NGOs (CCONG).

7 Among them, the Group of Argentine Foundations; the Group of Institutes, Foundations and Companies (GIFE) of Brazil.

8 Among them, the Ethos Institute of Social Responsibility of Brazil, the Abrinq Foundation; the Mexican Center for Philanthropy (CEMEFI).

9 Among them, the Latin American Association of Popular Organizations (ALOP), the Inter American Network of Foundations and Entrepreneurial Actions for Grassroots Development (RedEAmérica) and the recent informal network promoted by the GIFE and Worldwide Initiatives for Grantmaking Support (WINGS), among representatives of donors associations of 11 countries of Latin America.

10 See RedEAmérica, 2004. Building Together. A Proposal for Grassroots Development. Published by Fundación Corona, Colombia.

11 See RedEAmérica, 2004, Evaluation System. Draft. Not published.

12 In order to properly analyze this subject, see the paper by Enrique Peruzzotti and Catalina Smulovitz (2002).

13 On these issues, see, for example, World Bank, 2001. Chapters 2, 6 and 7; Narayan, Deepa, Narayan et al., 2000.

References

Associacão Brazileira de Organizacoes Não Governamentais. *Carta de principios de Associacao Brasileira de ONG's.* www.abong.org.br.

Beresford, Susan. 2002. *Aprovechar las posibilidades de la filantropía: La función clave de las organizaciones de infraestructura.* In www.wingsweb.org/SPANISH/ programs /LAC-Nov2002/index.html.

Brown, L. David, and Fox, Jonathan A. 1998. Accountability within Transnational Coalitions. In Brown, L. David and Fox, Jonathan A. *The Struggle for Accountability. The World Bank, NGOs and Grassroots Movements.* The MIT Press.

Brown, L. David, and Moore, Mark H. 2000. *Accountability, Strategy and International Non-Governmental Organizations.* Hauser Center for Nonprofit Organizations. Harvard University. (unpublished).

Brown, L. David, with Cohen, David; Edwards, Michel; Eigen, Peter; Heinrich; Martin, Nigel; Moore, Mark; Murillo, Gabriel; Naidoo, Kumi; Pongsapich, Amara and Scholte, Jan Aart. Civil Society Legitimacy: A Discussion Guide. In Brown, L. David (ed.). 2001. *Practice-Research Engagement and Civil Society in a Globalizing World.* Civicus and The Hauser Center for Nonprofit Organizations. Harvard University.

Mexican Center for Philanthropy (CEMEFI). 2003. *Distintivo Empresa Socialmente Responsable—2002.* In: http://www.cemefi.org/frames.cfm?ENC=2&ID =eventos/2002/enero/00.

Colombian Confederation of NGOs. 1998. *Declaración de principios de las Organizaciones No Gubernamentales (ONGs) de Colombia. (Declaration of principles of the Non Governmental Organizations (NGOs) of Colombia).* www.ccong .org.co.

Colombian Confederation of NGOs. 2002. *Acuerdo Programático por la Paz. (Program Agreement for Peace).* Bogota, July 2002.

Covey, Jane. *A note on NGOs and Policy Influence.* Institute for Development Research. vol. 9, no. 2. 1992.

Daubón, Ramón, and Saunders, Harold. 2002. Operationalizing Social Capital: A Strategy to Enhance Communities' "Capacity to Concert." In *International Studies Perspectives,* 2002, 3, pp. 176–191.

De Souza Briggs, Xavier. 2000 (a) *Community Building: The New (and Old) Politics of Urban Problem-Solving in the New Century.* Public Address, Second Annual Robert C. Wood Visiting Professorship in Public and Urban Affairs. University of Massachusetts, Boston.

De Souza Briggs, Xavier. 2000 (b) *The Art & Science of Community Empowerment.* Visiting Scholar Series. Poverty Reduction & Economic Management Network. The World Bank. Power Point Presentation.

Fundacao Abrinq pelos Direitos da Crianca e do Adolescentes. 2003 (a). *Programa Empresa Amiga da Crianca (Children's Friend Company Program).* In http://www.Abrinq.org.br/peac/programa/historico.shtml.

Fundacao Abrinq pelos Direitos da Crianca e do Adolescentes. 2003 (b). *Termo de Compromisso.* In http://www.Abrinq.org.br/peac/empresas/credencie .shtml.

Fowler, Alan. 2000. NGDOS as a Moment in History: Beyond Aid to Social Entrepreneurship or Civic Innovation? In *Third World Quarterly,* vol. 21, no. 4, pp. 637–654.

Ginsburg, Mark. NGOs: What's in an acronym? In: *Current Issues in Comparative Education.* vol. 1, no. 1. 1998.

Hulme, David, and Edwards, Michel. 1996. Introduction. NGO Performance and Accountability. In Hulme, David and Edwards, Michel (Ed.). *Beyond the Magic Bullet. NGO Performance and Accountability in the Post-Cold War World.* Kumarian Press.

Hulme, David and Edwards, Michel. 1997. Conclusion: Too Close to the Powerful, Too Far from the Powerless. In Hulme, David and Edwards, Michel (Ed). In *NGOs, States and Donors. Too Close for Comfort?* Save the Children.

Independent Sector. 2002. *Obedience to the Unenforceable. Ethics and the Nation's Voluntary and Philanthropic Community.*

Ethos Institute. Companies and Responsibilities. 2001. *Ethos Indicators of Entrepreneurial Social Responsibility. Version 2001.*

El Espectador. No somos la retaguardia de la guerrilla. (We are not the rearguard of the guerrilla). November 17, 2002.

El País. Y las ONG ¿quién las ronda? (And the NGOs who supervises them?) October 10, 2002.

Moore, Mark. 2002. *The "Public Value Scorecard:" A Rejoinder and an Alternative to "Strategic Performance Measurement and Management in Nonprofit Organizations" by Robert Kaplan.* (unpublished).

Najam, Adil. 1996. NGO Accountability: A Conceptual Framework. In *Development *Policy Review* vol. 14 (1996), pp. 339–353.

Narayan, Deepa et al, 2000. *Voices of the Poor. Can Anyone Hear Us.* The World Bank.

Nuñez, Alberto. Carta al Presidente Fox (Letter to President Fox). In *Coparmex-Entorno.* Year 14, no. 173. January 2003.

Oliveira, Anna Cynthia. 1999. La autorregulación de las OSC. (The Self-regulation of Civil Society's Organizations). Ponencia Magistral. Third Central American Regional Workshop "Un marco jurídico para la participación ciudadana" (A legal framework for citizen participation). In Fundación Arias para la Paz y el Progreso Humano (Arias Foundation for Peace and Human Progress). *Un Marco Jurídico para la Participación Ciudadana.*

Peruzzotti, Enrique and Smulovitz, Catalina. 2002. Held to Account: Experiences of Social Accountability in Latin America. In *Journal of Human Development,* vol. 3, no. 2, 2002.

Putnam, Robert. 2000. *Bowling Alone. The Collapse and Revival of American Community.* Simon & Schuster.

Raposo, Rebecca. 2003. *Fundacoes, desenvovimiento e mudanca social. O papel das associacoes de fundacoes. Um ohlar brasileiro.* (To be published).

Rueschemeyer, Dietrich. 1998. The Self-Organization of Society and Democratic Rule. Specifying the Relationship. In Rueschemeyer, Dietrich, Rueschemeyer, Marilyn and Wittrock, Bjorn (Ed.) *Participation and Democracy. East and West. Comparisons and Interpretations.* M.E. Sharpe. New York. Lond.

Semana. Las ONG: ¿héroes o villanos? (The NGOs: heroes or villains?) November 18, 2002.

Szazi, Eduardo. 2003. *Creating an Enabling Environment for Philanthropy and Civil Society: The Case of Brazil* (Unpublished).

Toro, Olga Lucía and Vila Moret, Elena. 2000. *Philanthropy and Volunteerism Programming in Latin America and the Caribbean.* W.K. Kellogg Foundation. Retrospective Evaluation 1994–2000.

Verba, Sidney; Schlozman, Kay Lehman and Brady, Henry E. 1999. *Voice and Equality. Civic Voluntarism in American Politics.* Harvard University Press.

World Bank. 2001. *World Development Report. 2000/2001. Attacking Poverty.* Oxford University Press.

SECTION

IV

REFLECTIONS FROM INTERNATIONAL PRACTICE

15

Organized Philanthropy North and South

Christine W. Letts

As in other regions around the world, philanthropy is not new to Latin America. There are long standing traditions among people of all classes of giving to the church and other selected charities. The Catholic Church has played a predominate role in channeling philanthropy from individuals to those in need. However, there are new trends in Latin American philanthropy that are emerging as a result of different forms of institutionalization. Authors in this book describe and comment on major features of the emerging shape of the philanthropic sector in several countries in Latin America and Mexico. While the focus of each chapter is different, and each presents different data to help us understand the state of organized philanthropy, together they illuminate several trends that are important to notice. The purpose of this chapter is to discuss such trends and suggest opportunities and cautions associated with them.

What impact do these trends have on enlarging philanthropy as a whole, on the strength of nongovernmental organizations, or the potential for social change? Many of these trends present contrasts to the features of the more established philanthropic sector in the United States. Stakeholders in the social sector in Latin America might take advantage of the emergent nature of the sector to establish policies and initiatives to enhance those trends that promise advancement and strengthening of the sector while adjusting those that do not. It is tempting for international and local players to encourage certain practices that we have found advantageous in the United States. But it is wise to notice that first, the Latin America trends are becoming increasingly linked, so influencing them will become more complex and second, that there may be advantages to the different shape of Latin American philanthropy and practices of the players and these may provide lessons for the United States.

1. The actors in organized philanthropy prefer development or strategic engagement, in contrast to traditional concepts of "charity," as the target for emerging philanthropy.

This trend is noticed in different ways by the authors. Several authors note that some forms of corporate responsibility and philanthropy are linked to notions of assistance, paternalism and social control, all of which have negative connotations. De la Maza chronicles how associations are advocates for corporate foundations to move beyond their traditional approach to philanthropy that centered on transferring material resources to their employees and those in need in their immediate environment. The argument for this is that this may satisfy needs, but not change the conditions that created those needs. This kind of philanthropy can be characterized as patronizing in the worst sense, in that it increases company control over workers and deprives them of voice. Turitz and Winder link the negative, paternalistic connotation of "donors" to the reluctance to adopt more grantmaking activities in favor of operating programs, another trend discussed below.

These are important cautions, but may be premature in the important movement to increase all philanthropy in Latin America. First, it is important to remember that the nature of needs and the context for organized philanthropy is evolving. Corporate social responsibility associations are making progress on encouraging companies to upgrade conditions for workers, but across Latin America these conditions have not improved to the extent that workers and their families should not remain an important constituency for attention. Second, individuals in North and South America have developed strong traditions of charitable behavior, primarily through their religious affiliations. These traditions won't stop, and rather than put any negative connotation on them, it is useful to encourage individuals to use various vehicles and methods in their giving to accomplish different purposes. We merely need to notice the outpouring of "charity" in response to the impact of the tsunami in Asia to remember how important this motivation is in mobilizing resources and engaging people in helping one another. Finally, most philanthropists who are considered strategic began with giving to charity. The evolution of the Fundación Carvajal in Colombia from charity to economic development and entrepreneur empowerment is a good example of this. Their strategy evolved not only as a result of noticing the limitations of this form of philanthropy, but also from becoming associated and knowledgeable about causes, problems and organizations through their charity. Since charity is so prevalent among all types of donors, North and South, it may be that eschewing simple "giving" to charitable organizations or needy causes will deter individuals, for whom this may be an important part of their contributions, from becoming a more visible force in organized philanthropy. This leads to the next trend.

2. There are a relatively small number of foundations that have been created by individuals.

All the authors point to statistics that show the number of foundations started by individuals to be the smallest percentage behind corporations and civic leaders (with the exception of the case of Peru, where at one time the number of family foundations outnumbered corporate foundations). This trend is certainly in sharp contrast to the evolution of foundations in the United States. There, the largest private foundations were, and are still, started by and endowed by individuals. The vast majority of foundations in terms of numbers are family foundations of all sizes that were started by an individual. In the early days of organized philanthropy in the United States, foundations were started to allow professionals to work on "root causes" of social problems. The Rockefeller, Carnegie and Russell Sage foundations were all founded in this spirit. Throughout the 20th century, individuals motivated by other factors continued to establish foundations. The United States has favorable tax treatment for the establishment of foundations, particularly when an estate transfers or there is a sudden generation of wealth. Second, individuals have always been motivated to create foundations in order to provide a mechanism for family engagement as generations within families are increasingly dispersed throughout the country. Individuals in Latin America exist in different social, cultural and regulatory environments that do not encourage the same kind of foundation formation.

Turitz and Winder do a good job enumerating some problems associated with this trend in Latin America. They provide data that show the low level of endowments in Latin American foundations. In the United States, endowments, while carrying the potential to avoid accountability, provide many advantages, particularly independence and longevity. As Turitz and Winder point out, foundations without endowments must rely on fundraising and fees to stay in operation and are quite fragile. This not only limits their flexibility, but also potentially puts them in competition with the operating social service organizations that they seek to support. As the philanthropic sector grows, individual wealth should become an active part of it, if not the driving force, in order to create more stability and plurality of interests in the sector.

3. Corporate foundations are emerging as the largest component of organized philanthropy and taking a leadership role in shaping the sector.

There are potential hazards to overcome and many benefits to harvest in this trend. Several authors explore problems that can emerge from corporate engagement in the public sector. One is the corporations' use of power in an undemocratic way. This is enabled by an environment characterized by the lack of transparency and structures that allow for self-dealing. Rojas cautions that public solutions dominated by corporate input "may be limited by excessive use of market logic." She provides as an example a corporation that in the spirit of comparative advantage is interested in transferring "know how" in addition to money and puts excessive emphasis on improving management processes and systems as the answer to public problems. It is important to note that, particularly in the world of philanthropy, corporations are not the only ones that may exercise power in a non-transparent, non-democratic way. Foundations in the United States have long been criticized for their insularity and inappropriate interventions into public policy or communities, and have come under extensive scrutiny in the last few years for self-dealing practices.

While there are many fine examples of corporate philanthropy in the United States, leadership and cooperation in the public sector among corporations seem to have as much, if not more, momentum in Latin America than in the U.S. There is great potential in corporations taking a large role in the philanthropic sector. First, it is important to recognize how commingled families, family wealth and corporations are, still, throughout Latin America. While we may be anxious about the reticence of individuals to step forward as leaders in philanthropy, in most cases it is these same individuals and their families who are the driving forces behind the growth and creativity in corporate philanthropy. It seems highly likely the growth in corporate philanthropy will be instrumental in the evolution of individual philanthropy.

Second, once a corporation enters the public realm, particularly drawing attention to itself for "good works," it is hard for it to retreat back into obscurity. This visibility invites scrutiny and commentary on the level, quality and impact of public ventures. Over time, it can increase the pressure to move beyond public relations and charity to a level of corporate responsibility that Rojas refers to as "good governance."

Third, the business sector already has extensive industry, community and personal networks that can be put to work on behalf of public causes.

For example, several years ago the American Chamber of Commerce in Argentina established a series of awards for inspired corporate philanthropy. It engages people from all the sectors as evaluators in the selection process and hold a large, well-publicized luncheon to make the awards each year. The World Economic Forum, which is largely funded by corporations, always includes many sessions related to corporate responsibility and philanthropy at its annual meeting in Davos, Switzerland.

Fourth, the leaders of corporations will inevitably be influenced by corporate engagement in the social sector. The top managers in the company, as well as the CEO, are destined to be involved where there is either prestige or risk. They will have the opportunity to engage and learn about public problems in a way that is not currently part of the culture for individuals, who will normally remain very private. They will be able to use their creativity and conscience to think differently about problems, and to observe how their corporation, in all its facets, contributes to the problems or the solutions. Their public engagement through the corporation is likely to influence their private engagement as well. This extends to a broader group as corporations include volunteering as an element of their corporate philanthropy initiatives, as noted by Fischer.

Fifth, while corporations can, and indeed have been, forces for the status quo of inequity in Latin American countries, Szazi points out how the corporations in Brazil became important proponents of reform. Finally, corporations can be a positive force in bringing pressure and support for the professionalism of social sector organizations. They can provide technical assistance through consultation, partnerships, conferences, training and participation on governing boards. In another Argentine example, corporate leaders were early supporters of Fundación Compromiso, a management support organization for social sector leaders and organizations.

There are strategies for optimizing the benefits and minimizing the hazards of corporate community involvement. Rojas advocates for "public governance" strategies, which essentially call for corporations to align their strategies associated with their people, products, politics and philanthropy. Strengthening the links between North American associations, such as BSR (Business for Social Responsibility) and Latin American companies is important. The development of associations of various kinds, which are covered in anther trend below, which develop standards and strategies among corporations, will be important not only to encourage good practices, but to call attention to less attractive ones.

4. Community foundations have become stronger in a few regions, but are struggling to become accepted and widely used in communities as an important vehicle for philanthropy.

Several of the authors discuss the emerging development of community foundations and their potential as a force for community social change. International foundations were the major impetus behind this development and provided the seed money for many of these institutions. While the chapter by Turitz and Winder shows growth in local support for these community foundations, they are all struggling to be recognized as an important community institution and to receive widespread community support. Several phenomena might account for this. First, successful community foundations in the United States rely on gifts and accounts set up by individuals, and these are largely in the form of endowment. We have already observed that there are not cultural precedents for either of these in Latin America. Second, those that have been more successful in raising local support have been enabled by local governmental support, as in the case of several Mexican community foundations. This is still a fairly rare phenomenon throughout Latin America.

Community foundations developed in the United States in a few cities with exceptional leadership among some individuals. They grew with the particular emphasis on getting people to donate money, to be dedicated to the local community, upon their deaths, from their estate. While many community foundations no longer emphasize bequests as their primary means of support, it is important to notice the particular cultural and technical origins of these now large and influential institutions.

5. Most foundations throughout Latin America devote a significant amount of their resources to operating programs rather than grantmaking.

This phenomenon is in sharp contrast to the United States, where operating foundations are few and far between, and where very few foundations operate their own programs, but is more consistent with foundations in Europe, that are predominantly operating. The authors tend to emphasize the negative reasons for this trend: foundation fears about being inundated with grant requests; a lack of trust or confidence in social service organizations; and a negative paternalistic connotation to the term "donor." This trend can hamper the development of social sector organizations that are strong and independent in Latin American communities.

It is important to understand the potential strengths and advantages of operating entities before we assume that grantmaking is a better way to use resources. Turitz and Winder point out that many operating programs are partnerships with other organizations and sectors. This is a positive phenomenon and one that we see too infrequently in the United States. Foundations with endowments can insulate programs from the instability of funding flows to create a more reliable context to test, develop and grow innovations. In the United States foundations have built and run programs that seem too risky (economic development) or too controversial (building capacity for gay and lesbian organizations) to attract sufficient funds elsewhere.[1] On the other hand, grantmaking is important for certain purposes. For example, grantmaking makes sense when it is not clear that there is a single idea or program that "works" and it is important to encourage more experimentation and experience. The most valuable attribute of private money for public purposes is its flexibility, and we should learn how to optimize the many different methods of philanthropy, rather than assume that one set is better than the other. The Latin American experience could be an excellent laboratory for learning since there seem to be more hybrid organizations than in other regions.

6. Foundations and foundation associations have great potential to be "bridgers" in Latin American society.

There is substantial evidence noted in this book of the record and potential for foundations and foundation and/or business associations to bridge across the government, business and social sectors. Aguero gives us a rich history of the role of associations in Brazil. Associations of foundations or businesses are emerging in several countries as important entities that will shape the philanthropic sector. Associations such as GIFE and Instituto Ethos in Brazil and CEMEFI in Mexico contribute to social advancement by bringing ethical and strategic frameworks to their members. Since the majority of the members are corporations, these associations might help to overcome some of the cautions about corporate philanthropy that the authors cite. These associations can provide legitimacy and visibility to corporate initiatives, while providing some "cover" for individual companies or individuals who do not want to be personally visible.

There are other arenas in which associations can be valuable: as learning communities to improve practices; providing legitimacy and advocacy for legal and regulatory changes; and connecting to global networks. Associations are the key entities that can coordinate activities with northern foundations or associations. The Synergos Institute and Kellogg Foundation have both supported and partnered with many Latin American associations in their work.

The associations that involve businesses as members may be particularly suited to playing a bridging role among the sectors, as well as provide other benefits in building the philanthropic sector. In addition to the benefits to corporate social responsibility, the leaders cut across many different networks in a community—political, religious, social and cultural. Mobilizing resources and consent from a multitude of sources is critical in any important initiative or social change strategy. And while this connection is often overlooked or not exploited, companies are connected at the grassroots levels of communities through their locations and employees. The leaders and their companies bring different skills, tools and perspective to bear on public issues. But, associations blunt the potential negative impact of extreme influence by too narrow power interests in the deployment of efficiency or resources.

All the authors point to the need to solidify the identity of the philanthropic sector and to improve the regulatory environment. It will be important that the leaders of these associations maintain their organizations' ability to challenge their members as well as support them. Associations in the United States have been criticized for protecting narrow interests, which can be a hazard for any member-serving organization.

Summary

The study of philanthropy in Latin America is as new as the phenomenon of organized philanthropy there. The authors in this book provide valuable insight into the structure and role of this developing sector. They call for attention to transparency, ethics and a focus on social transformation as the sector grows. These attributes will be critical if the philanthropic sector is to become a legitimate actor in social reform and development in Latin American countries. It will also be important for scholars and policy analysts to observe and document the innovative and unique features of organized philanthropy as it develops. Organized philanthropy will be an expression of the rich and distinct Latin American cultures and will ultimately have as much to share as to learn from other regions of the world.

Note

1 These refer to an economic development initiative of the Jacobs Family Foundation in San Diego, California, and a technical assistance program operated by the Gill Foundation of Denver, Colorado.

16

Building Civil Society Legitimacy and Accountability with Domain Accountability Systems

L. David Brown

Many aspects of the rise of philanthropy and civil society activity in social change in Latin America have been explored in earlier chapters. Civil society organizations (CSOs) during the last two decades have begun to play increasingly important roles in governance and social problem-solving in many countries and regions around the world. They have responded to disasters, delivered essential services, built local capacities, influenced policy choices and catalyzed multisectoral initiatives that bring to bear complementary resources of governments, businesses and grassroots organizations.

The rapid rise of CSOs as both national and international players has catalyzed interest in their legitimacy and accountability.[1] In part, this interest stems from a general "crisis in governance" that raises questions about the legitimacy and accountability of business and government institutions as well as civil society. In part, the interest is a consequence of CSOs' growing visibility as social actors on many important issues. In part, it has been generated by highly visible problematic actions by CSOs, such as Greenpeace's campaign based on a flawed analysis of the costs of disposing of the Brent Spar oilrig in the North Sea, or alleged self-dealing by the Nature Conservancy's Board of Directors. Perhaps most importantly, the questions have been raised by powerful actors, the very targets of civil society advocacy. Those targets have asked, "On what grounds do you have the right to challenge us?" and "Who do you represent?" Some have concluded that "unelected CSOs" are largely unaccountable and have set up an "NGO Watch" website to publicize CSO activity.[2]

Questions about the legitimacy of civil society organizations cut to the heart of their ability to mobilize resources, recruit volunteers and build alliances, as well as to establish their credibility as agents of constructive change. CSOs have neither the wealth of business nor the authority of government to generate influence, so they depend on credibility with the larger public to generate resources and influence. If critics successfully impugn that legitimacy and accountability, CSOs' roles in social development and change will decline dramatically. So strengthening the legitimacy of civil society volunteers, associations, foundations, partnerships and campaigns is central to their expanding contribution to constructive social change.

This chapter examines approaches to building the legitimacy and accountability of civil society organizations and alliances that will enable them to mobilize resources, recruit allies, and engage public support for social learning and innovation. It draws on experience from around the world to suggest ways in which CSOs can enhance their accountability to key stakeholders and their legitimacy as social actors in the Latin American context.

Background: Civil Society Accountability and Legitimacy

"Accountability" refers to the extent to which an actor can be held to his or her promises to perform some activity or service.[3] Accountability might be owed to oneself, as in acting consistently with strongly held values or principles. More commonly, accountability involves answering for responsibilities to others, and thus refers to a relationship in which some actors hold others accountable. A CSO that provides health and education services, for example, could be accountable to funders and clients for the quality of services it delivers, and an indigenous people's federation might be accountable to members for its effectiveness as a representative of their interests. Accountability typically requires some agreement on general goals, standards for performance, ways to assess that performance, mechanisms for communicating assessments to stakeholders, and sanctions by which stakeholders can create performance consequences.

"Legitimacy" refers to perceptions by key stakeholders that the organization's activities and roles are justifiable and appropriate in terms of the values, norms, laws and expectations that prevail in its context.[4] Institutional legitimacy can be framed in terms of prevailing value and normative expectations, or in terms of legal and regulatory requirements, or in terms of widely held expectations for good practice. The health and education CSO may develop legitimacy on the basis of years' service that meet regulatory standards and local norms. The indigenous peoples' federation may be recognized as the legitimate representative of politically marginalized groups, because it has elected leaders and it operates by locally accepted decision-making processes.

CSO legitimacy can be enhanced or undermined by its accountability to key stakeholders. Accountability systems that allow those stakeholders to assess and sanction CSO performance can also reassure the wider community that its activities are congruent with its mission. Service CSOs may claim legitimacy grounded in accountability to standards of service quality established by regulatory agencies and evaluated by clients. Capacity-building CSOs might argue for legitimacy based on demonstrated increases in client capacities. Advocacy CSOs might claim legitimacy from expertise on the issue, or articulating widely held public values, or as representing the affected group. Legitimacy is framed with reference to the values, norms, laws and expectations of larger publics and contextual forces, while accountability is focused on specific duties owed to particular stakeholders.

Standards for accountability and legitimacy may come from different sources. Sometimes standards are set by general agreement on explicit social policies, laws, values and norms. This might be called the *societal ideal* view of accountability. In the United States, for example, legislation requires that registered nonprofit organizations must provide a minimum level of financial information. However, neither legislation nor widely accepted norms define for CSOs the kind of primary stakeholder accountability enjoyed by owners of businesses or voters of democratic governments.[5] Indeed, many stakeholders may impose conflicting accountability claims on CSOs. Should donors take precedence over clients or government regulators or staff members? While societal ideals often set minimal expectations for CSOs, creating detailed accountabilities might undermine the flexibility, ease of entry, diversity and innovativeness that are central to the roles and value of civil society to the larger community.

When societal regulations and norms do not set clear standards, CSO leaders may have considerable latitude to define their accountabilities according to the moral, legal and practical demands of their missions and strategies. CSO leaders must develop strategies that simultaneously create public value, maintain authorization and support from stakeholders, and create the operational capacity necessary—and each of these strategic issues involves important external and internal stakeholders.[6] Leaders have some flexibility in prioritizing accountability to these stakeholders, though there are some moral, legal, and practical costs to their choices. This *organizational strategic choice* view of accountability offers CSO leaders opportunities to align expectations in ways that encourage stakeholders to press for strategic goals. A health and education CSO, for example, might increase the quality of its services by increasing its accountability to marginalized groups—which might require reducing its accountability to donors or other stakeholders. Organizational strategic choice is particularly important to building accountability for CSOs in problem areas for which tested solutions and "best practices" do not yet exist and innovations are vital.

A third source of standards may emerge when experience has begun to identify effective programs and challenges from powerful actors call for enhanced standards. Groups of organizations can draw on their experience to build agreement about standards for performance in critical domains of activity. This *negotiated domain standards* view of accountability can define standards of performance to which domain members agree to be accountable. Creating such standards involves effort and risk for domain members as well as compromising their autonomy—so it is not surprising that such negotiations are rare in the absence of external pressures that justify those costs. The Philippine Council on NGO Certification, for example, mobilized hundreds of civil society organizations to develop standards, provide peer reviews of compliance, and support a new organization to implement those standards—but did so in response to a government threat to abolish tax deductions for uncertified NGOs.[7]

This chapter concerns building legitimacy and accountability for two kinds of domains (areas) that are particularly relevant to the legitimacy and accountability of civil society and philanthropic activities in Latin America. *Sector domains* refer to communities of similar organizations that share a sectoral identity and interests such as corporate foundations or development NGOs. Sector domain standards include the development of codes of conduct, statements of principles and organizational or program standards that apply equally across sector members. Examples of such sector domain standards include the code of conduct of InterAction in the United States, the statement of principles of CCONG in Colombia, and the standards and assessment processes of the Philippine Council for NGO Certification.[8] Such sector standards set the stage for holding sector members accountable for violating expectations set up for the sector as a whole. In contrast, *problem domains* may involve dissimilar organizations from many different sectors, from civil society to business to government agencies, which share compelling interests in some issue or problem. The World Commission on Dams, for example, brought together business leaders, international financial institutions, government representatives, and grassroots activists concerned with assessing the performance of large dams and setting shared standards for future dam construction. Problem domain standards can establish how actors with very diverse interests can interact to deal with complex and conflict-ridden problems such as managing a sensitive ecosystem or preventing corporate marketing abuses in developing countries.[9]

This chapter focuses on the creation of accountability standards for sector and problem domains. This evolution is particularly important for strengthening the emerging roles of Latin American civil society actors in social innovation and problem solving.

Constructing Domain Accountability Systems

The construction of domain accountability systems has been receiving increasing attention in the last five years around the world. This section identifies several challenges to enhancing civil society legitimacy and accountability and describes initiatives to build systems to deal with these challenges in a variety of settings. The common challenges include: (1) identifying domains, goals and stakeholders, (2) negotiating performance standards and expectations, (3) building effective domain organizations, (4) measuring and communicating performance results, and (5) enabling consequences for that performance.

Identifying Domains, Goals and Stakeholders

Interorganizational domains are often loosely organized and poorly understood. One prerequisite to building domain accountability systems is identifying the domain, its members, the goals that justify investing in accountability systems, and the stakeholders that have compelling accountability claims. Sector domains are often composed of organizations that compete with one another for resources and their members may resist investing in systems that will undermine their autonomy. Problem domains often include organizations with histories of serious conflict, so identifying shared goals may require changing entrenched positions and stereotyped perceptions. Domains for joint action can remain unrecognized or with poor resources until external threats or dissatisfaction with the existing situation overcomes initial reservations.

Both sector and problem domains involve stakeholders with diverse accountability claims. Agreement on domain composition, problems and goals helps clarify the identities of domain actors and stakeholders. For example, Figure 1 depicts actors and stakeholders in a sector and a problem domain. Figure 1A represents the sector domain of child sponsorship NGOs in the United States. The domain has a wide range of external stakeholders—private and public donors, home and host country governments, general publics, children and family beneficiaries, their communities, program allies—as well as internal stakeholders—child sponsorship organizations and their staffs. Domain members invested substantial resources in developing shared accountability standards and an independent evaluation process after media criticism of their programs threatened to harm their reputations with private donors.[10] Sector goals include preserving relations with donors as well as creating value for children, their families, and their communities. Note that the domain organization requires members to be accountable to each other (small arrows) as well as to external stakeholders (large arrows). The domain must maintain legitimacy with and support from donors, the media and the general public. It also needs the operational capability provided by a sector association and an independent evaluation agency that can enforce compliance to the new standards.

Figure 1A. Sector Domain: Child Sponsorship CSOs

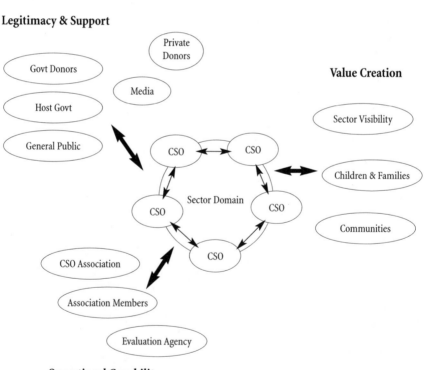

Figure 1B. Problem Domain: Applegate Valley Partnership

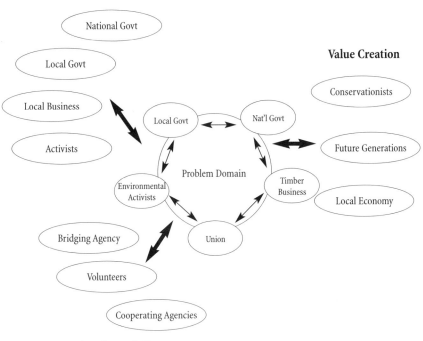

Legitimacy & Support

Value Creation

National Govt

Local Govt

Local Business

Conservationists

Activists

Local Govt ⟷ Nat'l Govt

Future Generations

Problem Domain

Environmental
Activists

Timber
Business

Local Economy

Bridging Agency

Union

Volunteers

Cooperating Agencies

Operational Capability

Figure 1B provides a similar map of the stakeholders of Oregon's Applegate Valley Partnership, which was organized to govern the problem domain of managing the valley's natural resources, after years of escalated conflict produced deadlocks that served no one's interests well.[11] The domain involved claims from diverse external stakeholders—local citizens, regional economic interests, local governments, cooperating agencies, labor unions, and future generations—as well as internal stakeholders within the Partnership—timber companies, environmental NGOs, labor unions and municipal government representatives. Environmentalists sought to end clear cutting to protect wildlife and ecologies; lumber companies and unions wanted to expand economic use of natural resources; local governments hoped to maintain order and public goods; and national government agencies wanted to meet long term needs while preserving voter loyalties. The Partnership was grounded in agreement on the importance of sustaining the Valley's natural resources and the need to end the existing deadlock.

Identifying the domain, its goals, and its internal and external stakeholders is a prerequisite to constructing ways to handle legitimacy and accountability challenges. Without agreement on problems that require joint action, key parties will not agree to invest resources to construct systems that will limit their future activities. Creating domain accountability systems requires balancing the claims of many different stakeholders, particularly in areas where there are relatively few standards established by existing laws, norms, values, and expectations.

Negotiating Performance Standards and Expectations

Domain standards provide benchmarks against which domain member behaviors can be assessed and held accountable. Standards may be difficult to establish in areas that are poorly understood or rapidly changing, but as experience accumulates and impacts are clarified, setting standards becomes more feasible. Setting accountability standards involves synthesizing experience to define appropriate standards and indicators and negotiating with stakeholders about how to assess compliance with them. Different stakeholders may focus on different standards: donors, regulators, beneficiaries, members, partners and targets have quite different interests at stake in the definition of good performance.

In sector domains, performance standards embodied in codes of conduct have been proliferating.[12] Sometimes standards emerge in response to private donors, such as the effort to create a code of conduct for child sponsorship NGOs—an initiative that built on an earlier effort by InterAction, the umbrella agency of U.S. international development NGOs.[13] On other occasions, sector standards respond to government concerns, such as the Philippine Council for NGO Certification's creation of a code and a peer review process to certify NGOs in order to preserve tax deductions for contributions to the sector.[14] In both cases, sector members created standards to enhance their legitimacy with and accountability to powerful external stakeholders.

In problem domains, the major conflicts may operate within the domain, rather than with external stakeholders. Problem domain actors with quite different interests may have to agree on domain goals and action plans in spite of histories of intense disagreements. Creating standards for managing the Applegate Valley forests and watershed, for example, required decisions about how much logging could be allowed while sustaining the local ecology—a controversy that had escalated into violent confrontations among timber companies, environmentalists and forest service agents.[15] Enabling economic activity while preserving the forest for future generations required negotiations among fierce opponents within the problem domain to craft standards and systems responsive to all their interests.

Building Effective Domain Organizations

Domain accountability systems often require new organizational arrangements, particularly when implementation of standards and accountability systems demand significant resources. Common organizational arrangements include sector associations, issue alliances and coalitions, independent accreditation agencies and watchdog information agencies. Those organizations use a variety of approaches to assessing and communicating member compliance with domain standards, including self-assessments, peer assessments by representatives of other similar organizations, certification by independent agencies or publication of information or external assessments.

Sector associations that develop codes of conduct can use a variety of tools to monitor and assess compliance. Many ask their members to do self assessments and report on their own compliance. For example InterAction in the United States and the Lesotho Council of NGOs require their members to assess and report on their compliance with the association code of conduct each year. This approach is inexpensive in association time and resources, but it relies heavily on the commitment and integrity of members to carry out a serious self-assessment. The Australian Council for International Development requires self-assessments, but adds a complaints mechanism so that external stakeholders have a vehicle for raising questions about compliance problems.[16] This addition increases the likelihood that members can be held accountable for inflated or fraudulent self-ratings. Associations are valuable for implementing standards when communities of organizations are subject to high costs for misbehavior by a few members.

When domain members are more diverse, as in problem domains, *issue alliances and coalitions* may be created to provide an organizational base for accountability. Alliances and coalitions can bring together diverse parties for joint action and mutual accountability. The Applegate Valley Partnership, for example, brought together stakeholders in conflict over managing natural resources, and built a system composed of formal institutional structures that support participation and collaboration; shared values and norms that support mutual respect, trust, information-sharing and influence; and management approaches focused on results and flexible response to many interests.[17] The Partnership has now evolved into a long-term co-governance arrangement that enables mutual accountability among its members as well as to external stakeholders affected by its decisions. Issue alliances and coalitions are useful when joint action by diverse actors with complementary resources is critical to governance or social problem-solving.

A third organizational arrangement for domain accountability is to utilize *independent accreditation agencies* to assess compliance with standards. Some accreditation agencies mobilize domain members for peer review, like the Philippine Council for NGO Certification. Others create review boards that include representatives of many stakeholders such as the Pakistan Centre for Philanthropy's NPO Certification Programme.[18] In both the Philippines and Pakistan cases, certification results in tax benefits and creates a significant incentive for compliance. The U.S. child sponsorship agencies are investing in certification by an independent agency in the hope that they can gain a "seal of approval" that is credible to prospective donors. Independent accreditation agencies can increase the credibility of compliance ratings, particularly when there are high stakes for distorting self-ratings.

A fourth organizational option for generating and communicating information about domain compliance with codes and standard is the creation of *"watchdog" information agencies* that make information available, with or without cooperation from domain members. For example, Guidestar publishes information online about nonprofit sector members in the United States that can be used by prospective donors, government investigators, journalists and academics. It is exploring providing similar services in other countries. From a more provocative perspective, the "NGO-Watch" website was established to publicize the activities of "unelected" and "unaccountable" NGOs by making media coverage of NGOs—particularly those involved in transnational policy advocacy—widely available.[19] Watchdog agencies may be particularly valuable in areas that are susceptible to conflict and negative outcomes if information is easily available.

As the risks and impacts of illegitimate or unaccountable behavior increase, there is more to be said for more independent and rigorous organizational arrangements to support domain accountability and legitimacy. The more CSOs are expected to be continuing players in governance and social problem solving, the more it makes sense to develop enduring systems for setting, monitoring, assessing and enforcing shared standards.

Measuring and Communicating Performance Results

Performance information indicates whether domain members are living up to standards and expectations. Getting unambiguous information about whether domain members have met domain standards can be difficult, particularly when domain goals involve complex, long-term changes that are affected by many factors. Some challenges involve domain members' willingness or capability to share information about their activities and performance—the problem of transparency. Other issues are raised by the difficulty of assessing consequences of domain activity—the problem of interpretation. Still other concerns grow out of the sources and validity of the information, particularly parties tempted to slant or distort information—the problem of credibility.

The question of *transparency* has produced varied approaches to systematic information sharing. Many CSOs use disclosure statements and annual reports to tell internal and external constituencies about their activities. Disclosure statements and reports make information about inputs (such as financial or human resources), activities (such as program activities or policy analyses) and outputs (such as products and services or policy proposals) available to stakeholders. Government regulations often require such reports, particularly with respect to financial management. For example, the Indian Foreign Contribution Regulation Act requires Indian NGOs that receive foreign funds to open special accounts so the state can monitor how those funds are used.[20] Many CSOs publish annual reports that provide information about their missions, strategies, and activities as well as their sources and uses of funds. The Internet has expanded opportunities for sharing information, although governments and corporations have been quicker to take advantage of that opportunity than many CSOs.[21] These statements are typically self-reports though independent outsiders may check and confirm them, as in external audits of annual financial reports. Constructing domain accountability systems requires clarifying what information is critical for accountability to key domain stakeholders, and then developing reports to make that information available.

Interpreting the results of CSO activities presents more complex problems. Many CSOs emphasize goals whose impacts are not immediately visible, such as improving the quality of life of marginalized groups or enhancing their capacity to affect government policies. Such impacts are difficult to measure unambiguously; they take months or years to materialize; and causal factors are so intertwined that CSO contributions are difficult to demonstrate. Donors and other stakeholders often call for evaluations and performance assessments, though they are less eager to financially support such activities. Some investigators are constructing systematic social audits that combine a variety of tools and processes to assess social programs, and others are developing widely-applicable reporting standards to assess social results.[22] While the costs of systematic performance assessment remain high, such research can identify processes, outputs and outcomes that produce desired long-term impacts for sector or problem domains.

The *credibility* of performance information is often linked to how it will be used. If performance information is used to punish CSOs, so that poor performance reduces funding or political space, then CSOs have incentives to emphasize positive and suppress negative results. In such circumstances, self-reports may be less credible than independent assessments. On the other hand, when performance information is used as a catalyst for organizational learning and improvement, CSOs may actively seek performance information in spite of discomfort caused by bad news.[23] Participatory evaluation processes may also help to get the perspectives of multiple stakeholders included in program decision-making as it evolves.[24] Domain accountability systems must balance the tradeoffs between uses of performance information and the quality of information generated by the system.

Collecting and communicating domain-wide information is probably more easily justified in problem domains, where the point of holding the domain together is to solve problems that all members agree are important. In sector domains, resources and commitment may become more available as members experience positive results from measuring and communicating performance information or they recognize negative consequences of accountability failures.

Enabling Performance Consequences

Identifying domain stakeholders, negotiating domain standards, building domain organizations, and assessing and communicating domain performance set the stage for enhancing civil society accountability and legitimacy. However, those elements must culminate in creating consequences for good and bad performance if accountability systems are to fulfill their promise. When domain members internalize the standards and their responsibility for meeting them, they may be internally motivated to be accountable.[25] But the accountability of many—if not most—organizations will be influenced by the possibility of sanctions by stakeholders, some within the domain and others outside of it. The prospect of more private donations to child sponsorship organizations or government tax breaks to NGOs in the Philippines and Pakistan are significant incentives for compliance with domain codes of conduct.

Sanctions for poor performance, however, depend on the power and resources of the stakeholder. Donors and government regulators often have power to hold domain members accountable, since they control important resources. Other stakeholders, such as program beneficiaries or low-status staff, may have claims that are less powerful in practice. The sector codes of PCNC and the child sponsorship organizations were designed with powerful government and donor stakeholders as primary audiences, and they offer fewer opportunities for leverage of other stakeholders.

Therefore, assessing domain power relations is important in designing accountability systems. Where the system is intended to increase accountability to stakeholders that might otherwise be ignored, explicit design to increase their voice is often necessary. While it may not be possible or even desirable to equalize influence across all stakeholders, structures and processes can be created to enable wide input and engagement. The Humanitarian Accountability Project International, for example, was created by humanitarian relief organizations to strengthen their accountability to grassroots groups affected by disasters.[26] It helps domain members construct and implement their own accountability systems and provides a vehicle for grassroots groups to safely raise issues about domain member performance. Accountability systems can balance power differences by explicitly designing to enable such participation. Otherwise they are likely to attend to a limited range of voices.

Sanctioning processes differ considerably across sector and problem domains. Sector domains, composed of relatively similar organizations, may replicate patterns of accountability invented by their members. Most child sponsorship organizations are vulnerable to donor pressures and media attention, for example, and less vulnerable to local communities and beneficiaries, so it is not surprising that this pattern recurs in their domain accountability systems. Sector domains may be to creating accountability systems that replicate inequalities common across the sector. Since they are composed of networks of peers, they may also have informal influence to sanction members who violate shared norms and values.[27] From this perspective, networks like Brazil's Instituto Ethos may be constructing new norms and expectations for work on social problems.[28]

Problem domains, in contrast, include members who are dissimilar in values, interests, and perspectives, so that many controversies are played out among domain members rather than between the domain and external stakeholders. Power differences may be less important in problem domains, since some level of mutual influence among members is a precondition for recognizing the domain. Timber companies, environmental activists and local government officials in the Applegate Valley Partnership had fought to a deadlock in the courts, and were forced to build organizational structures, processes and norms for cooperation to move beyond that deadlock. In the process, they developed the capacity to raise issues for voices not present, so they attended to the concerns of other stakeholders, including future generations, in their deliberations. Problem domains are initially more difficult to organize and manage than sector domains—but they are more likely to take multifaceted views of issues and accountabilities because of the different perspectives they bring together.

Possibilities for Latin American Philanthropies?

How is this discussion of civil society legitimacy and the construction of domain accountability systems around the world relevant to the emergence of philanthropy and its impacts on social change initiatives in Latin America? I want to suggest five areas in which this discussion might have useful implications for philanthropies interested in fostering social changes.

First, philanthropy is itself a domain of activity whose legitimacy and accountability may come into question. Indeed, if the experience of other civil society sectors is any guide, questions about legitimacy and accountability become more urgent as the sector becomes more visible and influential. The rise of Latin American philanthropies has already provoked some challenges to their legitimacy, and as they become more influential actors more questions can be expected in the future.

Latin American philanthropies should focus attention and resources on constructing domain standards and accountability systems that can preserve and strengthen the legitimacy of the philanthropic sector itself. To do so, philanthropies will have to grapple with the same threats to their independence and autonomy that have often hampered other civil society organizations in constructing domain accountability systems. Indeed, philanthropies that fail to build shared standards may pay a high price in terms of future leverage and opportunities available to institutions whose legitimacy is strongly rooted in the larger society.

Second, the rise of civil society initiatives on many social problems is likely to trigger increasing questions about their legitimacy and accountability in Latin American countries, particularly as they engage powerful actors who see them as threats to their position and power. Latin American philanthropies may be uniquely positioned to aid civil society organizations and sectors in responding to legitimacy and accountability challenges. While civil society leaders may recognize the importance of attending to legitimacy and accountability challenges, mobilizing peer organizations that are competitors for many resources to act on that recognition may be very difficult. Philanthropies may be able to act as relatively neutral conveners of civil society organizations to explore issues as well as sources of information and financial support for articulating shared standards, building systems to assess and communicate performance, and other aspects of accountability construction. Experience suggests that successful initiatives in accountability construction often have the unintended benefit of creating more sector-wide cohesion and coherence on other issues as well, so they may well have a general sector-building effect as well as constructing accountability systems.

Third, increased sector legitimacy depends not only on constructing systems that can produce and disseminate performance information, it also depends on negotiating expectations with key stakeholders for what is acceptable performance, particularly when different stakeholder may hold different or conflicting performance preferences.

Latin American philanthropies may be strategically placed to build bridges between civil society domains and critical external stakeholders, such as government agencies and businesses, to negotiate mutually acceptable standards and expectations. Philanthropies that have credibility across sectoral boundaries—government, business and civil society—and across social levels—local, regional and national—can make unique contributions to helping actors understand each others' concerns and synthesize mutually acceptable expectations. In the process, philanthropies can contribute to the education of all the parties and the possibilities for wider cooperation inherent in better mutual understanding.

Fourth, earlier chapters have described a variety of initiatives in Latin America that fall under the general heading of experimental, multi-sectoral initiatives to solve societal problems—or what has been described earlier as problem domains. Many problems simply cannot be solved with the resources available to one sector, be it powerful government agencies or wealthy corporations or compelling civil society campaigns.

Latin American philanthropies are positioned to catalyze and support intersectoral cooperation and domain accountability systems that can mobilize and legitimate otherwise unavailable resources for governance and social problem-solving. Philanthropies can have the political position and the material resources to focus multi-sectoral attention on complex problems and to encourage the emergence of problem domain cooperative initiatives that make use of complementary resources available to different actors. Technical and material support can help actors construct accountability systems that can support and institutionalize cooperative solutions to otherwise intransigent problems.

Fifth and finally, the construction of systems that enable accountability and legitimacy for civil society sector domains and cross-sectoral problem domains is underway in many regions on many different kinds of issues. Actors all over the world are struggling with challenges whose local details vary but whose underlying dynamics are similar if not identical. Latin American philanthropies could have global impacts in fostering and disseminating social learning about Latin American innovations in the strengthening of civil society and philanthropic legitimacy and accountability. Philanthropies often and with good reason focus first on having impacts on questions and issues that are close to home—but in this arena there are opportunities to catalyze new thinking on world wide challenges of philanthropy, civil society and social change as well as to apply ideas from other settings to the challenges of the Latin American region.

A Final Note

We live in a shrinking and increasingly interdependent world. We are confronted by a number of "wicked" problems for which existing institutions are increasingly inadequate.[29] CSOs have been important actors in raising problems, bridging differences, and proposing innovations to strengthen institutional arrangements for social problem-solving in many settings. Their importance as development actors is reflected in the rise of philanthropic and civil society initiatives described in earlier chapters of this book. But their increasing roles, some visible lapses and their challenges to powerful actors have led to questions about their legitimacy and accountability. These questions, left unanswered, can undermine their future contributions. Confusion about legitimacy and accountabilities undercuts the influence of civil society organizations with external constituents as well as their internal solidarity and shared commitment.

This chapter suggests that domain accountability systems can be designed to enhance CSO legitimacy and accountability as well as their capacity for learning and performance in both sector and problem domains. Building domain accountability systems requires identifying domain goals and stakeholders, negotiating performance standards and expectations, building domain organizations, assessing and communicating performance, and enabling performance consequences. Civil society actors can take the lead in this process, but donor, government and business support will be critical in what is inevitably a multi-sectoral process of negotiating the societal roles of civil society in relation to other participants in governance and societal problem-solving. Latin American philanthropies are uniquely positioned to foster strengthening of their own legitimacy and accountability systems as well as the legitimacy and accountability systems of civil society sector and problem domains in the region.

Accountability and legitimacy are key concepts in an age in which existing institutions are under intense pressure to adapt to globalization, technological change, and demographic shifts as well as the local manifestations of cross-sectoral "crises of governance." Philanthropies and other civil society organizations can be major actors in the processes of social and institutional innovation required to respond to these issues. Enhancing their accountability and legitimacy, in their own eyes as well as those of others, is critical to defining their roles in the social learning processes needed to cope with the world's emerging challenges.

Notes

1 See Clark, J. (2003). *Worlds Apart: Civil Society and the Battle for Ethical Globalization*. Bloomfield, CT: Kumarian Press; Edwards, M. (2000). *NGO Rights and Responsibilities: A New Deal for Global Governance*. London: The Foreign Policy Centre; and Kovach, H., Neligan, C., & Burall, S. (2003). *Power without Accountability?* London: One World Trust, Global Accountability Project.

2 See "Holding Civic Groups Accountable," *New York Times* editorial, July 21, 2003: and Naomi Klein, "Bush to NGOs: Watch Your Mouths," *Globe and Mail* (Canada), 6/20/03.

3 See Brown, L. D., & Moore, M. H. (2001). Accountability, Strategy and International Nongovernmental Organizations. *Nonprofit and Voluntary Sector Quarterly, 30*(3), 569–587; Cutt, J., & Murray, V. (2000). *Accountability and Effectiveness Evaluation in Non-profit Organizations*. London: Routledge.

4 See Edwards, 2000, *op. cit.*; Scott, W. R. (1995). *Institutions and Organizations*. Thousand Oaks, CA: Sage for perspectives on institutional legitimacy. For bases of legitimacy on particular issues, see Brown, L. D., & Others. (2001). Civil Society Legitimacy: A Discussion Guide. In L. D. Brown (Ed.), *Practice-Research Engagement and Civil Society in a Globalizing World* (pp. 31–48). Washington, DC: CIVICUS: World Alliance for Citizen Participation.

5 See Frumkin, P. (2002). *On Being Nonprofit: A Conceptual and Policy Primer*. Cambridge, MA, Harvard University Press; and Goodin, R. E. (2003). *Democratic Accountability: The Third Sector and All*. Cambridge: Hauser Center for Nonprofit Organizations.

6 Moore, M. (2000). Managing for Value: Organizational Strategy in For-profit, Nonprofit, and Governmental Organizations. *Nonprofit and Voluntary Sector Quarterly, 29* (1, Supplement,), 183–204.

7 See Chamberlain, R. A. (n.d.). *Regulating Civil Society: The Philippine Council for NGO Certification (PCNC).* Manila: PCNC.

8 See Villar, R., (2003) "Self Regulation as a Mechanism to Expand the Legitimacy of CSOs: Ideas for a Work Program," this volume.

9 See Weber, E. P. (2003). *Bringing Society Back In: Grassroots Ecosystem Management, Accountability and Sustainable Communities.* Cambridge, MA: MIT Press; and Johnson, D. A. (1986). Confronting Corporate Power: Strategies and Phases of the Nestle Boycott. In L. Preston & J. Post (Eds.), *Research in Corporate Social Performance and Policy* (vol. 8, pp. 323–344). Greenwich, CT: JAI Press.

10 See *Standards for Child Sponsorship NGOs*, Kennedy School of Government Case No. C16–02–1664.

11 Weber, E. (2003). *Bringing Society Back In: Grassroots Ecosystem Management, Accountability and Sustainable Communities.* Cambridge, MA, MIT Press.

12 See for examples Kunugi, T., & Schweitz, M. (1999). *Codes of Conduct for Partnership in Governance: Texts and Commentaries.* Tokyo: UN University.

13 InterAction, (2001). *InterAction PVO Standards,* Washington, DC: Interaction: American Council for Voluntary International Action.

14 Chamberlain, R. A. (n.d.). *op. cit.*

15 Weber, 2003, *op. cit.,* 107–140.

16 See Chapman, R. (2004). "Strengthening Australian NGOs: The Australian Council for International Development." *AccountAbility Forum* (2, Summer): 89–97.

17 See Weber, E (2003), pp. 70–105.

18 Rana, A. (2004). Improving Accountability: The NPO Certification Experience in Pakistan. *AccountAbility Forum* (2, Summer), 82–88.

19 See New York Times (2003) op cit. The website can be accessed at: http://www.nyt.com

20 See Ebrahim, 2003, *op. cit.* p. 816.

21 In a study that compared international NGOs, transnational corporations and intergovernmental agencies, investigators found that INGOs tended to score lower than the other two sectors in providing online information but higher than the others in member control. See Kovach, Neligan, & Burall. (2003). *op. cit.*

22 See, for a discussion of social audits, Ebrahim, A. (2003). Accountability in Practice: Mechanisms for NGOs. *World Development, 31*(5), p. 822–824. For

a brief treatment of the possibilities of common measures of social impact, see Bonbright, D. (2003), Ensuring Potential Winners Do Win. *Alliance*, 8:2.

23 Smillie, I., & Hailey, J. (2001). *Managing for Change: Leadership, Strategy and Management in Asian NGOs*. London: Earthscan; and Korten, D. C. (1980). Rural Organization and Rural Development: A Learning Process Approach. *Public Administration Review, 40*, 480–511.

24 See Estrella, M., & others, a. (2000). *Learning from Change: Issues and Experiences in Participatory Monitoring and Evaluation*. London: Intermediate Technology Publications.

25 Behn, R. (2003). Rethinking Accountability in Education: How Should Who Hold Whom Accountable for What? *International Public Management Journal, 6*(1), 569–587.

26 Callamard, A. (2004). HAP International: A New Decisive Step toward Accountability. *AccountAbility Forum* (2, Summer), 44–57.

27 See Goodin, 2003, *op. cit.*, for an analysis of networks as key sources of accountability for CSOs.

28 Medeiros Peliano, A.M.T., Beghin, N., & de Oliveira Neto, V. 2003, Philanthropy of Equity: The Brazilian Case, (this volume), p. 9.

29 See Rischard, J. F. (2002). *High Noon: Twenty Global Problems, Twenty Years to Solve Them*. New York: Basic Books; and Social Learning Group, *Learning to Manage Environmental Risks*, (vol. 2). Cambridge, MA: MIT Press; Clark, (2003), *op. cit.*

17

Strengthening Philanthropy and Civil Society Through Policy Reform: From Proposals to Action

Merilee S. Grindle

Good ideas and good research are essential to the promotion of philanthropy and the strengthening of civil society in Latin America. Just as important, however, is the ability to turn good ideas and the recommendations that stem from good research into practice. When such action means introducing new or improved public policies, knowledge of the policy process is a valuable tool for moving from ideas about what "ought to be" toward practice in the real world.

Many of the chapters in this volume provide eloquent testimony to the importance of public policy in support of philanthropy and strong civil societies in Latin America. Several review the ways in which government policies in specific Latin American countries affect the capacity of civil society organizations to promote social welfare, democratization, effective governance, and human rights agendas. They also point to ways in which such policies can be altered to increase these organizations' potential to contribute to the promotion of public welfare and democratic values and practices. Other chapters consider the role of laws in engendering philanthropic action; still others focus on the impact of tax policies on support for non-governmental activities. Finally, various chapters raise questions about appropriate regulatory policies that affect the activities and legitimacy of civil society organizations.

These chapters contribute much to our understanding of the content and impact of existing policies. They propose important ways in which policies can contribute to the public ends of philanthropy and civil society activism. An important question, then, is how reformers—in this case those who wish to introduce new policies or improve existing ones—can best advance their objectives in Latin America and elsewhere.

In terms of what we know about how various kinds of policies get on public agendas and are shaped, negotiated, approved, implemented, and sustained, what can we learn about turning the good ideas and research findings of this volume into effective public policies? In the following pages, drawing on literature about the politics of the policy reform process and on my own research, I'd like to propose some answers to this question.[1]

Certainly, policies are shaped by the stakeholders advocating them as well as by those opposing them, and certainly they are shaped by institutions of power in each society. But they are also shaped by the strategic choices of reformers who seek to find room to maneuver in often-contentious political environments. As the policy process unfolds, it provides significant opportunities for reformers (and their opponents) to intervene in strategic ways to shape the content of public policies and to promote or hinder their approval, implementation, and sustainability. First, though, policy ideas must become part of public agendas.

Agenda Setting. Throughout Latin America, major new policy initiatives were introduced in the 1980s, 1990s and 2000s to alter significantly the relationship between the state and the market, to change fundamentally the ways in which social services are produced and delivered, and to restructure the relationship between citizens and public organizations through democratization and decentralization of state power.

In some of these reforms, most notably the introduction of more market-oriented economic development policies, new ideas generally became part of public agendas because they were sponsored by political leaders and international financial institutions committed to restructuring the role of the state in economic development. In other cases, most notably the introduction of new social policies, these same actors were often those who promoted the need for change. But also, politicians responding to social protest over the impact of neo-liberal economic reforms and their implications for the extent and quality of public services frequently had reason to consider altering existing policies for the delivery of health, education, public health and sanitation infrastructure, and services for particularly vulnerable groups.[2] In still other cases, civil society organizations—national and international—pressed the need for reform on governments, most notably in the cases of service provision, improvements in environmental conditions, and human rights and equity concerns.[3]

No matter the source of pressure introducing new policies, the successful achievement of a place on a public agenda generally depended on the activities of policy "entrepreneurs" or policy "champions."[4] In such cases, politically powerful individuals—at times presidents, ministers of government, legislative actors, heads of important public commissions or agencies—were willing to take up an idea, commit their time and energy to promoting it, and use their political influence to ensure that it achieved a prominent place among the many other pressures on government or among the varied commitments of political leaders. This suggests that turning a proposal into an issue of prominence on a policy agenda generally requires identifying and even mobilizing those in politically influential positions who take on the difficult task of championing it through the policy process.

For those seeking to alter the policies that affect philanthropy and civil society organizations, then, an important first step in promoting change is to identify such individuals and to work with them to ensure that the idea is heard and taken seriously by other politicians and decision-making elites in government. How to do this needs to be a focus of strategic thinking on the part of reform proponents. Finding appropriate connections to political leadership, working through political institutions, considering how to "frame" the issue for political relevance—these are parts of initiating an effort to improve the policy framework for promoting the ends of philanthropy and civil society strengthening.

Designing New Policies. Policy champions also play an important role in the design of new policies. They take responsibility for appointing teams of people to work on developing a specific policy or piece of legislation, generating relevant information, consulting with important groups who will be affected by the reform, and assessing the budgetary, regulatory, capacity building, monitoring, and evaluation needs of the policy.[5] These tasks are as much political as technical. The work of the design team, for example, often involves specifying the content of new policy in ways that affect who will benefit and who might be harmed by it, who will be included and who will be excluded from its reach, and what procedures or activities are required of those who wish to benefit from it.[6] Thus, in what often appears to be a technical job of writing legislation or regulations, those active in this process are making a series of decisions about "who wins" and "who loses" from new policies. By making such choices, they are also foreshadowing the kind of conflicts that may surround the next phase of the policy process, that of negotiating and approving the reform proposal.

In addition, those involved in designing new policies often have considerable control over who participates in discussions about the content of reform. In the past two decades or so, for example, many governments in Latin America have been taken to task for the closed, top-down, and technocratic approach they have taken to designing many of the new policies that have been introduced.[7] Indeed, even in countries with relatively well-functioning democratic institutions, there has been a tendency for design teams to limit broad discussion of new policies. This practice stands in great contrast to current discourse in development circles about the importance of participation, inclusion, and bottom-up approaches to improved policies and governance.[8]

In general, experience to date suggests that a relatively closed process of policy design is likely to produce more coherent policies, but ones that are also vulnerable to rejection by those who believe their voices have not been heard in their development. Indeed, those who resent exclusion from the process may withhold their support for the policy after it is announced. In contrast, a more inclusive and consultative process of policy design helps build support for new policies and often results in ones more sensitive to the needs of different constituencies. At the same time, the cost of inclusion and consultation—the cost of consensus—can be policies that lack focus and clarity, that fail to achieve their objectives because they offer something to everyone, or that cost too much because of the need to serve many different interests.

Thus, for those who are concerned about improving policies for philanthropic action and civil society organizations, thinking strategically about the process through which a policy is designed can have significant consequences. Clearly, the process of designing policy will differ depending on the relative weight of technical issues—designing tax policy may require more technical input than does, for example, designing a policy for registering NGOs with government. Moreover, some policies naturally affect a wider range of interests than others and thus decisions about inclusiveness and consultation can vary considerably. Mechanisms and expectations about consultation will also differ by country. Democratic regimes tend to consult more than do authoritarian ones, although the range in democratic practice may be great. Expectations about what is appropriate engagement for public debate also vary among policy areas. Broad consultation is not likely in the management of macroeconomic policy, for example, but may be much more common in the design of urban development policies. Taking these and other factors into consideration, however, does nothing to diminish the strategic importance of choices about how to go about designing new policies.

Negotiating and Approving Reform. One of the most important activities that policy champions, design teams, and their supporters can take on is that of building support coalitions—inside government as well as within civil society—for important changes. This is particularly important for policies that need to have legislative approval and in countries in which the relationship between the executive and legislative branches is relatively equal. Increasingly, Latin American experience suggests that while executives often propose, legislatures may have considerable power to dispose.

Moreover, there may be organizations within government that do not support a particular reform. Ministries of finance, for example, may not be overly friendly to tax laws that promote philanthropy, viewing them as vehicles that divert resources from the public purse. Further, some policies directly affect the interests of particular groups in negative ways—new human rights regimes may not be welcomed by military and police forces, for example, and anti-corruption initiatives may be opposed by those threatened by exposure—and it can be expected that these groups will be active in trying to halt or alter the policy being promoted. Thus, policy champions not only need to build coalitions of support, they must consider how to neutralize or weaken opposition to the policy measures they are promoting.

Responding to these kinds of challenges is difficult and requires political skill and the ability to negotiate across organizations, parties, interests, and ideologies. It requires an ability to think creatively about how to compromise on the contents of policy without sacrificing its "soul" or watering down measures so much that they become ineffective as ways to achieve particular goals. It requires the ability to present compelling and relevant arguments to people in positions of authority who may not be enthusiastic about the ends or the means of the new policy. In dealing with reluctant legislative committees or party caucuses, it may be necessary to mobilize support outside of government through the media and civil society organizations to ensure that legislators are encouraged to vote for new approaches to public issues. In dealing with interests that might be threatened by the proposed reform, it may be necessary to offer concessions that moderate its impact on them or offer compensatory measures as a way of gaining approval for change.

Indeed, at times, when approval of a new policy seems doomed to failure, reform proponents face some very difficult choices. In the case of legislative approval that appears to be improbable, should reformers proceed instead through administrative decree?[9] In the case of interest group opposition, is it sometimes more effective to confront or ignore those who resist the policy than to negotiate with them? In both cases, is it better to wait until the timing is more propitious for change or to proceed in the face of strong opposition? There are no simple answers to these questions and reformers have to assess distinct situations carefully, try various ways of moving ahead, and understand the consequences of each choice.

Again, these difficult choices suggest that those concerned about improving the policy framework for philanthropy and civil society organizations must be strategic actors, carefully assessing the opportunities to advance their initiatives and realistically appraising their chances of success through alternative action scenarios.

Implementing New Policies. Too often, we assume that because a policy has been approved, it will be implemented.[10] Great attention tends to be focused on the very public phases of agenda setting and policy approval, and implementation is frequently considered to be an inevitable consequence of success in these earlier phases of the policy process. But in far too many cases in the real world, particularly in Latin America, a new law or regulation is announced—and nothing happens. In fact, the old Spanish colonial adage, "*obedezco pero no cumplo*" continues to characterize many public policies in a wide range of countries.

The reasons for this implementation gap are many. At times, policies are designed with little understanding of the context in which they are to be implemented and thus may be impossible to pursue even under the best of circumstances.[11] Some policies articulate an aspiration rather than an achievable goal—in some countries, for example, governments make commitments to provide jobs for all citizens regardless of the capacity to do so. In many other cases, policies affect the interests of groups that have the capacity to sabotage or subvert the implementation of policies—teachers' unions have frequently responded with protests and inaction to new policies that alter practices for hiring, firing, and promoting them, for example. In addition, some policies are based on assumptions about the incentives, capacities, and skills that implementers do not have. And, frequently, policies are affected by unanticipated events—the failure of logistical arrangements in delivering medicine to health clinics, for example, or a change in political leadership that alters the priorities of governments.

Thus, reformers ignore implementation at their peril. Realistically, it is no doubt impossible to anticipate everything that can go awry during an implementation process, but some actions can be taken to increase the probability that reforms will be implemented more or less as announced. Reformers, for example, can work to build support for new policies at high and middle levels within government. Public officials need to be motivated through incentives, accountability mechanisms, and understanding the objectives of new policies to carry out any new responsibilities that those policies anticipate.

Similarly, reformers can provide information about new initiatives to critical actors within the public sector and inform citizens more generally of the new policies and of the rights and responsibilities that these imply for them. Thus, communication strategies are essential to the successful implementation of new policies. It is equally important to consider carefully if the public sector has sufficient capacity to implement the new policy and to ensure that where capacity is lacking, training or other forms of capacity building activities are put in place. Alternatively, policies that require more capacity than exists can sometimes be redesigned in simplified ways or implemented through organizations in the private and not-for-profit sectors.

Implementing public policies is thus another arena in which reformers need to employ far more strategic thinking than is usually the case. They need to assess carefully what resources are needed to implement the policy effectively, recognizing that a failure to develop communication, logistical, incentive, monitoring, and evaluation systems can result in failed policy. In addition, reformers need to consider where problems are likely to arise and what can be done in advance to try to avoid such difficulties. They also need to think through implementation strategies that allow for flexibility and learning during implementation so that the policy itself or the mechanisms to put it into effect can be altered to respond to unanticipated problems or events. Indeed, monitoring and evaluation mechanisms are commonplace in public policies, but frequently what is learned through them does not feed back into the policy process—all too often, such information gathers dust on a shelf in some administrator's office.

Sustaining New Policies. Effective systems of implementation, and mechanisms that allow for learning and adaptation during implementation go a long way in ensuring that new policies are sustained over time. Clearly, to sustain a policy that has been introduced implies having the administrative capacity to implement it effectively. But other factors can also strengthen the sustainability of new policies, particularly in environments in which newly elected political leaders have considerable capacity to alter the priorities and policies that governments pursue.

It is important, for example, to work continuously to build commitment to new policies within government and by those who are responsible for implementing it. Incentives—particularly non-monetary incentives such as public recognition for a job well done, knowing that beneficiaries are being well-served, working in effective teams, and other such motivations—are important for the long term survival of commitment to new policies.[12]

Central to the provision of such incentives, and perhaps even more important than the incentives themselves, is the emergence of new stakeholders as beneficiaries of the policy. New stakeholders need to have the capacity to make their voices heard in providing feedback about the implementation of policy, to participate in decision making about how policies might be changed and how they are implemented, to demand performance and accountability from public officials involved in the process.[13] Thus, organizing stakeholders, or creating networks of stakeholders, and engaging them in the policy process can be an important way of ensuring they have the capacity to have a voice in policy and policy change. It can also be an effective way of ensuring that new policies remain in effect over the longer term as stakeholders develop the capacity to pressure government for their continuation.

A Simple Policy Framework. These observations, of course, oversimplify the ways in which good ideas can be turned into effective policies or can fail to become reality. They do, however, suggest a variety of ways in which reformers concerned about philanthropy and civil society can promote new policies through strategic political action, finding room to maneuver in often contentious political environments.

The framework in Figure 1 provides a schematic view of the policy process and the factors that are important in shaping the policy process and the strategic choices and actions that can promote new or better policy. At the first level of the figure are the various phases of the policy process we have considered, from agenda setting to policy sustainability. Of course, these phases are interrelated and there are important ways in which they affect each other. How an issue gets on the policy agenda, for example, can affect how it is designed. When civil society organizations press a policy issue on government, for example, it is likely that a more consultative approach to policy design will be followed than in cases in which policy makers or international organizations select particular policy priorities.[14] Similarly, policy is often redesigned as it is being negotiated and approved and it is sometimes redefined as it is being implemented. And clearly, how a policy is implemented affects its sustainability.

At the second level, the organization of civil society and the institutions of governance play an important role in determining who has access to power and how power and influence can be wielded in the policy process. At each phase of the policy process, particular interests are involved in promoting or opposing reform and particular institutions channel their activities and determine the extent of influence they have to affect the outcome

Figure 1. The Process of Policy Reform

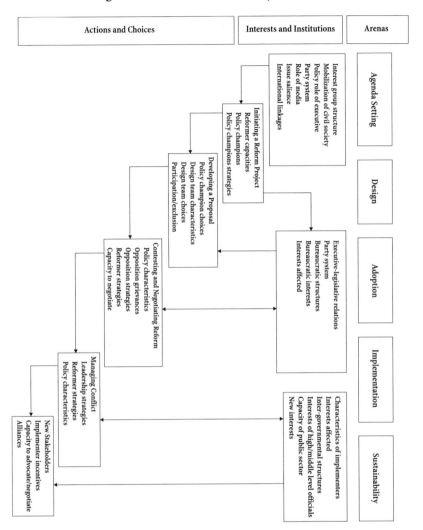

of policy discussions and debates. Organized interest groups such as those representing economic concerns may be part of debates about policy. For example, business elites may be particularly interested in promoting a change that would provide them with tax credits for philanthropic donations, but might lobby against a change that would increase their taxes even when the benefit to society is great. A union might oppose a proposal to strengthen the role of local communities in education or health provision, but support one related to increased protection of workers. At times, government organizations or public officials might act as an interest group in promoting or opposing a particular change.

At the institutional level, a tradition of executive dominance in policy making in Latin America often empowers those in the executive branch or those who have access to executive officials. Similarly, the responsiveness of public bureaucracies to various mandates may be central to the capacity to implement new policies.

At the third level in the figure are the strategic actions and choices that reformers may make at different phases of the policy process. Their decisions at each point along the way can enhance the opportunities to move ahead with the reform or may hinder them. It is at this level that the careful analysis of options for action by reformers and their supporters is most important.

This figure, of course, is only a general outline of the kinds of factors that can enhance or hinder reform of the policies that encourage philanthropy and the strengthening of civil society in Latin America. Indeed, history in every country is littered with failed attempts to improve or alter policy. At times, the reasons for such outcomes relate to the failure of reform proponents to think carefully about the challenges they face and to devise strategies that can respond to these challenges. Just as frequently, however, initiatives fail because governments have other priorities or are caught up in economic and other crises; because citizens do not understand the importance of change; because the opposition of important interests cannot be overcome no matter what strategies are followed; or because the time is simply not propitious for change.

Thus, the success or failure of reform is often contingent on factors beyond the control or influence of even very strategic reformers. The lesson they should learn from such experiences, however, is not that there is no reason for pursuing change, but rather that change in important policies is often a long-term process. The path to reform is often a rocky one and progress along it is sometimes halting. Nevertheless, those who wish to promote the practices of philanthropy in Latin America and the strengthening of the region's civil societies can look back upon recent history for considerable confirmation that positive change can happen and that successes in building more democratic and responsive societies do happen through the concerted efforts of reformers and their supporters.

Notes

1 The literature on policy reform in developing countries is extensive. See, for examples, Joan Nelson, ed., *Economic Crisis and Policy Choice: The Politics of Adjustment in the Third World.* Princeton, N.J.: Princeton University Press, 1990; Merilee Grindle and John Thomas, *Public Choices and Policy Change: The Political Economy of Reform in Developing Countries.* Baltimore, MD: The Johns Hopkins University Press, 1991; Stephan Haggard and Robert R. Kaufman, *The Politics of Economic Adjustment.* Princeton, N.J.: Princeton University Press, 1995; Merilee Grindle, *Audacious Reforms: Institutional Invention and Democracy in Latin* America. Baltimore, MD: The Johns Hopkins University Press, 2000; Ben Ross Schneider and Blanca Heredia, eds., *The Political Economy of Administrative Reform: State Building in Developing Countries.* Ann Arbor, MI: University of Michigan Press, 2003; Merilee Grindle, *Despite the Odds: The Contentious Politics of Education Reform.* Princeton, N.J.: Princeton University Press, 2004.

2 See Joseph Tulchin and Allison Garland, eds., *Social Development in Latin America.* Boulder, CO: Lynne Rienner, 2000.

3 See, for example, Deborah Yashar, "Indigenous Protest and Democracy in Latin America," in Jorge Domínguez and Abraham Lowenthal, eds., *Constructing Democratic Governance.* Baltimore, MD: The Johns Hopkins University Press, 1996.

4 On policy "champions," see Alejandra González-Rossetti, *The Political Dimension of Health Reform: The Case of Mexico and Colombia.* Ph.D. Dissertation, Department of Public Health Policy, London School of Hygiene and Tropical Medicine, 2001; Joe Wallis, "Understanding the Role of Leadership in Economic Policy Reform, *World Development,* vol. 27, no. 1, 1999. On "reform-mongers," see Albert Hirschman, "Policymaking and Policy Analysis in Latin America—A Return Journey," in Albert Hirschman, *Essays in Trespassing: Economics to Politics and Beyond.* Cambridge University Press, 1981. On policy "heroes," see Arnold Harberger, "Economic Policy and Economic Growth," in Arnold Harberger, ed., *World Economic Growth.* San Francisco: Institute for Contemporary Studies.

5 On design teams, see González-Rossetti, "*The Political Dimension of Health Reform*; Grindle, *Audacious Reforms*; and *Despite the Odds.*

6 See Grindle, *Despite the Odds,* especially Chapter 4.

7 See, for example, James Malloy, "Policy Analysis, Public Policy and Regime Structure in Latin America," *Governance: An International Journal of Public Policy and Administration,* vol., 2, no. 3 (July 1989).

8 See, for example, United Nations Development Programme, *Human Development Report, 1993,* New York: Oxford University Press, 1993.

9 See, for example, Alec Ian Gershberg, "Education 'Decentralization' Processes in Mexico and Nicaragua: Legislative versus Ministry-Led Reform Strategies," *Comparative Education,* vol. 35, no. 1, 1999.

10 See Grindle and Thomas, *Public Choices and Policy Change*, esp. Ch. 7.

11 This is a failure not so much of implementation but of policy making.

12 See Merilee Grindle and Mary Hilderbrand, "Building Sustainable Capacity in the Public Sector: What Can be Done?" *Public Administration and Development*, vol. 15, 1995.

13 For an excellent example of stakeholder engagement in policy, see Judith Tendler and Sara Freedheim, "Trust in a Rent-Seeking World: Health and Government Transformed in Northeast Brazil." *World Development*, vol. 22, no. 12 (1994).

14 Hirschman, in "Policymaking and Policy Analysis in Latin America" makes a distinction between "pressing" and "chosen" reforms, that is, those that are pressed upon decision makers and those they take up because of their own interests or concerns.

INDEX

INDEX